"Harry Dent has been among our most popular, stimulating, and controversial keynote speakers. Dent began predicting the huge tech stock-led run-up at the largest-of-all investor conventions in 1993. Dent's fresh perspective is the clearest and most actionable application of one of the most certain factors in our economic world: demographics. Because Dent's conclusions are so refreshingly specific and stimulate long-term strategic business and investment planning, I never miss his talks and written predictions. *The Great Depression Ahead* is a must-read for all of us."

—Kim and Charles Githler, founders, InterShow—The World Money Show,
   The Traders Expo, The Financial Advisor Symposium, Investment
   Cruises, and MoneyShow.com

"*The Great Depression Ahead* shows you how to position your retirement savings and other investments to take advantage of predictable market trends that could otherwise cause you to lose your savings just at the time you will be relying on them most for your future financial security. Harry Dent is a master at understanding these demographics and shows you how to have your money in the right place at the right time and when to make critical changes."

—Ed Slott, CPA, author, IRA expert, founder of Ed Slott's Elite IRA
   Advisor Group, creator of PBS Special *Stay Rich Forever and Ever*

"I have worked with Harry Dent since 1998. He is the only person I have read who makes sense out of why we had the boom in the 1990s and why we won't have it again, possibly for many years. His forecasts should certainly be seriously considered by any advisor or investor. He is an invaluable resource to many of my best clients in financial services."

—Bill Good, Bill Good Marketing

"I first came across Harry Dent's books in a book warehouse that was selling dated books cheaply. The great thing about reading dated books that make predictions is that you can instantly verify for yourself whether the author's predictions turned out to be accurate. Well, his predictions speak for themselves, and I have been an ardent follower of Harry's work ever since. Except now I pay full price to read them hot off the press."

—Dolf de Roos, author of the *New York Times* bestseller *Real Estate Riches*

"If you want to understand a topic, you should go to the best expert you can find. When I need to understand demographic trends and see how those trends will shape our economy in the years to come, I look to Harry Dent. Why? Because he has been right. For over a decade I have used his research and forecasts to help my clients plan for the years ahead. When I am training financial advisors, I always strongly suggest that they seek out Harry's research and incorporate it into their planning process."

—William J. Nelson, RFC, LUTCF, founder of the Learning Institute for Financial Executives

"Harry Dent has once again provided a clear and compelling view into our economic future. It is almost as if he has a time machine that sends back economic briefings from the future. By utilizing a good set of investment disciplines and Dent's road map for the future of the world's economy, investors now have the tools they need to profit, while at the same time protecting their portfolio. Without question, an essential component for any investor's library."

—Andrew Horowitz, money manager and author of *The Disciplined Investor—Essential Strategies for Success*, host of The Disciplined Investor Podcast

"Harry Dent has been our chief strategist for over fifteen years. Without him my clients and I would have gone down the wrong path years ago. His advice and leadership has added millions to our bottom line."

—Michael Robertson, Robertson and Associates

"Eighteen months ago I began selling personal real estate before the bottom dropped in Florida and stopped building a corporate campus in Ohio because of what was learned from the Dent Newsletter and Demographics School. These decisions have been critical in saving me millions of dollars both personally and corporately. Additionally, my business has expanded dramatically into the senior and baby boomer health care market due to the demographic research provided by the Dent group."

"On a regular basis I have clients, friends, and family commenting on how the Dent research has been so accurate in so many ways. Demographics are not a day-to-day aspect of what moves the market. But there is nothing I know of that affects the economy more long term. Harry's insight and effort is much appreciated and needed by everyone who wants to understand where we really are headed."

"I have been an avid reader of Harry Dent's books and newsletter for many years and have attended his Demographics School. That investment has turned out to be worth millions. His predictions led me to sell some real estate holdings in 2006 for significant profit and be disciplined enough not to acquire any new properties for almost two years. As Harry says, 'All bubbles deflate.' My investment partners and I are now in a position to take advantage of some significant distressed opportunities and not be saddled with losing positions. I can't wait to take advantage of Harry's updated predictions."

"Being with the HS Dent organization for almost ten years has been one of the best decisions I made for the growth of my financial planning practice. Not only have I used HS Dent as a research arm for the investments of my clients, but the organization helped in the development of my company. I was now able to offer a more complete planning package for my clients that encompassed their total financial picture."

"Introduction to the HS Dent demographic research has been one of the most beneficial events in my professional career. Being able to explain the economic power of demographic groups has been the most powerful tool

I have used to help clients understand the direction of the economy and look past the short-term volatility of markets."

—Donald Creech, Certified Financial Planner, Accredited Investment Advisor, Investor Resources, Inc.

"Two days in Harry Dent's Demographics School opened my eyes to the storm we're in and practical means to weather it . . . and now a book that demystifies the headlines and hands families a compass through the uncertainties. Every family needs what's in this book."

—Kathy Peel, America's Family Manager on AOL, author of many books including *The Busy Mom's Guide* and *Desperate Households*

"Working with affluent households in my financial planning practice, I found Harry Dent in 1995 and built an entire financial planning company around his macroeconomic predictions. The recent financial crisis came as no surprise to me or my clients; we were forewarned and therefore forearmed."

—Erin T. Botsford, CFP, CRPC, president, The Botsford Group

"Our association with Harry Dent has been both personally fulfilling and financially profitable for us and our clients. Harry's insights have become an integral part of our practice, both in the way we manage our client portfolios and in how we communicate the complexities of the current market environment with them. The type of information Harry provides makes people really stop and think about their current situation, and whether or not they are doing the right things. We constantly get feedback from clients and radio listeners alike telling us they are truly grateful someone is out there saying the things he says, and that although it may not be what they want to hear, they need to hear it."

—Dean Barber, Barber Financial Group

"Harry Dent's diligence and research has provided insight and information allowing our clients to be significantly better prepared for long-term investing. Additionally, it has provided our practice with a base of knowledge that is constantly monitored, updated, and communicated to us. In turn, we are able to effectively inform clients about the projected changes that are primarily driven by demographic trends. Harry's philosophy has helped our business evolve from an economic 'at the moment' reactionary stance to a 'big picture' proactive outlook that keeps the economic moments in perspective with the client's overall long-term objective."

—Daryl J. LePage, CFP, Brook Wealth Management, LLC

"When it comes to economics I look toward pundits who are controversial. Too many people put Harry Dent in the day-to-day advisor category, which is not what Harry is or has ever been. Many critics incorrectly label Harry Dent's forecasts as inconceivable; nobody knows the future! Personally I never took Harry's predictions at face value—i.e., the Dow hitting 30,000—partly because I comprehended his words, unlike many critics. Harry's humble predictions are in the form of questions that keep you on your toes. To the prudent investor and saver Harry's questions are invaluable. I'm more prepared to take advantage of current market conditions because I believed in Harry's forecasts, which have a solid foundation based on demographics."

—Darrell Catmull, KTKK AM630, Salt Lake City, UT

"In my 32 years of interviewing the world's leading investment authorities, Harry Dent's practical application of demographic trends as a powerful tool for investment allocation is without peer."

—Joe Bradley, Bradley Enterprises, LLC, dba Investor's Hotline

"When Harry speaks, we all need to listen. He was right on the money when he predicted the real estate boom of the 1990s. Each time he's been on my radio show, *Real Estate Today,* he knows what's happening and he has an uncanny ability to predict the future."

—Louis Weil, The Star Team, Star Team Real Estate

"When Harry gave me a copy of *The Great Boom Ahead* in the early nineties, I thought it was voodoo economics. Then I saw just how much he got right by way of demographic research—the stock market boom, the tech boom, then the real estate boom. In all my years following market prognosticators, I've seen that no one gets it right all the time, but very few can anticipate the market with the prescience and accuracy of Harry. Careful readers of *The Great Depression Ahead* will find lots of hope. The book is loaded with ways to grow wealth during these turbulent times."

"The economic and market analysis Harry Dent brings to my listening audience is of exceptional value. The absence of the usual Wall Street bias toward optimistic and self-serving predictions, along with fully supported historic trend research, is a gift to my listeners and fresh air for those willing to pay attention! Both short-term traders and long-term investors are well served by Harry Dent and his unique perspective."

"I've known Harry Dent for many years as a regular guest on my radio show, SmartMoneyTalks.com. His work is incredibly thought provoking. It's helpful in giving his readers a broadened perspective on how they view their financial matters."

"Three years ago, The Harvard Business School Club of San Diego hosted an evening with Harry Dent. We were all spellbound by his presentation. It's clear that Harry's insights can help you predict future trends with uncanny accuracy. Harry Dent's 'science of demographics' may be the most significant breakthrough in economic forecasting of our time. His work shows how a nation's economy is affected by the average age and size of its population. More important, Dent's insights can help you predict future trends with uncanny accuracy."

THE GREAT DEPRESSION AHEAD

HOW TO PROSPER IN THE DEBT CRISIS OF 2010–2012

HARRY S. DENT, JR.

FREE PRESS
New York   London   Toronto   Sydney

Free Press
A Division of Simon & Schuster, Inc.
1230 Avenue of the Americas
New York, NY 10020

Copyright © 2008, 2009 by Harry S. Dent, Jr.

All rights reserved, including the right to reproduce this book or portions thereof in any form whatsoever. For information address Free Press Subsidiary Rights Department, 1230 Avenue of the Americas, New York, NY 10020.

First Free Press trade paperback edition January 2010

FREE PRESS and colophon are trademarks of Simon & Schuster, Inc.

For information about special discounts for bulk purchases, please contact Simon & Schuster Special Sales at 1-866-506-1949 or business@simonandschuster.com.

The Simon & Schuster Speakers Bureau can bring authors to your live event. For more information or to book an event contact the Simon & Schuster Speakers Bureau at 1-866-248-3049 or visit our website at www.simonspeakers.com.

Manufactured in the United States of America

10 9 8 7 6 5 4 3 2 1

The Library of Congress has cataloged the hardcover edition as follows:
Dent, Harry S., 1950–
   The great depression ahead / by Harry S. Dent.
      p. cm.
   1. Economic forecasting—United States.   2. United States—Economic conditions—2001–   3. Population—Economic aspects.   4. Investments—United States.   5. Financial crises—United States.   I. Title.
   HC106.83.D458   2008
   330.973—dc22   2008030401

ISBN 978-1-4165-8898-6
ISBN 978-1-4165-8899-3 (pbk)
ISBN 978-1-4165-9527-4 (ebook)

To my mother, Betty F. Dent
To my wife, Jean-ne Carmichael Dent

Acknowledgments

THANKS TO MY literary agent, Susan Golomb; my partners at HS Dent, Rodney Johnson (President) and Harry Cornelius (Business Development). For research, Stephanie Gerardot and Charles Sizemore. For newsletter administration, Nicole Nonnemaker. For PR, Barbara Henricks and Nancy Lovell. For marketing, Arthur Labuvosky. For directing the HS Dent Financial Advisors Network, Lance Gaitan. Special thanks to the members of the HS Dent Financial Advisors Network and its board of directors: Bill and Phyllis Nelson, Mike Robertson, Beth Blecker, Joe Clark, Don Creech, and Daryl LePage.

Contents

Acknowledgments   xv

Prologue: Simple Principles Drive Complex Change   1

Chapter 1. The Debt Crisis of 2010–2012 . . . Why It Will Be
Very Good for Our Country   17

Chapter 2. The Fundamental Trends That Drive Our Economy:
Demographic and Technology Cycles   43

Chapter 3. New Geopolitical, Commodity, and Recurring Cycles:
With Likely Stock and Economic Scenarios for Years and
Decades Ahead   73

Chapter 4. The Greatest Bubble Ever in Real Estate:
The Demographics of Real Estate, the Greater Credit Crisis,
and the Likely Depression Scenario Ahead   107

Chapter 5. Echo Boomers Continue to Move to the Southeast,
Southwest, and Rockies: Opportunities for Businesses,
Developers, and Municipalities in the Downturn   139

Chapter 6. Changing Global Demographic Trends: The Rising East
and Emerging World Versus the Succession of Aging
Western Nations   175

Chapter 7. The Clustering of Risks and Returns: Why
Traditional Asset Allocation Strategies Will Fail Miserably
in the Decade Ahead   253

Chapter 8. Investment, Business, and Life Strategies for the
   Great Winter: How to Profit in a Deflationary Economy   281

Chapter 9. The Political and Social Impacts of the Next Great
   Depression: The Coming Revolution and "New Deal"
   in the United States and Globally   321

Index   363

THE GREAT DEPRESSION AHEAD

Simple Principles Drive Complex Change

ARE YOU PREPARED for the next great crash ahead?

Wouldn't it be nice to be able to predict the key economic trends that will impact your life, your business, and your investments over the rest of your lifetime?

Of course we would like to be able to predict all of these trends and have greater predictability and control over our lives. But what would any reputable economist tell you? No one can predict any major events or trends past the next election or Federal Reserve policy change, as we live in an ever-changing world with increasing complexity. "If a butterfly flaps its wings in Tokyo, we could get a hurricane in the Caribbean!" That's their interpretation of "complexity theory"—which misses the point of how that new theory actually increases the predictability of chaotic processes. Simple common sense would also tell you otherwise. Life clearly has become more complex over modern human history, yet we have learned to predict more events in all areas of life. As a result, our standard of living has gone up while our level of risk has actually gone down over time.

When people complain about how complex, unpredictable, stressful, and risky life seems to be getting, I always ask them to go back to the 1930s, the Great Plague of the mid-1300s, the Dark Ages, the last Ice Age, or almost any time in the past. Life was shorter, more brutal, and less predictable as a general rule the further you go back in history! For another, relatively recent example, try imagining that you are a secretary in the TV series *Mad Men,* depicting office life in the 1950s.

If you betrayed the king or a noble in the 1500s, you were hanged until nearly dead, and your intestines were cut out of you and burned while you were still alive enough to see it happen. Then you were killed. In a more merciful situation, you were burned alive at the stake. In the most merciful scenario (such as with Queen Anne Boleyn, a wife of Henry VIII), your head was cut off in public. That was justice back then. Your town or village could be raided at any time by vandals or bandits and they might throw your babies up to land on their spears for fun, rape the women, torture or kill the men, and make slaves out of those who weren't killed. If you were a lucky survivor, you perhaps just had to row boats for the rich or the navy until you passed out from exhaustion or were whipped to death. You've seen the movies—we don't need to go further here to make the point. We just don't accept the reality of the past: We prefer to see it as fiction and drama and watch movies about the few rich people who had it made.

Now people complain that the rich control over 40% of the wealth today and have too much influence—but wealth was ten times more concentrated in the glory days of Rome, and even more so before that. Most people were slaves, peasants, or barely struggling to survive for most of human history and were subject to sudden wars, plagues, famines, climate changes, and many other things that they could not see coming—even annual seasons and births on a nine-month lag from sex, if you go way back.

Understanding the cycles of life at more levels has given us greater predictability and control over our lives over time, despite rising complexity, greater populations and urban density—and now computers, nanotechnologies, and globalization. Scientists and professionals in many fields, including soft sciences like psychology and even more practical areas such as life insurance calculations, have been predicting more things with greater accuracy over time. It's time for economics and economists to join the party!

Successful Leaps in Science Finally Apply to the Dismal Profession of Economics

Successive breakthroughs in science, from Sir Isaac Newton's clocklike universe in the late 1600s through today's breakthroughs in quantum physics, create ever greater predictability, from macro to increasingly micro trends. The truth is that Newton was correct in his theory of simple and clocklike cycles. It's just that there are many cycles from macro to micro, and they interact differently over time—and that is what creates the "seemingly" random and complex world we live in. Newton identified some initial macro cycles, and scientists since have developed many more that often seemed at first to disprove Newton's cycles to some degree—but never really disproved them altogether. His theories and predictions still largely hold. Objects still fall with gravity at a certain rate, but Albert Einstein proved that objects in space warp gravity and create distortions that are meaningful on a macro scale.

A new group of scientists in quantum physics followed and proved that different dynamics work at the most micro levels—forces and patterns that have become more predictable despite seeming to be more random and that led to the information revolution in microchips, genetics, biotechnology, and so on. The truth is that such micro cycles are more probabilistic than deterministic (or cause and effect as in macro cycles), but those probabilities can be calculated very precisely, much as life insurance actuaries do today for average life expectancies, even though individual ones vary dramatically.

We're not going to get into all of that here, and this information may not seem to apply that much to your job or your life or investments. However, it is important simply to understand that there has been a scientific revolution since the late 1600s and 1700s that has brought one breakthrough after another and has created greater predictability in more fields of research (for example, from when the sun will burn out in 5 billion years to when tides will peak on any coast anywhere around the world, down to the minute). All of these predictions are based on life cycles and stages that occur at all levels large and small.

The problem with prediction is that there are many or even infinite levels of cycles. Hence the key to prediction is to identify which cycles are the most critical and in what hierarchy they occur for what you are trying to forecast. Complexity occurs from many simple cycles that interact and evolve over time and create ever-more-complex outcomes. The paradox is that greater complexity doesn't mean less predictability. We as humans have been capable of predicting more things over time due to our more complex learning abilities, and that has created progress and a higher standard of living. It's just that macro trends are the simplest and the least complicated in short-term complexity.

Economists assume the opposite: they think that long-term trends are not predictable due to ever-increasing complexity and that shorter-term trends are more predictable due to things like fiscal and monetary policies that have shorter time lags for effect, as a cup of coffee does. That is the great misconception!

Our economy has peaked every forty years like clockwork—and commodity prices have peaked every thirty years. The early part of most decades starts off weak, even in boom times. Every four years the stock market tends to take a significant correction, and about every four months it often does so again on a more minor scale. Every 500 years we see mega innovations like the printing press or computers that cause rising prosperity and inflation for 250 years or so to follow. Every 250 years we see major revolutions in institutions that promote greater freedom and human rights—such as the American Revolution and the Protestant Revolution before it. Every 5,000 years we make major leaps in civilization and urbanization, going from towns to city-states and empires to megacities and a global economy in current times.

Greater complexity leads to greater information and intelligence (including technology and now computers) that actually allow greater predictability over time from the macro to the micro arenas. Macro trends are the simplest and the least complex, as most short-term trends average out within their cycles. They dominate a grand hierarchy that is more predictable and for which greater information is available, but always more at the macro level than the micro level, wherein changes happen more rapidly and where there are infinitely smaller cycles to interact and create complexity. Yet changes are also increasingly more predictable at the micro level, especially since the advent of quantum physics and areas like technical analysis in financial markets. An overview of the more predictable macro trends paradoxically adds to the probability of predicting more complex short-term trends more accurately, as you can add a strong bias upward or downward to your probabilistic forecasts.

However, there is a greater error in forecasting that most everyday human beings share with economists: Human beings tend to project linearly, in straight lines, while real life and progress occur exponentially, in cycles up and down. Economists are trapped in a straight-line and short-term misconception of predictability, as they often make roughly right forecasts when cycles are headed in the same direction but almost always miss the major changes in cycles that most impact governments, businesses, and individuals. Hence, they tend to underforecast trends at both extremes—especially in bubble booms and bubble busts, as we are seeing today for the first time since the early to mid-1900s. We as individuals tend to do the same, and that is why contrarian indicators often work so well—they say "Do the opposite of what most people or economists think!"

How many economists forecast the unprecedented inflation of the 1970s, with $40 oil prices and the loss of U.S. corporate leadership to Japan? How many then forecast the boom of the 1980s during the recessions of 1980 and 1982? How many forecast the great boom of the 1990s and the resurgence of the United States when we were in debt over our heads and in a real estate slowdown and savings-and-loan crisis in the early 1990s much like today? How many forecast the surplus in the U.S. budget between 1998 and 2000 back when it had its greatest deficit in history, in 1992? How many forecast the long decline in Japan in the 1990s and early 2000s, when Japan looked invincible in the 1980s? Look instead at how many bestselling books forecast a great depression for the 1990s that never happened. How many forecast the crash of 2000–2002? How many forecast the boom that would continue into recent years after that crash? And how many forecast oil prices of $147 back in 1998, when they were at $11 a barrel?

I stood virtually alone in forecasting the great boom of the 1990s, with falling inflation and the surplus between 1998 and 2000—way back in late 1992 in *The Great Boom Ahead*. In that book I forecast that the U.S. would enter a depression from 2008 to 2022/2023. I also forecast the long downturn in Japan in 1989 in *Our Power to Predict*. My organization forecast the top in the stock and tech markets in early 2000 but did not at first anticipate how dramatic the crash that followed would be. We also forecast the boom that followed that crash in the 2000s, especially with the strongest buy signal in the history of our newsletter in October 2002, including the second buy opportunity in March 2003. But we overforecast the stock market in the 2000s by assuming that we would see a second tech bubble as strong as the first, as occurred in the 1920s, eighty years earlier, in our most important long-term New Economy Cycle. We have continued to be right about the direction of trends, but have missed the magnitude of some trends after the peak in early 2000. That has caused us to add some new long-term and intermediate cycles and indicators that are important for refining our forecasts, as we will describe ahead. However, these additions have not changed the importance of the fundamental indicators that are the very base of our research.

There is a logic to our economy that includes inflation and deflation, bubbles and depressions, growth and recession, and innovation and decline—just as in our broader world with the tides, the sun rising and setting, the 7 days in a week, the 12 months in a year, the 4 annual seasons, elections every 4 years, the average person moving every 7 years, 20-year hurricane cycles, and so on, even including ice ages every 100,000 years or so. The best economists identified a near-60-year cycle that occurred between the late 1700s and the early 1900s—but then it seemed to fail. The truth is that it was simply supplanted by a larger 80-year cycle, as we will describe in this book. Nevertheless, that 60-year cycle still occurs more in commodity prices than in broader economic cycles today and explains the recent commodity bubble. Every 4 years, as we approach the midterm elections, the stock market tends to correct, but every decade a broader cycle kicks in that tends to see stocks correct for 2 to 3 years in the early part of each decade—and that cycle can override and impact the 4-year cycle and other cycles. However, the 4-year cycle still persists pretty consistently.

The great insight for long-term forecasting comes from understanding the hierarchy of cycles from long term to short term that most affect the economy and your life. Our research is all about starting with the most fundamental macro cycles that actually drive economic growth and then refining those with other recurring cycles that impact the economy in the more intermediate term and with short-term technical analysis that better predicts the more probabilistic shorter-term wiggles. But the paradox is that the longer-term cycles are more predictable.

In your life-planning horizon, cycles as long as 500 years can be important, despite being beyond your horizon, as they show a certain direction that can be more positive or negative in your lifetime—and we, fortunately, have been in a major uptrend since the late 1800s that has encompassed the best trends within the last century and that should continue upward overall beyond your lifetime and even your kids' lifetimes.

However, the most important cycle is an 80-year New Economy Cycle that has four seasons, much like your life span and life cycle. That cycle is about to serve you the biggest surprise since the Henry Ford generation saw the Roaring Twenties suddenly turn into the Great Depression. But it is also the 500-year cycle that will likely make this coming depression less painful than the depression of the 1930s. The two most important inter-mediate-term cycles, the 40-year generation and 30-year commodity, just happen to be peaking around late 2009, creating "the perfect storm" just ahead.

The most important principle to understand is that your life cycle and the economy's life cycle are likely to coincide differently. You will tend to make logical decisions according to your own life cycle and seasons ahead: education, marriage, raising kids, peaking in your career, a midlife crisis, and retirement. You won't tend to see how the economy's life cycle will greatly impact yours, especially when it changes seasons, often dramatically at first, as in the early 1930s and mid-1970s—and the economy is the 800-pound gorilla!

Stumbling on a New Science of Economics Starting with Demographics

I started studying economics in college but quickly changed my major to finance and accounting—economics was vague and didn't seem to be predictable or useful on a practical level. I worked in accounting and finance for a Fortune 100 company for a few years and then decided to go to Harvard Business School to focus on broader and more strategic issues. I learned a lot there about product life cycles and how to fight for my ideas—that is what you had to do to survive "the case method approach," in which there was no right or wrong, just what you could best analyze and argue and what made the most sense at the time, and then compare that with what happened in reality afterward. I worked as a strategic consultant to Fortune 100 companies at Bain & Company at a time when the firm was young and I could learn directly from Bill Bain, from partners like Mitt Romney, and from many bright associates. I learned more there in two years than I did at Harvard Business School—but I didn't tend to agree with the consensus of the team most of the time. I tended to think, "Let's duplicate the innovative new, decentralized minimill strategy of companies like Nucor rather than trying to emulate the Japanese at reengineering larger, more centralized steel mills"— which wasn't as realistic for the more mature companies we were consulting to.

I knew my days were numbered at Bain & Company. My greatest accomplishment was that I was assigned to develop a forecasting model for tire demand for a major tire company simply because I had an accounting and finance background. I was into that, given that I had an interest in long-term cycles even back in college. However, I had never had any training in forecasting nor had I ever actually developed a forecasting model, other than projecting profits forward like any good accountant. Well, I had a short-term deadline and my manager told me that he knew that the present models were too optimistic based on past extrapolations of trends and given rising oil prices, a slowing economy, and the shift to radial tires, which lasted twice as long—which all strongly suggested a slowing trend in tire demand rather than an ever-rising one. He also told me to focus on the fundamentals and to keep it as simple as possible, since I had only a few weeks to develop this model.

There's nothing like urgency and focus to force clear results! Within two weeks I had developed a two-variable model on a time lag that forecast a change in direction that ended up being right, while the industry models were wrong. To make a long story short, that is where I learned about the S-curve principle of new products overtaking old ones (radial versus bias tires) and about the demographics of when people drive more or less and who buys products like tires by age and income. Those two principles drove a very simple model that not only tracked the past as well as much more complex models did, but also forecast a major change in trends that such complex models did not.

What I really learned was that simple trends drive long-term growth and changes in cycles and that demographic and technology cycles are critical in predicting business and economic trends.

Of course, we refined that model for shorter-term variables once it proved correct for predicting longer-term trends and cycles, but the fundamentals—not the shorter-term and more varied indicators that drove and fed the more complex econometric models in the industry— came first. That is how most economic models currently work: they start from the complex and work backward rather than starting from the simple or macro and working forward.

In the 1980s, I started working with more entrepreneurial companies that fit my leanings toward a new, more decentralized economy and business model. In my consulting with these companies, I kept seeing that members of the large and emerging baby-boom generation were creating new product and technology trends; that confirmed the demographic and S-curve life cycles I learned at both Harvard Business School and Bain & Company. Naturally, I kept researching demographic and technology trends until I arrived at a number of breakthrough models that ended up applying more to the macro economy than to trends within the markets in which I was consulting.

In 1988 I discovered a strong correlation between the Dow and S&P 500 adjusted for inflation and a 45- to 49-year lag for the peak in spending of the baby-boom generation and the past Bob Hope generation back to the 1950s. This simple model would forecast macroeconomic and stock trends 50 years in advance! In 1989 I discovered a clear correlation between inflation and young people entering the workforce at the peak of their expense cycle for education, workforce training, and investment. Then I looked back and saw that the same economic cycles were occurring in radical new technologies that were first innovated and started to move mainstream on an S-curve cycle on an 80-year or two-generation lag back to the early 1900s and Roaring Twenties. We were clearly in the dynamic early stages of a new economy.

I started to see that *demographic trends* were the greatest driver of our economy, along with *radical new technologies* that changed the foundations of our economy and that followed a four-stage life cycle of innovation, growth, shakeout, and maturity. I also saw that demographics seemed to be increasingly driving the innovation and adoption of new technologies, as increasingly affluent consumers had much more impact on our economy than in past eras, when a relatively few people controlled politics, wealth, and business. Hence, demographics were destiny!

I will explain much more about these simple principles and how powerful they are, but let me first explain how my firm's research has evolved over time, starting with the simplest fundamentals and refining those with other important cycles that affect our economy and your life.

It took some time and experimentation to get to where we are today, and it hasn't always been easy. I will explain the confidence levels we now have in our forecasts for years and decades ahead, after many refinements to our most fundamental indicators in demographic and technology cycles.

The Evolution of Our Forecasting Methods

Starting in the late 1980s, we predicted the slowdown in Japan for twelve to fourteen years, a two-year slowdown in the U.S. economy in the early 1990s, and then the greatest boom in U.S. history for the 1990s, which would continue into the end of this decade. We even predicted in the early 1990s that the unprecedented federal deficit would turn into a surplus between 1998 and 2000! We at first overforecast the downturn of the early 1990s in the United States, but we were pretty much right on about everything else, including falling inflation and interest rates in the 1990s. We did this on the basis of two simple indicators: the Spending Wave (a 44- to 48-year lag on births for the peak in spending of the average household) and an 80-year New Economy Cycle that would see radical new information technologies move mainstream suddenly from around 1994 to 2008, much as autos, electricity, and phones did from 1914 to 1928 on an S-curve cycle. Most economists and people said we were nuts! The truth is, we were and we weren't! There were no other major cycles to interfere, and our new fundamental cycles won out, with the Dow going to 10,000+ in the greatest bull market since the 1920s in the 1990s, with Japan continuing to slow and the great federal deficit disappearing and turning to surpluses from 1998 to 2000, all as we forecast in *The Great Boom Ahead*.

Since we were tracking the Dow on an exponential correlation with the growing boom, our "Dow Channel" forecast a peak between 32,000 and 40,000 between 2008 and 2009. That channel also forecast that stocks were extremely overvalued in late 1999 and early 2000—which we warned about in *The Roaring 2000s Investor* (1999) and in our newsletter in early 2000. We forecast that the Internet bubble was peaking in February 2000, and in April 2000 we forecast that the Nasdaq and broader tech stocks were peaking as well. The problem is that we thought that this would be another 20% to 30% correction on the way up to 32,000+. It was not! By late 2000 and early 2001 our growing base of shorter-term technical indicators suggested that the downturn could see the Nasdaq and Dow go back to their late 1998 lows but that much of the damage was already done. Our challenge at that point was to figure out how such strong demographic and technology S-curve trends could result in such an extreme crash in an ongoing bull market.

From late 2000 onward, we reexamined our fundamental indicators and any other cycles and indicators that could explain the extreme 2000–2002 crash in the midst of such strong long-term trends in demographic and technology cycles—and we discovered a new twist on the technology and New Economy Cycle as well as some important new recurring cycles.

The first insight we got was from a Decennial Cycle from Ned Davis suggesting that the first few years of most decades start off weak with substantial and often extreme stock corrections in good and bad times. The second and bigger insight came from going back 80 years to the last New Economy Cycle and seeing that there was a first bubble in automotive and technology stocks from 1914 to 1919 that crashed in a manner very similar to the 2000–2002 crash. That represented a shakeout cycle after overexpansion into fast-growing new S-curve markets that was very much in line with our longer-term cycles but that occurred on the more intermediate S-curve of radical new technologies first entering the mainstream markets from 1914 to 1928. So the crash of 2000–2002 and its severity actually were predictable! Hence, as in the early 1920s crash, we were expecting a second strong bubble to follow, as occurred between 1925 and 1929. We also gave the strongest buy signal in our newsletter's history in late 2002, after giving a premature buy signal in late 2001, near the ultimate bottom.

After the markets closely followed a crash and slow recovery cycle before the next bubble that was at first similar to the 1990s and 1920s bubble booms, we got a strong divergence in the summer of 2006, as oil prices suddenly shot up to $78. Stocks were still heading upward but no longer in the bubble-like trajectory we expected. That forced us to look for reasons why oil prices and the geopolitical environment were differing from those in the 1990s, despite earnings and growth trends that were still clearly in line with our fundamental demographic and technology cycle indicators. Out of that analysis, we discovered two important new long-term cycles: a clocklike 29- to 30-year Commodity Cycle and a 32- to 36-year Geopolitical Cycle, which alternates between favorable and unfavorable environments pretty reliably every 16 to 18 years.

In our September and October 2006 newsletters, we cut our 2008–2009 forecasts for the Dow at the peak from 32,000 to 40,000 down to 16,000 to 20,000 based on these new cycles, suggesting that the markets had been and would continue to trade at half their valuations compared with the 1990s, even in a growing economy. When the subprime mortgage crisis started to hit in late 2007 and early 2008, we cut those forecasts back to 14,000 to 16,000, out of a belief that that some and likely more indices had already reached long-term highs as the financial sector had done in mid-1997, and others would come close to retesting their highs into mid-2009 and some could reach slight new highs after corrections into mid- to late 2008.

What we present in this book is, first of all, a more sober forecast than our bullish forecasts of the early 1990s and early 2000s. However, our fundamental long-term indicators have forecast consistently since the late 1980s that this boom would end around the end of this decade, as the massive baby-boom generation finally peaked in its productivity, earning, and spending power and as the new Internet and information technologies saturated our economy at or near 90% adoption. Thus we are not being inconsistent here—and people should listen more to a long-term bull that is turning bearish than to the perennial bears who forecast a great downturn or depression after every strong advance and excess borrowing cycle.

What we have learned over the evolution of our research is to incorporate a hierarchy of cycles that even better explains the most important trends that drive our economy, exponentially, up and down in cycles. We still find that our most fundamental new long-term cycles from generational spending trends and new technology cycles primarily drive the trends, but we now include new cycles, such as the Geopolitical Cycle and the Commodity Cycle (in Chapter 3). We've also incorporated some new twists in our longer-term 500-Year Cycle from past books, including a 250-Year Revolutionary Cycle and an even broader 5,000-Year Civilization Cycle, which corresponds to the new globalization trend.

Whether you have been exposed to our research in the past or you are a new reader, we strongly suggest that you keep an open mind and

carefully consider the arguments, logic, and hierarchy of cycles presented in this book. We have missed the magnitude of some trends, but we have successfully predicted the key trends and cycle changes over the last two decades. The most important cycle change for your wealth, health, life, family, business, and investments is just ahead during the first and last depression you are likely to experience in your entire lifetime—as they occur only every 80 years in current cycles.

How to Use This Book: How It Is Organized

Because many readers will have had some exposure to our past books or seminars, Chapter 1 gives a quick, summary overview of the dramatic change in economic trends ahead and how we have changed our forecasts over the past several years. Everyone should read that chapter first. Our more seasoned readers can skim or review Chapter 2, in which we look at and update the most important fundamental trends that drive our economy. New readers should be sure to study this chapter in depth, as it is most basic to our research. Chapter 3 brings the newest insights for past readers who have not subscribed to our newsletter. This chapter looks at the hierarchy of cycles from long term to short term and highlights the most important new cycles we have added in the last five to ten years. Chapter 4 addresses the issue most critical to many people today: the housing slowdown and the subprime crisis. We forecast well in advance that baby boomers would peak in their housing expenditures ahead of the broader economic peak due to definable spending trends by age. We also forecast, along with and using Robert Shiller's analysis, that housing was the most overvalued in U.S. history and ultimately due for a 55% to 65% longer-term decline, not just the 30% to 40% experienced so far in 2008. The worst decline will come from late 2009 or 2010 onward, when the longer-term baby-boom spending cycle finally collapses.

Next, we look at the silver linings in the downturn. In Chapter 5, we'll see that continued demographic-driven migration patterns will augment certain states and areas while hurting others. The biggest beneficiaries will continue to be in the Southeast and Southwest, but the trends toward states there are shifting after the bubble made many attractive areas too expensive. In Chapter 6, we take a look at the global trends in demographics, which differ greatly among various areas around the world. Asia will continue to rise, while many commodity-oriented emerging countries will bust at first. Long term, the global economy will see a new paradox: the economies of most developed Western countries, Japan, and, on a lag, China, will age and slow long term, while the economies of many emerging countries, such as India, will continue to rise for decades.

We then look at strategies for surviving and prospering for individuals, businesses, and governments. Chapter 7 starts with a better understanding of risk: why returns are not normally distributed, as most investors and financial advisors assume, and why traditional asset allocation models will fail in the coming "winter season." In Chapter 8, we will look at more specific strategies in stages for investors and businesses, including personal and family strategies in all aspects of your life. Finally, in Chapter 9, we will look at the critical issues facing our government and institutions as they are forced to restructure more radically and face the realities of an aging population versus ever-rising benefits promised. A "New Deal" will come in national politics, but we will also see a "New Deal" between the affluent developed countries and the emerging ones. New global institutions will be required to deal with a truly global economy that will finally emerge more in the early 2020s into the next boom—but only after a major revolution from failed policies in trade, pollution and global warming, and terrorism.

Longer-term historians, economists, and students should go to www.hsdent.com, to "Free Downloads," and download "The Long Wave." Therein we reconcile one of the great paradoxes in recent economic history: why did the 60-year Kondratieff Wave suddenly fail in the 1990s after two centuries of success as an economic model? We show conclusively how a larger 80-year generation-based cycle supplanted that model, and why global trends are in fact likely to return us back to that near-60-year cycle in the future. In fact, it seems that our broader New Economy Cycle gets stretched from 60 to 80 years every 250 years on our new Revolutionary Cycle (see Chapter 3).

This book is organized so that you can start with the first chapter as an overview and then go more directly to the chapters that most apply to you or that you are least familiar with if you have followed our work in the past. The most important chapters to focus on are Chapter 1 (overview), Chapter 3 (new cycles), Chapter 4 (real estate and depression cycles), and Chapter 8 (strategies for family, investment, and business). Our most astounding and long-range forecasts come in Chapter 6 as we look at trends around the world for the rest of this century! The rest is more optional or to scan, or to get to as you please. You don't have to read this book in a linear sequence.

Welcome to the first comprehensive forecast for the trends that will affect you for the rest of your lifetime. Most economists don't dare to do that. We do! But we also recognize that there will be divergences and continued refinement of our research as well. Hence in the back of this book we are offering free periodic e-mail updates, and we have a monthly newsletter you can subscribe to that will give in-depth updates to our research and shorter-term market and economic forecasts.

The greatest lesson we have learned in more than twenty years of comprehensive research and forecasting is that there are important cycles that occur in a hierarchy that can allow you to plan for the key trends that will affect your life, your business, and your investments over the rest of your life. We have been very good and have gotten better at timing those key cycle changes. The most difficult challenges come in the more exact timing as these cycles interact in more complex ways, and in the magnitude of the booms and busts, particularly in the stock markets. We have a very high confidence level in forecasting that our economy will worsen and that we will see the worst downturn since the 1930s between mid- to late 2009 and 2012. Whether the Dow falls to 3,800 (our best target) or lower is harder to forecast. And whether the actual bottom comes in late 2010 or mid-2011 or mid- to late 2012 or even late 2014 is also a question mark. Whether unemployment reaches 15% or higher is also to be seen.

Best of success to you in the great crash and depression ahead! We want to help you get through the most difficult period in the economy's natural life cycle. "You can't change the winds, but you can reset your sails." Now let's turn to Chapter 1, which has been totally rewritten, and get a quick overview of our "very contrary" forecasts and where and how they have changed in recent years. Also note that major revisions have been made to Chapter 6 for new research into emerging country trends globally.

The Debt Crisis of 2010–2012

. . . Why It Will Be Very Good for Our Country

WE ALL WATCHED our banking and financial systems melt down out of nowhere in 2008 from things most of us never heard of: credit default swaps, collateralized debt obligations, collateralized mortgage obligations, and so on. Some of our largest financial institutions, including Lehman Brothers, failed, and many more would have if it hadn't been for the massive government bailout and rescue program. The Dow crashed 7,840 points, from 14,280 to 6,440, slashing our retirement plans. But unlike the 2000–2002 crash, the 2008 crash saw real estate and commodities crash as well. Most baby boomers finally felt how vulnerable their retirement plans were and they have become very conservative in spending and more savings-oriented, which hurts the economy. Since March of 2009 the stock markets have rallied back above 9,800, which we predicted as "the eye of the storm" in the first edition of this book, with signs of stabilization in the banks, the economic slide abating, and leading indicators pointing upward again.

Major magazines like *Newsweek* and *BusinessWeek* have had cover stories pegged to the notion that "the recession is over." Most economists now agree, but note that the recovery will be slow at first. Such broad consensus is almost always wrong! By contrast, a majority of people in this country feel that the government has gone too far in its bailout and stimulus programs, and we think your intuition is correct. **More debt cannot be the answer to an economy that is suffering from excessive debt and leverage!** There also are much more important reasons that this recovery will not be sustainable and that we will see the banking crisis return stronger than ever in 2010:

1. The largest generation in history, the baby boom, has peaked in its long spending cycle, which started in the early 1980s. The boomers will increasingly be saving for retirement and retiring in increasing numbers for many years to come. How does the government regenerate spending in this environment?

2. We have just seen the greatest credit and real estate bubble in modern history and it has only begun to deleverage and deflate. It can't complete that process unless we allow a lot of failed debts to be restructured rather than propped up in support of a failed system. Isn't it a good thing to eliminate a lot of debt?

3. The U.S. government is trying to stimulate the economy out of a meltdown and downturn when the U.S. is now the greatest net debtor in the world. But it simply won't have the capacity to keep borrowing to stimulate without driving up interest rates. Domestic and foreign bondholders will start to question the U.S. government's ability to repay, with deficits approaching $3 trillion, and higher interest rates would kill the real estate markets again anyway.

The most important view from our very objective and long-term research is simply that our economy has always followed a four-season cycle that fluctuates around new technology and generational boom and bust cycles. Think of consumer prices or inflation like temperature. We come out of a cold winter like 1930–1942, see spring with temperatures rising to comfortable levels again and a boom like 1942–1965, with a rising Bob Hope–generation cycle of spending. Then temperatures rise more rapidly into a summer season that produces high inflation and extreme interest rates, which are not good for the economy or stocks, as we saw from 1966 through 1982. Then inflation subsides and we see the fall season bring temperatures back into a very comfortable range again: technologies flourish with low interest rates and the massive baby boom generation spending its way into a great bubble, as it did from 1983 to

2000. Then winter starts to set in, slowly at first. Then it gets very cold around 2010–2012, with many banks and businesses failing, which eventually clears the decks of excessive debt and failed business models to set the stage for spring again, around 2020/2023.

The biggest surprise ahead is that we will see deflation in prices, not inflation, despite the greatest government stimulus program in history. That changes investment and business strategies in ways that are contrary to what most bullish and even bearish economists expect. From late 2009 or early 2010 into late 2010 stocks, real estate, bonds and commodities will fall dramatically again, cash will be king, and the U.S. dollar will paradoxically rise, not crash, as it did in the stock crash from May 2008 into March of 2009.

Is there something wrong with the universe or our Creator? These seasons are pervasive in life, including our own human life cycles, and each season has its purpose. Depressions, or winters, are not an accident of bad business or government policy, although bad government policies or lack of effective regulation can make them worse. They are the essence of economic cycles, which flourish the most under a free market capitalist system—with some obvious rules and regulations required. Any game needs good rules to work, and that is where our government may have failed most in the recent cycle. But free market capitalism is not failing now any more than it did in the 1930s. Remember the simplicity of these seasonal cycles, as we will refer to them briefly in the sections ahead, and then summarize this most senior of cycles at the end of this chapter.

You can't change the winds . . . you can only reset your sails. There is a way that you can not only survive but prosper in this winter season ahead. And many long-term benefits will come from this winter season, such as lower debt levels, lower housing and real estate costs, a lower cost of living and retirement, and many more efficient businesses to continue to make new technologies and products/services more affordable. Our children and the next generation will benefit the most from this necessary and inevitable winter and debt deflation cycle. It was no accident that the greatest mass prosperity boom in history, from 1942 to 1968, followed the Great Depression.

Why listen to us? We predicted this downturn in the early 1990s in our first published book, *The Great Boom Ahead*. On page 16 of the paperback version, published in 1994, we stated: "The next great depression will occur from 2008 to 2023." And later we added that "no amount of government stimulus will prevent this." We also predicted the great boom of the 1990s and beyond when most best-selling authors back then were predicting a depression. And our predictions had nothing to do with government policies. The government thinks it created this unprecedented boom and now it thinks it can prevent the next winter, or great depression. But the cycles are immutable: the greater the bubble boom, or fall season, the greater the depression—with no exceptions in modern history!

We will show in this first chapter and in much more depth ahead that predictable generational and technology cycles drive our economy—and earlier in our agriculture-based history (and in many third world countries today), commodity cycles drove our economy. Good government and infrastructures can set the stage, but it is consumers and businesses that drive our economy and free market capitalism tends to allow them to create the greatest standards of living. But such free market cycles tend to thrive precisely because they allow extremes in innovation and failure. That is why the U.S. leads in new technologies and has created the highest standard of living in the world of any major country. And that's why we saw the most extreme bubble and will now see the most extreme crash and debt restructuring before we boom again.

The same predictable generational cycles also allowed us to predict the long decline in Japan in the late 1980s just as most economists thought Japan was the new up-and-coming leader in the world economy. Now Japan is the society that is aging the fastest with the highest debt ratios of any major country. Japan's stock market crashed 80% from 1990 to 2003 and real estate 60% to 70%. The Japanese will never see those peak levels again in our lifetime! We should not repeat Japan's mistake of allowing government stimulus and debt to replace private sector deleveraging and restructuring of debt.

We have predicted many other major cycles, including the peak in the housing bubble, which we noted back in 2004–2005 in our newsletter, *The HS Dent Forecast*. But we also admit where we have been off in the past. Our biggest miss was in magnitude only, but it was a big one. We predicted correctly that stocks would boom again from October 2002 onward, but we predicted a much greater advance: as high as 32,000 plus in the Dow, not 14,280. We were looking at a similar technology and generational cycle back in the early 1900s where a first technology bubble from 1914 to 1919 and crash was followed by a second bigger bubble from 1922 to 1929. This time the bubble and speculation expanded onto a world stage, with bigger bubbles in housing and real estate, emerging markets and Asia, and commodities like oil. But the U.S. stock markets still doubled between late 2002 and late 2007, so our investors were headed in the right direction and Asia was one of our biggest recommendations, with the biggest bubbles occurring in countries like China and India. Hence, this last decade was "roaring," as we predicted in our best-selling book *The Roaring 2000s* (1998).

In this first chapter we will keep it simple and explain the most important trends that are both highly projectable and intuitively understandable. It is the family life cycle of earning and spending that most drives modern, middle class economies, and we can predict such trends by moving forward the birth index 46 years for the peak in spending, after we adjust for immigration. Credit bubbles in the past have followed very predictable stages of deleveraging and deflation. And deflation (or winter) has always followed such bubbles—again with no exceptions in modern history! Our economy follows four simple seasons just like our annual weather cycles. We cover these principles in more depth in Chapter 2.

The theme of our research is that you can see today all of the key economic trends that will impact your life, your family, your business, and your investments over the rest of your lifetime! No one else dares to do that. We do. Read further to see how simple and common sense our cycles and methods are—and how unexpected the changes will be in the next few years.

Principle 1: The Largest Generation in History Has Peaked in Its Spending Cycle . . . Why This Is Not an Ordinary Recession

Economists have missed the simplest and most important cycle driving modern economies like that in the U.S. New generations come along about every 40 years and move up a predictable family life cycle of earning, spending, and productivity. These people then do predictable things as they age from entering the workforce (age 20, on average) to getting married (age 26) to having kids (ages 28–29) to buying starter homes (age 31) to trade-up homes (ages 37–42) to peaking in spending (ages 46–50), then peaking in savings rates (age 54) and net worth (age 64). They retire at age 63 and have the highest debt at ages 41–42, most of it mortgage debt. These are all average statistics like our life expectancies from life insurance actuaries. We are all different, but on average we are highly predictable.

The simplest logic is that our economy booms as new generations move up this predictable spending cycle. All you have to do is lag the birth index, adjusted for immigration, by 46 years for the peak in spending. It's Homer Simpson who drives our economy, not Ben Bernanke or Barack Obama!

Contrary Insight 1: The government's stimulus plan will not work for more than a very short time due to the slowing spending and rising

Figure 1.1: The Spending Wave
Births Lagged for Peak in Family Spending

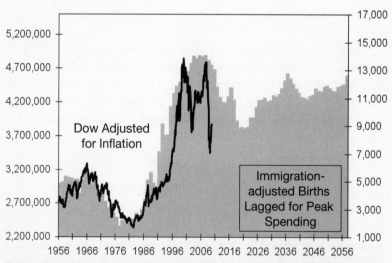

Figure 1.1 shows the correlation with the S&P 500 adjusted for inflation with this simple lag. We call it the Spending Wave and we came up with this indicator back in 1988 after the 1987 crash, when many thought the stock market boom was over. In 1988 and in our first book, *The Great Boom Ahead*, we predicted this boom would last until late 2007 or a bit later and then we would see an extended downturn and depression, from 2008 into 2023 or so, as the massive baby boom generation turned from spenders to savers for retirement.

savings of the largest generation in history. And baby boom savings trends are being amplified by the sudden, simultaneous collapse of stocks and real estate at the same time. This is not an ordinary recession. It is the beginning of a long slowdown in a cycle of approximately 40 years. Japan already saw its baby boom peak nearly 20 years earlier, around 1990, and its stock market and economy declined for 14 years, as we forecast with similar indicators back in 1988 and 1989.

Most European and developed countries are peaking in demographic spending trends along with the U.S. and that is the first reason this is a global downturn. In Chapter 2 we cover the family life cycle in more depth and show how consumer spending varies in different categories, from potato chips to housing to prescription drugs, and how the broader spending waves vary around the world. In this chapter we are trying to simply demonstrate the most important points to stimulate you to learn

Figure 1.2: 39–40-Year Generation Cycle
S&P 500 Adjusted for Inflation Log Scale

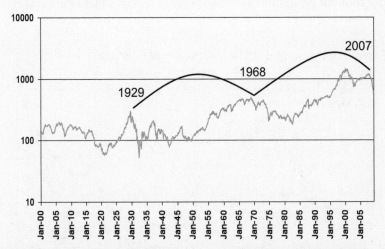

Figure 1.2 shows how the stock market has seen major long-term peaks every 39 years, with those highs not being achieved again for 24 to 25 years. The 39–40-year cycle is simple: the economy and stocks boom for about 25 to 27 years and then decline for 12 to 14 years. We have seen long-term declines between late 1929 and early 1942, late 1968 and late 1982, and now late 2007 to 2020 or late 2022 or so. Japan is the only major developed country to not have a baby boom after World War II. We are fortunate to have that country as an example of what will occur ahead of the larger baby boom peaks in the rest of the developed world. The results in Japan were clear: a deleveraging of debt, stocks, and real estate—and deflation, not inflation!

more and get serious about changing your investment, business, and life strategies ahead of the deeper debt and demographic crisis ahead.

Principle 2: The Greatest Credit Bubble in Modern History Will Continue to Deleverage . . . Deflation, not Inflation, Is Just Ahead

The biggest trend driving the unexpected meltdown of our banking and financial systems that started in 2008 is the fact that we have seen the greatest credit bubble in modern history, which began to develop way back in the early 1980s but accelerated dramatically between 2000 and 2007. Figure 1.3 shows how debt as a percentage of GDP in the U.S. has skyrocketed during this period even more than it did during the Roaring 20s. Private debt is approaching 300% of GDP vs. 270% back in 1932, and total debt is nearing 400% of GDP vs. 310% in 1932. But note how much private debt was eliminated in the 1930s and 1940s winter season: it fell from 270% to 50% of GDP. What a massive relief! Figure 1.4 shows how private debt is decelerating much faster than the public debt from the stimulus program is growing. Figure 1.5 shows that household net

Figure 1.3: Private and Public Debt as a % of GDP, U.S.

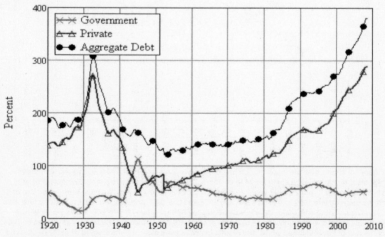

Figure 1.4: Change in Private and Public Debt, U.S.

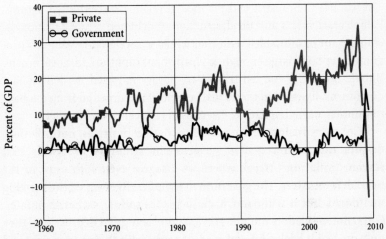

Source: Steve Keen's Debtwatch July 2009

Figure 1.5: Total Household Net Worth, U.S.

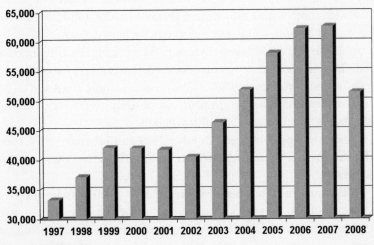

Source: Federal Reserve

worth fell $12 trillion in 2008 alone, not counting early to mid-2009. The total decline in household net worth will likely be closer to $25 trillion. This dwarfs the present and planned government stimulus programs! Falling asset values and the destruction of debt will create deflation—a contraction of available credit that would outweigh any stimulus program except one large enough to clearly bankrupt the U.S. government. Bubble booms in the fall season are always followed by deflationary downturns, like that in the 1930s, in winter. You don't go from fall back to summer, or high inflation. That has never occurred in history.

Contrary Insight 2: We will see deflation in prices, not inflation, despite the unprecedented government stimulus programs that scream "inflation." Here's where we disagree even with most of the bearish forecasters. The government temporarily stopped the banking meltdown, but it will come back in spades sooner rather than later. Government leaders did not prevent "the next great depression," they only pushed it back a bit and made it worse with their added debt and stimulus. Deflation implies very different investment and business strategies than an inflationary downturn of the sort that happened in the 1970s.

We predicted in the first edition of this book that we would see a first deep recession and then a strong government stimulus program that would create "the eye of the storm" with a stock rebound into the summer of 2009. But then the real depression would hit between 2010 and 2012, with another major stock crash between late 2009 and late 2010. In this revised edition, and in our newsletter, we have examined all of the great bubble and credit booms in history. There are no exceptions: once credit bubbles go to extremes they always deflate, and they are followed by deflation in prices, not inflation. Why? Because more assets and credit are destroyed than the government can possibly counteract, without going bankrupt, through a stimulus program.

Stocks will peak between October 2009 and February 2010, then fall to between 2,300 and 4,500 by late 2010, with 3,350–3,800 our most likely target.

Most economists now see a recovery in 2010, albeit a milder one than in the past due to the obvious damage to the banking system and due to heightened consumer fear and savings. Leading indicators are looking at the rising money supply and stimulus, but are missing the dramatic decline in Money Velocity in Figure 1.6. Consumers and businesses are not spending the stimulus and banks are not lending like they did in the past—for obvious reasons. We see a very brief recovery that is followed by a resurgence of banking crises and geopolitical tensions around the world. Consumers and businesses will then retreat even faster than they did in 2008 and early 2009 and the banking crisis will resurge again even harder than it did in late 2008. By other reliable cycles, the odds are strong that the next banking and geopolitical cycles will hit again between late 2009 and the summer of 2010.

Our government's policy is that downturns and debt crises like this are to be avoided at all costs. That means they are willing to rack up $10s of trillions in debt if necessary. This is absurd. No household or business would try to borrow their way out of excessive debt when their jobs or market prospects turn down. They cut costs and restructure their debts to survive and ultimately prosper again. The bankruptcy process is one of the cornerstones of modern free market systems. If everyone had to pay their debts no matter what after taking risks and innovating, innovation would suffer and be less attractive. Chapter 11 is a legal process wherein individuals or businesses can restructure their debts after failure if they have enough potential to grow again.

Contrary Insight 3: This debt crisis will allow massive restructur-

Figure 1.6: Money Velocity
GDP to Adjusted Monetary Base

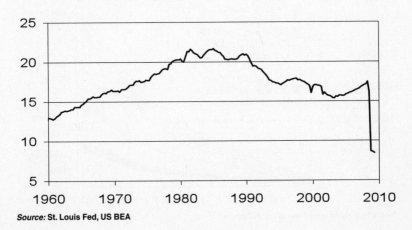

Source: St. Louis Fed, US BEA

ing of debt that will make individual households and businesses more viable and efficient again, with lower debt and borrowing costs and with lower interest rates as well from the deflationary environment. That is good for our country and economy in the future! Figure 1.3 above shows how much debt was eliminated in the 1930s and 1940s, setting the stage for the greatest mass prosperity boom in history after World War II. The winter season clears the decks for renewed growth in spring, a time for the country to emerge again with innovations, more efficient businesses, and lower costs of living.

In contrast, Japan followed the same "stimulate with public debt" strategy to offset the private decline and debt deleveraging that our government is proposing. Public debt largely offset private debt destruction. Now Japan is an aging society with declining growth prospects and the highest government debt ratios in the developed world—a recipe for disaster. Japan is a retirement community in hock. Its stock market peaked in 1990, and its stocks are still down 75%, while real estate values are down 60%, and the country will see worse ahead in this global downturn.

There is much concern about the rising federal debt in this country, which doubled from $5 trillion to $10 trillion in 8 years under George W. Bush. Figure 1.7 shows the big picture with $57 trillion in total debt, or

Figure 1.7: Total U.S. Debt, 2008

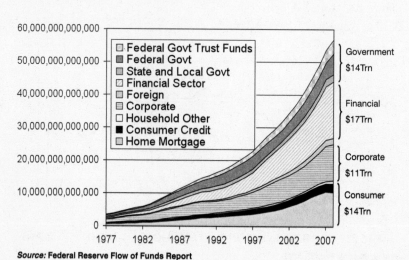

Source: Federal Reserve Flow of Funds Report

400% of GDP, as we showed earlier. The largest part, $17 trillion, is simply leverage within our banking and financial system. This is the reason that the big banks and investment banks got together with the government and demanded the massive bailout program. Our financial system made major bets with massive leverage—sometimes as high as 30:1—and now many of its players are bankrupt. The system started to melt down and would have without government intervention. But we need to get rid of most of this $17 trillion. The next largest sector is consumer debt, at $14 trillion, with $10.5 trillion of that home mortgages. More than $5 trillion will be written off in this sector before the crisis is over. Then there is $11 trillion in the corporate sector, which will see $5 trillion plus in commercial mortgages and business loans written off. We should see at least $20 trillion of debt vanish. How could that not be a good thing? The government and financial institutions are merely hoping that the economy can return to normal and that they won't have to admit they were so stupid and went so far in unregulated leverage and debt. The big question is how much the government debt rises. We are already at almost $12 trillion for the federal government and $2 trillion for state and local. Federal debt could rise to $20 trillion by 2013.

In addition to nearly $12 trillion in government debt in late 2009, we have $43 trillion in unfunded liabilities for Medicaid, Medicare, and Social Security, according to the U.S. Treasury—and $53 trillion according to the Pete Peterson Foundation. That means we have total debt, including private debt of $100 to $110 trillion, or 700% to 800% of GDP. Enough is enough! It's time we admitted we are nearly bankrupt and go through a Chapter 11 process of eliminating debt and cutting costs—not stimulating and propping up an already overleveraged economy. That is precisely what occurs in a depression.

We encourage voters to revolt against the massive stimulus program, as it won't work anyway and will only add trillions in long-term government debt. Imagine a $20 trillion plus government debt that starts our annual budget process with $1 trillion plus in just interest costs on the debt! We think that the next stage of the downturn will cause voters to lose faith in the stimulus approach, and foreign creditors like China, Japan, and Saudi Arabia will have a similar change of heart. We see a series of $2 trillion–$3 trillion deficits between 2010 and 2012 that will force the government to get its house in order and stop its unlimited stimulus policy. But surprisingly, we don't see a further collapse in the U.S. dollar! How could this be? The credit bubble occurred more in the U.S. and dollar-denominated assets than assets and currencies elsewhere in the world. Hence, this deflationary process will destroy more dollars than any other currency and paradoxically make the remaining dollars in the world worth more! That's why you have to think deflation instead of inflation. Deflation creates the opposite outcomes for currencies and investments than inflation.

Contrary Insight 4: The U.S. dollar will tend to appreciate, not collapse, in the stock crash and debt crisis of 2010. Why? Our trade deficits decline dramatically in a downturn like 2008 and early 2009 and that is good for the dollar. But more important, the dramatic deflation of debt and assets actually creates fewer dollars in the world financial system and they are then worth more. Again, deflation has the opposite consequences of inflation, and even most bearish forecasters have and will continue to miss this. Deflation is a good thing. It will dramatically lower long-term consumer and business costs and strengthen the U.S. dollar again.

The dollar has already collapsed 60% since its long-term peak in 1985 and 40% since 2001. We will deflate debts and assets faster than Europe or Asia and that will, paradoxically, support the U.S. dollar. We have also led this downturn, but the rest of the world follows. Other economies suffer on a lag and face banking crises, business failures, and rising unemployment as well. So why are their currencies worth so much more currently? In a downturn our trade deficit with foreign countries also declines and that is good for the dollar. In the last stock crash, from May 2008 into March 2009, the dollar actually rose, as we show in Figure 1.8. Eventually the dollar could fall again, depending on how this downturn plays out, but your last worry should be a crash in the dollar in 2010!

Principle 3: The Greatest Real Estate Bubble in Modern History: 2000–2005 . . . Further Declines and Massive Banking Fallout Are Inevitable

We can have major stock crashes and not see major bank failures or deep downturns like we saw in the 1930s and started to see in 2008 and 2009.

Figure 1.8: S&P 500 vs. U.S. Dollar, May 2008–March 2009

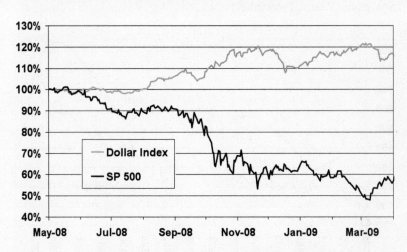

The 1987 crash saw no recession or even a marked slowdown in the economy, and the 2000–2002 crash saw only a very minor recession. Why? Bank loans generally are not made against stock holdings. The early 1990s saw major bank failures because real estate was declining and there was a minor credit bubble in real estate tied to S&L lending in the 1980s. It wasn't primarily the stock crash that caused the Great Depression. It was the failure of farms—back when most of us were still farmers— where most bank loans were extended, along with the collapse of regional real estate bubbles in places like Florida, New York, and Chicago. We have seen real estate bubbles many times in the past. In fact real estate tends to run in 17–18-year cycles (Figure 1.9). We saw minor peaks in 1972 and 1989 and then a much larger real estate bubble heading into 2006. This was no ordinary real estate bubble, it was the greatest in modern history!

Robert Shiller from Yale restated home prices back to the late 1800s by adjusting them for inflation, the average size of homes, and the quality of their features. (We will show his analysis in Figure 4.2 in Chapter 4.) We tend to think that real estate goes up even more than it has in our lifetimes as we forget that homes used to be both smaller and far less well-equipped with modern features and appliances. To make a long story short, home prices don't rise with the economy and earnings like stocks do. Housing prices follow building costs and replacement values

Figure 1.9: 17–18-Year Real Estate Cycle
Real Estate Values, 1946–2009

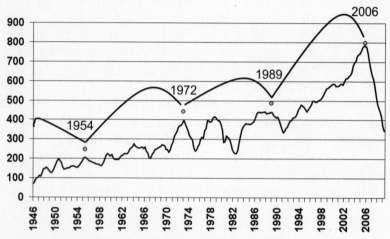

Source: The Foundation for the Study of Cycles, Inc. and HS Dent Foundation

when adjusted for inflation. They have been mostly flat since the late 1800s, with declines for advances in mass manufacturing and building techniques in the early 1900s. The Great Depression brought prices down temporarily. But housing shortages during World War II and the return of soldiers with generous GI Bill benefits geared toward buying homes brought prices quickly back into line with long-term trends.

Then the greatest bubble in modern history occurred: home prices doubled on average between 2000 and 2005, and banks lent more aggressively than ever against those inflated prices. The Federal Reserve lowered short-term interest rates to 1% to stimulate the country out of the recession of 2001, and helped create the next great bubble in real estate. The dramatic failure of stocks also encouraged households and investment managers to speculate in real estate as well.

The banks were already dead in 2005, when they lent aggressively against real estate values that doubled in just five years. This is not merely a subprime crisis, it's the deleveraging of the greatest global real estate bubble in modern history.

Many middle and upper-middle class and affluent households bought homes and/or borrowed against their inflated equity. As home values continue to deflate back to reality, approximately half of home-owners will have homes worth less than their mortgages, with rising unemployment stimulating defaults well into early 2011, when most short-term mortgage incentives reset back to normal, higher rates.

Contrary Insight 5: Home values will continue to fall back at least to 2000 year price levels and possibly as low as 1996 price levels. This will put half of the homes in the U.S. in negative equity, further increase defaults, and will be the final nail in the banking system coffin, along with rapidly collapsing commercial real estate values, which always fall later and farther. One of the classic rules of bubbles is that they always deflate at least back to where they started and sometimes a bit lower. Home prices will have to fall 55% to 65% vs. the 30% to 40% fall thus far. Did the banks factor that—or 15% plus unemployment—into their stress tests?

Japan offers a great example. Japan went through the same peak in its baby boom generation nearly two decades ahead of the U.S. and Europe, and saw an equally dramatic housing bubble between 1986 and 1991. Then the bubble deflated right back to where it started in 1986, as we show in Chapter 4. Normal rates of appreciation after 1950 were not wiped out—just the gains accrued because of the bubble. But the correction required a 63% decline in housing, a 70% decline in condos, and an 80% decline in commercial real estate. Real estate stopped falling generally in 2005. But it has not bounced back because Japan's older citizens are preparing for retirement or life in nursing homes, offsetting the demand for new homes by the country's smaller younger generation.

Commercial real estate in the U.S. inflated a bit more than even the residential bubble, and now commercial prices are falling faster. Both need to fall at least back to 2000 year levels, and that means more declines to come—25% to 40%. Commercial is likely to fall even farther than residential, as it did in Japan in the 1990s. This real estate downturn is not over. And default rates on subprime, prime, commercial loans and credit cards have continued to rise even as the economy has started to recover. Unemployment and business failures naturally lag stock market declines and economic slowing. Normally that is expected and OK. But in this downturn, the banking system has been mortally wounded and housing and real estate prices are very fragile. Continued defaults on a lag are likely to generate further banking crises by July or August 2010 even though the economy is appearing at first to recover. And if the recovery happens to be stronger than expected, short-term and long-term interest rates will rise more dramatically, killing the real estate recovery.

Contrary Insight 6: We see the next, greater banking crisis unfolding in the summer of 2010, just when most economists see a recovery. We haven't even felt the effects of most of the foreclosures that have already occurred because they are still in process and negotiation. As real estate defaults continue to rise, banks will fail to a greater degree than they did in late 2008 and early 2009—a failure that was as scary as anything we have seen since the early 1930s. The next Great Depression will finally hit between mid- to late 2010 and 2012, just as we originally forecast in the first edition of this book in late 2008.

Principle 4: A 29–30-Year Commodity Cycle Has Peaked . . . Impacting Emerging Countries and Creating a Truly Global Crisis

The U.S. stock market saw its greatest bubble in the 1990s around the strong emergence of new technologies, much like the Roaring 20s for automobiles and electricity and phones. But the developing world saw its greatest bubble in the dramatic growth of countries like China and India, and more broadly around a major commodity boom in everything from agricultural products to industrial metals to energy and precious metals. That is one trend we missed at first. That commodity bubble and skyrocketing oil prices in recent years hurt the stocks of developed countries like the U.S. despite strong earnings trends that were as strong as those in the 1990s. And the speculative money ran not only into real estate but into commodities and stocks in emerging markets. Hence the U.S. stocks did not bubble like they did in the 1990s, they merely doubled rather than quadrupling, as we forecasted.

Commodity cycles tend to run on a different clock than the generational boom and bust cycles: 29–30 years vs. 39–40 years, as we demonstrate in Chapter 3 in Figure 3.5. This commodity cycle just happened to peak in mid-2008 and collapsed more sharply and a bit earlier than the projected late 2009 or early 2010 dropoff. The banking meltdown forced a lot of highly leveraged hedge funds and speculators to dump their commodities when the slowdown caused weakness.

Between July 2008 and February 2009 we saw the sharpest market declines in history, especially in oil and natural gas. These declines were greater than we expected when we wrote the first edition of the book. We have been forecasting a rebound in oil prices back to $80–$100 during "the eye" of the storm, just as we expected in stocks. But that rebound is likely to be over by early 2010. And the banking and geopolitical crises ahead are likely to cause one more round of spikes in the crisis commodities like gold and silver, and likely oil and natural gas. Mid-2008 will almost certainly represent a long-term peak in commodity prices, and that impacts many of the emerging countries that helped generate one of the most concerted global bull markets in history, from 2003 to 2007.

Contrary Insight 7: Oil and other commodities will not rise for years into the future, despite forecasts of growing demand in emerging countries. Commodity prices will deflate with everything else in 2010–2012 and off and on into 2020–2023. We see oil going back to near $10 between mid-2011 and early 2015. We saw the greatest concerted bull market in global history, with all major emerging and developed countries rising and booming from 2003 to 2007. Now we are seeing a concerted global bust with falling stock markets, real estate, bonds, and commodities. Deflation causes all assets to fall . . . and that means that normal asset allocation strategies for investment fail miserably!

We wouldn't want to be a typical stockbroker or financial advisor in this environment, as most will steer their clients wrong and be hated for decades! In an inflationary downturn and crisis like the 1970s, stocks and bonds fell but real estate, commodities, and emerging countries rose, so diversification paid off to some degree. Experts who recommend commodities past early 2010 as a hedge to this crisis will see losses similar to or even greater than those in the stock markets. Advisors who see the dollar collapsing or recommend emerging country stocks will be penalized heavily as well.

When we do see a more concerted global boom again, from the 2020s forward, we are likely to see the greatest commodity boom in history because growth will be driven more by emerging countries like India and China, which are far more commodity intensive. During the global bust, of course, these countries will be set back as exports decline to developed countries, whose economies will be in comparatively worse shape. The next great commodity boom, featuring emerging countries who are strong exporters, will occur from the early 2020s to 2039–2040.

Principle 5: Geopolitical Cycles Are Adverse from 2001 into 2018–2019—They Are Likely to Accelerate from Late 2009 into 2010

When the recent U.S. stock market bubble proved to be less bubbly than the market was in the 1990s, we uncovered another important cycle. Somehow after 9/11, things just weren't the same. The stock market likes economic growth, low inflation and commodity prices, and geopolitical stability. Not only did commodity prices accelerate, the geopolitical environment has seen one challenge after the next since 2001. When we looked back in history we saw that about every 16 to 18 years, the geopolitical environment seems to switch from being generally favorable to unfavorable, as we show in more depth in Chapter 3 in Figure 3.6.

From 1983 to 2000 (18 years), there was generally peace in the world, no major government tensions, and low inflation. Since 9/11 we have seen two failed wars in Iraq and Afghanistan with no apparent chance for victory or resolution. We have seen scares over nuclear weapons development in Iran and North Korea, whose leaders are highly irrational. We have seen growing violence and drug wars along the U.S. border with Mexico, exacerbating an already rising discontent with illegal immigration. Major tensions between Pakistan and India complicate the Afghanistan war, and tensions are rising again between the U.S. and Russia. And now the worldwide banking crisis that started in the U.S. is disrupting currencies and creating incentives for trade protectionism. We had a similar adverse cycle, from the early to mid-1960s into the early 1980s, starting with the Cuban missile crisis and the assassinations of the Kennedys and Martin Luther King, then the escalation of the Vietnam War and the broader Cold War with Russia and China—and rapidly escalating inflation to boot.

But before that, from 1945 to 1962/1965 (17–20 years), things were great, especially during the "Happy Days" boom of the 1950s. Before that, from 1930 to 1945, the geopolitical environment was as bad as it had ever been. We have found that this cycle has repeated roughly all the way back through the 1800s. The current cycle points to a down stock market until 2018 or 2019. The geopolitical environment and our ability to combat terrorism are unlikely to improve during this period, and a falling worldwide economy will only aggravate tensions among countries. In fact, within these 16-to-18-year alternating cycles, we have seen shorter term half-cycle peaks of about 8.5 years in such geopolitical events as the first terrorist attack on the World Trade Center in early 1993, coordinated attacks in Bombay that year, and the much larger terrorist attack on the Twin Towers in September of 2001; the next events would be due between very late 2009 and mid-2010, most likely between January and July. It is likely that banking crises will start to strike again by July or August of 2010 and geopolitical events could precede and exacerbate the banking and economic crises.

Contrary Insight 8: Geopolitical events will continue to be largely unfavorable into 2018 or 2019, with shorter-term geopolitical cycles, suggesting that major negative events, on the scale of 9/11, will occur between late 2009 and early to mid-2010. Such events will eventually favor crisis commodities like gold, silver, oil, and natural gas, but likely only into early to mid-2010 and spike more unpredictably. The deflation environment to follow will hurt all commodities as well.

The banking crisis is likely to resurge by the summer of 2010 and geopolitical tensions earlier; hence geopolitical tensions could first instigate economic reactions that stimulate further banking crises. We don't know if it will be another major terrorism event or a war between Iran and Israel or something else totally unexpected. But our cycles strongly suggest something is about to occur that will be unfavorable for the world economy, the banking system, and stocks.

Principle 6: The Seasons of Our Economy—We Are Moving into the First Winter Since the 1930s

At the beginning of this chapter we gave a brief description of a seasonal cycle that is pervasive throughout life and analogous to cycles apparent in economic, sociological, human, and even geological contexts. The simplest and easiest analogy is to our annual seasons: spring, summer, fall, and winter. In technology, industry, and product life cycles those seasons might be called innovation, growth, shakeout, and maturity. Applied to human life, these seasons might be described as youth, adulthood, midlife crisis, and old age.

When we look back at history—and we have done so more comprehensively and farther back than any economic researchers we know—we see these four seasons repeating economically in 50- to 80-year cycles. Currently these cycles are closer to 80 years. But we also see smaller and larger cycles over time. We have a 500-year cycle that stems from mega-innovations like the printing press, tall sailing ships, and gunpowder from the 1400s forward, and a more recent innovation cycle propelled by the use of electricity and the development of information technologies from the 1900s forward. From around 1820 to 1945, we saw the most concentrated succession of depressions in modern history, in the 1840s, 1870s, 1880s, 1890s, and 1930s. But we are now in the spring season of that longer-term innovation cycle, hence this depression is not likely to be as devastating as the Great Depression of the 1930s or the Great Depression of the 1840s even though the credit bubble is larger and the demographic downturn more potent. Strong demographic trends in the larger populations of emerging countries will generate growth again, as we will explain in much greater depth in Chapter 6.

The most important cycle in current times has been an 80-year economic cycle, shown in simple terms in Figure 1.10, that includes the emergence of the computer, jet travel, TV, and nuclear power. Further innovation—powerful PCs, wireless phones, the Internet, and broadband services—accompanied the bubble boom. Think of the price index or inflation like seasonal temperatures, with high inflation like summer and low inflation like winter. During the seasons with more-comfortable, moderate temperatures, like spring and fall, we also see generation-based spending and boom cycles, as we did in 1942–1968 and 1983–2007. We cover this part of the economic cycle in more depth, and relate it more to the emergence of new technologies, in Chapter 2.

Figure 1.10: Simple Four-Season Economic Cycle

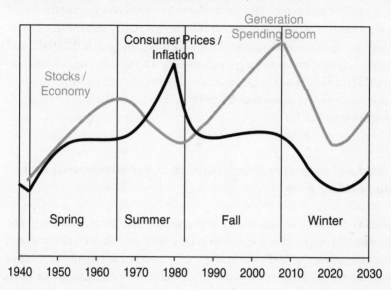

Spring: New Technologies First Emerge with Modestly Rising Inflation = Happy Days and Mass Prosperity

Our last winter season saw deflation in prices, like a drop to wintry temperatures, from 1930 to 1942. Then the rising spending of the Bob Hope generation and World War II pulled us into spring, with inflation that rose moderately from 1950 into 1965. As spring emerged from winter and radical new inventions like computer mainframes were adopted by corporate America, a new generation was earning and spending. New technologies also tended to revitalize older technologies, like cars and electrical appliances, and push them further into the mainstream. Spring—"The Happy Days" of the 1950s and early 1960s—is the best of the seasons for most people.

Summer: New Technologies Stall While Inflation Escalates = Stagflation

But technological innovation in things like computers started to stall as minicomputers failed to keep up with the demand for technology productivity and members of the Bob Hope generation slowed their spending and became savers. That generation's low productivity and the cost of raising and educating the massive baby boom generation led to inflation and recession, or "stagflation." That is summer, and it is hot, humid, and very sluggish. Inflation hit as high as 14% and interest rates as high as 16%. That was very bad for stocks, bonds, borrowing, and the economy. But stocks finally bottomed in late 1982, the start of the wonderful, cooling fall season.

Fall: New Technologies Move Mainstream and Inflation/Interest Rates Fall = Bubble Boom

Fall is the best season for entrepreneurs, risk-takers, and company builders as new technologies—first PCs, then cell phones, the Internet, and broadband services—are adopted by mainstream users due to leaps in user-friendliness and affordability. Productivity increases while inflation and interest rates fall. This strong growth and very low interest rate environment encourages growing speculation in new companies and business models. The new, more innovative baby boom generation is rising in its spending cycle and you see the most dramatic booms in stocks and the economy. Bubble booms like 1914–1929 or 1983–2000 encourage and maximize innovation in new business models when no one really knows what the new business models will be. That requires many trials—and many failures! And that leads to winter.

Winter: Deleveraging of the Credit Bubble and a Shakeout in Business Models = Deflation and Depression

Then we hit the worst season for most people and businesses, but it is actually the most productive and decisive in the entire long-term economic cycle—proof of the "no pain, no gain" concept. After so many new companies go public and so much debt is built up in speculation, winter quickly shakes out the debt, leaving only those companies that, by accident or by brilliance, are truly successful. That process started with the Internet bust between 2001 and 2002 but wasn't in full swing until 2008.

The destruction of assets and credit from the credit and bubble boom leads to deflation, not inflation, even though the government tries to stimulate its way out at first. The winter season destroys massive amounts of debt and shifts market share to the most efficient businesses during this "survival of the fittest" shakeout. Those businesses become even stronger in market share and scale, and, consequently, become more efficient. This lowers the costs of maturing technologies. The winter season also sees the next radical technological innovations. Just as we saw computers, jet engines, TV and nuclear power emerge in the 1930s and 1940s, green energy, nanotechnology, robotics, and biotechnology will emerge in the 2000s and 2010s. During the next spring, from about 2020 to 2036, maturing technologies will expand further into the mainstream and new technologies will expand into niche markets.

Contrary Insight #9: If you understand the four seasons of our economy, you can see the longer term economic future, just as you anticipate and prepare for the major changes in weather each year. We are entering into the worst of the winter season and you need to prepare now by selling unnecessary assets, cutting costs and saving, and waiting to benefit from the greatest sale on financial assets of a lifetime— just as the government is trying to convince you to borrow and spend again! Cash, cash flow, and credit are critical in the winter season. The businesses and individuals who merely survive will inherit the future. The younger, echo boom generation will see much lower housing, borrowing, and living costs from this winter restructuring (which will be much like the Chapter 11 process in business) and thrive again in the next spring season, from 2020/2023 onward.

In Chapter 2 we will start our more thorough explanation of how very simple cycles drive the most important trends long term, starting with demographic and generational cycles of earning and spending, which anyone can intuitively understand but economists virtually ignore.

The Fundamental Trends That Drive Our Economy

Demographic and Technology Cycles

IN CHAPTER 1, we outlined a bold forecast for the next several years and for many decades to come. Any "reputable economist" will tell you in a heartbeat that this just can't be done in our increasingly complex global economy with its rapidly changing technologies and trends. However, as we briefly discussed in the Prologue, this unprecedented information revolution has given us much greater insights into historical cycles and patterns that create greater long-term predictability, even though we are hit with even more short-term curveballs and changes from such rapid change and progress. For past readers of our books, Chapter 3 will be critical to understanding why and how we have changed our forecasts from previous books between 2006 and 2008, especially with regard to our new Geopolitical Cycle and the 29- to 30-Year Commodity Cycle. The present chapter reviews and updates information on the fundamental forces that drive our economy—those forces that are far beyond monetary policies, fiscal policies, random events, and other recurring cycles.

Like scientists in many fields, we have uncovered basic cycles that delineate the fundamental causes of economic growth and progress rather than just the symptoms of such growth and progress that most economists tend to track and follow. We can project these cause-and-effect cycles not just for years, but for decades into the future, and even further to some degree. From the longest view, climate is the greatest cycle that drives growth and innovation—as we will begin to address more in Chapter 9—and we are facing a potential climate crisis that could have a great impact in the coming decades. Even here, scientists have uncovered three long-term climatic cycles that can project temperatures far into the future. One of the hints of man-made global warming is that we have diverged from these natural cycles to a major degree in the last five decades and to a much more minor degree over thousands of years since the Agricultural Revolution in biblical times.

However, in modern times, the greatest fundamental factors that have driven and will continue to drive our economy and progress are demographic and technological innovation cycles—which also flourish naturally within longer-term favorable climate cycles—like the one since the advent of the Agricultural Revolution, and increasingly since the late 1800s. The first major factor we will address here, as we have in all of our past books, is demographic trends—but with major updates for global trends in Chapter 6. When most people hear the term *demographics,* they think population growth. Of course, rising population growth naturally would create economic growth. That doesn't take a doctorate to understand. But the key insight is this:

It is the aging of a population that is most critical to economic growth and progress in the time cycles that we are most concerned with. It is like the difference today between an 18-year-old and a 48-year-old. Young people cost everything and produce very little. Young people are the greatest cause of inflation in modern societies. People in their late 40s are the most productive and highest-spending people in developed countries; hence they drive productivity, growth, and a growing economy. The simplest principle is that new generations, such as the massive baby-boom generation in the United States, cause increases in the predictable family earning, spending, and productivity cycles that cause extended boom periods—as occurred from 1942 to 1968 (the Bob Hope generation) and, more recently, from 1983 to 2007. Eventually, the new generation peaks in spending, saving more and spending less into and after retirement. It is not people's retirement that causes great booms to peak initially, but their savings for retirement and their kids leaving the nest, which allows them to live well while spending less and less. In modern times, these generational cycles occur about every 40 years along birth cycles that date seemingly back to biblical times.

Generational Birth and Spending Cycles:
Forecasting the Economy Fifty Years in Advance

Let's start with the simplest logic ever in economics. New generations are born about every 40 years. They grow up and earn and spend more money until their spending peaks—between the ages of 46 and 50 today. Our life expectancies were lower the further we go back in history, so the median age for this peak in spending was lower decades and centuries ago and will be higher in the future. Let's also qualify this by saying that third-world countries typically do not have the infrastructures and political/legal/economic systems to leverage their people as they age. Hence these countries do not tend to follow the demographic spending cycle we will discuss ahead.

Figure 2.1 shows births adjusted for immigration in the United States from the time that they first were recorded annually, beginning in 1909. We see birthrates in the Bob Hope or World War II generation rising until 1921–1924 (likely since the very late 1800s) and then falling into about 1933–1936. We see a peak at much higher levels with the massive

Figure 2.1: U.S. Immigration-Adjusted Births, 1909–2007

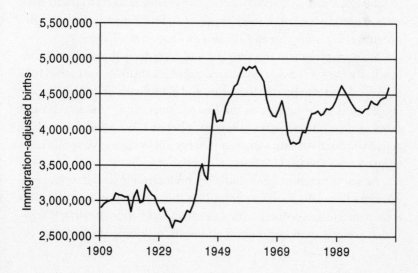

baby-boom generation rising from 1937 into 1957–1961. Note that the peaks in the births of these two generations were about 40 years apart—1921 and 1961. In biblical times, generations were cited as occurring in 40-year cycles. In recent years, the echo-boom birth wave has seen a more-complex "double top" first in 1990 and again in 2007 or so, but the echo-boom generation is still in this rough 40-year cycle overall if you average out these two tops. U.S. birth trends for past and future immigrants are adjusted on a computer model that uses past and present immigrant information to determine on a historical curve when such immigrants were born.

The most important insight from birth trends is that the baby-boom generation dwarfs both the generation before and the generation to follow in size (and more so in relative magnitude). In North America, this generation was greatly augmented by immigration from abroad, especially from Mexico. Such large generations seem to occur about every 250 years and have the mass to create great revolutions in innovation, growth, and political/institutional change in the leading nations—such as the American and French revolutions and the Industrial Revolution in Great Britain 250 years ago. We are in a time of radical and accelerated change and growth led by the United States but expanding rapidly toward East Asia and beyond. That is the greatest reason we are witnessing such a massive bubble boom, and why we will at first see a massive bubble bust to follow before we see longer-term progress that is likely to dwarf what we have seen in the last century. However, in future decades, more of this progress is likely to come in Asia, as we will cover in Chapter 6.

Now we bring you the simplest and most factual insight, which is much like the average life expectancies that life insurance actuaries have used for decades to predict the future and bet trillions of dollars. The average family or household in the United States (and, similarly, in most developed countries) peaks in spending between the ages of 46 and 50, actually around 46 with a plateau into age 50, as Figure 2.2 shows from annual surveys by the U.S. Bureau of Labor.

As new generations move into their peak earning, spending, and productivity years, the economy booms on about a 48-year lag today. This creates the greatest economic indicator in history—the Spending Wave—which projects economic booms and busts, including stock market cy-

Figure 2.2: Average Household Spending by Age, United States

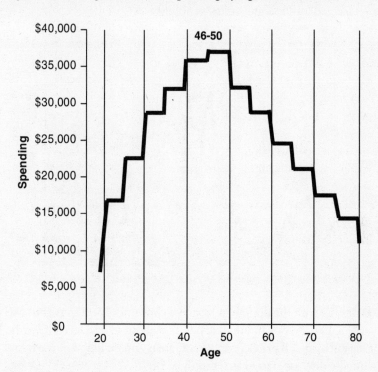

cles, five decades into the future. Is that long enough for your planning horizons?

Figure 2.3 shows how the Dow and the broader stock market, adjusted for inflation, have correlated with a lag in the peak spending of the average household in the United States in the past and into the future. This boom, which started around 1983 with rising baby-boom spending, should peak between late 2007 and late 2009, and then turn downward into the early 2020s. This would represent a 12- to 14-year downturn similar to 1968–1982 and 1930–1942 in past generational cycles in modern U.S. history and similar to the recent downturn cycle in Japan from 1990 to 2003, with an off-generational cycle there after World War II. Figure 2.4 shows the reality of what occurs when a generational spending trend peaks and turns downward. The Nikkei 225 fell 80% from 1990 to

Figure 2.3: The Spending Wave
Births Lagged for Peak in Family Spending

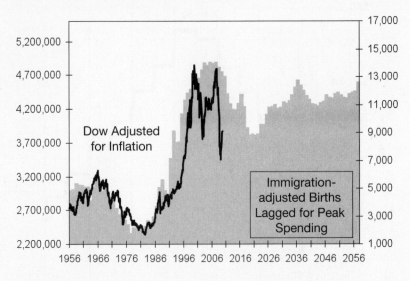

2003, in line with the decline in Japanese consumer spending. Thus this great U.S. baby boom and bubble boom is about to end, even if we did not have soaring oil prices or the credit crisis and deflation of the housing bubble that has started to set in since late 2007 and 2008. The Western world has Japan as an example of what occurs when a stock and real estate bubble deflates.

In Chapter 5, we will show how such generational and demographic trends will continue to cascade forward around the world in countries such as China, India, Brazil, South Africa, Vietnam, United Arab Emirates (including Dubai), and many others that follow a development path out of relative poverty into more capitalistic economies and markets. However, many maturing Western nations in Europe, Russia, and Eastern Europe will decline in such trends after 2009 for many decades to follow, whereas North America will see a final resurgence with its more substantial echo boom from the early 2020s into the early 2040s and finally into the mid- to late 2050s or so. China and East Asia will start to slow by 2020 or so for many decades to follow, with more substantial declines after 2035—long ahead of North America. However, the next boom in the United States will not compare with the boom we have just witnessed

Figure 2.4: Japanese Nikkei 225 Versus Consumer Spending, 1981–2007

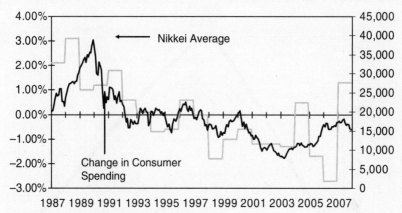

Source: Japanese Family Income and Expenditure Survey.

from 1983 to 2009, partly because the echo boom will be the first generation to be smaller than the last. But also, more of the gains and advancements will come in Asia in the coming decades and in the rest of the emerging world, from the Middle East to Africa to Latin America, after the next commodity bubble deflates by the early 2020s (see Chapter 3).

Before we look at such macroeconomic trends from demographics, let's look at some of the almost infinite microtrends that accrue as well, found in the annual *Consumer Expenditure Surveys* of the U.S. Bureau of Labor. Demography is the *key* factor driving our economy from macro to micro, not just *a* factor! It impacts trends at the everyday level, such as potato chip consumption (Figure 2.5). The average household spends the most money on potato chips when the parents are age 42. Why? On average, the first kid is born when parents are age 28. Kids reach their highest calorie intake at age 14, according to documented health studies. Twenty-eight plus 14 equals your kids eating you out of house and home when you are age 42!

Just think of all of the things we do as consumers as we age—most of which we can measure from government and marketing surveys. We enter the workforce between ages 20 and 21, on average. That number ranges from ages 15 to 28 and includes people who are high school dropouts, graduates, college graduates, and everything in between, in-

Figure 2.5: Potato Chip Spending by Age

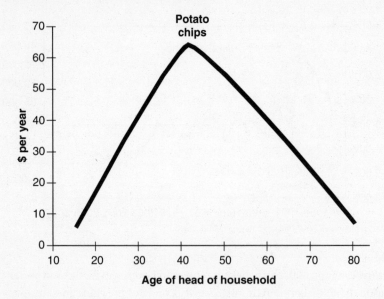

cluding a small percentage of people with master's degrees and Ph.D.s, etc.—but again, age 20 to 21 on average. We actually start to earn money and to contribute to the economy in our 20s and beyond. We as individuals switch from being an expense and investment in the future to contributing to the future and actually creating it.

We get married at age 26 on average today. The average age of marriage was 22 back in the 1950s and has been increasing by a little less than a year every decade. However, even that average age for marriage is split strongly between people who graduate from high school and get married more in their early to mid-20s and those who go to college or beyond and get married more around their late 20s or early 30s. Marriage is a strong motivator for building households and becoming major new consumers. Hence development of shopping malls and other new retail outlets peaks in correlation with the marriage cycle, 25 years after the peak age of marriage, as occurred around 1986 (1961 + 25 = 1986).

We have kids on average at age 28. Then, of course, we want to buy a home and become even more motivated as workers and consumers to raise our families the best we can. The greatest acceleration in household

spending comes in the 25- to 29-year age range, as does the greatest likelihood of moving to a different region for economic and job prospects
(as we will cover in Chapter 5). Starter home purchases peak around age
31, and rentals peak around age 26, just as people get married on average.
People in more educated, upscale households get married and peak in
such cycles later; less educated people peak earlier. As our incomes grow
and our kids grow up, we need a larger home. Hence, trade-up home
purchases peak in the latter 30s, between the ages of 37 and 42. The highest mortgage debt occurs today between the ages of 41 and 42 and then
declines for the rest of our lives, much like spending on potato chips! It's
all about kids for most of us. We will look in more depth at spending on
housing and at the future for housing and real estate in Chapter 4.

Our peak in spending still comes years after our largest home purchase. We want to improve our homes through furnishings and pools
and buy more cars (kids hitting driving age) and better ones—and many
of us need to get our kids into college and support them there, and so on.
We even buy sports cars and motorcycles in our midlife crisis between
ages 45 and 49, as Figure 2.6 shows for motorcycles. The peak in spending for the average family finally occurs between ages 46 and 50, as Figure

Figure 2.6: Motorcycle Spending by Age

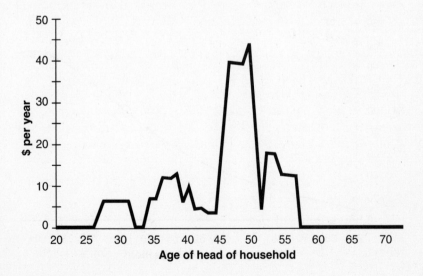

2.2 showed previously. However, even in spending, the top 1% of households peak in their income and spending between ages 55 and 59, and the top 10% peak between ages 50 and 54. Spending on magazines peaks a little later in life, between ages 60 and 64. An example of a major category of spending that increases over a person's entire life is prescription drugs (Figure 2.7).

The turning point in household spending comes for the economy after we reach our late 40s in age, at which point on average we spend less for the rest of our lives. It's not that we live less well, but that we don't need a bigger house; we don't need to support the kids, with all of their food and car insurance needs; and we don't drive our cars as much once we don't have to take the kids to school and to soccer practice. The savings cycle (often to fund college for the kids) actually starts in our late 30s and early 40s after we have bought our largest house, but this cycle accelerates into our mid-50s, when we save at the highest rate (and buy the most stocks) while we still have higher incomes and lower expenses from the kids leaving the nest. We continue to save at lower rates into our retirement around age 63, on average today (and we continue to buy more bonds from our mid-50s onward). Then our average net worth

Figure 2.7: Prescription Drug Spending by Age

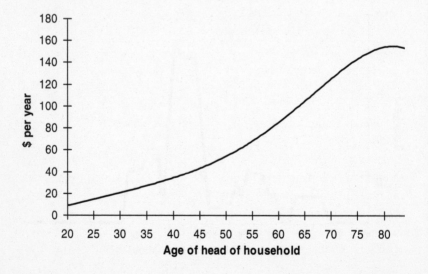

peaks around age 64, just after we retire. One of the biggest factors driving lower earning and spending rates after age 50 also occurs as women drop out of the workforce, earlier than men, once the kids are educated and out of the household and the need for extra income is not as pressing.

If we know when the average person enters the workforce, gets married, has kids, buys houses, earns and spends, borrows and retires debt, saves and invests, retires and dies— why can't we predict most key trends in our economy decades in advance? The answer is that we can!

As we will show in Chapter 6, we can predict such trends in all developed countries around the world, and increasingly in the countries that enter a sustainable development path out of third-world status. Global demographic trends show that most countries in the Western world, as well as Eastern countries like Japan, China, and South Korea, are aging and slowing over the coming decades, just as emerging countries enter an accelerated development path with spending trends that can grow out to the 2040s to 2060s and beyond. India, not China, is the largest potentially developing country and has a long growth path ahead into the mid- to late 2060s. Brazil is the next large country with growth potential for many decades ahead. The Next Great Depression probably will come during the late 2060s into the 2070s, when India and world population trends are projected to peak and slow down. We will look at the potential peaking of the long-term bubble in human population in Chapter 9.

Technology Cycles: The Greatest Source of Productivity over Time

Yes, we gain substantially in productivity as we age into our 40s or so, but in modern nations we do so largely because of the incredible and growing technology infrastructures that we have inherited and that are constantly advancing and becoming more affordable and accessible. The technologies we have developed just over the last century are simply astounding: phones, electricity, automobiles, flush toilets and plumbing, the whole array of electrical home appliances from refrigerators to washing machines, radio, television, superhighways, airplanes and jets, nuclear energy, computers and personal computers, cell phones and handheld computers, the Internet, broadband, biotech, and on and on. Nanotechnologies that make things from nothing—or from the inside out—are coming in the next few decades, as are functioning robots and robotics, alternative energies, and far greater advances in biotech. How could we imagine living without these conveniences—and how much have they changed our lives and our standard of living? The major difference between a person in Papua New Guinea and a person in the United States is the level of technologies and infrastructures available, including education and information access.

There is always innovation in new technologies, but the key insight is that every 60 to 80 years we get clusters of radical new technologies that change the very infrastructures for communication, transportation, and automation of work. Such technologies change how and where we work and live and change business and political models of production and organization. The last such revolution came between the late 1800s and the early 1900s, with electricity, phones, autos, movies, and radio. The most recent revolution has revolved around personal computers, cell phones, the Internet, broadband, high-definition TVs, and digital cameras. New technologies have life cycles just as people do. That makes them predictable. Bubble booms occur when such radical technologies first move mainstream on an S-curve progression. The last such bubble boom was from 1914 to 1929, exactly 80 years from the present one, from 1994 to 2007 to 2009.

The S-Curve: The Predictable Path of New Technologies

Automobiles were perhaps the best-documented technology of the early 1900s. Figure 2.8 shows the S-curve progression of autos into urban households in the United States. The key to understanding technologies is that they grow exponentially until they hit limits. Most businesspeople intuitively assume a straight-line growth pattern instead, and that's not good business! It takes the same time to go from 0.1% to 10% of businesses, customers, or households as it does to go from 10% to 90%. As

Figure 2.8: Automobile S-Curve, 1900–1942

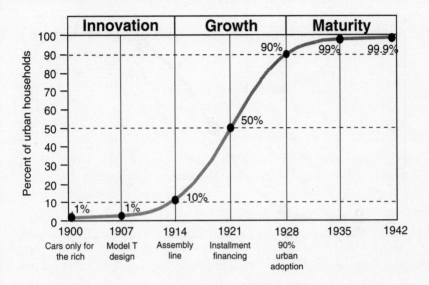

more households get the technology, there are fewer persons to market to. Growth naturally slows down in the latter half of the cycle, and then it takes the same time to go from 90% to 99.9%.

Automobiles took 14 years to go from commercialization to 10% of urban households. Cars were still a luxury product in 1914. The first innovation was the Model T in 1907, which brought costs down by standardizing the design. But the big innovation that took cars mainstream was the assembly line at Ford in 1914. Cars then moved from 10% to 90% of urban households in just 14 more years—making eight times the progress. The last bubble boom in technology stocks occurred during that 10% to 90% progression from 1914 to 1928. By 1928–1930, 90% of urban households also had electricity and lighting, telephones, and radios. The basic infrastructures were in place for the greatest advance in middle-class standards of living in U.S. history from the 1940s into the 1960s. However, first that bubble boom had to deflate in the 1930s and those leading new technology companies had to shake down to the few leaders that would bring those technologies even lower in cost and much further mainstream in the next great boom to follow.

Figure 2.9: Four-Stage Technology Life Cycle

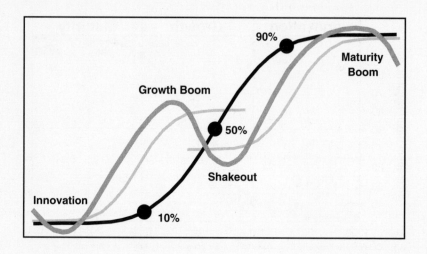

Figure 2.9 shows the stages of the life cycle around the S-curve progression. The first phase is the Innovation Stage, between 0.1% and 10%, wherein many car models, the Model T, and the assembly line appeared. In this stage, the product or technology is expensive and more difficult to use and hence penetrates only to more upscale or sophisticated users. In marketing terminology, we move from the opinion leaders to the early adopters in this stage. Once the technology is proven in such niche markets and starts to become more affordable, it accelerates rapidly into the mainstream from the early majority to the late majority—going from 10% to 90%. The first phase of this acceleration is called the growth boom stage. Exponential growth continues as we move from 10% to about 40% of households or the early majority. This phase attracts many new products and companies, and they eventually expand too quickly and create excess capacity. This causes the shakeout stage, from about 40% to 60%, wherein many companies go under and market share is shifted to the strongest companies and products. This consolidates market share and scale and makes the products even more affordable. Then we see the maturity boom stage, which takes the product to 90%, or the late majority. Thereafter, growth slows down rapidly, since there are so few new users to market to.

If you know which stage of the technology or product life cycle you are in, you will know what is coming next. The Shakeout or Depression season naturally follows the Growth Boom season or bubble boom.

We saw bubble booms from 1816 to 1835, 1865 to 1872, and 1914 to 1929. They were all followed by depressions in the 1840s, 1870s, and 1930s. The Roaring Twenties bubble was the most extreme, as was the Great Depression of the 1930s. As automobiles slowed from 90% to 99.9% penetration of urban households between 1929 and 1942, there was a major shakeout, which left only a few surviving companies and culminated in a depression. Actually, the shakeout started after the first auto bubble burst between 1920 and 1922, 80 years before the tech bubble of 2000–2002 burst. Figure 2.10 shows the first bubble in automotive stocks from 1912 to 1919, a major crash from late 1919 to early 1922, and then a greater bubble into late 1929. There were two bubbles: a growth boom and a maturity boom, with a shakeout in between. Figure 2.11 shows Intel from 1992 to 2000 and General Motors 80 years before in the first bubble of each revolution. So don't say history doesn't repeat itself!

Figure 2.12 shows how the number of automotive companies grew in

Figure 2.10: S&P Automotive Index, 1912–1932

Figure 2.11: General Motors Versus Intel 80-Year Lag

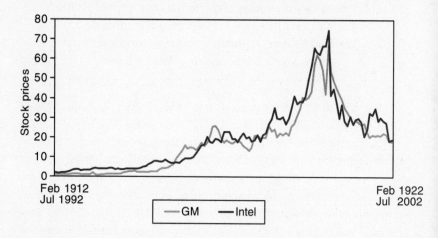

the first growth boom and bubble, declined sharply in the first crash in the early 1920s, and then declined further to the few surviving leaders in the second crash in the early 1930s.

Businesses need to understand that a "survival of the fittest" battle is coming between 2008 and 2012 that will determine the leaders for many decades to come. The businesses with the largest market shares or niche dominance and with the lowest costs and strongest balance sheets and liquidity will grow stronger and gain long-term market share, but many more will fail or be taken over by the stronger companies. Banks need to understand that they haven't seen anything yet when it comes to home foreclosures and business failures.

This extreme shakeout process in business, along with the great over-expansion and credit expansion in the bubble boom, will cause this downturn to see much higher unemployment than in the recessions of the 1970s and early 1980s; our best estimate is 12% to 15%. Many banks will fail, have to merge with others, or be bailed out by the government, making the 2008 credit crisis look like nothing. The Fed will have to cut short-term interest rates to near zero by 2011, and the 30-year Treasury bond will eventually fall to something like 2% in yields. The federal deficit will soar to over a trillion dollars, likely between 2011 and 2013. The U.S. government will have to raise taxes dramatically on businesses

Figure 2.12: Number of Auto Companies, 1910–1935

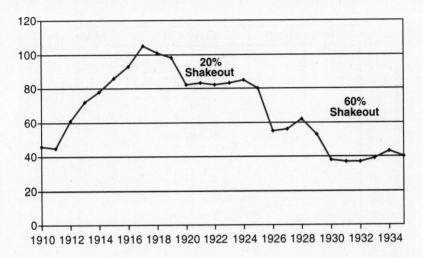

and the more affluent, as it did from the 1930s into the 1940s to finance the Great Depression programs and World War II. We will comment on taxes more in Chapter 8.

Present-Day S-Curves

We can measure the S-curve progress on the key radical technologies of today and see that we are nearing the end of this bubble boom in technologies just as we were in 1928, when autos and most key technologies were at or near 90% penetration of households. Figure 2.13 shows the cell phone or wireless S-curve, which hit 10% of households in 1994 and is due to hit 90% by late 2008—exactly 80 years after cars! Figure 2.14 shows the Internet hitting 10% slightly later and already flattening out by 2007 at just over 70%, as many older households don't care and some younger ones find ways to get access free elsewhere. The most critical trend is in broadband, which really makes the system effective (Figure 2.15). Now broadband is coming at twice the speed of the Internet, much as radios did versus cars in the 1920s. Broadband should hit 90% of Internet users by late 2008, or 2009 at the latest. Digital cameras are

Figure 2.13: Cell Phone S-Curve

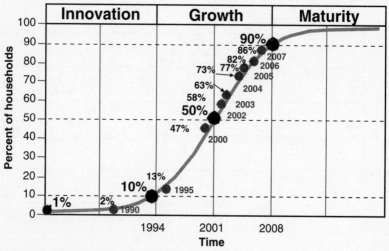

Source: Forrester Research; U.S. Census Bureau.

also due to hit 90% by late 2008. The only major consumer technology not yet near 90% is high-definition TVs, which are on target for around 2013.

By late 2008 or late 2009 at the latest, the U.S. economy will likely be saturated with the new information infrastructures of the future, just as it was between 1928 and 1929. Thus, these high-growth tech industries will slow down and we will see the next crash led by tech stocks begin by mid- to late 2009. The Nasdaq could be back at or below its 2002 low of 1,108 by late 2010 or mid-2012!

The 80-Year New Economy Cycle

When we take our 40-year generational cycles in productivity and spending and combine them with the four-stage technology life cycle, we get a comprehensive model for how our economy grows and evolves over time. We call this the 80-Year New Economy Cycle, and it is displayed in Figure 2.16. Now we are looking at the same four-stage cycle over a tech-

Figure 2.14: Internet S-Curve

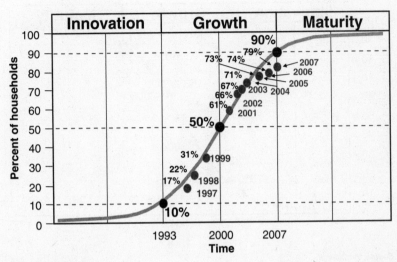

Source: **Pew Internet.**

nology S-curve that is typically 14 to 28 years and we show that the same progression of stages occurs over one human life span or two generations today. This chart breaks down into four stages or what we like to call "seasons." One line shows the generation boom/bust cycles and the other shows how price levels vary from inflation (summer) to stable (fall) to deflation (winter) to stable (spring), just like the temperature in our natural seasons. In Chapter 1 we gave an overview of this simple four-season cycle, but in the natural order we are used to: spring, summer, fall and winter—with inflation like temperatures. In Figure 2.16 we arrange the same seasons around the historical technology cycle, whose four stages are innovation, growth boom, shake-out, and maturity boom. In the new technology cycle, they initially emerge in winter, but are very limited in application—like mainframe computers in the 1940s and 1950s. They first enter niche markets in spring, but more important, help extend the maturing technologies into lower cost markets and broader applications. Then they emerge themselves mainstream for the first time in the fall after more critical innovations in summer (and hence come down in price with greater scale), and then mature more fully in spring again.

Figure 2.15: Broadband S-Curve

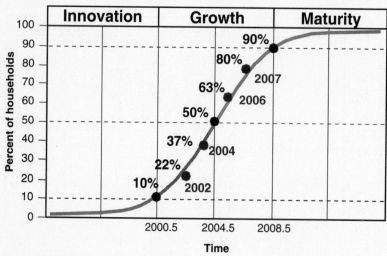

Source: Pew Internet.

Readers who are familiar with the Kondratieff Wave will recognize the pattern on the price index line and for good reason. The Kondratieff Wave follows the same four-stage (or four-season: spring, summer, fall, and winter) progression and best represented this New Economy Cycle in the time before the early 1900s, when 29- to 30-year Commodity Cycles and 58- to 60-year basic Innovation Cycles drove our economy more than did 40-year Generation Cycles. We will discuss the Commodity Cycles in Chapter 3. To see how the new Generation Wave stretched and overwhelmed the Kondratieff Wave over the last century, visit www.hsdent.com, go to "Free Downloads," and download "The Long Wave."

The Innovation Season: Inflation and Radical Innovations That Create the New Economy

In Figure 2.16, we start with the Innovation Season, where there is rising inflation but a falling generational spending trend. This was our econ-

Figure 2.16: 80-Year New Economy Cycle

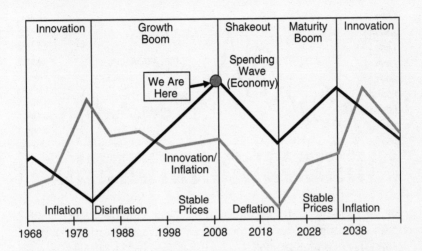

omy from 1969 to 1982: rising inflation, rising recessions and unemployment, low productivity, major innovations in technologies, and many start-up companies that ended up being major growth companies in this bubble boom. Why inflation? The maturing industries and technologies of the past were slowing in growth and losing their luster. The new industries were not large enough to counter with their new high productivity and they required a high level of investment to get off the ground. But most critical was the effect of the massive baby-boom generation entering the workforce.

Young people are expensive to raise. The government has to educate them and businesses have to make large investments in work space, technologies, and training when they first enter the workforce. Young people cost everything and produce very little! In modern economies, in which commodity prices are a small percentage of GDP, it is the expense of incorporating or—better put—the investment to incorporate young, new workers that is the greatest driver of inflation. Once they enter and become productive, they bring down costs and inflation. Figure 2.17 shows the best correlation with inflation we have found: workforce growth on a 2.5-year lag. Apparently it takes about 2.5 years for the average new worker to generate more than he or she costs.

More important, this indicator gives us a rough forecast of inflation

Figure 2.17: Inflation Indicator

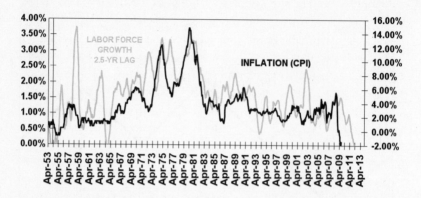

for 2.5 years forward. This indicator has been telling us since late 2007 that inflation pressures would rise to around 5% into early 2010. We've seen rates that high in 2008 despite the slowdown. The likely minor recovery in 2009 will almost certainly see inflationary pressures resurging quickly unless there is a modest rebound. The greater point here is:

It was the expense or investment involved in incorporating the massive baby-boom generation into the workforce that was the main cause of the unprecedented inflation bubble of the 1970s. On our 80-year New Economy Cycle, inflation accompanies the Innovation Season when the radical technologies that will drive our long-term productivity first emerge into niche markets and the new generation that will drive such radical innovations when they are young.

And that is the real point to this stage of the economy's life cycle. Almost every company or technology that has been growing and driving this bubble boom since 1983 first emerged as a start-up between the late 1950s and the early 1980s. In fact, small-cap stocks outperformed large cap between 1958 and 1983 by six times in returns, as radical new companies were favored over maturing larger ones in this dynamic Innovation Stage! Think about some key companies: Intel, Dell, Apple, Microsoft, Federal Express, Wal-Mart, and Charles Schwab, to name a few, and key technologies like microchips, personal computers, and cell phones—the building blocks of the digital and Internet revolution.

This innovation revolution was to be expected as the auto, phone, and electrical revolution of the past had fully saturated our economy by the 1960s—way beyond urban households to all households and two cars per family instead of one. Such innovations also occurred in this period because a large, more rebellious generation was coming along. History, elaborated through the groundbreaking research of William Strauss and Neil Howe in their 1992 book, *Generations,* shows that every other generation is more individualistic and radical in its innovations—throwing out the baby with the bathwater at first—as occurred with the baby-boom generation (and with the Henry Ford generation before the Bob Hope generation). The second generation is more conformist, and its innovations when young tend to extend the industries and technologies of the past rather than re-create the wheel. In both cases, it is young people just entering the workforce, especially the most educated, who most drive new innovations. The outperformance of small-cap stocks from 1958 to 1983 was no accident. That simply represents a 22-year lag on the Birth Index or young new people coming out of college into the workforce.

We can project when large-cap stocks are likely to do better on a 48-year lag today for peak spending. We also can project when small-cap stocks will likely do better on a 22- to 23-year lag for peak innovation, or what we call "the yuppie effect." We will cover this more in Chapter 8.

The Growth Boom Season: The Radical New Innovations Move Mainstream with the First Generation's Spending Wave

The second stage is the Growth Boom Season, similar to 1983–2009 in today's economic cycle. The new, individualistic generation has fully entered the workforce and now its rising productivity and rising spending drive an extended economic boom. During this boom, the new generation increasingly adopts the very technologies that it innovated in the Innovation Stage before. These new technologies then tend to see S-curve after S-curve go from 10% to 90%. Personal computers were first; they hit their shakeout phase in the mid- to late 1980s and matured more in the mid-1990s. The real revolution and bubble came with the Internet and wireless technologies, from 1994 into 2008. Productivity rates surged to the highest levels since 1914–1929, and the baby boomers kept moving up their Spending Wave.

Growth booms are where technology bubbles always emerge, especially in the last half of the boom—as in 1858–1872, 1914–1929, and 1994–2008. They are dynamic, like the Innovation Stage that comes before. In these periods, we see a booming economy, rising productivity, falling and/or low inflation rates, the emergence of the new radical companies and technologies into the mainstream for the first time, and large-cap stocks increasingly outperforming small caps. However, such bubble-like growth creates unsustainable asset and stock valuations and excess expansion and capacity. Just as these trends hit their extremes, the economy gets saturated with the new technologies and the individualistic generation peaks in its Spending Wave. That situation leads to the worst stage.

The Shakeout Season: Depression, Deflation of the Bubble Boom, and the Real Business Leaders of the Future Finally Emerge

The 1930s were the worst depression in U.S. history. However, that terrible time set the stage for expanding the new technologies that had first moved mainstream into the late 1920s but became much more mainstream from the 1940s to the 1960s—bringing further progress more to the middle class and not just to the rich and innovative. Economists constantly tell us that we should prevent bubbles and that they are bad for the economy—but the economy would disagree! Bubble booms like that in 1994–2009 allow entrepreneurs to experiment with many new products and services and new business models. The more experimentation, the better! Bubbles in assets create a lot of temporary capital to do that with. Only a small fraction will survive, but a wide array of experimentation only augments the chances of finding better applications and business models for the new technologies. The truth is that no one—governments, businesspeople, or consumers—really knows what will be the best applications for new technologies that are so radical. Experimentation is critical. The best applications will become more obvious in the latter stages of the Growth Boom Season and concrete during the Shakeout Season.

The bubble boom necessarily will create excess asset valuations and a lot of products and business models that will not work, like tadpoles in a pond where only a few ultimately survive. All of this has to be flushed out in a depression—like a junkie coming off a big high. The economy finally slows, because the new technologies have saturated their markets for now. The new generation slows as its members age past their peak spending years (in their late 40s today). That slowing forces asset prices, from real estate to stocks to commodities, to deflate in price and for banks to have to write off bad business and real estate loans from the bubble. That contracts the money supply, despite government efforts to stimulate the economy through cutting interest rates, undertaking public works projects, etc. That leads to deflation, not inflation, as most economists will expect after living through the inflationary bust of the 1970s and seeing inflation rise in the last few years of this boom.

A resurgence of inflation will be one of the fears in late 2009, just before the worst deflation crisis since the early 1930s! It's not that the government will not try to inflate its way out of this next crisis. It's that the massive write-off of real estate and business loans will outweigh those efforts and contract the money supply—which means fewer dollars chasing goods or deflation in prices.

In addition to the painful process of deflating the bubbles in business, real estate, stocks, and commodities, the increasing retirement of

Figure 2.18: Inflation Forecast

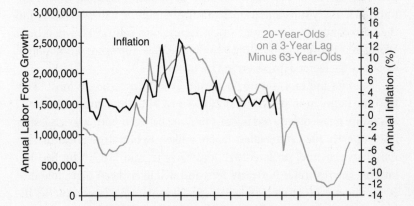

Source: U.S. Census Bureau and U.S. Bureau of Labor and Statistics.

the massive baby-boom generation will also cause deflation trends. We can extend Figure 2.17, the Inflation Indicator, two decades into the future by projecting the number of people who will enter the workforce on average at age 20 and subtracting the number that will exit on average at age 63, as we do in Figure 2.18. This chart projects deflationary trends to set in by 2010 onward, as the echo-boom generation hits its first peak in workforce entry and the larger baby-boom generation starts to retire in much larger numbers. In fact, we should see deflationary trends on this indicator alone into the early 2020s, and this is very good news for high-quality long-term bonds and bad news for stocks, real estate, and commodities.

The worst of the unemployment, business, and bank failures in this most difficult deflationary and Shakeout Season should occur between mid-2010 and mid-2011 but also extend off and on into 2012 and possibly even into 2013 to 2014. We will see a second round of slowing and more minor deflation, as spending downtrends continue into around 2023. Most depressions have three phases: a first severe crash and collapse, a bear market rally and renewed economic growth from government stimulus, and then a final slowdown and deflationary phase that is not nearly as extreme. After the bubble boom from 1858 to 1872, there was a more severe downturn and depression from 1873 to 1877 and then a second milder depression phase from 1882 to 1886. In the Great Depression, there was a severe crash with 25% unemployment from 1930 into 1933, a very substantial stock rally from mid-1932 to early 1937, and then a second slowdown and stock decline into mid-1942, when both World War II and the Spending Wave of the Bob Hope generation pulled us out of the worst depression in U.S. history.

The first and most severe phase of this next depression is most likely to come between mid-2010 and 2012—or 2014 at the latest. The final, less severe phase downward is likely to come between mid-2017 and early 2020, or early 2023 at the latest. There is likely to be a strong bear market rally between mid- to late 2012 and early to mid-2017. The Fed has lowered interest rates to nearly zero and will likely keep them low into 2012. The president-elect in late 2012 will initiate the largest public infrastructure projects in history and usher in legislation that increasingly protects the everyday worker and raises taxes on the more affluent and businesses as we will cover more in Chapter 9. Barack Obama may not survive the debt crisis and depression of 2010–2012 unless his leadership qualities are stellar and the economy at least starts to rebound more strongly by the second half of 2012—which is possible in our cycles. We expect the worst of the downturn around early to mid-2011, but continued off and on weakness into mid- to late 2012. He will have to overcome the disappointment that the massive government stimulus failed in 2010 after his economists promised we would come out of the crisis at least moderately, even though he did not initially cause the banking meltdown.

Whoever is elected in 2012 will likely be the next FDR and a popular president for decades and centuries to come—and will almost certainly be a Democrat or even an Independent!

Stocks are very likely to see their ultimate lows between late 2010 and mid-2012, and begin a more sustainable long-term bull market by the end of our Geopolitical Cycle (Chapter 3) in late 2019 to early 2020 or by late 2022 at the latest. Any recovery is likely to be slow at first in the early 2020s, as the Spending Wave will still be pointing downward into around 2023 and the next technology revolution (nanotechnologies, robotics, and biotech) will not be due to accelerate mainstream until between 2023 and 2036. We will see the strongest region of the world economy by then—East Asia (China, Japan, and South Korea)—weakening by 2021 to 2022 just as the United States and the West start to reemerge. From about 2023 on, the next maturity boom and concerted global advance are likely to begin.

The Maturity Boom Season: The New Technologies Move Fully Mainstream with the Next Generation's Spending Wave

The most revered and beloved of times tend to come in the Maturity Boom Season, as in 1942–1968, especially the "Happy Days" of the 1950s and early 1960s before the Cuban Missile Crisis. This period represents the crescendo of technological progress that now moves fully into the mainstream economy, benefiting everyday people and workers much more than the rich and innovative. This is a time when the economy is less volatile and the world is most at peace. The greatest benefits actually emerge from the ashes of the Shakeout Season or depression. But wars like World War II often usher in this season, which generates the most broad-based progress in the 80-year New Economy Cycle.

The larger business corporations that survive the shakeout have greater economies of scale and are forced to innovate to the extreme just to survive. That brings not just lower prices for the new technologies but the mainstream application of broader new organizational models, like the new corporate model at GM by Alfred Sloan in the 1920s that decentralized product decisions and profitability while centralizing large-scale internal functions. In the 1950s, that model was decentralized even further by leaders like General Electric and spread to most corporations, not just the innovators in the 1920s and 1930s. New technologies create rising productivity in the Growth Boom Season, but organizational innovations and new infrastructures from the government in the Shakeout Season create the basis for extended productivity in the Maturity Boom Season.

Businesses need to recognize it is not just the attributes of strong market dominance and financial liquidity that will be necessary in the coming economic seasons. Organizational innovations that increasingly allow bottom-up decision making to create customized products and services at lower costs will be the key to growth in the Shakeout Season ahead and the next Maturity Boom Season to come from 2023 into 2036 and beyond.

The echo-boom generation will be driving our economy upward and buying larger houses from the early 2020s into the early 2040s. After a slowdown into the mid- to late 2040s, they will see a final surge in spending into the mid- to late 2050s. However, global demographic trends and our Commodity and Geopolitical Cycles will shape the world economy increasingly beyond the Generational cycles in North America, as we become even more global in this Maturity Boom Season ahead.

The next Maturity Boom Season should occur from around 2023 into around 2036, when we will finally see the crescendo of the globalization trends that began in the 1970s in the Innovation Season of this New Economy Cycle—after we see greater protectionist and terrorist trends into the Shakeout Season between 2010 and 2019.

As we will discuss in Chapter 9, we need more effective global governmental structures for dealing with a truly global economy, as multinational companies have already developed. Terrorism, trade protectionism, and threats like global warming cannot be dealt with otherwise! The next U.S. and global boom is not likely to be as dynamic as the great bubble boom from 1983 to 2009. Even though the populations of major emerging nations will continue to grow and technologies will continue to advance exponentially, the most prosperous nations of the world will slow in both innovation and spending growth as they inevitably age in the coming decades, especially after 2035 for major regions like Europe, Russia, and China/East Asia. We will discuss these global trends in Chapter 6.

Before we move to Chapter 3, where we will discuss the most important recurring cycles that have greatly reshaped our forecasts for the latter stages of this bubble boom and the timing of the great bust to follow, let's summarize the key points in this most basic chapter:

1. Demographic trends are the most critical driver of our economy in modern times, as they predict not only peak spending and productivity but also innovation early on and retirement later through consumer and work life cycles.

2. The most important demographic trends from inflation to economic growth can largely be predicted two to five decades in advance.

3. Technology innovation is exponential in nature and is the greatest driver long term in our standard of living and progress.

4. Technologies and the new economies that they create have life cycles just as people do. Hence we can predict such cycles many decades in advance.

5. Both demographic and technological cycles predict a deflationary shakeout or depression between 2010 and 2020–2023.

6. The worst of this downturn is likely to occur by mid- to late 2012, with the greatest stock crash between late 2009 or early 2010 into late 2010.

7. The leaders for decades to come in business will be created

by the more liquid and dominant businesses that survive this
cruel "survival of the fittest" challenge.

8. In this most difficult cycle, all assets outside of cash and
high-quality bonds—real estate, stocks, and commodities—
will deflate substantially, and traditional asset allocation
models will fail, as will many businesses and banks.

9. You need a very different investment strategy for the
Next Great Depression, as we will discuss in more detail in
Chapter 8.

CHAPTER 3

New Geopolitical, Commodity, and Recurring Cycles

With Likely Stock and Economic Scenarios for Years and Decades Ahead

FOR OUR PAST READERS this will be the most important chapter to focus on. When we gave our strongest buy signal ever in our newsletter in October 2002, we expected the next tech and stock bubble potentially to be as strong as the second bubble in the last revolution from 1922 to 1929, after a more modest trading range at first for years. The recovery from the crash of 2000–2002 initially correlated very closely with both the early trends in the 1920s and in the 1990s booms, before those bubbles accelerated in 1925–1929 and 1995–1999. However, we got a clear divergence in such trends in mid-2006, when oil prices hit $78. Earnings were soaring, as we would have expected with the second stage of the S-curve productivity cycle and continued strong spending by the baby-boom generation. But surging oil and commodity prices and the increasingly adverse geopolitical events have kept the valuations or price/earnings (P/E) ratios on stocks more conservative since 2001, especially after the terrorist attacks of September 11.

In the latter part of 2006, we cut our forecasts for the Dow from 32,000 to 16,000 to 20,000 and continued to trim back our estimates in 2007 and 2008 to 14,000 to 16,000, due to a rising commodity bubble—and even more so an adverse geopolitical environment. From the 1980s

Figure 3.1: S&P 500 Earnings Growth, 1988–2008

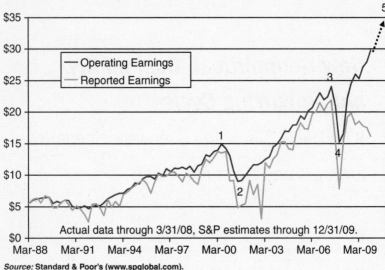

Actual data through 3/31/08, S&P estimates through 12/31/09.

Source: Standard & Poor's (www.spglobal.com).

through the 1990s, our fundamental cycles in demographics and technology largely explained the advances in the economy and markets. But since the early 2000s, something was changing, and this suggested some important new cycles for us to incorporate into our long-term forecasting methodology.

Let's start by showing this divergence in Figure 3.1. This chart shows earnings growth for corporations in the 1990s and 2000s. Note that the growth was even greater in the 2000s boom than in the 1990s boom, until 2008. Figure 3.2, a stock model constructed by Arthur Laffer and Stephen Moore, shows the divergence between stock performance and earnings (adjusted for interest rates) back to the 1970s. Here we see a clear divergence in the 1970s and in the 2000s. Stocks are approximately 50% lower than they would have been in the growth trend of the 1990s.

Figure 3.2: Capitalized Earnings Versus S&P 500

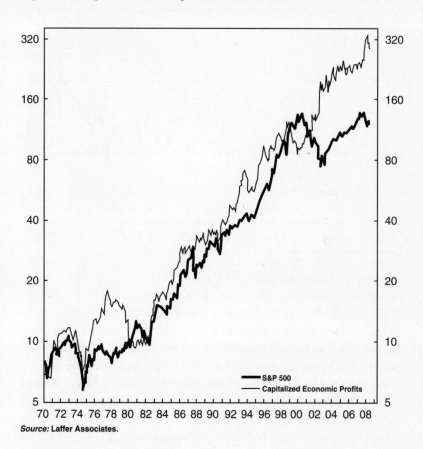

Source: Laffer Associates.

The 29- to 30-Year Commodity Cycle

The most obvious culprit was oil and commodity prices. We have recently seen a commodity bubble that is rivaling that of the 1970s even
when adjusted for inflation. Oil prices in Figure 3.3 saw a massive bubble, especially from 1972 to 1980. On Elliott Wave chart patterns, that
bubble would have represented the major third-wave advance. Then we
saw a major bear market or fourth-wave correction into 1998, when oil
prices hit $11 (as they also did initially in 1986). Now we have seen a

Figure 3.3: Historical Price of Oil 1946–Present

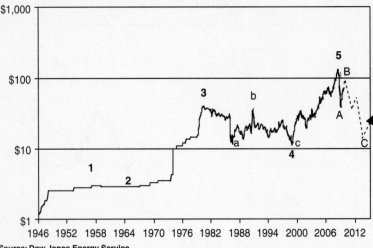

Source: Dow Jones Energy Service.

final fifth-wave advance that then saw a dramatic crash that bottomed at $32 and the bear market bounce that followed to $81 in October of 2009 could see a final advance to $90–$100 in late 2009 or early 2010. Figure 3.4 shows how oil is likely to continue to see a downturn toward $10 to $11 a barrel between 2011 and 2013, and then prices are likely to remain in the $10 to $100 range for many years until we see a broader commodity and global boom again from the early 2020s forward. By then oil may not be the leading energy source for transportation. We should then see a major crash in oil prices back toward $10 that starts in 2010 and continues for years, with most of the damage between late 2010 and early 2013. It is harder to estimate how fast and how far oil prices will fall, as there will still be strong demand in commodity-intensive emerging countries that resume growth even after this next stock crash and more extended downturn in developed countries. But we should see prices fall back more into the $10–$40 range between 2012 and 2020. Many alternative technologies will not be that attractive in this range.

The same is true for commodities in general, not just for the record gold price of $1,070 we saw in October 2009. The Commodity Research Bureau index showed a similar bubble in the 1970s and a new bubble

Figure 3.4: Crude Oil

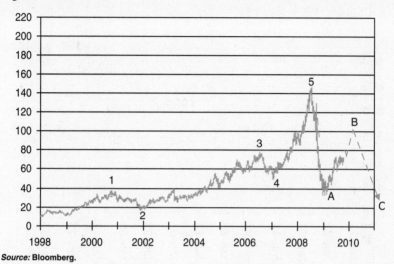

Source: Bloomberg.

starting in 1998. This bubble in commodities and oil has been hurting the stock market, as it both raises inflation trends modestly and raises costs for many businesses. This caused us to review past commodity cycles and our old Kondratieff Wave research, and we found that there has actually been a regular 29- to 30-year cycle in commodities over the past 200 years. Figure 3.5 shows this 29- to 30-year Commodity Cycle over the last century, with regular peaks in 1920, 1951, and 1980. Previous peaks occurred in 1834, 1864, and 1892. The next peak would be due between late 2009 and mid-2010 and in 2039–2040 after that.

This cycle represents an important addition to our recurring cycles, especially in this boom. Most past booms, such as the 1920s, 1950s to 1960s, and 1980s to 1990s, did not see commodity bubbles to interrupt, nor significant inflation pressures due to strong productivity from rising generational and technology trends. However, a commodity bubble and World War I worked against strong advances in the broader stock market, while technology stocks had their first major bubble between late 1914 and late 1919.

The last bubble to peak was the Treasury bond bubble into late 2008 at near 2.0% yields. From 2010 on, we will see the bursting of all three major bubbles: stocks, real estate, and commodities. Hence, com-

Figure 3.5: 29–30 Year Commodity Price Cycle
CRB Index (PPI before 1947)

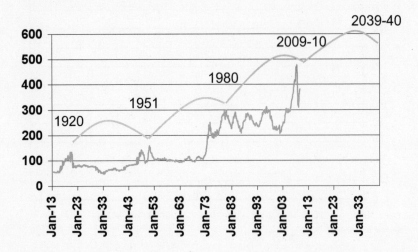

modity and energy stocks will be the last sector for investors to sell between late 2009 and early 2010. The final bursting of the commodity
bubble will be most painful to emerging and third-world countries, especially to the Middle East, Russia, Latin America, Africa, and select Asian
countries like Indonesia. The next commodity crash is likely to hit between mid- to late 2010 and early 2015, but it will probably be 2020 or
2023 before we see the next sustained commodity boom and bubble,
which should last into around 2039–2040.

The New 32- to 36-Year Geopolitical Cycle

The most important new cycle we have added is a new Geopolitical
Cycle. Every 32 to 36 years, we tend to see alternating periods of 16 to 18
years when the general geopolitical trends and environment are first favorable for stocks and valuations and then unfavorable. This cycle has a
much bigger impact than the 29- to 30-year Commodity Cycle on developed countries such as the United States, given that commodity prices
are such a small percentage of GDP in modern times. Figure 3.6 shows
this cycle over the last century, with peaks in stocks and valuations in

Figure 3.6: 34–36 Year Geopolitical Cycle Dow Industrials

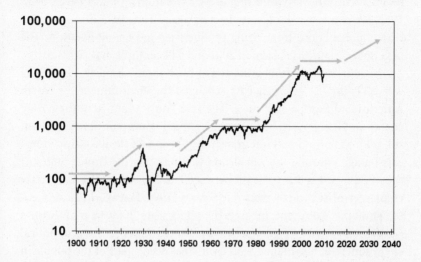

1929, 1965, and 2000. The next cycle peak will come around 2035–2036, in line with some important peaks in global demographic trends for China, Russia and Eastern Europe, and Europe (Chapter 6). Past cycle peaks in the last century before came around 1834, 1866, and 1898. The only major peak that came off cycle would have been the stock market peak in early 1873, which was followed by a depression. There was a major stock market peak between late 1834 and early 1835 that led to a major depression that was right in line with this cycle.

In 2006, we started feeling as if the trends were becoming like the 1960s and 1970s. There was the Cuban Missile Crisis, JFK was assassinated, the Vietnam War escalated yet we couldn't win it, and Bobby Kennedy and Martin Luther King, Jr., were assassinated. There was the recession of 1970 and a worse recession from 1973 into early 1975 (with the greatest crash in stocks since the early 1930s). The Cold War escalated, with creeping inflation that became the largest inflation surge in modern history, into 1980. Finally, between 1980 and early 1983, we saw the worst recession and unemployment since the 1930s. The economy continued to be strong due to demographic and technology trends into the late 1960s, but stocks advanced much more slowly than they had in the 1950s and early 1960s. During 1961–1962, stock valuations or P/E levels actually peaked at levels similar to those in 1929 and then declined even in the boom. Overall, the last unfavorable cycle was from around 1966 through 1982. We experienced a favorable cycle again from 1983 through 2000, with a global boom from rising productivity and falling inflation. The next unfavorable cycle began in 2001 and will continue into 2018–2019.

In 2001, the tech bubble started to crash more seriously. Then there was 9/11, the big event that has changed the environment for North America and Europe ever since. The Iraq War was aimed at the wrong enemy and has gone as badly as the Vietnam War up until recently, but still it looks hard to pull out gracefully. There have been continued terrorist attacks around the world, and we think that the United States or the Middle East is due to be hit between late 2009 and 2010 on a pretty regular terrorist cycle of every 8 to 9 years (1993, first World Trade Center bombing; 2001, the major 9/11 attack; late 2009 to mid-2010, a Mideast crisis or a greater attack on the United States?). This geopolitical environment of heightened risks clearly has been a part of the bubble in oil prices, but more so has been the rapid expansion of the more commodity-intensive emerging countries, such as China, India, and Brazil. As Figure 3.2 showed previously, stock prices literally have been 50% of what they would have been with the earnings and interest rate trends in the 1990s. This one new cycle alone caused us to cut our stock estimates for the peak of the boom in half in September 2006.

This Geopolitical Cycle continues to point downward into 2018 or 2019. We expect world events and terrorism to get worse, not better. We expect stocks to continue to underperform their earnings and valuation trends of the 1980s and 1990s, even more so in the extended slowdown from 2010 into about 2023. We expect the commodity bubble to first create higher tensions in the Middle East, and then its collapse to create greater problems and unrest in the Middle East and the third world that could then create an even greater backlash against North America and Europe. Expect the next major terrorist attack to occur between late 2009 and mid-2010, and expect for the overall trend in terrorism to likely peak by 2014 or 2015, but to continue on and off into the end of the next decade. Finally, we expect greater protectionism in trade to continue into the latter part of the next decade as well as environmental challenges from pollution and global warming.

The next global boom on this cycle would come between approximately 2020 and 2035 or 2036. Stocks could bottom out by 2020, even though demographic trends in the United States don't start to point upward again until at least 2023. That boom also will coincide with a rising Commodity Cycle and bubble again; hence stocks are not likely to see the same bubble-like environment from falling interest rates and easier speculation. This next boom will also fall into the Maturity Boom Season of our 80-Year New Economy Cycle covered in Chapter 2. Such booms do not tend to be bubble booms but tend to be more orderly and civilized, with mildly rising inflation trends.

The combination of extreme demographic trends, radical new technologies moving mainstream, and a positive Geopolitical Cycle into 2000 should make 1983 to 2000 the greatest bull market run in history for a long time to come. We are not likely ever to see a boom of the magnitude of 1983 to 2009 in the Western world in our lifetimes—and maybe not even in the emerging world after 2009, with some likely exceptions in leading emerging countries such as India. We very likely have just lived through the greatest boom in world history!

These two new cycles have greatly reshaped our forecasts for the present decade, and they occur more in the time frames of our 40-year Generation or Spending Wave and our technology and S-curve cycles. There are some important long-term cycles that bring additional perspective to the magnitude of today's advances and progress that we will cover next. Then we will look at some intermediate- to shorter-term cycles that will be important to predicting how this bubble boom will unwind in the next few years and decade ahead.

A Brief History of Long-Term Cycles: 5,000 Years, 2,500 Years, 500 Years, and 250 Years

Villages and Towns to Cities and Nation-States to a Global Economy: The 5,000-Year Civilization Cycle

Since the dawn of perhaps the greatest revolution in human history, the Agricultural Revolution, around 10,000 years ago (8000 BC), we can see an astoundingly clear 5,000-year cycle (Figure 3.7). In the first stage of the Agricultural Revolution, people first settled down into small vil-

Figure 3.7: 5,000-Year Civilization Cycle

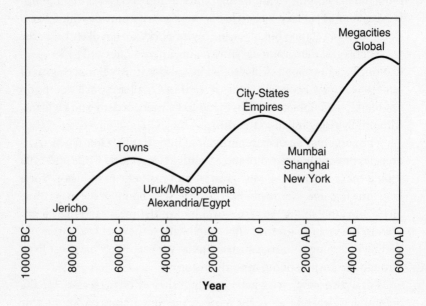

lages and towns, like Jericho in the Fertile Crescent in the Middle East between 11,000 and 10,000 years ago. Jericho is the first by clear archaeological evidence. About 5,000 years later, around 3000 BC, we see the emergence of larger cities; trading centers and city-states like Uruk in Mesopotamia and Cairo, Egypt, emerged with the advent of writing and the wheel. These city-states ultimately evolved into the nation-states and expanding empires of the past centuries from the Indus Valley (Pakistan) to China to Persia to Greece to Rome to the dominant Western nations from Spain to the Netherlands to England, France, and Germany since the Renaissance—and especially England and the United States in the last two centuries.

Today we are witnessing the very early emergence of the next 5,000-year cycle, with the first truly global economy in history, which is based initially on the Internet as the integrating communications and transactions system. This is a major step forward, and it should not be surprising that there is a major cultural clash and much resistance (terrorism, immigration, and outsourcing) to this leap in history. Globalization probably will take 5,000 years to integrate fully and to create the peak efficiencies from this new broadest market and environment, which ultimately will include space as a new frontier at some point in time. As we will discuss in Chapter 9, we have yet to develop effective global governmental systems to deal with terrorism, global warming, environmental degradation, and global trade rules and regulations, and space and satellites are likely to be the next arena of confrontations.

The coming global downturn at first will continue to cause a backlash to globalization that will in turn force important global institutional innovations over the next few decades, likely starting more around the early 2020s, as a greater crisis in these areas and others unforeseen finally drive these issues above many individual countries' interests.

2,500-Year Empire Cycles

Within the very broad City-State to Empire Cycle of the past 5,000 years existed two apparent 2,500-year Empire Cycles. The first was the increasingly expanding empire in the Middle East from Uruk to Babylon to Egypt—culminating in the Persian Empire, which developed increasingly from 3000 BC to around 500 BC. In 480 BC came the famous battle of Thermopylae, wherein the massive Persian army of Xerxes was defeated by a very small army of highly trained and independent Spartans from Greece. From around the 500s BC onward, there was a cultural, philosophical, and scientific revolution in Greece that created the greatest advances prior to the 1700s Enlightenment revolution and beyond in Western Europe. Greece established the very foundation of democracy, even though it extended to only the most elite property owners at first.

Figure 3.8 shows a rough approximation of rising prices (and, hence, progress in standard of living) over the last 2,500 years based on our broad gauge of historical academic research. This 2,500-year cycle follows the same four-stage, two-boom technology life cycle we covered in Chapter 2. The Greeks represented the Innovation Season; the Roman Empire, the Growth Boom Season; the Dark Ages, the Shakeout Season; and the Western boom in Europe and North America up until around 2009, the Maturity Boom Season.

From the coming decade forward, we should see much more poten-

Figure 3.8: 2,500-Year Western Civilization Cycle

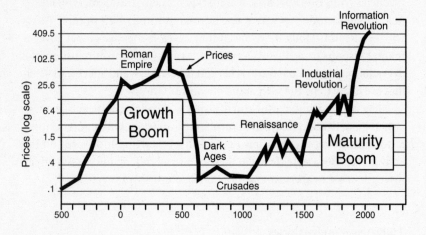

tial demographic growth and a likely shift in technological and innovation leadership to Asia and ultimately to other developing areas that may simply extend this Maturity Boom Season.

The 500-Year Mega Innovation Cycle

Computers, television, nuclear power, and jet travel were invented in just a few decades between the 1930s and 1940s—and they, along with many modern technologies just before and after, are the basis for this new information-based global economy. If you go back five hundred years, you will find the last mega technologies that changed the world and helped to build the largest nation-states and empires in history: the printing press, tall sailing ships, and gunpowder. The current 500-year cycle, which originated with the telephone in the late 1800s and accelerated with PCs and the Internet in the late 1900s, could be called the Information Revolution or the Global Revolution.

The previous 500-year cycle was called the Capitalist Revolution. It originated in the late-1300s Renaissance era in northern Italy, accelerated in the late 1400s to early 1500s with the mega technology revolutions mentioned above, and was extended by the new work ethic and cultural trends of the Protestant Revolution (250-year cycle ahead), which first challenged the iron authority of the Catholic Church and then created the "Puritan" work ethic and pioneers who moved to America and ultimately created the greatest democratic revolution in history in the late 1700s. The Capitalist Revolution was exemplified by the Dutch East India Trading Company in 1602, when capital was raised from many individual investors to finance long-term sailing expeditions for profit. This was the very beginning of stocks and the stock market—hence, the Capitalist Revolution at its most core trend.

Figure 3.9 is a historical chart of prices in England for the past thousand years, which shows this 500-year cycle and the broader revolutions that followed such mega technologies. Paradoxically, in the long term, inflation (rising prices) is actually a sign of progress and a rising standard of living—although we are taught in modern economics that inflation is a bad thing! New technologies allow greater specialization of labor, which means that we subcontract more tasks to others while producing much more by specializing ourselves (more in "The Long View" at www.hsdent .com). Hence the prices of goods rise for the value added of others, but our own incomes rise even faster from doing what we do best and getting

Figure 3.9: 500-Year Mega Innovation Cycle

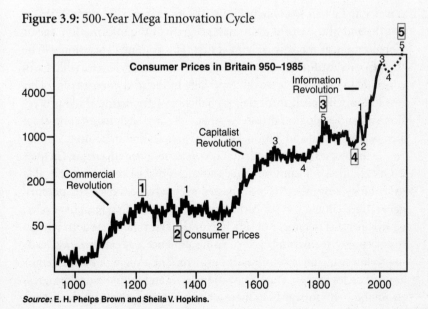

Source: E. H. Phelps Brown and Sheila V. Hopkins.

very good at it—creating a net gain in our standard and quality of living, despite rising prices overall. This is one of the greatest paradoxes of economic progress!

This 500-year Mega Innovation Cycle is the most important long-term cycle beyond our 80-year New Economy Cycle. The more deflationary trends and series of depressions from the 1840s into the 1930s actually represent the long-term bottoming of that cycle, which centered in the late 1890s. Since then, inflation and economic cycles are heading up again into as late as 2150 (500 years after the last long-term peak around 1650). Hence this deflation cycle may be sharp and devastating near term, but the longer-term trends are headed up and the massive demographic growth ahead from billions of people in emerging countries will buoy this downturn despite extremes in the credit bubble in this great boom. This is another reason to expect that the worst of this deflation cycle, banking crisis, and depression will occur by 2012 or early 2015 at the latest.

As we go into this near-term depression cycle from 2010 to 2023, it is important to understand that this is just a shakeout, first on a powerful 80-year cycle, but more on the way upward within a massive 5,000-year Globalization Cycle that is just beginning and a 500-year Information Revolution that is still in its early stages and should be advancing for a century and a half to come before it hits its peak momentum. So this is not the end of the world or human progress or the Information Age or globalization, as many will claim at first. This coming depression will be the key catalyst for the next 250-year Revolutionary Cycle, which will continue to change our world, especially in the next two decades. This revolution will result from major challenges—terrorism, trade protectionism, and ecological disasters—that will force such major long-term advances in global and national political policies and structures.

Technologies grow exponentially over time, as we covered in Chapter 2. Our children will continue to see advances that would be unbelievable to us today, just as we have witnessed such advances over our parents' generation. Of greatest concern in this century are demographic cycles, which are most in danger of slowing for the first time in modern human history due to the natural cycle of rising affluence and urbanization leading to lower births and long-term growth. The slowing of such demographic cycles tends to slow innovation cycles and technological progress (from the 2040s forward), as there are fewer young people to innovate or to challenge the established systems—which is what they do best and how they most contribute to the economy.

The 250-Year Revolutionary Cycle

Within these 500-year Mega Innovation Cycles we tend to get two 250-year Revolutionary Cycles to create the environment for technologies to continue to advance human progress through more advantageous organizations at the broader political and business levels. Thus these revolutions tend to be more cultural and institutional in nature. The last such clear revolution was in the mid- to late 1700s, with the American Revolution and the Industrial Revolution—obviously the most important revolutions before the present information and global revolution. If we go back in Figure 3.10, we can see that there was another important cultural revolution 250 years before that: the Protestant Revolution in the early to mid-1500s, which established the work and saving ethic that ultimately made the Industrial Revolution possible and most opportune in Western Europe. This revolution also accompanied the broader Capitalist Revolution in business on the 500-year Mega Innovation Cycle above. Before that there was the Merchant Revolution in northern Italy, which created the origins of modern finance and the base for the broader Capitalist Revolution from the 1400s onward. Before that there were the Crusades of the early 1000s, the advent of Islam in the mid-700s, the fall and rise of Rome in previous cycles, and so on.

To summarize the longest-term recurring cycles, we are in the very early stages of a major 5,000-year Globalization Cycle, in the early stages of a powerful 500-year cycle, and just about to enter a new 250-year Revolutionary Cycle that will represent the second American Revolution and the next network revolution in industry and business in organizational and institutional terms, as opposed to just advancing technologies. In the emerging world, this should represent the first real democratic and capitalist revolution that allows more countries to begin to catch up to Western standards of living in the coming decades and to perhaps trump our lead in innovations over time. That ultimately should mean the fall of more corrupt, dictatorial regimes over the next decade or two.

In their prophetic but underappreciated book, *Natural Capitalism*

Figure 3.10: 250-Year Revolutionary Cycle

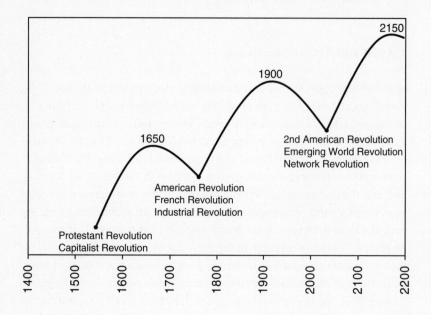

(1999), authors Paul Hawken, Amory Lovins, and L. Hunter Lovins fore-saw a second industrial revolution in which the elimination and total re-cycling of waste through real-time production to demand organizational and business models would create the next leap in innovation. We agree nearly 100%, but our cycles show that this will occur more in the next few decades, with the incubating innovations stemming back from the late 1990s and 2000s. The last organizational and production revolution on our 80-year New Economy Cycle began in the early 1900s with Frederick Taylor's "scientific management," which redesigned the very nature of work and specialization of tasks; continued with Henry Ford's assembly line, which automated production and moved the work to the worker; and culminated in Alfred Sloan's brilliant new corporate model at Gen-eral Motors in the early 1920s, which centralized the greatest scale func-tions but decentralized product and customer decisions and profit accountability.

That model expanded increasingly in the Shakeout Season of the

1930s and beyond to greater perfection at General Electric in the 1950s, with an even more decentralized product division and profit-oriented model. This next Shakeout Season of the New Economy Cycle will create the longer-term business and government models for decades to come with more radical decentralization of decision and profit models. This broader organizational and institutional revolution will stem from *Reengineering the Corporation* (Michael Hammer and James Champy, 1994) to the real-time production-to-demand model at Dell in the mid-1990s. Don Tapscott's book *Wikinomics* (2006) best correlates with the Alfred Sloan revolution at GM in the 1920s and even goes beyond our bottoms-up model in *The Roaring 2000s* (1998) by extending research and decision making to other organizations and independent people. On our longer-term cycles, the next 250-year Revolutionary Cycle between the 2010s and mid-2020s will be the basis for a greater advance in global corporate and government institutional and cultural reforms, based on the growing influence of all of these new models moving more mainstream and being accelerated by the great shakeout and depression ahead. This cycle could also see a world war in its latter stages, which would also correlate with an 80- to 84-year Generation Cycle in wars that include the American Revolution, the Civil War, and World War II. Such a war would be due not in the coming decade, but more likely between 2022 and 2026 just as we are emerging out of this long slowdown. It could be fought more between rising Asian powers.

In *The Roaring 2000s,* we introduced a simple overview of the new corporate organizational model of the future that will emerge slowly in the 2000s and accelerate afterward. The guiding principle is simple. Companies and governments will organize around the customers, not the producers, and operate increasingly from the bottom up, not the top down. They will also innovate and collaborate horizontally. Or as we have always said, "Management is the problem, not the solution!" That would, in essence, represent the next American and democratic revolution from the everyday lives of consumers and workers to the political process of government and citizens. Unresponsive and bureaucratic, top-down management models will be replaced with network systems that bring both information and accountability for results right down to the front-line workers who serve unique segments of customers and access all of the specialty functions and servers in the company and its partners.

Such network, real-time information-based systems already exist today in information-intensive businesses such as the modern stock exchanges. Where is the management of these systems? Does anyone see the managers or their efforts? Someone rings the bell at 9:30 AM Eastern Time and runs and gets out of the way! Users drive the system with their trades in as real-time a system as you will find almost anywhere today. The system instantly reflects the profitability of every trade and the P&L and balance sheet of each account at the end of the day. The job of management is to design the organizational and information systems that allow highly accountable interactions between customers/users and frontline automated or human browsers where required. The browsers allow the users to access whatever servers are available in the system in real time, not hours or days or weeks or months later, as in the old batch-and-queue assembly line system of the past. And now, in *Wikinomics,* Don Tapscott documents how the best corporations are outsourcing parts of even their core research and problem solving at all levels to outside organizations and individuals by bidding out problems and solutions and rewarding the best responses inside or outside their companies—especially outside.

The history of human evolution has been about a consistent and exponential trend away from dominance by the few to more inputs, productivity, and gains for the many, although the top 1% in the United States still control well over 40% of the wealth. However, it was ten times that concentrated in Roman times. The advent of capitalism and democracy actually are two opposing trends that achieve this continued common end and goal.

Most people tend to think that democracy and capitalism operate on the same principles. Mostly they do not! Capitalism operates on the Darwinian principle of survival of the fittest. The strong get stronger through success and attract more wealth and capital—causing increasing inequality. The best, "most fit" innovations get a lot of capital and the worst get starved and die. In other words, the rich get richer and the poor get poorer. And the more conservative economists and politicians who support this philosophy generally favor a minimum of government interference in the economy and minimal government support for the "less fit." This may seem harsh to many, but it is clearly the favored policy of nature and the universe. That was clearly the trend in the long hunting and gathering era of human evolution that has most shaped our genes long term.

Since the Agricultural Revolution, people have lived in increasingly stable, urban, and higher-density environments, where cooperation among people of different families, clans, tribes, and ethnic groups was critical for both survival and rising specialization of labor and standards of living (and that is where strong political dictatorships, religion, and military power first emerged). That ultimately brought the more liberal principle of democracy—greater equality and sharing of "the power and spoils" to ensure the common interests to make such a more complex social and political network for greater scale, specialization, and productivity sustainable.

In the old mobile, tribal model it was a win-lose proposition. It was us versus the animals and us versus other tribes in the area. It was bands of hunter-gatherers in areas that won or lost or moved on to a new territory to escape the competition for scarce resources. On a broader scale, it was *Homo sapiens* versus the Neanderthals, and we won! The principle of survival of the fittest was critical. However, even within such migratory clans there was the principle of equality or teamwork. Though there were obviously individual hunters or clan leaders who contributed the most, the spoils were distributed more equally to keep the team together and motivated.

In the new culture of towns, cities, and nations—and now even more so in a global economy—both win-lose competition and win-win propositions with progressive social and political structures are increasingly required for survival. Cooperation versus competition, liberal versus conservative, capitalism versus democracy—those are the dualistic principles that are necessary to create successful structures as we evolve and our organizations become more complex and interdependent. It is not that one view is superior to the other.

The survival of the fittest or conservative principle paradoxically fosters innovation, and often the most radical, out of sheer stress, desperation, and random mutations, even though such principles are often considered less progressive. The more democratic and liberal principles foster cohesion and a minimum of unrest and rebellion, which allow a growing scale of cooperation and interaction. This also greatly fosters innovation, especially incremental innovation through the adoption of successful new behaviors—which is the principle of both expanding demographics and the S-curve of technology adoption. This greater social interaction and adoption of successful behaviors are also the key characteristic that differentiates humans from even the highest primates and more so from the broader animal kingdom. The important point is that we need both conservative and liberal principles in our economies and societies, not either/or. They are like the positive and negative poles that make our planet, relationships like marriage, and even basic batteries work.

It is important to understand that in all cycles—including our generational, technology, geopolitical, commodity, cultural, and civilization cycles, both long term and short term—there are alternating stages that bring both radical and incremental innovations, conservative/survival of the fittest and liberal/inclusive phases, and booms and busts that create the best long-term evolution for our lives and for the economy. We cannot get birth without death, innovation without complacency, growth without recessions, inflation without deflation, pleasure without pain, and so on! The very principle of life is duality, or the play of opposites. Life and energy at its very core cannot be created without opposite positive and negative poles, again as in a simple battery.

The more we look at history from the broadest to the shortest-term spans, we see clear, recurrent cycles. Such cycles occur in a hierarchy with both more and less powerful and longer-term and shorter-term effects. It is the inability to see this "grand hierarchy" of cycles that causes even so many astute cycle analysts to seem to prove wrong eventually. A larger or more powerful cycle simply starts to trump the present cycle they were tracking and using for forecasting.

Again, the very intelligent forecasters who saw a great depression in the 1990s were tracking the 29- to 30-year Commodity Cycle and a broader 58- to 60-year Kondratieff Cycle and simply missed the more powerful 40-year Generation Wave and an 80-year New Economy Cycle, as we covered in Chapter 2 and cover more on our website (download "The Long Wave" at "Free Downloads" at www.hsdent.com). That Kondratieff Cycle is still in force and is most evidenced by the continued effects of the 29- to 30-year Commodity Cycle we covered earlier in this chapter.

We believe this new, more powerful Generation Cycle finally will create the Next Great Depression in the coming decade. But even this depression will represent a down cycle in a broader 500-year cycle upward into around the middle of the next century (2150). Hence its deflation impacts are likely to peak early on and we are likely to see continued growth in Asia before the slowdown of most Western nations ends.

To create a better forecast for how this next depression will play out nearer term, we need to focus on the shorter-term to intermediate-term cycles that have continued to recur predictably in modern times.

Shorter-Term Recurring Cycles: 20-Year, Decennial, 4-Year, and Annual Cycles

The 20-Year and 40-Year Cycles

We noted in our previous book, *The Next Great Bubble Boom* (page 22, Figure 1.3), that major long-term bottoms in the stock market have occurred about every 20 years, like 1903, 1942, 1982, and next around 2022–2023. This cycle may simply be a subcycle of the 40-year Generation Cycle or Spending Wave in modern times, but we can see it in Figure 3.11. The 20-year cycle bottoms every 40 years tend to lead to broader booms again. Even though we may see the worst of the next crash into late 2010 or 2012, we are not likely to see another sustained upward bull market cycle until after late 2022.

The Most Powerful Decennial Cycle

After the 2000–2002 crash proved to be more severe than we originally expected, given such strong demographic and technology trends into 2008–2009, we began to focus more on the Decennial Cycle in stocks and the economy, which has been documented for years by Ned Davis. Figure 3.12 shows the average gains in the stock market (Dow) over the last century. The markets tend to peak late in the ninth year, correct into the middle part of the second year, and then recoup modestly into the end of the fourth year. Most or all of the net gains then tend to occur in the second half of the decade.

We back-tested this cycle over the last century. By getting defensive in

Figure 3.11: 20-Year and 40-Year Cycles

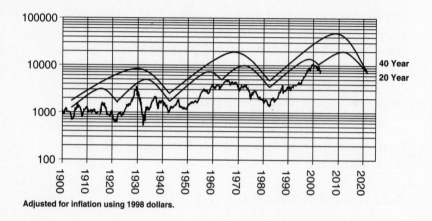

Adjusted for inflation using 1998 dollars.

the first 2.5 years of every decade, investors could have created greater risk/return benefits than in any other cycle, including our Spending Wave. This cycle alone strongly suggests that investors and businesses should be more defensive between late 2009 and mid-2012.

What is behind this cycle? It seems that there is a natural corporate and real estate planning cycle in which companies have 10-year plans to achieve new targets by the end of the decade. They all then tend to expand—and overexpand—into the end of each decade and then have to consolidate or shake out in the early years of the decade that follows. Whatever the cause, this cycle has been one of the most consistent in the past century, and we should continue to take it into account unless it fails and then continues to fail miserably over a few decades.

Although this long-term average was affected substantially by the great crash of late 1929 to mid-1932 and by the extreme 1987 crash, we still see a strong consistency over time. The greatest stock crashes other than 1973–1974 have occurred in the early years of the decades: late 1919 to early 1922; late 1929 to mid-1932, late 1937 to early 1942; 1960–1962; 1970; 1980–1982; 1990; and early 2000 to late 2002. Even the crash of 1973–1974 occurred in the first half of the decade and was preceded by a substantial crash in 1970. Similarly, the greatest bubbles have occurred in the second half of the decade: 1914–1919; 1925–1929; 1985–1989

Figure 3.12: Decennial Cycle

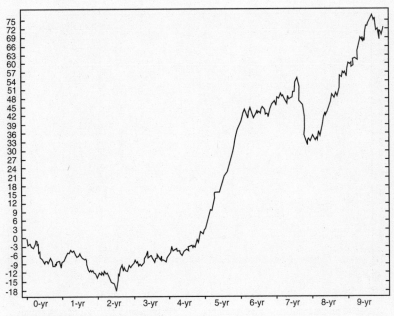

Source: **Ned Davis Research, www.ndr.com.**

(United States and, more so, Japan); 1995 to early 2000; and 2005–2009 in emerging markets and commodities today. In U.S. history there have been no overall down periods in the second half of any decade in the twentieth century, even during the broader bear markets in the 1970s and 1930s. As an investor, you still could have made money from late 1934 to late 1939 and late 1974 to late 1979 in the stock markets!

The Most Consistent 4-Year Presidential Cycle

It is well known among most stock analysts that the markets tend to see minor to substantial corrections every 4 years into the midterm election cycles in the United States, with stocks tending to hit natural intermediate-term bottoms between the summer and fall of years like 1962, 1966, 1970, 1974, 1978, 1982, 1986, 1990, 1994, 1998, 2002, 2006—and next—

Figure 3.13: The Four-Year Presidential Cycle

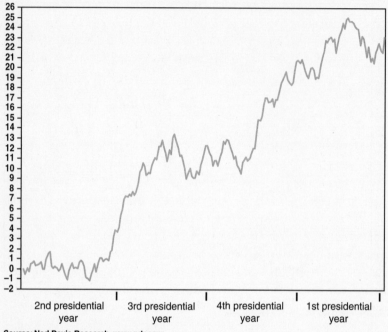

Source: Ned Davis Research, www.ndr.com.

mid- to late 2010! This cycle has been documented best by Ned Davis, as is shown in Figure 3.13.

What is behind this cycle? The Federal Reserve and U.S. government tend to be more stimulative in their monetary and fiscal policies building up to the presidential elections to support the present administration or party—and then have to deal with the excesses by use of tightening and cutbacks into the midterm elections, when there is less at stake. Investors also tend to get optimistic in the first year of a presidency, with so many promises having been made during the election, and then realize that not much will change by the second year. There may be other influences that we have not yet identified, but this is another consistent cycle.

This four-year Presidential Cycle is the most consistent. It's just a matter of whether the correction will be more or less substantial. The greatest two corrections and long-term bottoms occurred into late 1982 and late 2002, as have other major long-term bottoms like that in 1942, which points back to the twenty-year cycle discussed above. The next downward cycle is likely to occur from late 2009 to late 2010. Every major cycle we have points downward from late 2009 into late 2010. That's why we expect the greatest part of the current crash and most of the damage to the stock market for the next decade to occur then!

A New 3.3-Year Cycle?

Robert Prechter, author of *Conquer the Crash* (Wiley, 2002), in his newsletter *The Elliott Wave Theorist*, has postulated a new 3.3-year cycle that may have merit. The last one bottomed in mid- to late 1998 with that sharp correction; then the next one hit in late 2001 right near 9/11; then the next came in very early 2005. The last cycle bottom would have hit around the March bottom in 2008, although many indices made new lows in October 2008. The next cycles would bottom around mid-2011, late 2014, very early 2018, and early to mid-2021. This cycle would suggest that it could be mid-2011 before the stock market bounces back strongly from the 2009 to 2010 great crash, and it would give more weight to a low and buying opportunity in late 2014—and even suggest a possible ultimate low in late 2014 with the 3.3- and 4-year cycles coinciding. But this cycle is not as proven as the 4-year and Decennial, so we will give them more weight for now. Prechter also has noticed that in every other Decennial Cycle that we tend to see bottoms more in the −0 and −4 years like 1970 and 1974 and 1990 and 1994. Hence, we could see a major crash into late 2010/mid-2011 and then a final bottom in late 2014. We will keep that open as an alternative scenario, but the greater weight of our cycles more suggests a major bottom between late 2010 and mid-2012.

The 8.6-Year Armstrong Cycle

Another cycle that we have tracked historically is the 8.6-year Armstrong Cycle in Figure 3.14. This cycle oscillates more between primary and secondary momentum moves up and down. It is supposed to correlate more with global business cycles but has correlated more closely with the stock market in recent times. Here you can see that a primary momentum top occurred in early 2007—and we saw a series of increasing stock market corrections to follow into March 2007, August 2007, November 2007, and March 2008. The secondary momentum bottom was due to bottom on March 22, 2008, just five days from the actual bottom on March 17. The next secondary momentum top would be due for mid-April of 2009, right near when the Annual Cycle is due to peak by May, and then the primary bottom occurs in mid-2011, when we expect the worst economy and unemployment to follow the sharp crash of 2009–2010. The next primary bottom in this cycle would occur in early 2020 near the bottom of our 32 to 36-year Geopolitical Cycle. Given that 8.6 × 4 = 34, we wonder if these two cycles are related.

The Annual Cycle: Sell in May, Buy in October

The stock market tends to have an annual cycle that is less consistent but over time is quite powerful. Because investors receive more dividends in the early part of each year and then receive tax refunds into April or May,

Figure 3.14: The 8.6-Year Armstrong Cycle

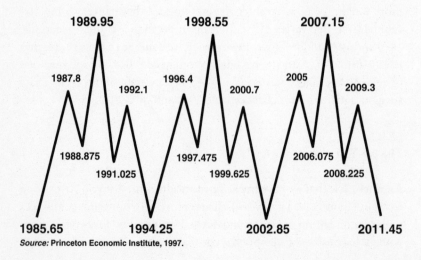

Source: Princeton Economic Institute, 1997.

there tend to be greater flows of funds into the stock market between the tax-selling season (to take advantage of losses between October and December) and April or May of each year. The markets tend to have less relative cash flow from May or June to September or October. There is also a tendency to sell losing stocks toward the end of the year (September/October) for tax losses and then to rebuy in January onward. Figure 3.15 from Ned Davis shows that over the last century, almost all of the stock gains on average have come from November to April, with May through October pretty much a wash.

This cycle suggests that the peak of the bear market rally in 2009 should occur between late 2009 and early 2010, most likely between mid-October of 2009 and late December 2009/early January of 2010. The worst of this cycle should hit between May and October 2010.

Figure 3.15: Annual Cycle in Stocks

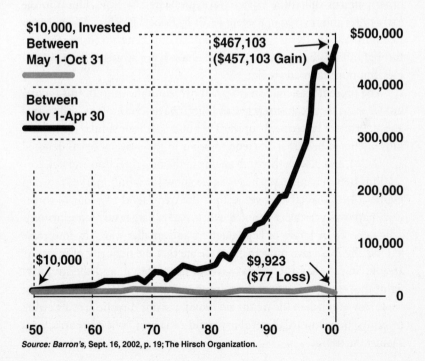

Source: *Barron's*, Sept. 16, 2002, p. 19; The Hirsch Organization.

Seasonal Four-Month Cycles

We also tend to see cycles within every year with corrections between January and March, May and July, and September and November. Timing of these cycles tends to vary, but they occur on average around three times a year or every four months. The next cycles should hit around March 2010, July 2010, November 2010, and so on.

On these shortest-term seasonal cycles, the top in the choppy bear market rally that likely began in October 2008 after the first crash is likely to come as early as April 2009 or as late as September 2009 on the annual cycle or September/October 2009 at the latest on the Decennial and four-year Presidential Cycles.

If we put together all of our long-term and short-term fundamental and recurring cycles, we can start to integrate the most likely scenarios for the great crash ahead and the depression to follow. First, however, we will summarize a wave or pattern recognition approach to stock and other patterns called the Elliott Wave, pioneered by R. N. Elliott in the early 1900s and revived in the late 1970s by Robert Prechter. We will refer to Elliott Wave patterns and wave counts in our scenarios just ahead and throughout this book. Most technical analysts are aware of these principles, but most laymen are not.

The present explanation is a great oversimplification of this theory, but we want to give an overview of Elliott Wave terminology and counts ahead. Primary movements upward in bull markets or similar downward movements in bear markets tend to occur in five-wave patterns denoted as 1, 2, 3, 4, and 5, with three advancing in the new direction and two corrections between such advances, as we show for a bull market move in Figure 3.16. Corrective waves against the trend tend to occur in three-wave patterns, which are denoted as a, b, and c. Larger waves are customarily denoted by larger or capital letters and smaller waves by lowercase letters. The five-wave movements indicate that the majority of investors are moving toward the primary trend, up or down, and the minority fights the trend. At any time there are always bullish and bearish points of view. However, when the trends are moving in one direction, more swing investors move toward the primary trend and fewer fight it in corrections against the trend.

Figure 3.16: Basic Elliott Wave Patterns

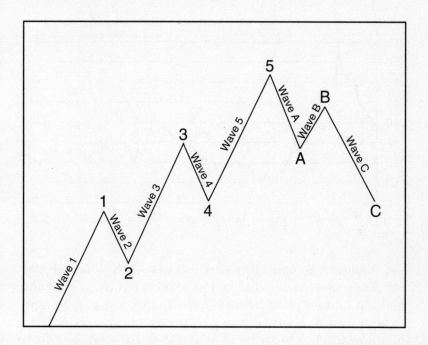

Likely Stock and Economic Scenarios Ahead

We will now look at the most likely scenarios for the stock market in the next, very critical, few years and for the decade ahead during the Next Great Depression. We will start with the stock scenario of the last depression in the United States, with Figure 3.17 as a guide. The Dow peaked in late 1929 and then declined 87% into April 1932. That was the worst crash in U.S. history! During a bubble bear market rally into April 1937, the Dow advanced 300%, or four times in five years! Wow! That's not bad in bad times. However, the Dow peaked then at lower levels than in late 1929 in early 1937 and down 50% to an ultimate low in early 1942 as World War II became a reality. The war actually advanced growth in major U.S. companies despite sacrifices in consumer demand and inflationary trends from the war. Stocks trended upward mildly during World War II but then exploded from 1948 onward.

Figure 3.17: Dow, 1928–1942

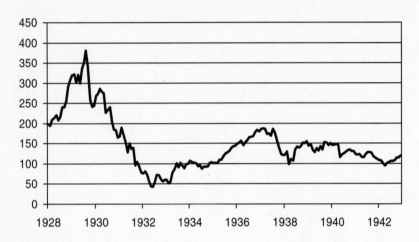

The most likely scenario for the Dow and stocks is shown in Figure 3.18, taking into account all of our cycles. The first crash occurred into March of 2009 and took the Dow to 6,440. The next major crash is very likely to occur from late October 2009 at Dow 10,119 or, more likely, from a peak as high as 11,300 or so by mid- to late February 2010. If the Dow peaks higher, then the crash is likely to be more severe and we have targets as low as 3,350–3,450 in either scenario. The least bearish pattern here would see the next crash being more modest, from lower levels of 10,119 with a target as high as 4,600. Ultimately we expect the markets to correct back to at least where the bubble began in late 1994 at around 3,800. The most likely pattern here is that we see 3,300–4,600 by late 2010 and then roughly retest those levels around mid- to late 2012.

The less likely or worst case scenario 2 is shown in Figure 3.19. In this case, the market is likely to peak earlier in late October at 10,119 and we see adverse geopolitical events or signs of the next banking crisis earlier. In this scenario, the next crash could take us from 10,119 in October to as low as 2,275 in late 2010, or perhaps as high as 3,500. Then we would see a fifth wave down to new lows between 800 and 2,300 in mid- to late 2012. The longest term support for the markets comes between the 1974 and 1982 lows, at 575 and 775 respectively.

Figure 3.18: Dow Forecast: 2009–2023
Scenario 1

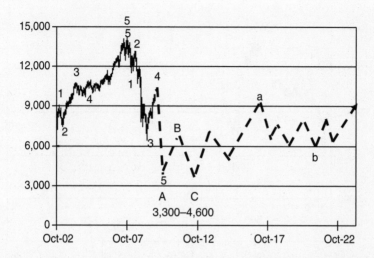

Again, we are making very bold forecasts and offer in the back of this book free periodic e-mail updates to readers so we can keep you posted on major changes in cycles and scenarios. Scenario 2 discussed here is one of the biggest changes that could occur.

In Chapter 4 we will bring the last dimension into our economic forecast: housing and real estate. We will look at how the deflation of the housing bubble will impact our economy and banking system and the three-stage progression that depressions tend to follow.

Let's review the summary principles from this chapter:

1. Since our last book, *The Next Great Bubble Boom,* we have added two important long-term cycles: the 32- to 36-year Geopolitical and the 29- to 30-year Commodity Cycles.

2. The Geopolitical Cycle has caused U.S. stocks to underperform in the 1990s by 50%. But this means less of a bubble to deflate between 2008 and 2012.

Figure 3.19: Dow Forecast: 2009–2023
Scenario 2

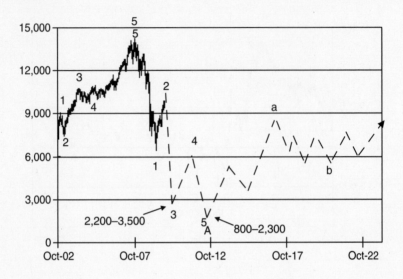

3. The 29- to 30-year Commodity Cycle has been on a perfect collision course with the peak of our Spending Wave. This is not typical. The last cycle peaked just before this great boom began in 1980 and the previous one partway into the 1942–1968 bull market, in 1951.

4. The commodity bubble peaked in mid-2008, ahead of schedule due to the credit meltdown, and was followed by a bubble in Treasury bonds into late 2008 that will finally likely revert again into a final bubble in hard assets like gold, oils, and commodities, likely by early 2010.

5. The largely consistent Decennial Cycle points down from late 2009 into mid-2012 and the next great stock crash is likely to bottom long term and reverse by mid-2012. The next Decennial Cycle would hit from late 2019 to mid-2022, but our Geopolitical Cycle will be pointing up from 2020 forward and may offset that cycle a bit.

6. The four-year Presidential Cycle also points down from late 2009 into late 2010, making that the most dangerous period

with all of our intermediate and long-term cycles pointing down simultaneously.

7. The 4-year cycle also bottoms in mid- to late 2014, mid- to late 2018, and mid- to late 2022. These will likely represent advantageous buying opportunities for stocks. With the conjunction of a new 3.3-year cycle, late 2014 could also represent a long-term bottom in an alternative scenario, instead of around mid- to late 2012.

8. If we take all of our cycles into account, the greatest near-term buy opportunity for stocks is likely to come in mid- to late 2012 and possibly earlier, between late 2010 and mid-2011. The greatest long-term buy opportunity is likely to come between late 2019 into early 2020 and mid- to late 2022. Late 2014 should also mark a key buying opportunity intermediate term.

CHAPTER 4

The Greatest Bubble Ever in Real Estate

The Demographics of Real Estate, the Greater Credit Crisis, and the Likely Depression Scenario Ahead

The Housing Bubble Follows the Tech Stock Bubble from 2000 to 2005

WE HAVE SEEN stock and commodity bubbles as large as the current ones over the past 200 years, but we have never seen a real estate bubble like the one we just experienced—and certainly we have not seen one with so much leverage in borrowing against it! Housing in 2005–2006 reached roughly double the price it should be compared with historic inflation and replacement cost trends, rents, and consumer incomes. Such a bubble simply is not sustainable and will continue to deflate, as we've been forecasting since 2003 in our newsletter. The years 2006 to 2009 represented the first deflation cycle, occurring during the first deep downturn, due to the demographic and technology trends covered in Chapter 2. The next, more severe deflation cycle in housing will begin by the summer of 2010, when we begin to enter a more serious downturn and our demographic and technology cycles turn down in unison with our 4-year and Decennial cycles (Chapter 3).

The greatest collateral for bank loans is against real estate. When real estate prices inevitably fall to long-term fair values, the banking system will experience much worse failures and fallout than occurred in 2008. The Next Great Depression will be most sensitive to continued falling real estate values, as stocks already took a major deflation in 2000–2002. Commodities, the bubble that has already burst, are a much smaller percentage of our economy—they will see deflation largely between 2010 and 2015 but could bottom initially by late 2012 or early 2013.

Our theme during the decade of the 2000s has been "bubble after bubble." It was no accident that as soon as the stock bubble burst, beginning in 2000, housing prices accelerated upward more rapidly, as we can see in Figure 4.1. Not only were the baby boomers moving into their peak house-buying years, but the huge flows of investment funds shifted suddenly from stocks to housing while interest rates plummeted dramatically with Fed easing and a slowing economy—making housing affordability and speculation even more attractive. To add to that, banks and mortgage companies competing in this bubble offered increasingly liberal financing with little or no money down, short-term ARM rates, and teaser loans with low interest rates that would ratchet up later. And many immigrants and low-income households were told to lie about their jobs

Figure 4.1: Average Home Prices 1994–2009

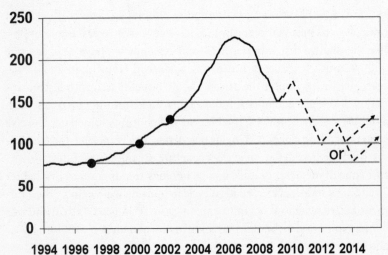

Source: Case-Shiller U.S. 10-City Index.

and income since nobody cared anyway with house prices going up so consistently. Now that housing has slowed down since late 2005 and 2006, investment funds have shifted more into commodities, energy, and emerging markets for stocks and the banks are seeing steadily rising defaults and foreclosures. Since bubbles usually return to where they start, home prices could fall to 1996 to 2000 levels, or 55% to 65% from the top.

Let's start with the overvaluation issue in housing and then look at how demographics drive real estate cycles in all sectors. Robert Shiller of Yale has done the best work on housing valuations in the two editions of his *Irrational Exuberance* (1999 and 2005). His most important analysis is given in Figure 4.2, which shows home prices in the United States adjusted for inflation, size of house, and quality of features. This approach deserves to be applauded, because it represents a clear look at housing. Most housing data are skewed by vast improvements in the size and quality of houses over the last century, which make housing look as if it has appreciated more than it really has. The astounding insight here is that except during the extreme bubble after 2000 and the deflation cycle of the early 1900s and 1930s, housing has remained essentially flat when adjusted for inflation.

Figure 4.2: Long-Term House Prices vs. Inflation

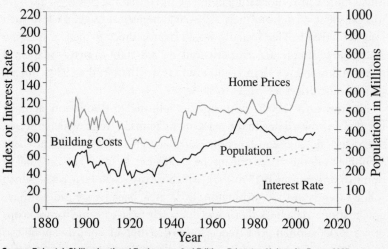

Source: Robert J. Shiller, *Irrational Exuberance*, 2nd Edition, Princeton University Press, 2005.

Figure 4.3: Median Asking Price for Existing Houses in Washington, D.C., 1918–1941

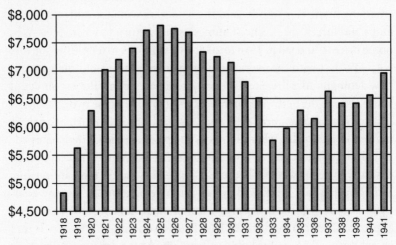

Source: Historical Statistics of the U.S., Colonial Times to 1970, 1975.

Home prices and real estate do not grow with the economy and earnings like stocks do. They correlate long term with inflation or replacement costs. If you can build a new house down the road at a certain price, how much more can your existing house be worth? Home prices would have to fall 55% to 65% from their 2005–2006 highs just to get back to such long-term trends. That scenario would create a shock to the U.S. banking system far greater than we experienced in 2008/2009, as well as in the real estate and mortgage sectors, and even greater than in the 1930s, during which house prices fell closer to 30%.

In the early 1900s, home prices adjusted for inflation actually trended downward due to the mass manufacturing trend, which lowered the price of housing construction. Note that in the 1920s, we did not have a bubble in home prices during the great stock bubble. The 26% fall in nominal prices from 1925 to 1933, which we can see in Figure 4.3 (which follows trends in the Washington, D.C., area, because we did not have good national data back then), was due solely to an extremely poor economy and deflation in price trends, not to deflation of a housing bubble as today. We see similar trends in Figure 4.4, with housing starts first peak-

Figure 4.4: Housing Starts, 1918–1941 (in Thousands)

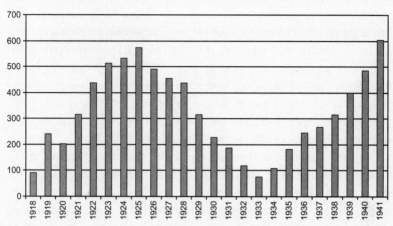

Source: Historical Statistics of the U.S., Colonial Times to 1970, 1975.

ing in 1925, five years ahead of the downturn in 1930, and a downward acceleration from 1930 to 1933, when the economy collapsed.

Figure 4.2 shows that house prices were about double what they should be due to the extreme bubble from 2000 to 2005. In the coming years, housing will fall both from overvaluation and from rising unemployment and deflationary trends. The downturn will not likely be as extreme as in the 1930s, but overvaluation in housing and real estate now is much more extreme than it was then. Yet the current housing bubble in the United States and in many Western nations is not as extreme as what occurred in Japan. Thus we feel that housing prices on average will drop at least 50% and as much as 65%. That means lesser drops in undervalued areas with higher in-migration rates and greater drops in overvalued markets with falling immigration or rising out-migration rates. In Chapter 5, we will discuss migration and immigration rates and will consider how many states in the Southeast, Southwest, and Rockies will experience demographic growth even in the downturn and fall less than most areas.

Most people we talk to just cannot conceive of home prices going downward more than a minor amount, as we saw in the mid-1970s, early 1980s, and early 1990s. That is natural, because we haven't seen housing prices decline dramatically in the United States since the 1930s. Even that downturn was less than 30%. However, if we look at Japan over the last two decades, we get a very different picture (Figure 4.5). Land prices in Japan experienced an extreme bubble, especially between 1986 and 1991, fell nearly 60% over 14 years into 2005, and are still recovering only modestly, with its smaller echo-boom generation coming through to bid housing prices back upward. As we note in that chart, Japanese real estate prices crashed back down to where the bubble trend started in 1986. Home prices similarly fell just over 60% from 1991 to 2005, as we show in Figure 4.6, whereas condo prices fell closer to 70%.

Japan's bubble was even more extreme than the situation in the United States and most major Western countries today, since its land for development was scarcer, its inflation and interest rates were lower, and the Japanese government actively supported a system of borrowing against real estate to finance expansion. Japan also experienced a stock market bubble into late 1989 and a crash of 80% between 1990 and 2003. Two bubbles deflated, but Japan did not experience a commodity bubble

Figure 4.5: Japan Land Price National Index, 1955–2005

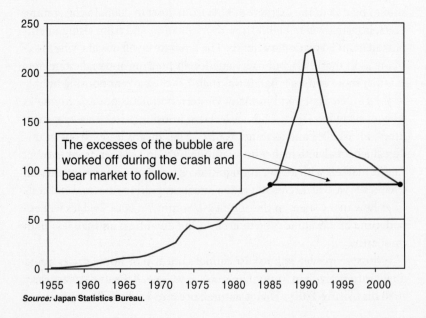

The excesses of the bubble are worked off during the crash and bear market to follow.

Source: Japan Statistics Bureau.

Figure 4.6: Japan Residential Housing Price Index,
23 Tokyo Wards, 1989–2004

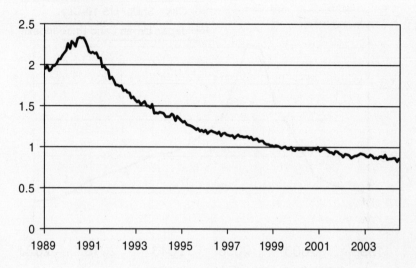

as we are seeing today in the United States. The Japanese government was very slow to force the write-off of loans, so real estate prices had a much slower long-term slide than did the United States in the 1930s (Figure 4.3). The U.S. system is much more likely to resolve this crisis faster, between 2010 and 2015. Note in Figures 4.5 and 4.6 that almost 90% of the damage to home prices in Japan occurred in the first five years, from 1992 through 1996, as we expect between 2007 and 2012 or 2013 in the U.S. depression ahead. Figure 4.7 shows what would happen if the U.S. deflation in housing prices were more parallel to the one in Japan (to see this, follow the dark line down)—but we think this is less likely, as the United States also has a much larger echo-boom generation to regenerate demand first for starter homes and then for trade-up homes to follow. We show the more likely path of home prices with the gray dotted line with a decline of 55% to 65% into 2012–2013 before heading up again more modestly.

Most of the damage to U.S. home prices is likely to occur from mid-2010 into early 2013, or early 2015 at the latest. Rising mortgage rates will hit by mid-2010 with a failing economy to follow. The first round

Figure 4.7: U.S. vs. Japan Deflation Cycle

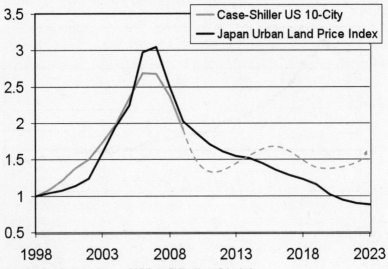

Source: Japan Statistics Bureau, S&P/Case-Shiller Home Price Index.

of declines hit more in areas with high speculation for second homes, such as Florida, Arizona, Nevada, and Southern California. The next round will hit more across the board, and in major cities like New York and San Francisco, when the economy, employment, and immigration weaken. Unlike Japan, we are likely to see a faster resolution to the banking crisis. Prices for starter homes are likely to bottom between mid-2011 at the earliest and early 2013 at the latest, with late 2012 to mid-2015 as the most likely time period for broader sectors. Then they could advance again, but a bit more slowly at first, especially for larger homes, which could lag for years. There could be a second mild slow-down around 2018 to 2019 before the next, broader advance into the 2020s and 2030s.

The Demographics of Real Estate

The continued slowdown in house prices will come not just from the deflation of the unprecedented bubble from 2000 to 2005. The largest generation in U.S. and Western history peaked in its home-buying cycle in the middle part of this decade, and we will see weaker home markets until the middle of the next decade, when the next generation moves into its long home-buying cycle. Here we look at the demographic trends that drive home prices and see many different real estate markets that will boom and bust at different times. The apartment and rental markets will hold up the best at first, and the starter home markets will be the first to rebound in the early part of the next decade, along with the second stage of baby-boom vacation and retirement home buying shortly thereafter.

Figure 4.8 shows the different sectors of real estate that boom and peak as we age over our consumer life cycle. The cycle starts with the birth wards in hospitals and extends into kindergartens, elementary schools, and high schools. Here, we start with colleges, which peak in growth when we turn 18 and on average enter college. We enter the work-

Figure 4.8: The Real Estate Life Cycle

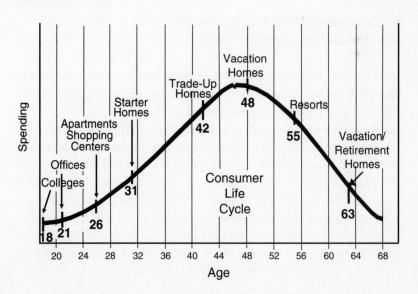

force around age 20 to 21 on average, and that drives offices and industrial or commercial real estate. As we get married (at an average age of 26, today), the demand for rental apartments and new retail stores peaks, as new couples become major new shoppers and household spending accelerates at the fastest rate.

Once we have kids, in our late 20s on average, we start to buy homes. The starter home cycle peaks around age 31 but accelerates between the ages of 26 and 33. This begins the home-buying cycle, from age 26 to around age 42. As our kids grow and our incomes rise, we buy our largest or trade-up home, typically peaking between the ages of 37 and 42 as our kids are nearing or entering high school. The trade-up purchase represents the peak in spending on housing for the average household (although a minority of households spend more later in life by adding a vacation home). Note that this occurs several years before the overall peak in spending, which occurs between the ages of 46 and 50. That is why home prices and spending trends peaked in the 1920s in 1925 and the economy didn't collapse until 1930. This time around, we saw a peak in home buying in 2005 and the economy is set to collapse around 2010 onward by our forecasts. That is when the current housing crisis will accelerate due to economic weakness and rising unemployment.

Multifamily Housing and Shopping Centers: Marriage and Family Formation Cycle

If we look at the Consumer Expenditure Survey and some association data from the real estate industry, we can document these demographic trends. Figure 4.9 shows spending on rental housing by age. It peaks at age 26, when we get married today on average, and then falls off sharply, rising only modestly in the late stages of retirement. Past trends in real estate strongly suggest that the growth of retail stores and shopping malls also peaks with new family formation around age 26, given that shopping centers peaked back in 1985 on a 25-year lag on the Birth Index, when marriages occurred on average at age 25. Ages 25 to 29 represent the fastest acceleration in consumer spending, as we get married, form new households, and need all types of new stuff. Figure 4.10 shows a 26-year lag on the Immigration-Adjusted Birth Index for peak cycles in multi-

Figure 4.9: Rental Housing Spending by Age

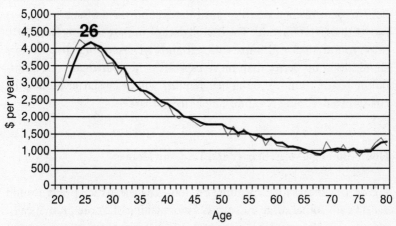

Source: Consumer Expenditure Survey, 2000; U.S. Bureau of Labor Statistics.

Figure 4.10: Apartment Rental and Retail/Shopping Center Cycle, 26-Year Lag

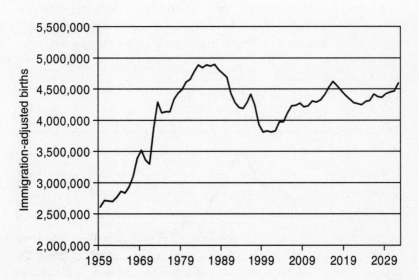

family/rental housing and retail shopping centers. The trends here point toward continued growth at first with the echo-boom generation into 2017 or so and then declines until the second wave of echo boomers moves this trend forward. The overall decline in the economy from 2010 into around 2023 will impact these trends adversely, but these sectors should hold up better than most, especially the apartment and multi-family sector, as more young new families will delay starter home purchases in a declining economy and housing market.

Home-Buying Cycles: Starter and Trade-up Homes

Figure 4.11 shows total spending on homes by age, which peaks around age 37 with a final surge into age 42 before falling off more dramatically. Figure 4.12 shows mortgage interest by age, which peaks between ages 41 and 43, or 42 on average. This trend tends to confirm that the bulk of money is spent on housing by ages 41 to 42. Note that housing spending and mortgage interest fall dramatically after age 42. This is a highly cyclical and concentrated consumer market leveraged highly by borrowing that occurs largely between the ages of 26 and 42. It is also the largest area of consumer spending. Hence the continued real estate slowdown due to the aging of the massive baby-boom generation will be the greatest force

Figure 4.11: Total Home Purchases by Age

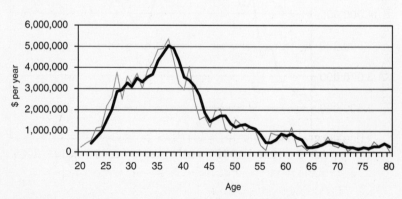

Source: Consumer Expenditure Survey, 2000; U.S. Bureau of Labor Statistics.

Figure 4.12: Mortgage Interest by Age

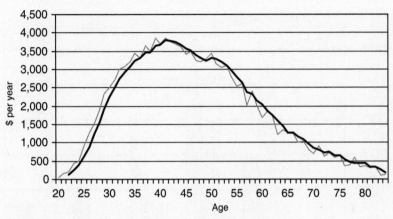

Source: **Consumer Expenditure Survey, 2000; U.S. Bureau of Labor Statistics.**

in bringing down the banking system in the great depression ahead. Banks will have to write down more and more loans, including business loans collateralized by real estate and failing business loans.

A look at statistics from the National Association of Realtors shows a better refinement of starter home buying versus trade-up homes (Figure 4.13). This chart shows that the typical first home buyer is age 31 and the trade-up or repeat buyer is age 41. Note in Figure 4.14 an approximately 31-year lag on the Birth Index for starter home buying that shows that baby-boomer spending peaked between 1987 and 1991. That peak led to the S&L crisis of the early 1990s and the minor decline in real estate values. The next starter home buying cycle for the echo boom generation is just beginning and will rise sharply into 2020–2022, just as our overall economy and housing market fall further in the next downturn. Hence, this is the best sector for home builders in the coming decade.

The greatest opportunity for home builders will be to convert failing trade-up home zoning plans into more affordable starter home developments in the next decade, including rentals that can be converted to purchases.

Figure 4.13: First and Second Home Buying Trends

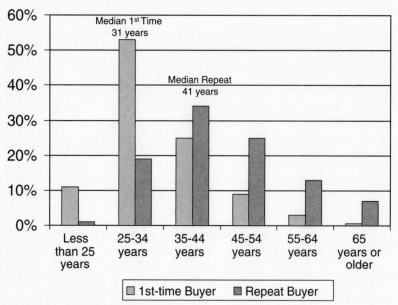

Source: **National Association of Realtors.**

There was an even greater trade-up home-buying cycle in 2005. The massive baby-boom generation moved into its peak home-buying cycle on about a 42-year lag into 2003. Speculation in housing and vacation homes stretched this cycle a bit into mid-2005 in the great housing bubble from 2000 to 2005, as we discussed earlier in this chapter. Figure 4.15 shows a 42-year lag for peak overall trade-up housing and mortgage interest cycles (think McMansions).

This cycle has already clearly peaked, and the echo-boom generation will not see an upward trend in this cycle until between 2015 and 2020. So this will be the worst place for home builders and home values in the coming decade. Housing trends for larger homes should start to rise again in the late part of the next decade and then lead house buying and appreciation into the early to mid-2030s in the next concerted global boom. There should be a second stage of such peak or trade-up home

Figure 4.14: Starter Home Buying Cycle, 31-Year Lag

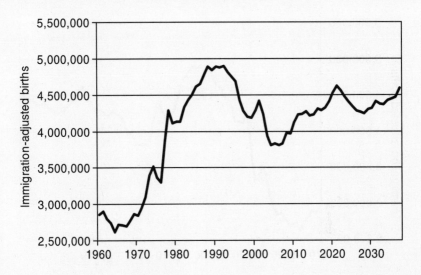

buying from the early 2040s into the early 2050s or so with the second and final wave of echo-boom trends.

The greatest theme of the Next Great Depression will be the deflation of real estate and the credit bubble that revolves around it, just as the major theme of the 2000–2002 crash was the bursting of the tech bubble. Large, trade-up homes or McMansions and high-end vacation homes will be the hardest hit. The slowing in the predictable baby-boom spending cycle for homes will create a greater credit crisis between 2010 and 2012 and will sustain a long-term, slow recovery for years to follow, until the next extended boom from the early 2020s onward. Banks, mortgage companies, and investment banks will fail on a much wider scale than we have already seen in 2008. The unwinding of this real estate and credit bubble will become a global trend and impact real estate in places like London, Paris, Frankfurt, Barcelona, Moscow, Sydney, Auckland, Vancouver, Shanghai, Mumbai, and Dubai as well.

Figure 4.15: Trade-up Home Buying Cycle, 42-Year Lag

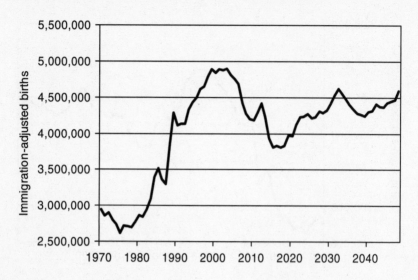

The Vacation/Retirement Home Cycle, Peaking in Late 40s and Mid-60s

Vacation home buying is a smaller, luxury segment of the home market—typically averaging around 10% of the total market—that is growing with our rising affluence and our aging society. The most extreme bubbles in housing typically have come in recent years in this segment as many more than the normal 10% participated. More aging baby boomers speculated in vacation homes and condos after the stock market peaked in early 2000, exaggerating this trend. Figure 4.16 shows average spending on vacation homes by age, with a first surge and peak into around age 48 and a second surge into around age 63 to 65. So there is a first trend of buying from the mid-30s into the late 40s, and then a second trend from the mid-50s into the mid-60s.

Figure 4.17 shows that the average purchase price for such vacation home or retirement home buyers at the peak among persons in their mid-60s is approximately double the price paid by those in the late 40s. This trend indicates a trade-up cycle as well. The first, broader round of vacation home buying is among households that have seen their kids

Figure 4.16: Vacation Home Purchases by Age

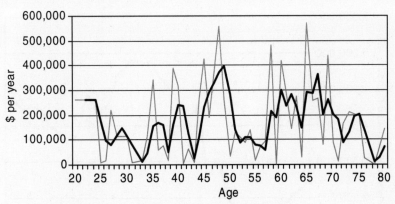

Source: Consumer Expenditure Survey, 2000; U.S. Bureau of Labor Statistics.

Figure 4.17: Average Purchase Price of Vacation Homes by Age

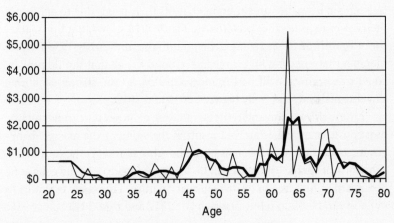

Source: Consumer Expenditure Survey, 2000; U.S. Bureau of Labor Statistics.

starting to leave the nest but may still be funding college educations and have less to spend. The second round is about the "ultimate dream home away from home." This cohort has more assets and discretionary income to afford something even better—and more often will buy it for cash. Alternatively, people in this group may be looking at retiring part-time or

Figure 4.18: Vacation/Retirement Home Cycle, 63-Year Lag

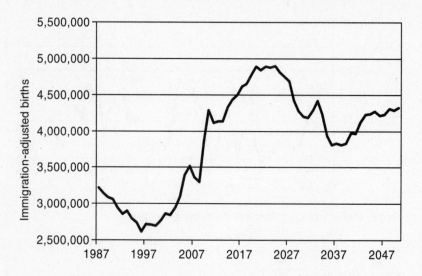

full-time in a smaller dream home that fits their needs due to aging and their lower maintenance preferences. Figure 4.18 shows that this market should continue to see strong demand into the mid-2020s. However, remember that there is a first surge into around age 48 that should peak by 2009; this segment will be the most sensitive to the strong economic slowdown ahead, especially between 2010 and 2012.

Although vacation and retirement home demographic trends are the most positive in real estate as a result of the aging of the massive baby-boom generation, this segment of the housing market is the most overvalued from speculation and will be the most sensitive to the economic downturn at first due to its discretionary nature. This is the best area to sell now; and look to rebuy between late 2012 and mid-2013.

Commercial Real Estate and Other Sectors

Commercial real estate, both office and industrial, has two significant drivers. The first obviously is a growing economy with lower unemploy-

Figure 4.19: Commercial Real Estate Cycle, 20-Year-Olds Minus 63-Year-Olds

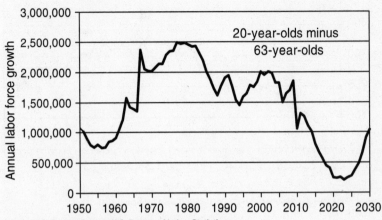

Source: U.S. Census Bureau; U.S. Bureau of Labor Statistics.

ment, which causes businesses to add employees and upgrade the quality of their workspace as they prosper. The second is the demographics of workforce growth, as new young employees enter the workforce and older workers retire. Figure 4.19 shows the workforce growth cycle, which adds new 20-year-olds (average age for workforce entry) and subtracts 63-year-olds (average age of retirement). Even without the long slowdown in baby-boomer spending ahead, commercial real estate would enter a long period of slowing, as baby boomers begin to retire faster than echo boomers enter the workforce, from 2010 to around 2023. With rising unemployment, especially into 2011 or mid-2013, this sector will be one of the worst hit, as it is falling faster than residential and is likely to bottom lower and later.

Commercial real estate and business hotels will be hard hit, especially into 2011 or late 2012 to mid-2013. They have held up better in the late stages of the economic boom than residential real estate, but rising unemployment and business failures will take a high toll, as will rapidly rising baby-boomer retirement. Light industrial parks that are more flexible and affordable will hold up the best, as will commercial real estate ori-

Figure 4.20: Spending on Leisure Travel by Age

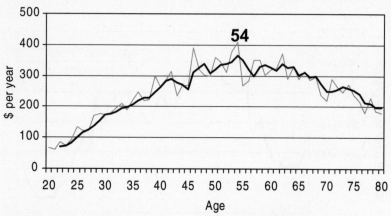

Source: Consumer Expenditure Survey, 2000; U.S. Bureau of Labor and Statistics.

ented toward health care and assisted living. Resort hotels will hold up a bit better, as the baby boomers continue to travel into their mid-50s, with obvious offsets for a strongly declining economy.

Leisure travel peaks around age 54, as is shown in Figure 4.20. Resort hotels will have continued rising demographic demand into around 2015 or 2016, as Figure 4.21 shows. Obviously, as stated above, a declining economy will curb demand substantially, especially in the higher end of the market.

Summary for Real Estate

Two key areas at the two extremes of the real estate spectrum will bring opportunity after the crash of 2010 and the real estate depression into 2011–2012 and beyond. The first will be affordable apartments and starter homes for the new echo-boom generation, especially between around mid-2011 onward. Affordable rental apartments should hold up the best at first. The second will be higher-end vacation and retirement homes for the aging baby boomers, between late 2012 and mid-2013. Commercial real estate and McMansions will be the hardest hit and very

Figure 4.21: Resort Hotel Cycle, 54-Year Lag

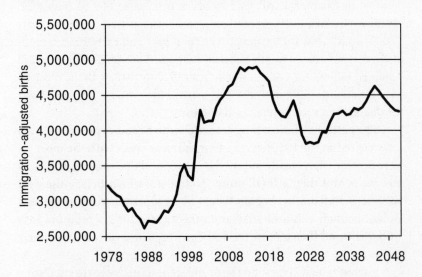

slow to recover, starting between late 2012 and mid-2013, and more so from 2020 onward. There will continue to be pockets of growth due to migration trends in parts of the Southeast, Southwest, and Rockies, as we will cover in Chapter 5 ahead. Hospitals, health-care facilities, and basic infrastructure like water, wastewater, alternative energy, and transportation will be attractive and receive strong government funding to counter the downturn—as in the 1930s.

The Deflationary Economic Environment Ahead: A Replay of the 1930s?

Beyond the demographic cycles for various sectors of real estate and other sectors of our economy and stocks, we also must consider the impacts of the overall economy from declining baby-boom spending and changing interest rates, especially from the rare deflation cycle ahead. The Spending Wave (Figure 2.3 from Chapter 2) predicts that spending will trend downward generally from around 2010 into around 2023. A weak economy will obviously affect unemployment and foreclosures and will create greater caution in spending, especially for large durable goods such as housing, furnishings, and cars. The weakest cycles in the downturn examined in Chapter 3 will tend to occur from late 2009 to mid-2012. These cycles will likely strengthen again between mid-2012 and early 2017, turn downward again between mid-2017 and early 2020, and, finally, may slow down mildly between 2021 and 2022–2023. Figure 3.17 in Chapter 3 shows the cycle in stocks from 1928 to 1942, with the most severe crash bottoming in mid-1932, a strong bear market rally into early 1937, and then a less severe crash into early 1942.

The patterns of most long-term downturns and depressions, such as occurred in the 1930s, have a first, extreme crash with the most severe downturn, typically followed by a rebound that can last as long as five years and then a final, more modest slowdown before the next long-term bull market begins. We are likely to see the worst of the next downturn between mid-2010 and mid- to late 2012, a rebound into mid-2017, and then a more modest downturn into early 2020 or early 2023.

Interest rates will vary long term and short term due to the oscillating economic environment noted above, falling inflation rates with deflation for much of this period, and anticipation of default rates. We showed the general deflation trend from the retirement of the baby boomers slowing workforce growth in Figure 2.18 in Chapter 2. As a general rule, deflationary trends will be the most extreme between mid-2010 and mid-2013, and give way to some inflation again into 2017. Deflation will then likely continue to a lesser degree from 2017 into as late as 2023 before we see the resumption of mild inflationary trends longer term. The deepest deflation should by this chart come toward the end of the downturn cycle in the early 2020s, but rising trends in Asia are likely to offset that, and we should see more modest deflation trends after a rebound in inflation between 2012 and 2017. The banking crisis from the bursting of the real estate, commodity, and stock bubbles will create the most severe deflation in the early years of the next decade, a more moderate deflation between 2017 and 2020, and a lower level of deflation in the early 2020s, as the dotted line in Figure 2.18 shows. Again, these are rough forecasts.

Interest rate cycles will be volatile during the times of greatest fear and deflation, will be different for short-term versus long-term rates, and will vary greatly by credit quality. Figure 4.22 shows three-month T-bill rates and six-

Figure 4.22: Short-Term Treasury Yields, 1928–1942

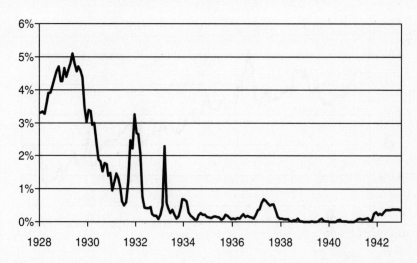

month Treasury note rates from 1928 to 1942. Rates rose a bit as the economy bubbled from 1928 to 1929 and then dived to nearly zero between 1930 and 1936–1940, as the Fed stimulated the economy during the worst crisis and unemployment ever. There was a spike in late 1931 as the crisis first looked so ominous. Hence, from 1936 on, investors earned no returns on safe cash investments. How did that affect retirees living on fixed incomes? Their only consolation was that the cost of living went down due to the deflationary trends. The best place to make modest gains and some capital appreciation was in high-quality long-term bonds.

Trends in long-term interest rates were different. Figure 4.23 shows long-term Treasury yields from 1926 to 1942. They spiked upward in the early stages of the sharp downturn into late 1931. However, "a flight to quality" sent these yields downward into the worst of the crisis in early to mid-1932, as bond yields on corporate and municipal bonds continued to spike higher. Yields continued downward from 1933 to 1942, to as low as 1.7%. That level was still much higher than 0.1% on three-month Treasury bills, but the real advantage was that the value of the bonds appreciated substantially in that period as deflation set in, as we will discuss in more depth in Chapter 8. The steepest drop in yields came from 1933

Figure 4.23: Long-Term Treasury Yields, 1926–1942

Figure 4.24: Consumer Price Index, 1928–1943

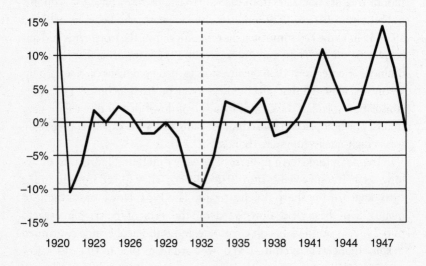

into 1936, in the aftermath of the stock crash and highest unemployment, when continued deflation was accompanied by improvements in the economy.

To get a better look at the broader economic picture in the Great De-

Figure 4.25: Gross National Product, 1921–1946

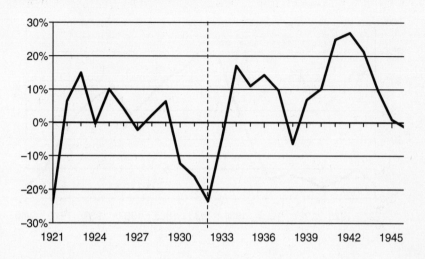

Figure 4.26: Fixed Investment, 1929–1943

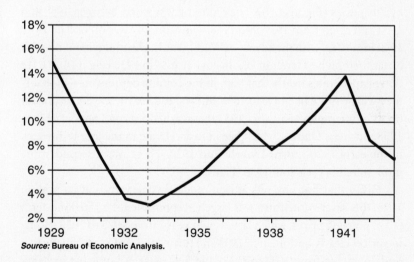

Source: Bureau of Economic Analysis.

pression, let's look at some key economic statistics. Figure 4.24 shows the Consumer Price Index annually, with the strongest deflationary trends occurring from 1930 into 1932 and a second, milder round from 1937 into 1938–1939. Gross domestic product also declined more sharply at

Figure 4.27: Unemployment Rate, 1923–1943

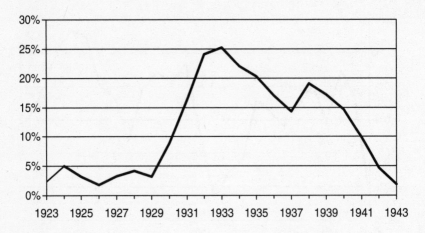

first, with a second, milder drop from 1937 into 1938 (Figure 4.25). The swings in the economy are best shown by changes in capital investment by businesses (Figure 4.26). The economy was worse between 1930 and 1933 and again from 1937 into 1938. The economy was off and on from 1940 into 1943, with the advent of World War II. Unemployment rates hit by far their highest levels in U.S. history at 25% in 1933 (Figure 4.27). We don't expect rates nearly that high in the coming depression—probably they will be more like 14% to 16%. But you can see there were secondary bouts of unemployment after 1937 that reached a second peak at 18% in 1938. Business failures, which began to accelerate in the first tech wreck in the early 1920s, turned severe into 1932. There was a second, more modest failure cycle into 1938 (Figure 4.28).

Given that housing was at best modestly overvalued at its peak in 1925, this severe downturn was largely responsible for a rare long-term fall in housing prices, which lasted eight years, from 1925 to 1933. Housing prices clearly bottomed in 1933 and turned upward even into the second downturn from 1937 to 1942, due to the starter home buying wave of the next, larger generation ahead. The housing crash contributed much to the deflationary environment of the 1930s, as banks had to write off real estate loans in addition to business loans, as in the early 1920s tech wreck (this situation is echoed in the 2000–2002 tech wreck). Figure

Figure 4.28: Number of Business Failures, 1921–1946

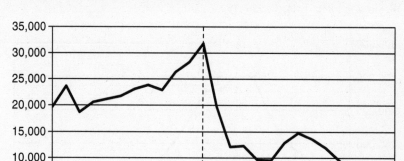

4.29 shows how mortgage foreclosures first started to rise in 1926 but then accelerated to much higher levels during the worst of the slowdown in 1933. As shown in Figure 4.30, the number of banks started to decline after the business and tech wreck of 1920–1922; this decline accelerated into 1933. The number of banks fell 40% from 1929 to 1933.

Deflation in prices from the massive write-off of business and real estate loans and bank failures was the hallmark of the 1930s depression, and this deflation is what most set apart the 1930s depression from the extended 1970s inflationary recession. Writing off loans contracts the money supply even as the government tries to inflate the economy with lower interest rates and liquidity. Most economists will expect inflation in the next slowdown when it finally occurs in 2010, especially after the resurgence of commodity prices in 2009—and we believe that they will be dead wrong!

Expect higher levels of social unrest, terrorism, and crime in such an extreme and extended downturn, especially during a deflationary depression with high unemployment levels. The greatest correlation with crime and social unrest is simply unemployment. Figure 4.31 shows how suicides peaked at the highest levels in 1932 with the worst of the stock crash; homicides peaked between 1933 and 1934 with the highest unemployment rates. Our Geopolitical Cycle from Chapter 3 predicts contin-

Chart 4.29: Number of Mortgage Foreclosures of Nonfarm Residential Real Estate, 1926–1947

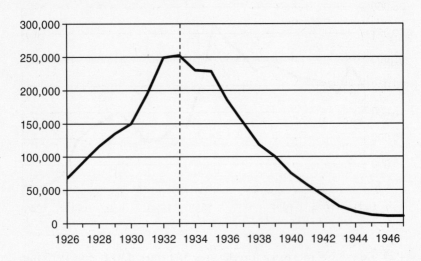

Figure 4.30: Number of Banks, 1920–1947

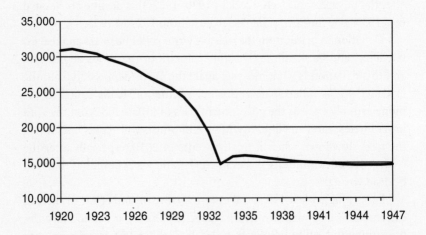

Figure 4.31: Number of Suicides and Homicides, 1920–1945

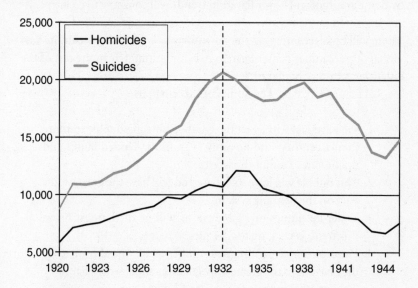

ued worldwide unrest and conflicts into 2018 to 2019, including rising terrorism.

We have been warning for a long time that where you live is important in this Next Great Depression. It is better to live in the outer suburbs and exurbs of major cities and better to live in larger cities (inland especially is better) in the Southeast, Southwest, and Rockies, which have high migration rates—cities such as Phoenix, Tucson, Las Vegas, Denver, Atlanta, Austin, San Antonio, Dallas, Raleigh, Charlotte, Nashville, Tampa, Orlando, Jacksonville, and Richmond. If you can, it is even better to live in more remote inland towns with high recreation and culture, such as Santa Fe, New Mexico; Prescott, Arizona; Saint George, Utah; Telluride, Colorado; Ashland, Oregon; Asheville, North Carolina; Fayetteville, Arkansas; Madison, Wisconsin; Ann Arbor, Michigan, Bloomington, Indiana; Gainesville, Georgia; Gainesville, Florida; Woodstock, New York; or Burlington, Vermont; or in these not-so-inland cities: Wailea, Hawaii; Sarasota, Florida; or Virginia Beach, Virginia.

We will look in more depth and detail at how to take advantage of this downturn in investments, business, and life strategies in Chapter 8, including for your kids' education and career opportunities. However, in the next chapter we will look at how domestic migration rates are driven by demographics and how migration trends will continue to create pockets of growth in the regions, cities, and towns we have referred to above. There will be silver linings in the downturn, as we will see, including vast global opportunities nearer term in Asia and ultimately in the rest of the emerging world (Chapter 6).

Let's summarize the key points of this chapter:

1. We have just witnessed the greatest housing bubble in more than a century, and possibly ever, in the United States and major cities around the world.

2. This bubble will have to deflate and will have the greatest impact on the banking system.

3. Trade-up homes or McMansions will be the hardest hit as this trend is peaking for decades to come.

4. Vacation/retirement homes will be hit very hard initially as they have seen the greatest speculation and mostly peaked by 2006 or 2007 in their first cycle of buying.

5. Commercial real estate will also be hard hit by rising unemployment, business bankruptcies, and downsizing—and the fact that it has only begun to deflate in 2008, faster than residential housing has. Opportunities there should begin to emerge by mid-2013 and again around 2023.

6. Apartments will hold up best as more young households will be forced to rent first, and that rental cycle is still on the rise demographically into 2017.

7. Affordable starter homes will be the first great opportunity starting by mid-2011 to late 2012 for home builders and young buyers, especially with falling mortgage rates and a rising demographic cycle into around 2022.

8. Vacation/retirement homes will be the next to rebound, between mid-2013 and early 2015, due to a baby-boom cycle that doesn't peak until around 2025.

9. Larger homes and McMansions may first resurge around early 2015 and then boom more sustainably from around 2020 to 2023 onward.

10. A concerted long-term boom in real estate more across

the board will occur from around 2023 into around 2036.

11. This banking crisis and depression cycle will very likely come in three stages: the first a severe downturn and bubble collapse into late 2012 to mid-2013; the second an interim boom and rally for as much as five years from mid-2012 to early 2017; and the third a less severe slowdown and deflation cycle from mid-2017 into early 2020 or as late as early 2023.

CHAPTER 5

Echo Boomers Continue to Move to the Southeast, Southwest, and Rockies

Opportunities for Businesses, Developers, and Municipalities in the Downturn

IT DOES NOT MATTER what angle you take in describing the economy, it always comes down to one thing: people. In a modern, industrialized nation, the economy can be described as nothing more than a group of people, or a population, earning and spending (or not spending, as the case may be) money. At the end of the day, there are four things about people that drive the economy: how many people are there, what age they are, what they are buying, and where they live or are moving. When we have the power to see how these four variables will change over time, we have the power to see what is potentially in our "economic future," years before it ever happens. This chapter will show the effects of where people are moving; such migration flows are highly demographic driven.

Here are the key summary insights:

1. Young, new households and not retirees will drive immigration and domestic migration.
2. The echo boom will increase domestic migration trends to the Southeast, the Southwest, and the Rockies, despite a

slowing in our economy after 2009, creating the best opportunities long term in selected states and cities in these areas.

3. The cities that are most attractive to domestic migrants are
   those with populations between 1 million and 2 million and
   (more recently) slightly smaller cities.

4. Immigration, mostly into large coastal cities, will slow dramatically with rising unemployment in the downturn after
   2009; this will exaggerate the real estate downturns in these
   areas.

5. Our current and future policies to restrict immigration will
   make our inevitable slowdown after 2009 more severe, as
   immigrants contribute to economic and demographic
   growth beyond their social costs.

Domestic Migration: The Zero-Sum Game That Will Only Grow in the Decade to Come

Given the economic challenges facing the United States over the next fifteen years, domestic migration will become all the more important, especially as we show ahead that immigration will fall dramatically in a bad
economy. The states and cities that attract the most domestic migrants
are the ones that will prosper the most in the downturn; those that lose
population will suffer more dramatic falls in real estate values, a falling
tax base, and an exodus of high-quality companies and households. Businesses and real estate developers will want to refocus their businesses in
the areas that will slow the least and/or actually still grow in the coming
extended downturn.

To get an idea of the impact we are describing, consider that domestic
migration out of state has three times the percentage impact of immigration. Contrary to popular belief, these domestic migrants are largely
young, productive new households, not retirees. Most older people, if they
relocate at all, do so near their families and grandkids. From 1995 to 2004,
a full eight times as many people aged 20 to 29 years moved as retirees
aged 60 to 69 years (Figure 5.1). From 1995 to 2000, that ratio was even
larger, 11 times. Even though the number of moving retirees will increase
dramatically in coming years, the overwhelming majority of migrants will

Figure 5.1: Young Households Dominate Moving and
Regional Migration

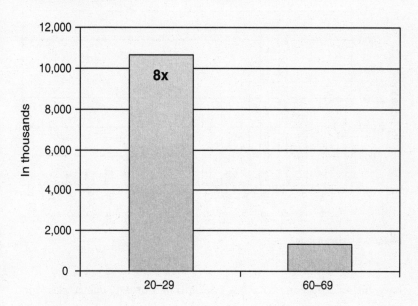

Source: U.S. Census Bureau.

continue to be young families looking for good job opportunities, better
climate, and a lower cost of living. It is the echo boomers—*not* the baby
boomers—who will dominate these domestic migration trends.

Figure 5.2 shows the truth about domestic migration and moving altogether. People who move to other regions are highly concentrated between the ages of 20 to 29, with the peak between ages 25 and 29. The age
demographics are similar even for those who move locally or within the
same state or region. These are people coming out of school, getting married, and looking to have kids—that is, when they move for better job opportunities, lower living and housing costs, better schools, better
climates, and so on. It is easier to move when you have less furniture and
fewer relationships. The actual peak age is probably closer to age 26,
when people get married today on average. Note that the percentage of
people who move declines steadily after age 34, and there is not a notice-
able rise around retirement age. Hence only minor numbers of people
move to a new region for retirement. However, the ones who do move

Figure 5.2: Movers to Different Regions, by Age

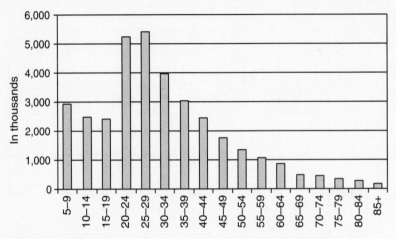

Source: **U.S. Census Bureau.**

have historically gone to a few concentrated areas, such as Arizona, Nevada, and the coasts of South Carolina and Florida.

Again, it won't be the aging baby boomers who reshape our country as a result of domestic migration, it will be the echo boomers, who have just started their moving cycle in this decade, as we can see in Figure 5.3. Here, the Immigration-Adjusted Birth Index is lagged for 25 to 27 years for the peak in moving rates. The echo-boom generation will continue to move in higher numbers into around 2017, allowing for the average age of marriage to advance toward 27 by then. There will be a minor slowing in moving rates until around 2024 and a second advance into around 2034 or 2035.

Knowing where the next generation of echo boomers will be moving will allow you to see opportunities for growth even in the worst economy of our lifetimes. These people will represent new consumers at their highest growth rates in spending for businesses; they will need apartments and starter homes; and they will create new tax revenues for municipalities.

Figure 5.3: The Migration Wave, 25- to 27-Year Lag for Peak Movers

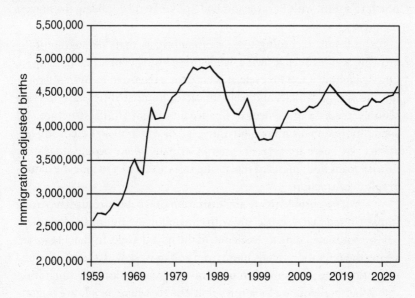

Among cities, the biggest winners from domestic migration—those likely to continue booming in the downturn—are medium-sized, typically inland cities with 1 million to 2 million in population. The states that have been benefiting the most from domestic migration patterns are in the Southwest (Nevada, Arizona, and Texas); in the Southeast (Florida, Georgia, North Carolina, coastal South Carolina, and northern Alabama); and in the Rockies (Oregon, Colorado and Idaho)—and more recently in New Mexico and Utah. In the coming years, the greatest number of migrants will move to the Southeast, but the greatest percentage rates of growth will continue to occur in the Southwest, as we will cover ahead.

In March 2006 *The Economist* ran an article titled "Cradle Snatching" showing that the United States is not alone in its migration trends. Traditionally, Europeans have always been far less mobile than Americans. However, demographics and economics have created a new trend in Germany as well. Because German birthrates have been extraordinarily low for decades now, young workers are in short supply. As a result, fierce competition has developed between the various regions of the country, resulting in what has been dubbed "demographic theft." The German convection current is moving the population from east to west and from north to south, with Bavaria and Baden-Württemberg being the biggest recipients.

The result, according to *The Economist,* is that "demographically growing regions keep growing, while those losing people go on doing so. Once caught in a vicious cycle, it is hard for a region to recover: after losing the young, female, and well-educated, municipalities have to close schools, increase utility fees to finance an oversized infrastructure and spend more on an aging population—all of which makes them still less attractive." There are areas in eastern Germany where people are tearing down vacant buildings and replanting trees and parks to hide the demographic contraction.

Germany's problems are an illustration of what is already happening in the United States, especially with the hollowing out of the Rust Belt. These trends are going to accelerate in the next decade. In Canada we are seeing the migration trends more from east to west, with the greatest immigration into British Columbia and the greatest domestic migration into Alberta. Before we look further at exactly where people are migrating, let's look at immigration trends, which have been very significant for growth in the United States in the past but are likely to fade far more dramatically than most people (even those strongly anti-immigration) would expect.

Immigration: Adding to the Demographic Fire, but Set to Decline Dramatically

Immigration, along with domestic migration, is highly age driven, just like almost every trend in economics: inflation, innovation, spending, borrowing, investment, and so on. Economically, immigration is a winning proposition for the receiving country. Although immigration does create social costs, including costs of education and medical care, immigrants on average add a net $80,000 more in taxes over their lifetimes above these social costs. It takes an investment of about $250,000 to raise the average kid before he or she works and becomes productive, not counting government schooling costs. On the other hand, immigrants come in raised and ready to work, albeit typically with lower educations and incomes at first. Essentially, we bypass the unproductive years of their lives and get them in their prime.

Furthermore, immigrants are an immediate boon to the areas to which they move because many of the things they consume, such as food, clothing, and shelter, are purchased locally. As a result, immigrants instantly add consumer demand just by moving to a town. Immigrants tend to be drawn to areas that are already booming, because it is in such boomtowns that the best opportunities exist for high-paying jobs. This creates a self-reinforcing cycle in which new immigrants are attracted to areas by growth that has already been partially fed by immigration.

Right now there are estimated to be between 10 million and 20 million illegal immigrants in the economy, and the figure is probably closer to 20 million. The number of service workers we have who are in this group is obviously in the millions. The U.S. unemployment rate in the last expansion got as low as 4.7%. If we removed millions of service workers from the economy today, two things would happen. First, some jobs would simply go unfilled, and those services would die out. To give an example, in parts of Western Europe, dry cleaners are almost nonexistent, and those that do operate are extremely expensive. European immigration laws, designed to favor labor, place a tremendous burden on employers, thereby making low-end service businesses unprofitable to operate.

The second eventuality would be higher wages for these jobs, and therefore higher prices for consumers—meaning inflation. It is precisely the flow of workers to our economy, workers who perform services as well as consume goods and services while here, that helps us to grow and to do so without the curse of inflation.

As with domestic migration, immigration is driven by the 20- to 29-year-old age group, with the peak age of immigrants being closer to 26, like that of domestic migrants, as Figure 5.4 shows. The same forces that encourage new American households to move to a new state also motivate foreigners to move to a new country. Immigration to the United States (Figure 5.5) has been growing steadily since World War II and peaked in 1991, with a temporary spike that followed amnesty programs in 1986. Note that immigration peaked similarly between 1907 and 1914, two generations or almost 80 years ago, and then fell to nearly zero in the Great Depression, when the economy collapsed and unemployment rose more dramatically.

Figure 5.4: Immigrants to the United States by Age, 1945–2000

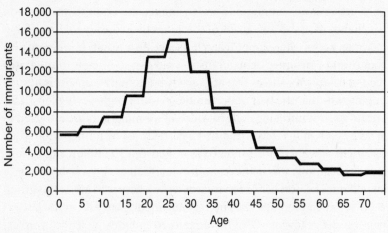

Source: U.S. Census Bureau.

These immigrants were generally the same age as the baby-boom population here at that time. This means that these newcomers effectively made the baby-boom generation even bigger, amplifying its effects. Immigration peaked at 1.8 million in 1991 and has now settled back to between 800,000 and 1.2 million, plus at least 500,000 per year in illegal immigration, which adds nearly 0.5% in population growth per year. But now that immigration rates seem to have stabilized at lower but still robust levels, we are proposing to further restrict immigration and make the present illegal immigrants here earn their way to proper documentation. This means that not only will growth continue to slow, especially with the slowdown of 2008, but also that the bust years of our economy will be all the more severe when immigration comes to a halt, just as Figure 5.5 shows it did in the 1930s through World War II.

In the economic slowdown that we forecast from about 2010 into 2023, based on our demographic analysis (Figure 2.3, The Spending Wave, in Chapter 2), there should be a significant rise in unemployment, at least to 15%, between 2011 and 2012. We can expect immigration to be restricted dramatically, much as it was in the 1930s, due to a backlash in public sentiment toward immigrants who are "stealing American jobs" and due to falling opportunities in a deteriorating economic environ-

Figure 5.5: Immigration to the United States, 1820–2006

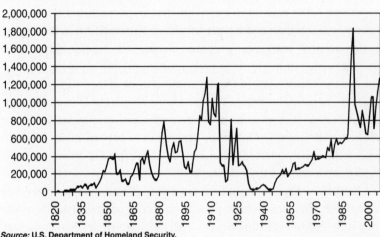

Source: U.S. Department of Homeland Security.

ment. Although this certainly will lessen the number of workers chasing jobs, it will have little effect on the problem of a slowing economy. Our immigrant population tends to join the workforce in low-end service jobs. Reducing the number of applicants for these jobs will not do very much to create new opportunities for engineers or MBAs. Nevertheless, anti-immigrant sentiment is already high and will obviously rise more dramatically as our economy slows.

Even now, in the midst of an economic boom as measured by expansion in GDP and consumer expenditures, our government has already initiated several new policies that make immigration, both legal and illegal, much more difficult. Some of these policies were related to security and terrorism, although nearly all reflect a general feeling of unease among Americans about the high levels of immigration in recent decades. To give some examples, the Immigration and Naturalization Service recently instituted a "catch and return" policy, in which undocumented immigrants are deported without a formal hearing. Meanwhile, citizen groups such as the Minute Men have taken to patrolling the U.S. border with Mexico themselves, citing national security and job competition as their concerns.

In mid-2006, the House of Representatives proposed legislation that would make illegal immigration a *felony,* and would impose criminal penalties on companies that hire undocumented workers. The Senate and the president have taken a more moderate approach, but both nevertheless have felt the need to "get tough" on immigration in a congressional election year. The proposed Senate bill would allow some undocumented immigrants to stay in the country after paying a $2,000 fine and their back taxes, but it also requires some of the more recent immigrants to leave altogether. This is only the beginning. When our economy stalls after 2009 and unemployment rises, anti-immigrant sentiment will get much stronger. Out of the depression of 2010 to 2012, we would expect the newly elected president to usher in the strongest anti-immigration reforms since the early 1930s.

Partially as a result of our forecasted drop in immigration, real estate and growth prospects in high-price, high-immigration coastal cities like New York, Boston, Washington, D.C., Miami, Los Angeles, San Francisco, San Diego, Seattle, and Vancouver will be the hardest hit after 2009. Dallas and Houston are likely to be hit hard as well due to high immigration rates into Texas, although domestic migration into Texas has been improving in recent years and real estate valuations in Texas are affordable.

As we showed just above, the echo-boom generation will peak in its moving cycle around 2017, decline for several years, and then peak again with its second wave around 2034 to 2035. At that point our country will become more sedentary and begin aging more rapidly, becoming less innovative and less mobile—like Europe and Japan today.

So, with regard to immigration, we have bad news and good news. The bad news is that we are not going to have enough immigrants to boost consumer demand by a meaningful amount once the downturn begins, and this will make the downturn worse, especially in high-immigration areas. The good news is, at least relative to the other developed countries, the United States will be far more likely to assimilate existing immigrants into our system. In the first half of 2006, pro-immigrant rallies brought hundreds of thousands of marchers into the streets, many waving the flags of foreign countries (although many waved American flags as well). Many Americans found that sight to be troubling, but it must be kept in perspective. It might be helpful to compare our situation to the one currently facing Europe. Compared to the problems of our European contemporaries, our "problems" look quite bearable.

*The Convection Current: Continued High Migration into the Southeast,
Southwest, and Rockies from the Northeast, Midwest, and California*

Figure 5.6 shows a simplified overview of the key migration patterns in
the United States. Immigrants from abroad tend to come into large cities
in the Northeast, like New York; large cities in the Southeast, like Miami;
and the larger cities in Texas. In the West, they come statewide in California. Domestic migration tends to occur from the Northeast, especially
from New York and New Jersey, into the east coast of Florida and into
Georgia, North Carolina, and South Carolina. People from the Midwest
tend to move more to the west coast of Florida and to northern Alabama,
Georgia, North Carolina, South Carolina, and Texas. The other great migration trend is from California into Arizona, Nevada, Colorado, Texas,
Oregon, and Idaho.

The largest coastal cities are losing much of the benefits of their high
foreign immigration by rapidly losing domestic migrants to medium-to-
large growth cities that are typically more inland. There are three obvious
motivations for these migration trends: better climates, lower housing

Figure 5.6: Migration Flows

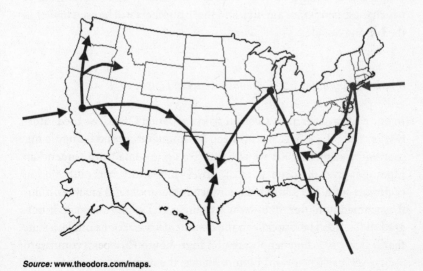

Source: www.theodora.com/maps.

costs, and growing jobs. Immigrants to our country certainly benefit their new states, but the higher incomes and spending are clearly moving with the domestic migrants. This will be particularly problematic in the downturn, when states and municipalities are facing serious revenue shortfalls. Some of the states that are losing population, such as California and New York, also have some of the worst state budget problems.

The United States is an extraordinarily mobile society, as evidenced by the fact that 414 million people, or 152% of the population, moved in the last decade. It is often stated that the average household moves every 7 years, or in this case, 1.4 times every decade. Approximately 79% moved within the same state and 60% within the same county. These trends are not as significant for this analysis of regional migration trends, but they are important for expanding exurban areas and counties just outside growing city suburban areas.

The key group for migration trends is made up of the 10% or 42 million who moved to a different region or division (subregion) in the last decade. This group was 3.0 times the nearly 14 million legal and illegal immigrants in the same period. This large group of regional migrants creates 1.5% in population shifts per year, which is greater than our current population growth at 0.9% and exceeds our current birthrate at approximately 1.4%. Needless to say, the movement of *42 million people* creates a major trend for real estate and business growth in the areas to which these people are moving, and those numbers will be even higher in the coming decade.

Domestic Migration Trends from United Van Lines

In our past special report *Demographics in Motion* (2006), we used information from the U.S. Census Bureau for immigration and domestic migration by state. In 2008 we were able to access data from United Van Lines that gives the percentage of movers inbound versus outbound of each state back to 1978, which is much better for trend analysis in domestic migration over time—which again will be more relevant as immigration likely falls drastically in the coming decade. For example, a state that is strongly losing net population may show 60% of moves outward bound versus 40% inward bound. Hence, the numbers are relative and

Figure 5.7: Top Ten States with Net Out-Migration, 2003–2007

State	5-year Average
North Dakota	66.4%
Michigan	63.3%
New Jersey	60.9%
Indiana	60.0%
New York	59.5%
Illinois	58.5%
Pennsylvania	56.3%
Ohio	55.2%
Wisconsin	54.6%
Massachusetts	54.5%

Source: United Van Lines.

will always add up to 100% in any year. Figure 5.7 shows the top ten states by percentage of out-migration between 2003 and 2007. The weakest states in order are North Dakota, Michigan, New Jersey, Indiana, New York, and Illinois. The four other weaker states—Pennsylvania, Ohio, Wisconsin, and Massachusetts—are similarly in the Midwest and Northeast.

Figure 5.8 shows the states attracting the greatest net in-migration in the last five years. The strongest have been North Carolina, Nevada, Oregon, South Carolina, Idaho, Alabama, and Arizona, with strength in Tennessee, Delaware, and New Mexico as well. But the trends over time have been very different, as the charts in the next section show. Over the last decade or two, it has been Florida that has seen the greatest numbers in domestic in-migration, with Texas second and then Georgia and North Carolina. Nevada and Arizona have seen the highest rates of growth in the past decade, but are falling off after the housing bubble bust began, and now North Carolina leads in growth rate, with Nevada a close second.

Figure 5.8: Top Ten States with Net In-Migration, 2003–2007

State	5-year Average
North Carolina	62.0%
Nevada	61.7%
Oregon	61.0%
South Carolina	59.8%
Idaho	59.3%
Alabama	58.3%
Arizona	58.3%
Tennessee	55.3%
Delaware	55.2%
New Mexico	54.6%

Source: United Van Lines.

Long-Term In-Migration Trends in the Southeast

When we look at the region with the greatest overall volume in domestic migration, we see very different trends in the Southeast. Florida (see Figure 5.9) had very high rates of in-migration in the 1970s and 1980s and then another revival during the housing bubble from 2000 to 2007. But house prices bubbled too much and reached the highest levels by far in the Southeast, which has generally remained very affordable. Since 2004, in-migration rates have slowed to almost a balance in 2007. Is the migration boom in Florida over? This state will likely become more attractive again as prices there fall more than in other areas during the downturn and as it continues to attract retirees. But it is likely to be the northern part of the state, the north side of Tampa and Orlando, Jacksonville, and the Panhandle that continue to grow. The devastation in southern Florida real estate is likely to scare off buyers there for a number of years and this state could actually start to see some out-migration in the years to come before it rebounds again, as it did briefly in 2006.

Figure 5.9: In-Migration Rates: Florida, North Carolina, and South Carolina, 1978–2007

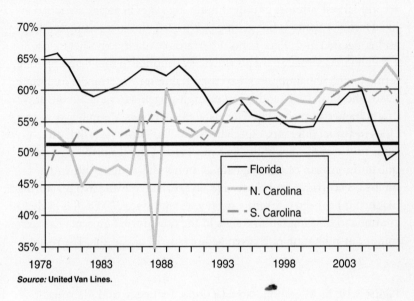

Source: United Van Lines.

When real estate values get very low again, likely between 2011 and 2014, southern Florida will rebound strongly as a hot spot as it attracts retirees, young families, and immigrants. Miami in particular will attract yuppies looking for a hip place to live after prices fall from the extreme excess building of condos, especially just north of the city in the new Performing Arts district.

North Carolina is now the top state for in-migration rates, very close to Nevada. The trends here were rising steadily in the 1990s and have gone to extremes in this decade. Given its affordability and two attractive emerging cities, Charlotte and Raleigh-Durham, this state should continue to be the strongest in the years ahead. South Carolina has great beach areas, but suffers from having no cities greater than 1 million—"the sweet spot." The most attractive cities tend to be 1 million to 2 million in population, as we will discuss in the next section. But South Carolina has been rising more strongly since 2000 and looks to continue to do so as its larger cities get closer to the 1 million mark in the coming years.

Figure 5.10 shows the other key migration states in the Southeast. Georgia has been the star here due to the large city of Atlanta, with the second-largest volumes of migrants among states in recent decades. Unlike Florida, Atlanta is not getting overpriced, but it is getting too large and congested and there is no other attractive city anywhere close to 1 million in Georgia. So trends will likely continue to cool here a bit long term, though remaining above average. Tennessee was stronger in the late 1980s and early 1990s and is just resurging again after the bubble drove prices higher in places like Florida. Tennessee has a number of larger cities to attract migrants, especially Nashville. This state is likely to continue to rise in the downturn. The most recent star is northern Alabama due to the growth of Birmingham as an up-and-coming "little Atlanta" on the I-85 corridor, and Huntsville, an exurban tech and manufacturing magnet. It has been one of the strongest states since 2003 and is likely to continue to lead migration trends in the downturn. Louisiana has seen minor out-migration rates, even before Hurricane Katrina. The rebuild-

Figure 5.10: In-Migration Rates: Georgia, Tennessee, and Alabama, 1978–2007

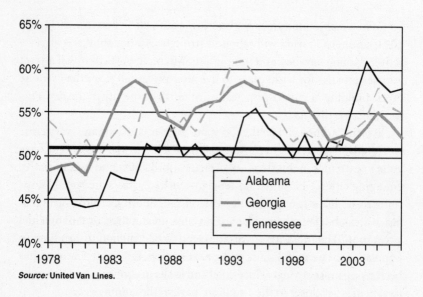

Source: United Van Lines.

ing of the southern part of the state will give it an opportunity to become attractive to domestic migrants if they do it right.

In-Migration Trends in the Southwest

The Southwest has seen the highest rates of growth, since the leading states there, such as Nevada and Arizona, are smaller in population than the larger states in the Southeast. Nevada continues to see the highest growth rates in migration (Figure 5.11), although the trends there have cooled a bit since 2003 with the growing bubble and falloff. But in-migration rates there are still near 60% and second only to North Carolina's. Arizona has been the second-fastest-growing state for migration for a long time, but has cooled even more than Nevada since 2005 due to the real estate crash and now hovers at a respectable 55% level. Both of these states are likely to suffer from continued home price declines worse than the nation's, and it may take a while for home buyers to have confidence in these markets, much as in Florida. But Arizona and Nevada should continue to see above-average in-migration, especially in the second half of the coming decade.

Texas is the largest state in the Southwest (or Southeast by some classifications). Hence it has high numbers of migrants, but not nearly the same percentage growth as Nevada and Arizona. Texas was stronger in the late 1970s and early 1980s before the final oil crash hit in 1986. Texas migration rates have been weaker since, but have risen since 2005 as the bubble in Florida, Arizona, and Nevada has made its largest cities, Dallas and Houston, look more attractive—and it has two growth cities in the sweet spot, Austin and San Antonio. But Texas will be hard hit by a strong fall in immigration in the downturn ahead, making it more likely a mildly positive growth state rather than a leader in growth like North Carolina or Nevada. Utah and New Mexico are states in the Southwest that have had low in-migration rates over the last few decades but may be showing signs of growth due to affordable housing versus Arizona and Nevada and new sweet-spot cities like Salt Lake City and Albuquerque. Provo/Orem has been one of the top-growth smaller cities in the country. These two states are worth watching in the next few years.

Figure 5.11: In-Migration Rates: Nevada, Arizona, and Texas, 1978–2007

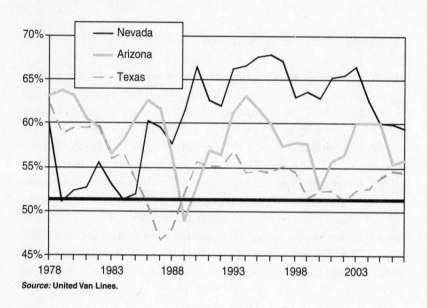

Source: United Van Lines.

In-Migration Trends in the Rockies and Northwest

The Rocky Mountain and northwestern states all tend to have net in-migration most of the time. The most critical states are shown in Figure 5.12. Oregon is the leading state in this area, taking over the lead after Washington State became congested and overpriced after 1998. Oregon picked up steam in the 1990s and has accelerated to number three in migration growth rate in the last five years, although it has dropped off in the last two years. Is it getting too overpriced now as well? Home prices have held up well there (as well as in Washington) and Oregon could rise again as California experiences some of the worst falls in prices due to extreme overvaluation and a dramatic fall in immigration rates ahead. This area looks good, but somewhat questionable into 2012 or so due to high prices in Portland.

Idaho is the other strong state in the Rockies, with Boise as a minor high-tech hub with very mild weather. Idaho's migration rates have re-

Figure 5.12: Migration into Western States:
% of Interstate Migration That Is Inbound

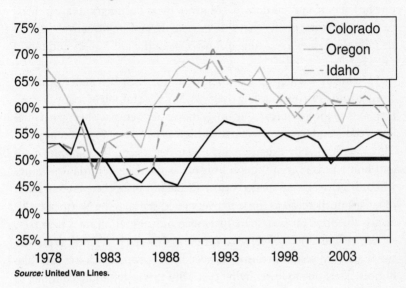

Source: United Van Lines.

mained strong, but declined into 2007 as well. We're not sure whether this represents a short-term fluke or a change of trends. The tech bust ahead could hurt Boise for a number of years, but Idaho should continue to be at least a moderately leading state for domestic migrants. Colorado had stronger trends in the 1990s but has cooled off a bit in this decade. We would guess this state will continue to attract migrants but not quite as fast as in the past. Denver remains an attractive city for young households.

Out-Migration Trends in the Midwest

The states with the strongest out-migration trends are typically in the Rust Belt or Midwest due to the long-term trend in falling manufacturing jobs. These states also have colder winters that motivate people to move south. Figure 5.13 shows the worst states of magnitude in this region. North Dakota, not shown, is actually the worst, as it has the worst weather and no sizable cities that attract industry and jobs. With out-migration rates recently as high as 66% to 68% the question is, will any one be left here in a few decades? Many of these out-migrants are moving to South Dakota, giving that otherwise cold and unattractive state net in-migration rates averaging around 54% in the last 5 years and recent rates at 57%.

Michigan is suffering the worst of all the Rust Belt states from declining auto jobs, outsourcing overseas, and the shifting of many domestic plants to the Southeast. Out-migration rates here have been near 60% for decades and have worsened to as high as 66% to 68% in recent years. This state is already experiencing a near depression in unemployment and home prices, even though housing is relatively affordable. Things will only get worse in the downturn ahead, but prices here are not likely to fall as much ahead as those in overvalued states in the Northeast. Illinois is the other large state that has seen out-migration rates near 60% for decades and this is likely to continue, as Chicago is the most expensive city in the Midwest. Wisconsin has been losing people at a lower rate than Illinois, likely due to lower living costs. But this state should continue to

Figure 5.13: Out-Migration Rates: Michigan, Illinois, and Wisconsin, 1978–2007

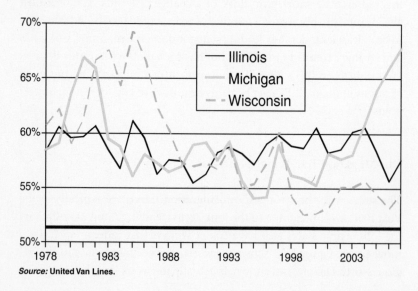

Source: United Van Lines.

decline as well in the downturn ahead. Pennsylvania, Ohio, and Indiana (Figure 5.14) have all been consistent losers in out-migration for decades, but at lower rates than Michigan and Illinois. Indiana was the worst a few years back, but Ohio's rates worsened in 2006 and 2007, and that does not bode well for the downturn years to come.

Out-Migration Trends in the Northeast

The states that have the greatest potential to see rising out-migration rates are in the Northeast, since the costs of living here are the most expensive outside California. As the downturn sets in, major cities like New York, Boston, and Philadelphia will see greater layoffs from financial and service industries, as will California. The falls in real estate prices in these areas will be much greater going forward, as prices have held up relatively well this far due to a good economy and limited development options, but will not hold up in a deflationary downturn and real estate crash. Figure 5.15 shows the trends in the key states that are losing (except Pennsylva-

Figure 5.14: Out-Migration Rates: Pennsylvania, Ohio, and Indiana, 1978–2007

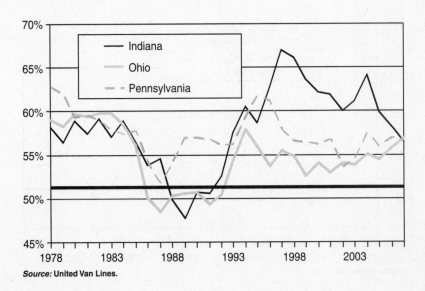

Source: United Van Lines.

nia, which was included in the Midwest and is in truth part Rust Belt, part urban Northeast). New Jersey has seen the highest out-migration rates in recent years and like New York has been consistently near 60% for decades. Both of these states will feel the fall of Wall Street between 2010 and 2012, much more than the minor hit in 2008. Massachusetts has seen less serious out-migration rates after seeing worse trends in the late 1980s and early 1990s, with the real estate crunch hitting strongly at that time. This will occur again, as Boston has a high quality of living but is still substantially overvalued, though not as much as New York. Hence Massachusetts is likely to weather this downturn better. The bright spots in the Northeast are, in order: Delaware, Rhode Island, and Vermont.

To summarize: The best states for continued growth due to domestic in-migration are the ones with both recent high rates and more affordable housing: North Carolina, South Carolina, Alabama, Nevada, and Oregon—and perhaps up-and-coming New Mexico and Utah. Arizona, Idaho, and perhaps Colorado are likely to continue to see good rates of in-migration, with Arizona hurting somewhat from falling immigration rates. The worst states for out-migration are likely to be the ones that are

Figure 5.15: Migration Out of Northeastern States

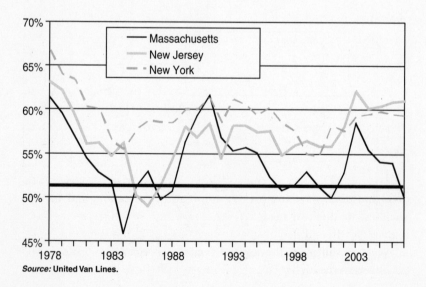

Source: United Van Lines.

the most expensive and have not yet seen their worst housing declines: California, New York, New Jersey, eastern Pennsylvania, and Massachusetts. The Rust Belt states that are losing the most now—Michigan, Illinois, Indiana, Ohio, and Wisconsin—will likely continue to do so but their relative fall in real estate prices will be less, given that they are not typically overvalued and have already fallen a good bit in 2008.

The Size of Cities That Are Benefiting: New Megacities and Up-and-Coming Ones

One of the broader impacts of migration patterns has been the impact on the types of cities that people are shifting to, as we have been hinting at in the previous section. Figure 5.16 shows migration patterns by size of metro areas from 1995 to 2000. The first insight is that metropolitan areas in total lost 510,000 people from 1995 to 2000. This represents the long-term (80-year) shift from suburban to exurban areas, similar to the shift from cities to suburbs from the 1920s to the 1980s, which we covered in depth in *The Roaring 2000s*, Chapter 9. But the most compelling insight is that over 2 million people moved out of very large cities in just 5 years, mostly into growth cities with populations between 1 million and 2 million, and to a lesser extent to new megacities with populations between 2 million and 5 million.

These migrants are downsizing from the largest cities with the highest living costs to somewhat smaller large cities with more affordable housing and job growth. The new megacities such as Atlanta, Dallas, Houston, and Phoenix have attracted the greatest numbers, but smaller-growth cities have seen the highest growth rates. These cities, such as Austin and Charlotte, still offer an array of entertainment, services, and amenities but often have the atmosphere more of a quaint exurban resort or college town in their earlier growth stages. Cities "in the middle," with populations of 250,000 to 1 million, which offer no great cultural attractions and don't have the back-to-community, recreation, and nature qualities, are the least attractive. Yet Figure 5.17, which shows the percentage growth to different areas from 2000 to 2003, indicates that more migrants are shifting to the next tier of cities between 250,000 and 1 million, likely to the higher end of this range, with the highest total migra-

Figure 5.16: Migration by Size of Metro Area, 1995–2000

	Total Metro	<250k	250–1,000K	1–2mm	2–5mm	>5mm
Net Domestic Migration	–510K	142K	218K	714K	527K	–2,111K
% Change	–2.5%	8.0%	5.3%	21.7%	14.8%	–27.4%
Immigration	6,876K	318K	881K	898K	1,438K	3,342K

Source: U.S. Census Bureau.

tion rates at 11.1% and the highest domestic net migration at 4.8%. Many cities 2 million to 5 million in size started to get too expensive or congested in the recent bubble.

> **The greatest insight into where most growth will occur due to migration is the new sweet-spot cities with populations between 1 million and 2 million, especially in the Southeast and Southwest, where the migration is already naturally heading—and more recently in cities slightly smaller.**

In Figure 5.18, we look at the metropolitan areas that are now in the sweet spot. They are listed in order from smallest to largest, since the ones that are just hitting the sweet spot are likely to be growing fastest and to be less noticed by businesses and developers at first. The ones in the Southeast and Southwest include Salt Lake City, Birmingham, Oklahoma City, Richmond, Louisville, Jacksonville, Orlando, Memphis, Nashville, Austin, San Antonio, Charlotte, Virginia Beach, and Las Vegas. Figure 5.19 shows the cities in southerly areas that are over 750,000 and approaching 1 million; they include Raleigh, Tucson, Honolulu, Tulsa, Fresno, and Albuquerque. If the trend toward smaller cities is indeed a longer-term one, then the cities approaching the sweet spot in Figure

Figure 5.17: Migration by Size of Metro Area, 2000–2003

	Total Metro	<250k	250–1,000k	1–2.5mm	2.5–5mm	>5mm
Net Domestic Migration	−0.1%	0.3%	4.8%	2.1%	1.2%	−5.2%
Net International Migration	5.2%	4.0%	6.3%	3.8%	5.5%	8.8%
Total Net Migration	5.1%	4.3%	11.1%	5.9%	6.6%	3.6%

Source: U.S. Census Bureau.

5.19 should become even more attractive. Cities such as Greenville-Spartanburg, Columbia, and Charleston, South Carolina, could become more attractive as well with the recent growth in that state. Note that Raleigh-Durham combined would already fall in the sweet spot, with around 1.4 million in population.

Figure 5.20 shows the larger megacities that have had the highest numbers in population growth. Eight of ten are in the Southeast and Southwest. The top five—Atlanta, Dallas, Houston, Phoenix, and Riverside–San Bernardino, California—were all just above or below 800,000 in the last ten years. Only two northern mega business centers, New York and Chicago, even made it into the top-ten growth list—and this was due to immigration, not domestic migration—and immigration trends will decline sharply ahead. The smaller up-and-coming cities with the highest percentage rates of growth are attractive, smaller cities in the Southeast and Southwest, which include Phoenix and Las Vegas (Figure 5.21).

When we take into account both total volume and growth rates, the growth from migration has been concentrated in a few states in the Southeast and Southwest: Florida, Georgia, Texas, Arizona, North Carolina, and Nevada. The strongest mega-growth cities have been Dallas, Atlanta, Houston, Phoenix, and increasingly Charlotte and Las Vegas—which have both favorable job growth and more affordable housing. However, these large cities are getting more congested, and that may cause migrants to choose cities in the next tier of just below or above 1 million.

Figure 5.18: Cities in the Sweet Spot,
1 million–2 million

Metropolitan statistical areas	July 1, 2004
Salt Lake City, UT	1,018,826
Rochester, NY	1,041,499
Birmingham-Hoover, AL	1,082,193
Oklahoma City, OK	1,144,327
Richmond, VA	1,154,317
Buffalo-Niagara Falls, NY	1,154,378
Hartford-West Hartford-East Hartford, CT	1,184,564
Louisville, KY-IN	1,200,847
Jacksonville, FL	1,225,381
Camden, NJ	1,237,773
Memphis, TN-MS-AR	1,250,293
Nashville-Davidson—Murfreesboro, TN	1,395,879
Austin-Round Rock, TX	1,412,271
Charlotte-Gastonia-Concord, NC-SC	1,474,734
Milwaukee-Waukesha-West Allis, WI	1,515,738
Indianapolis, IN	1,621,613
Providence-New Bedford-Fall River, RI-MA	1,628,808
Virginia Beach-Norfolk-Newport News, VA-NC	1,644,250
Las Vegas-Paradise, NV	1,650,671
Columbus, OH	1,693,906
San Antonio, TX	1,854,050
Orlando-Kissimmee, FL	1,861,707
Kansas City, MO-KS	1,925,319

Source: Population Division, U.S. Census Bureau.

Figure 5.22 lists the twelve metro areas most affected by traffic problems. Not surprisingly, Los Angeles and the San Francisco Bay area top the list. Quality-of-life issues concerning traffic are yet another reason (in addition to high living costs and taxes) for the exodus from California into the other western states. The real story in California is that it has seen many lower-income immigrants from Mexico and Asia but has been slowly losing higher-income households to other states. This trend

Figure 5.19: Cities Approaching the Sweet Spot, 750,000–1 million

Metropolitan statistical areas	July 1, 2004
Raleigh-Cary, NC	914,680
Tucson, AZ	907,059
Honolulu, HI	899,593
Tulsa, OK	881,815
Fresno, CA	866,772
Lake County-Kenosha County, IL-WI	851,330
New Haven-Milford, CT	845,694
Dayton, OH	845,646
Albany-Schenectady-Troy, NY	845,269
Omaha-Council Bluffs, NE-IA	803,801
Albuquerque, NM	781,447
Allentown-Bethlehem-Easton, PA-NJ	779,816
Worcester, MA	779,488
Grand Rapids-Wyoming, MI	767,539

Source: **Population Division, U.S. Census Bureau.**

should worsen more dramatically when real estate values plummet much more and immigration falls sharply in the years ahead.

California is likely to see the greatest shock in falling real estate values and rising out-migration, with the most overvalued real estate and dramatically falling immigration rates.

The leading California cities increasingly share the traffic congestion list with several of the new growth cities of the Southeast, including Atlanta, Houston, Dallas, and Orlando. We are sure that the Miami–Fort

Figure 5.20: Cities with Highest Population Growth, 2000–2006

Atlanta-Sandy Springs-Marietta, GA	890,211
Dallas-Fort Worth-Arlington, TX	842,449
Houston-Sugar Land-Baytown, TX	824,547
Phoenix-Mesa-Scottsdale, AZ	787,306
Riverside-San Bernardino-Ontario, CA	771,314
Los Angeles-Long Beach-Santa Ana, CA	584,510
New York-Northern New Jersey-Long Island, NY-NJ-PA	495,154
Washington-Arlington-Alexandria, DC-VA-MD-WV	494,220
Miami-Fort Lauderdale-Miami Beach, FL	455,869
Chicago-Naperville-Joliet, IL-IN-WI	407,133

Source: U.S. Census Bureau.

Lauderdale area is close to being on this list. The congestion in these major southern cities should accelerate the movement of migrants toward larger cities like Tampa and emerging growth cities like Austin, San Antonio, Jacksonville, Raleigh-Durham, Charlotte, Birmingham, and Nashville—and to smaller, exurban areas within their high-growth states. Other attractive growth cities outside the Southeast and Southwest that are attracting young professionals include Denver and Minneapolis.

Total In-Migration in Key States and the Impacts of Volume and Immigration

The greatest volume of total migration has occurred and will continue to occur into the Southeast over the next decade or more, and immigration has been a substantial factor as well. In this section we will look at the key growth areas in the Southeast, Southwest, and Rockies, using Census Bureau data on both immigration and net domestic migration. Figure 5.23 shows southeastern states in order of their total in-migration rates bro-

Figure 5.21: Cities with Highest Percentage
Growth Rates, 2000–2006

St. George, UT	39.80%
Greeley, CO	31.00%
Cape Coral-Fort Myers, FL	29.60%
Bend, OR	29.30%
Las Vegas-Paradise, NV	29.20%
Provo-Orem, UT	25.90%
Naples-Marco Island, FL	25.20%
Raleigh-Cary, NC	24.80%
Gainesville, GE	24.40%
Phoenix-Mesa-Scottsdale, AZ	24.20%

Source: **U.S. Census Bureau.**

ken down into net domestic migration and immigration from 1995 to 2004. Florida, Texas, Georgia, and North Carolina clearly dominate in that order in total numbers of migrants. Arkansas, Kentucky, Alabama, Mississippi, and Louisiana trail in that order. Louisiana was already losing population before Hurricane Katrina in 2005.

Florida has had the largest absolute numbers and percentage growth rates. Florida attracts retirees as well as younger households, and that is another reason it has been the kingpin in total volume in the past. South Florida attracts the most affluent retirees and migrants, in part due to its low taxes and favorable weather. It also attracts a lot of immigrants from South America. In the last ten years, 32% of the total immigration has come from immigrants, mostly into the Miami–Fort Lauderdale area. Because of this massive migration and limited space due to the Everglades inland, South Florida has become very expensive and crowded, a situation that creates opportunities in northern and western Florida and in other Atlantic and Gulf Coast states, like North Carolina, South Carolina, and northern Alabama. That is why Florida's net domestic migration rates have slowed to nearly zero recently and why Florida is likely to

Figure 5.22: Top Twelve Cities for
Traffic Congestion

1. Los Angeles, Long Beach, Santa Ana, CA
2. San Francisco, Oakland, CA
3. Washington, DC
4. Atlanta, GA
5. Houston, TX
6. Dallas, Fort Worth, Arlington, TX
7. Chicago, IL
8. Detroit, MI
9. Riverside, San Bernardino, CA
10. Orlando, FL
11. San Jose, CA
12. San Diego, CA

Source: Texas Transportation Institute.

see some net out-migration during the worst years of the real estate crash ahead.

Texas is the next state that stands out in total volume, and a whopping 52% of that is from immigration, largely from Mexico. Texas has grown faster recently as a result of flight from New Orleans and Louisiana after Katrina and affordability compared to Florida for domestic migrants. This state has some of the lowest living costs in large cities with high job growth and cultural attractions. However, the high immigration component is Texas's Achilles' heel in the coming decade and could make it a very moderate growth state at best in the downturn. Georgia is the third in total volume but with much lower rates from immigration. Georgia will continue to slow in migration trends simply due to the congestion of Atlanta and the lack of any other major attractive cities, as we discussed above. It should also be a modestly growing state in the years ahead and has seen its major growth surge. Virginia is the other state that relies even

Figure 5.23: Migration and Immigration into
Southeastern States, 1995–2004

	Domestic Net Migration	Immigration from Abroad	Total
Florida	1,766,342	825,388	2,591,730
Georgia	726,879	212,590	939,469
North Carolina	650,103	146,627	796,730
Texas	997,634	930,539	1,928,173
South Carolina	217,445	34,954	252,399
Tennessee	296,101	56,045	352,146
Virginia	242,715	179,965	422,680
Arkansas	85,836	22,908	108,744
Kentucky	85,998	27,937	113,935
Alabama	47,333	26,299	73,632
Mississippi	19,450	9,729	29,179
Louisiana	(145,247)	26,061	(119,186)

Source: **U.S. Census Bureau.**

more on immigration than Texas, at 57% of the total in the past 10 years. Those people obviously come into the D.C. and northern Virginia area. This area will be hit hard by falling immigration and very high real estate prices in the coming decade. The domestic migration has been focused more on Richmond and Virginia Beach/Norfolk/Newport News, which should continue to be good areas in the downturn.

The rest of the southeastern states, which are lagging in growth, have the potential to benefit from their similar warm climates if they can improve their image for quality of life and attractive business environments, as they represent the most affordable areas in the southern half of the country. The Gulf areas in southern Louisiana, Mississippi, Alabama, and the panhandle of Florida must demonstrate after Hurricanes Katrina and Rita that they will make the investments (supported by FEMA funding) to ensure that they will not be as threatened in the future. These coastal areas are the least developed warm coastal areas in the country but obviously are the most prone to hurricane damage. Thus far, only northern Alabama and the panhandle of Florida have proven attractive to domestic migrants.

Figure 5.24 shows the southwestern states, including California. Here it is very clear that California's growth has come overwhelmingly from immigration, with a decline of 287,000 from domestic out-migration. Immigration should drop dramatically in the coming years while domestic out-migration grows from the more extreme real estate crisis ahead in this state. Arizona and Nevada have more modest growth from immigration, both under 20%, so the impact there should be more minor. Utah and New Mexico trail by a large margin, and have greater impacts from immigration, which is a negative, but they have higher recent rates of domestic migration, which is a positive.

Despite boasting the highest percentage growth rates in states like Nevada and Arizona from the ongoing exodus from California, the Southwest has a huge challenge in water access as it continues to grow, and more expensive real estate in Arizona and Nevada. The Southeast has much higher rainfall and much more developable land, but even it occasionally suffers from droughts and water shortages. The Southeast continues to look like the best overall area for growth and development in the downturn.

Figure 5.25 shows migration trends in the Northwest and Rocky Mountain states outside California. The states here with the greatest exposure to immigration are Washington, Oregon, and Colorado. Washington has already lost its edge in domestic migration and will see further downward pressure in growth and real estate prices from a serious decline in immigration as 39% of its growth in the last ten years has come

Figure 5.24: Migration and Immigration into
Southwestern States, 1995–2004

	Domestic Net Migration	Immigration from Abroad	Total
Nevada	512,330	90,824	603,154
Arizona	794,827	190,931	985,758
California	(286,775)	2,330,174	2,043,339
Utah	31,521	59,093	90,614
New Mexico	12,784	42,911	55,695

Source: U.S. Census Bureau.

from immigration. Oregon has been hot in recent years from domestic migration but will see some slowing from its 30% contribution from immigration, as will Colorado with 27% immigration. Hence Oregon will likely be modestly positive in the years ahead and Colorado could see only very mild growth ahead.

Vancouver and British Columbia are the areas in Canada that attract the greatest immigration and will see their very hot real estate market finally slow in the years ahead. Vancouver will be hit very hard if immigration from Asia slows as much as immigration into California from Mexico. Calgary and Edmonton in Alberta have the highest domestic migration but will likely be hit moderately hard by falling commodity prices from mid-2010 onward.

The Northwest and western Canada have had some of the strongest real estate markets since the broader bubble peaked in 2005–2006. But falling immigration rates and commodity prices are likely to finally burst these bubbles from late 2009 or 2010 onward.

One Last Thought on Those Old Boomers . . . and the Taxes That They Pay

As we have already elaborated in this report, it is the echo boomers, not the baby boomers, who will create the biggest geographic growth opportunities in the coming years. Still, the original baby boomers' impact will be felt. Remember, the echo boomers are young, and as a generation they have little in the way of assets and lower but rising incomes. This young generation may be pulling up stakes to make their fortunes in another state, but the full benefits to those other states will not be felt for years—when those fortunes are made and they buy their largest houses.

The baby boomers, however, have already amassed a fortune as a generation and are at their peak in earnings. It is the boomers who currently pay the most in income, sales, and property taxes, and—perhaps morbidly—the eventual death of the boomers stands to provide a windfall in estate taxes to those states that levy them. Not surprisingly, some of the states that are providing the best growth opportunities in numbers for the young echo boomers—Florida, Texas, Nevada, Arizona, etc.—are the same ones providing the best tax savings to the older baby boomers, as those states generally have no or very low income and estate taxes.

Figure 5.25: Migration into Northwest and
Rocky Mountains, 1995–2004

	Domestic Net Migration	Immigration From Abroad	Total
Colorado	347,179	129,329	476,508
Idaho	103,694	22,372	126,066
Oregon	225,298	96,219	321,517
Washington	298,538	194,100	492,638
Montana	24,099	2,623	26,722
Wyoming	(8,523)	2,223	(6,300)

Source: U.S. Census Bureau.

The incoming retirees will *not* necessarily provide a large tax windfall for their new states, as many of these retirement-oriented states generate most of their revenues from sales taxes. As we know, older retirees consume less and will thus pay less in sales taxes going forward. These new retirees will have a greater impact on property taxes. These retirees *will,* however, be a major loss to the states they leave, which typically have higher income and property taxes.

The key insight is that while the number of migrating baby boomers may be relatively small, the financial impact on the states that they leave behind will be substantial. After all, it is the richest people—and most valuable would-be taxpayers—who have the means and the incentive to migrate. This means that, with regard to state tax revenues, the migration of the baby boomers actually will be a *less* than zero-sum game. Expect the states left behind to become desperate and tax hungry after the demographic downturn we expect in 2010 onward.

Summary of Migration Trends and Opportunities

As the present housing bubble deflates over the next few years, the greatest long-term trend for real estate and business growth will come from increasing echo-boom migration into large and affordable growth cities and largely into the Southeast and Southwest. The states with the greatest present momentum are Nevada, Arizona, Oregon, North Carolina, Idaho, and South Carolina. The southeastern coastal states will continue to see the largest volume of migration. The most attractive states, such as Florida, Nevada, and Arizona, have gotten expensive in the recent real estate bubble. That makes way for greater gains in other southeastern and southwestern states if they can attract businesses and jobs, especially in cities that are nearing or in the sweet spot of 1 million to 2 million.

The downturn after 2009 will weaken immigration sharply, while strengthening domestic migration trends a bit. States like New York, Massachusetts, Illinois, Washington, Florida, Virginia, Texas, California, and British Columbia will be hit hardest by this decline in immigration. The areas that will see the greatest declines after 2009 will be those with a combination of high prices and high immigration: the Northeast, California, South Florida, and British Columbia. These same areas are hence likely to have the most severe real estate declines in the coming years, whereas real estate prices will decline substantially, but more modestly, in most of the country.

Remember from Chapter 4 that the real estate sectors with the greatest opportunities in the downturn after the first major crash between 2010 and 2012 will be (1) affordable rental apartments and affordable starter homes for the high-migration echo boomers and (2) vacation and retirement homes for baby boomers. Once the worst of the real estate crash occurs between 2011 and 2013, starter homes will be the strongest segment, with a strong revival in vacation/retirement housing as well.

When we consider how many people are in our economy, how they spend, and where they spend, it is clear that significant changes are in front of us. For twenty-six years our country has prospered because of the ever-increasing spending of baby boomers, coupled with strong productivity gains from new technologies. This economic engine attracted immigrants eager to work. With the changes we've outlined throughout this report, we can expect to see a deeply slowing economy and an even greater decline in immigration after 2009. With the help of demographic trend analysis we can pinpoint areas that are best positioned to weather the coming economic storm, as well as those that will prosper the fastest once the lean years are behind us.

We will keep you updated on migration trends in the free periodic updates that you can sign up for in the back of this book and in our monthly newsletter that you can subscribe to.

The other major area of opportunity in this broader depression and deflationary downturn between 2010 and 2020–2023 will come overseas, where there are massive demographic growth trends for decades to come. But this growth at first will be concentrated in the Asian economies that are rising in industrial and information/service sectors and are not so dependent on the commodity bubble. In Chapter 6 we will look at demographic trends around the world and how there will be a greater divergence between developed and emerging countries, and East and West, in the coming decade and beyond.

Changing Global Demographic Trends

The Rising East and Emerging World Versus the Succession of Aging Western Nations

OVER THE LAST thousand years, improvements in the quality of life for leading-edge countries have moved forward at what seems to be light speed, mostly in Western Europe, North America, Australia/New Zealand, and Japan. Although ancient and medieval societies experienced some progress in their standards of living, particularly under the Roman Empire, the true momentum began with changes in how populations were organized in political systems, the protection of individual rights under the law (starting with the Magna Carta in AD 1215), the Renaissance in Europe, and the development of more sophisticated political and financial systems especially since the American and Industrial Revolutions in the late 1700s. After this, technological innovations and scientific discoveries have built upon themselves in an exponential fashion in country after country and region after region—and this is now occurring in more emerging countries around the world, especially in Asia.

With the development of free markets and even greater individual rights in the last 200 years, there has recently been a race for economic leadership in modern, industrialized nations. The countries of Western Europe and North America and the country of Japan, as well as Hong Kong, Singapore, Taiwan, and South Korea, have been in the lead and have enjoyed tremendous benefits as they have industrialized, urbanized, and modernized—in that order. The results have been overwhelming in terms of the standard of living of their average citizens.

One of the tremendous benefits of this race in leading countries has been that other nations, those that are not as open in political systems or as developed economically, have been able to adopt a "follow-the-leader" strategy and move their own standards of living forward in a fraction of the time it took the leading Western countries to develop. Countries such as Israel, South Korea, Hong Kong, Taiwan, Singapore, and now China are all moving through, in just decades, very distinct stages of development that took the Western world hundreds of years! The stages of transition that a nation goes through are clear and can be identified by the distribution of its population by age groups. Countries begin as rural and agrarian, marked by low incomes and high birthrates and mortality rates. That situation creates high numbers of young people and comparatively fewer maturing and older people—a perpetual cycle of poverty, as young people tend to cost more than they produce and, by their nature, create more wars and chaos.

As stable political, legal, and financial systems emerge, industrialization takes hold and more people prosper. They migrate to urban areas for the new jobs being created, which produces growing generational waves into the adult and middle-aged years of the population, as such urban and more affluent people have fewer children. These consumers eventually mature into their peak spending and productivity years around their late 40s today, but this happens only when an economy has developed the political, legal, financial, and technological infrastructures that make a modern consumer economy possible. These infrastructures first educate workers and then leverage their productivity as they age and accumulate technical skills.

As urbanization and modernization progress, populations tend to increase their levels of education and move the base of their economy further up the ladder of knowledge through rising skills and specialization of labor. All these changes further enhance the standard of living of the population. It is important to note that if a country is not on such a path to development, there is no timetable for when it will break the bonds that contain it. The obstacles to development—dictatorships that keep the power and economic gains to a tiny fraction; lack of stable financial systems, political systems, education, and individual rights; etc.—can remain in place indefinitely if the people are insulated from the outside world and its opportunities. However, once the yoke is cast off, the modernization of a country takes on a life of its own.

But for all the positive effects of this progress, there is a caveat: a downside for which there is no historical precedent and therefore no example of what will fully happen next. This downside is the seismic shift in how populations actually replace themselves or, in this case, *choose not to*. Ultimately, broad prosperity and urbanization create a sharp drop in the birthrate that, with the passing of time, pushes the population more and more into the older age ranges. This creates a trap of perpetual aging, as there are progressively fewer and fewer younger people to have kids and sustain population growth or to rebel and push radical new innovations in technologies, lifestyles, and business models for the future. And even with government incentives for having more kids, older populations are increasingly physically unable.

Around the world we are now facing the reality that once populations have moved from being agrarian-based societies to being urbanized societies that have industrialized and modernized, having children is actually a drain on the economics of the individual family. In the United States, the Department of Agriculture estimates that it takes approximately $250,000 to raise one child, not including college education. As populations become more urban and modernized, families within those populations choose to have fewer children, and this choice keeps the standard of living of the family high, the social opportunities more advantageous, and the potential through higher investment in education per kid higher as well. This seems rational to the individual household, but it works against the growth of the larger society or nation.

This condition has now started to reach critical mass. Mature countries such as Japan and most countries of Europe and the former Soviet Union are actually set to decline in population in the coming decades—and China is not far behind. What does this mean for those countries and for the world? It means first a slowdown in innovation, then a slowdown in economic activity, and eventually a declining standard of living. All these things are foretold by demographics and have a tremendous impact on the economies of developed countries.

How Our Research Is a New Science in Economics
for Longer-Term Trends

Spanning over twenty years now, our research has proved increasingly effective for predicting major shifts in economic growth and slowing in developed countries (DCs). The basis of our approach is the development of new demographic forecasting tools that track and project the peak spending of new generations of educated and technology-empowered consumers and workers. This approach is not that useful for less developed countries (LDCs), because there have not been sufficient legal, political, financial, and technological infrastructures developed to leverage the productivity of workers as they age. Therefore, the wealth of the nation tends to be centered in a small percentage of people who tend to have a strong interest in exploiting the broader population and its ignorance of its potential.

Once a country begins to urbanize and modernize, the wealth produced gets distributed more widely throughout the population, creating a society of mass affluence, and the spending and innovation habits of the population become the driving force in the economy. In modernized first-world countries, consumer expenditures tend to account for 60% to 70% of all economic activity. Using this new approach, we were able to forecast both the unexpected decline of Japan back in the late 1980s and the incredible boom of the United States and the rest of the developed world, excluding Japan, during the 1990s.

As we continue to expand our research to include in-depth analysis of more countries, it becomes obvious that the world is approaching the greatest demographic and economic shift in modern history. These changes will not occur all at once, as countries are developing, growing, and maturing at different rates. However, there will be a culmination of these changes, marked first by an economic peak in many of the most affluent nations in the world by 2010, then by a second slowing around 2035, and ultimately, much farther down the road, by a global decline in population and economic activity starting around 2065–2070— unless there are big changes in birthrates or longevity, which could occur in the coming decades of continued technological progress but not likely in time to impact the life spans in emerging countries that will increasingly dominate.

This chapter forecasts the changes ahead not only for developing and mature countries, but, more important, for many larger populations in countries that have the potential for moving from LDC status to DC status over the coming decades, as many are already doing. These estimates, which are based on clear demographic trends already in place, will allow you to identify those areas of the world and specific countries that are poised to see the greatest growth over the next five to fifty years and even beyond—and the ability to see which countries and regions could suffer long periods of decline and when. Finally, we will estimate when these events will reach their apex and will mark a global decline in population and economic growth, with all of its implications.

By 2010, the populations of Europe and North America, the economic engines that have driven world growth for centuries, will be set to age and will begin slowing long term, following the example of Japan's peak and slowing since 1990. At the same time, most Asian and many emerging nations will continue to grow explosively in a catch-up cycle for many decades to come. In just two generations, or about eighty-five years, China is on track to make progress in GDP per capita similar to what it took Western Europe over a thousand years to achieve—but China's spending trends will start to peak between 2015 and 2020, and the country will age rapidly and lose population faster than the United States starting around 2035. China's development relative to the West may never fully materialize, as the country will age along with the West, despite never having achieved its full potential wealth.

We foresee a cascading global boom wherein more affluent Western nations increasingly age and slow while new larger populations and nations continue to emerge rapidly, especially in East, Southeast, and South Asia, where just over half of the world's population now resides (and a greater majority will emerge in the next fifty years and beyond). This is important to understand, as the coming decades will not see a concerted, strong global boom as in 1983 to 2009, wherein most nations were growing simultaneously. From here on out some nations will be slowing and others will be growing—with a clearer shift toward the East.

Here's the big picture: Japan began to age and peak first in 1990; Europe, Eastern Europe, Russia, the United States, and Australia/New Zealand will follow around 2010; China, between 2020 and 2035; Southeast Asia around 2040; Latin America around 2040; and then India, South Asia, and the Middle East around 2065–2070. North Africa and sub-Saharan Africa may continue to emerge into as late as 2085 to 2100—but only if they modernize and join the globalization party. Also note that North America, Australia, and New Zealand have a substantial echo-boom generation and are more in a long-term plateau into the 2050s rather than a long-term decline from 2010 onward, as in Europe and Russia.

We predict a major economic slowdown will occur in North America and Europe from 2010 into 2020–2023, which will be marked by a series of dramatic stock crashes between late 2009/early 2010 and mid-2012, as we covered in Chapters 1 through 4. Despite that slowdown, broader Asia and many other emerging countries will continue to grow, but those with high exports to the West and commodity-based economies initially will suffer in reaction to this Western slowdown and the likely resulting commodity/energy price peak between late 2009 and mid-2010 at the latest. The emerging market bubble in stocks also will have to deflate between 2007 and 2010–2012.

Due to strong demographic trends and continued development cycles, Asian stocks should represent the greatest buying opportunities for equity investors as early as late 2010 or mid- to late 2012 at the latest. This region will be the quickest to recover from the bubble bust and grow again, especially as it is less dependent on the 29 to 30-year Commodity Cycle, which is likely to be especially weak between 2010 and late 2012 or 2015 and then off and on into 2020–2023—with greater impacts on most Latin American, Middle Eastern, and African countries.

After this period of global economic cooling, there will be another, more concerted world growth surge from around 2023 into around 2035–2036, when China finally slows and Russia and all of Europe slow even more dramatically. But even this boom will see China and East Asia lagging between 2020 and 2024 and Europe continuing to slow long term—so we won't be firing on all cylinders. Our next positive Geopolitical Cycle will also peak around 2035–2036, after bottoming around 2019. Hence we should see a slowing in global growth again between 2036 into the mid-2040s and perhaps into the early 2050s, but it will not be nearly as dramatic as the downturn we expect between 2010 and 2020–2023.

The slowdown in the West after 2009 will exacerbate the antiglobalization backlash. Growing unemployment, social unrest, and a general condition of financial hardship and lack of opportunity around the world will be caused by the economic slowdown in both Western regions and the nations that export heavily to them.

The combined challenges of economic slowing, growing trade protectionism, increased times of terrorism, war, and unrest, and growing issues such as pollution and global warming finally will cause leading and rising nations to realize that global cooperation and much more effective international political institutions and agreements are needed for continued prosperity. Thus we expect to see globalization come back with a vengeance in the 2020s, with countries in Southeast and South Asia (not as much China and East Asia) taking the lead for the first time.

After the final economic peak in the United States, caused by the spending of the echo-boom generation (children of the baby-boom generation), along with Brazil and Indonesia around the mid- to late 2050s, world population will peak around 2065–2070. At this time, India is likely to be the largest and leading economy in the world and at the peak of its spending and growth potential. From that point on, we will truly enter a new era of slowing demographic trends for the first time since the last Ice Age, although there will still be potential for demographic-based economic growth in large pockets of the Middle East and Africa, but only for the countries in those areas that make a successful transition to modern economies.

Continued innovations in technology as well as global infrastructures and institutions will be critical for continuing to advance our standard of living in a world of flat-to-falling population—and very likely major environmental threats and challenges from the rapid modernization of Asia and many emerging countries. Aging populations around the world will make such innovation more challenging, as a result of another demographic-based fact of economic development: younger people are the primary drivers of innovation, and there will simply be fewer and fewer of them. This, in turn, slows future innovation and economic growth in a slow but vicious cycle of decline.

The challenge in this unprecedented global demographic shift for maturing countries will be "How do we continue to innovate in tech-nologies, lifestyles, and political/business organizational structures to ad-vance our standard of living in aging and even declining populations?" For the emerging countries the challenges will be "How do we rapidly put into place the political, legal, and financial institutions and basic infra-structures necessary to leverage the economic potential of our people as they age from their young to peak productivity years?" and "How do we attract foreign investment from the aging, affluent nations in order to catch up to the developed countries before the whole world slows down and we miss the opportunity?"

Again, we will discuss later in this chapter how a new baby boom could develop in emerging countries and how a more rapid advance in longevity could develop in more developed countries in the coming de-cades due to progress in biotechnologies.

The Spending Wave on a New Global Perspective

The Spending Wave is our simplest and most powerful forecasting tool, as discussed in Chapter 2 (Figure 2.3). We simply move forward the number of births (adjusted for immigration) in a developed country like the United States for the quantifiable peak in spending (at the age of 46 to 50 today) of the average household and the correlation with the econ-omy and the stock market long term is remarkable.

When we apply the Spending Wave to countries other than the United States, it is important to note that while it is still effective for esti-mating economic growth, it might not be quite as effective at estimating changes in financial markets in those countries as it is in the broader and more self-sufficient U.S. economy.

Although many of them maintain and are rapidly expanding global operations, U.S. companies are still overwhelmingly geared toward sell-ing to the American consumer, just as Japanese companies were despite the more highly visible export companies. Furthermore, the sheer size of this market means that more everyday American companies often have ample room to grow within the country's borders and have no com-pelling need to expand abroad. It is therefore not particularly surprising that demographics—which drive consumer patterns—can accurately forecast stock market trends. In many of the more developed countries in Europe and in Asia, such as the Netherlands and Singapore, respectively, there isn't always as close a correlation between the Spending Wave and the stock market as there is in the United States, as the companies in these smaller markets cannot depend as much on domestic consumption and must depend instead on exports. Many also have government policies in place that actively encourage exports. Countries with higher governmental direction and/or with international trade flows of 20% or more of GDP will be influenced by global factors rather than by purely domestic demographic patterns.

The United States and Japan have collected annual birth data over most of the last century, but many countries don't readily provide data at that level of detail or history. Luckily, the United Nations does provide past and future projections of age distributions in five-year cohorts for all major countries around the world, which give us a comparable standard to use for demographic projections worldwide. Birthrates are now declining in all major regions of the world—on a predictable downward slope—although such rates are still much higher in areas like South Asia, the Middle East, and Africa (Figure 6.1). Life expectancy is increasing in a predictable upward slope similarly, with the exception of a very small number of countries like Russia. This allows the UN to project population and age distributions many decades ahead in all countries and for the world as a whole with a pretty high degree of reliability.

Figure 6.2 shows the world population projections out to 2100, with a projected peak in 2065 and a gradual slowing thereafter. The peaking and mild decline around 2065 may look relatively harmless, but that is deceptive. If this slowing occurs as projected, it will represent the first decline in world population in modern history! The last time world population declined on any extended basis would have been between 12,000 and 25,000 years ago, in the last Ice Age. When world population merely flattened between around AD 1 and AD 1000, we experienced the dreaded Dark Ages—or what would have been like a nearly 500-year bear market after the fall of Rome for the more developed world back then.

However, the nice, steady slope upward into 2065 does not tell the real story, either. The more interesting dynamic comes from the fact that increasing numbers of maturing, affluent countries will be slowing dramatically while larger populations of emerging countries will be acceler-

Figure 6.1: Declining Birthrates Around the World

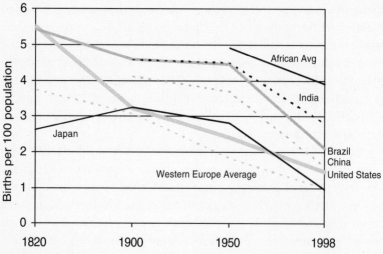

Source: **Angus Maddison,** *The World Economy: A Millennial Perspective,* **Development Center Studies, OECD, 2001: Table 1-5A, p. 30.**

ating faster than the West did—catching up in accelerated booms, like China today. Hence we need to look at the demographic and spending trends for the key regions—and the leading countries within those regions around the world—to really see how dynamic and contrasting this continued massive global boom will really be and how the overriding trend will be moving from the United States primarily in an eastern direction, and secondarily to the Southern Hemisphere.

By combining the past numbers of people moving into the peak spending ages of 45 to 49 with the future UN population projections of 45- to 49-year-olds, we can construct a Spending Wave for any country in the world and for the world in total, including an Innovation Wave for younger people in the 20- to 24-year range.

Most people naturally assume that China is still in an early stage of development and that it will grow for many decades or even centuries ahead, just as the West has grown for centuries. China's larger baby boom will peak in spending around 2015–2020, just five to ten years after the United States and most of Europe, as we show later in Figure 6.24. There will be a very moderate slowing into 2020, then a stronger slowing into

Figure 6.2: World Population Projections: 2010–2100

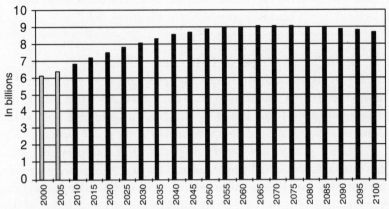

Source: *Investor's Business Daily*, April 22, 2004, p. A16.

around 2025, followed by a smaller echo boom that will peak in its spending around 2035. After that, China's spending trends will be down for many decades ahead. The UN projects that China's population will peak around that time as well and then actually start *declining*!

Some would counter that China will still see massive movement from rural areas to cities and that this urbanization will keep its standard of living and economy growing. This is certainly true up to a point—but demographic statistics suggest otherwise. From our research, we know that it is primarily young people between the ages of 20 and 34 (especially 25 to 29) who move to new regions of opportunity (as we indicated in Chapter 5), and that this will be a quickly shrinking segment of Chinese society. Similarly, China's Innovation Wave from its younger, age 20–24, segments already peaked back in the mid-1980s, with the smaller echo-boom Spending Wave peaking by 2020 if not before. Hence China will slow down in urban migration and in innovation, lessening the chances that strong new leadership will develop in new technologies and industries. This will even reduce the likelihood of a major revolution toward democracy and greater human rights in its political system—which is needed for further growth in productivity and for the standard of living to catch up fully with the West.

As a few astute demographers such as Phillip Longman have noted, "China will grow old before it grows rich."

We think that GDP per capita in China is likely to approach that of the Western world about the time China peaks and begins a long decline around 2035, but it is unlikely to reach or exceed it. Also, migration to the cities probably will have slowed by that time, if not before, with lower numbers of young new families who tend to be the prime movers.

Figure 6.3 shows how rapidly newly emerging countries like China can catch up to Western living standards, because the Western countries have already paved the way. And yes, China is catching up to the long exponential rise in Western living standards, mostly in a matter of decades since the 1950s. At the rate that China's GDP and Western Europe's GDP per capita are growing, they would converge around 2050 and possibly sooner as Europe's progress rapidly declines in the coming decades. But China's progress is likely to slow as well, first after 2020 and more so after 2035; hence it is likely never to catch up fully. This is likely to be the case for many emerging countries as well; their rapid urbanization and growth in standard of living also accelerate their declines in birthrates.

This transition to modernization is not a process that all countries and cultures master equally. We cannot assume that all countries and regions will emerge successfully or fully until they have reached a certain stage, such as that reached by Israel, Singapore, Hong Kong, South Korea, Taiwan, and urban China today.

Mexico, India, Brazil, South Africa, Botswana, Thailand, Vietnam, United Arab Emirates, the Czech Republic, Slovakia, Poland, and Turkey are clearly showing such potential, whereas countries such as the former Yugoslavia, North Korea, Iran, Sudan, Nigeria, and Burma are not. Major emerging countries such as Indonesia and Pakistan are showing the possibility of such potential but are not clearly on the path yet. Countries that have become suddenly rich, for example Saudi Arabia and Iran, are not likely to develop significantly if oil prices retreat long term—as they are likely to do after 2009—unless they invest more in the development of their people and infrastructures and in diversifying into broader in-

Figure 6.3: GDP per Capita, China Versus Western Europe, AD 400 to 1998

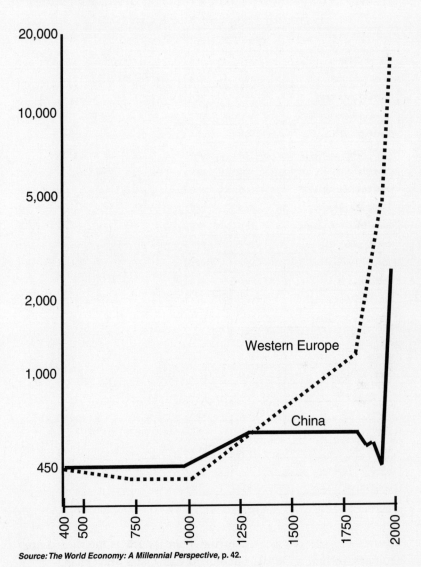

Source: The World Economy: A Millennial Perspective, p. 42.

Figure 6.4a: Populations of Global Megacities in Millions
(2007 Population over 9 Million)

	2007	2025
Tokyo, Japan	35.7	36.4
New York, USA	19.0	20.6
Mexico City, Mexico	19.0	21.0
Mumbai (Bombay), India	19.0	26.4
São Paulo, Brazil	18.8	21.4
Delhi, India	15.9	22.5
Shanghai, China	15.0	19.4
Kolkata (Calcutta), India	14.8	20.6
Dhaka, Bangladesh	13.9	22.0
Buenos Aires, Argentina	12.8	13.8
Los Angeles, USA	12.5	13.7
Karachi, Pakistan	12.1	19.1
Cairo, Egypt	11.9	15.6
Rio de Janeiro, Brazil	11.7	13.4
Osaka-Kobe, Japan	11.3	11.4
Beijing, China	11.1	14.5
Manila, Philippines	11.1	14.8
Moscow, Russia	10.5	10.5
Istanbul, Turkey	10.1	12.1
Paris, France	9.9	10.0
Seoul, South Korea	9.8	9.7
Lagos, Nigeria	9.5	15.8
Jakarta, Indonesia	9.1	12.4
Chicago, USA	9.0	9.9
London, UK	8.6	8.6

dustries and services, as is occurring in areas such as the United Arab Emirates (including Dubai), Bahrain, Kuwait, Qatar, and Oman.

With rapid globalization in recent decades, a number of megacities (which we define as cities over 9 million in population) have emerged as major hubs in the fastest-growing areas, as Figure 6.4a shows. Since 1975, cities with over 10 million in population have already grown from 3.6% of world population to around 10%. Note that five of the twenty-five megacities are in South Asia: three in India, one in Bangladesh, and one in Pakistan. There are four in North America, counting Mexico City; five in East Asia, two in China, two in Japan, and one in South Korea; two in Southeast Asia; two in the Middle East and North Africa (including Istanbul despite Turkey's application for European Union status); three in South America, and one in sub-Saharan Africa. There are only three in Europe if you count Moscow and London (just shy of 9 million but included due to its overwhelming world status). If we include the cities that are projected to be greater than 9 million by 2025, in Figure 6.4b, East Asia adds four (all in China), South Asia adds five (three in India), South America adds two, and sub-Saharan Africa adds one.

By 2025, ten megacities will exist in South Asia and nine in East Asia, dwarfing all other regions.

The world is likely to continue to group into six larger trading zones from the ten major regions we cover ahead: (1) North America, including Mexico, Central America, and the Caribbean; (2) South America; (3) Europe, including Eastern Europe and Russia; (4) East Asia and Southeast Asia; (5) western Asia, including South Asia, the Middle East, and North Africa; and (6) sub-Saharan Africa. As Europe and China age more rapidly in the decades ahead, it is South Asia that is clearly most likely to become the leading region of world growth not just in demographics, but in large megacities—if India can continue to develop successfully, and especially if Pakistan and Bangladesh follow. South Asia will ultimately have ten megacities, and the broader block of West Asia, including the Middle East and North Africa, takes it up to twelve versus ten in East and Southeast Asia combined. Now you see why Dubai aspires to be a growing hub for this broader region!

The megacities that increasingly dominate global demographic growth will continue to concentrate in Asia, but ultimately in South Asia even more than East and Southeast Asia. India, Pakistan, and Bangladesh will have five super cities out of ten worldwide with nearly 20 million or

Figure 6.4b: Populations of Emerging Megacities in Millions (2025 Population over 9 Million)

	2025
Kinshasa, Congo	16.8
Guangzhou/Guangdong, China	11.8
Lahore, Pakistan	10.5
Shenzhen, China	10.2
Chennai (Madras), India	10.1
Tehran, Iran	9.8
Bangalore, India	9.7
Bogotá, Colombia	9.6
Lima, Peru	9.6
Wuhan, China	9.3
Tianjin, China	9.2
Hyderabad, India	9.1

more by 2025. China will have only one. This is another reason that India is likely to ultimately be the dominant country in Asia, and in the world, especially as China slows dramatically after 2035.

Global Demographic Spending Trends

In this chapter, we will first look at the big picture and then at the prospects for the ten key regions in the world and the leading countries within those regions. The questions we ask: Where is the global boom headed? When will global growth be stronger or weaker in the decades ahead? Which countries will be more dominant or peaking, or newly emerging at each stage? Figure 6.5 looks at the Global Spending Wave for the entire world based on the number of people projected to move into the peak spending ages of 45 to 49 for decades ahead.

A few things must be understood when using this approach. First, this chart makes no allowance for differences in incomes and spending power across countries and assumes that most emerging countries will achieve living standards approaching that of the West today, which many or most clearly will not. Otherwise, the more developed countries would have to be weighted more, making the projection more complex, and would lean toward slower growth as well as more accentuated declines between 2010 and 2025—which is more realistic. Second, this chart assumes that the peak in spending for most countries remains about the same, when the peak in spending has been moving forward about one year per decade due to mildly rising life expectancies (and we adjust for that in our more detailed U.S. Spending Wave).

Although life expectancies will continue to advance in the developed countries (especially with potential advances in biotech further out), the emerging countries have lower life expectancies, which will catch up to those of the developed countries based on rising standards of living; the UN data may not fully reflect this. Hence, while our global projections are likely to be in the ballpark, this world Spending Wave probably has a slight bias to the upside and the actual peak in spending power eventually may come a few years later for these reasons.

Finally, the UN's birth and age distribution projections could be

Figure 6.5: Global Spending Wave

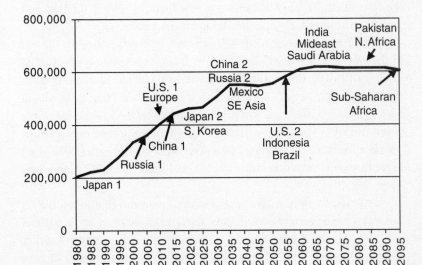

Source: United Nations.

off here and there due to changes in birthrates, but more due to immigration rates, which are much more cyclical and thus not as steady as birthrate declines. However, most countries do not have immigration or outward migration as a significant factor, as the United States does. The good thing about demographics is that we can see these trends changing, and most of the impacts are well into the future—so we can make adjustments to our forecasts and still be well ahead of the trends. Given these caveats, we can adjust for changes in the data as they occur.

So let's step back and look at the global demographic trends over the rest of this century, which our kids and grandkids will experience even if we don't!

The obvious trend is that world growth flattens between around 2010 and 2025 as the United States and Europe peak and slow. Given the dominance in the overall size of these economies and the strong export markets they represent for most emerging countries, the world will initially slow much more than this chart indicates. Note that Japan already experienced the peak of its larger baby-boom spending cycle between 1990 and 1996. Japan's economy declined—along with its stock and real estate markets—even while the rest of the world (especially Asia) continued to boom. Japan is a good model for what will likely occur during the decline cycles of the West and other affluent, maturing economies while the continued, larger global boom moves forward toward the East and toward more southerly emerging countries over time.

The impact of the slowing of Japan after 1990 was minor for the rest of the world, which continued to grow from demographic trends. The slowing of North America and Europe by 2010 will have a major impact, despite growing trends in most emerging countries! Hence, the global boom from 2023 onward will not be as dynamic and pervasive as the boom from 1983 to 2009, with the exception of leading emerging countries like India. Global demographic trends clearly slow after 2010, then move in shorter advances, such as 2023–2035 and 2052–2065, and then wane after 2065.

Japan led the way with a peak and decline in the 1990s, and Russia and many of the countries of Eastern Europe will be next. These nations should have seen a peak around 2005, although booming commodity and oil prices into late 2009 to mid-2010 have offset that slowing at first. Then the first big tsunami hits: the United States and most of Europe peaking by 2010—which should finally force a major slowdown in oil prices and commodity prices—affecting Latin America, Russia, the Middle East, Africa, and many other emerging countries as well. China sees its first larger baby-boom peak between 2015 and 2020, followed by Japan's final echo-boom peak and South Korea's larger peak around 2020 (China's decline is only minor through 2020). Hence East Asia should continue to be relatively strong during the downturns in the United States and Europe. Between 2020 and 2025, the United States will see its final echo-boom generation begin to emerge, while China and East Asia will surprisingly see a slowdown, start to lag, and see a major recession in the early to mid-2020s. Countries like India will continue to emerge rapidly. From around 2025 to 2035, China's final echo-boom generation will kick in.

We will see a more concerted global boom from around 2020 to 2023 into 2035–2036, with China and East Asia lagging at first and Europe lagging altogether.

The next key transition point comes with a flattening from 2035 to 2050, when China sees its final echo-boom peak and Russia, Japan, and Europe decline more dramatically due to extreme aging. As we mentioned earlier, our major long-term 32- to 36-year Geopolitical Cycle that alternates between more favorable and less favorable trends every 16 to 18 years (Chart 3.6 in Chapter 3) would also peak around 2035 to 2036 or so, adding to the flattening or slowing of global growth trends after this next series of declines sets in. A less favorable cycle between 2036 and the early 2050s would tend to add to economic slowing and stock corrections around the world, especially midcycle into around 2043–2045 after countries like Mexico, Chile, Malaysia, and Vietnam peak around 2040. We predict that global growth will flatten again between 2036 and around 2050, with a final growth surge centered in India, the Middle East, and Africa into around 2065, and likely into 2068–2069, into another peak in the Commodity Cycle.

The world cycle should turn upward again by the early 2050s, if not sooner, on a more positive Geopolitical Cycle, led by countries like India,

Pakistan, Brazil, Argentina, the United States (with its final wave of echo boomers), Australia, Saudi Arabia, South Africa, and others in the Middle East and Africa. India should be the largest and most dominant country in that phase and should peak around 2065 to 2069. At that point, the world population finally peaks and we will likely shift into the first cycle of world slowing in modern history (since the last Ice Age, 20,000 years ago). After that peak, there will still be the potential for demographic-based growth into 2085 or beyond in countries like Pakistan, Egypt, and Saudi Arabia and even further potential in sub-Saharan Africa into 2100 or so—if these countries and regions successfully transition into modern development. But too much of the world is likely to be declining or slowing by then to offset such new growth.

Another important demographic indicator that we track is the number of 20- to 24-year-olds in the economy, which we call the Innovation Wave, because it tracks the number of people in the economy who are at their most creative point—the young adults, or yuppies, just entering the workforce out of college. They are the ones who bring new lifestyle trends and technological breakthroughs that will increase productivity for decades to come and move forward our standard of living as increasing numbers of people adopt those new trends in an S-curve fashion. In fact, we have found that small-cap stocks correlate more with a 20- to 24-year lag on the Birth Index, as they represent the most innovative sector of business (as we will cover in Chapter 8). The strongest Innovation Wave in the United States occurred from 1958 to 1983 on this lag, with small-cap stocks greatly outperforming large caps in that time frame. The Innovation Wave tells us something else: it tells us when economies are more likely to experience inflation from rising workforce entry. The reason is that young people, while very innovative, are also very expensive to raise, educate, and finally incorporate into the workforce, as we noted in Chapter 2.

The global Innovation Wave is depicted in Figure 6.6. Although the innovation and inflation trends peaked for the West (which clearly dominated back then) in the late 1970s to early 1980s, the peak for the world should come in the late 2030s to the mid-2040s and plateau after that. Note that our next 29- to 30-year Commodity Cycle peaks around 2039–2040, meaning that inflation trends worldwide are likely to be rising from the early 2020s (slowly at first) into around 2040, sixty years

Figure 6.6: Global Innovation/Inflation Wave

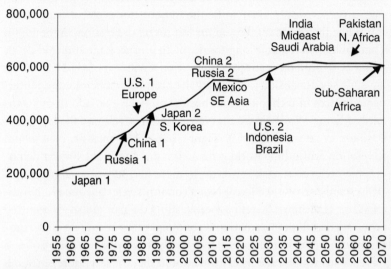

Source: United Nations.

after the last major peak in 1980. The next strong bubble in inflation and commodity trends is likely to occur from around 2035 into 2039–2040. That peak clearly should be led more by countries like India than China at that time, as we will show later in this chapter. As we review key regions of the world and individual countries, we will put these two indicators, the Spending Wave (solid line) and the Innovation Wave (dotted line), on the same chart for ease of comparison.

There was an acceleration in demographic-driven innovation globally, especially from 1965 into 2010. That trend continues up into around 2045 before peaking long term. We will not see technological progress as strong in the second half of this century due to slowing demographics since young people are the key drivers, unless we see an emerging world baby boom, which would be more likely in the 2080s and 2090s and would impact innovation trends into the early 2100s.

Global innovation and technology trends should peak in momentum by the early to mid-2040s and global spending/population growth by the mid- to late 2060s. That means the next depression after this one will very likely occur from the late 2060s into the 2070s (back on a 60-

year cycle) and be worse than this depression in the 2010s. Growth and progress will clearly be slower in the last four decades of this century, and that is paradoxically likely to be the impetus for a global baby boom much like the one that followed the last severe depression, in the 1930s. That could then rekindle long-term growth prospects into the mid-2100s in line with our 500-year Mega Innovation Cycle.

One key dimension (which we will only touch on here) is the continued advances in technology and business models that add to our standard of living. We discussed the New Economy Cycle and the four-stage business cycle in Chapter 2 (Figure 2.16). The massive baby-boom generation around the world generated more dominant 40-year demographic cycles to stretch this cycle to more like 80 years, supplanting a well-established 58- to 60-year New Economy Cycle called the Kondratieff Wave. The United States has been leading the new global, customized economy based on information technologies that allow real-time communication and bottom-up, network organizational structures—and these trends will ultimately expand around the world to more emerging countries.

However, our new global demographic projections strongly suggest that demographic trends are reconverging around this 58- to 60-year Kondratieff Wave New Economy Cycle, with the peak in innovation/inflation around 2040. This has affected our longer-term projections with a shorter Maturity Boom from 2020–2023 to 2035–2036, but not that of the slowdown between 2010 and 2020–2023. At www.hsdent.com we discuss further how stronger demographic forces on 40- and 80-year cycles have supplanted the Kondratieff Wave Cycle of the past 200 years and how it looks as though this occurs every 250 years on our Revolutionary Cycle (go to "Free Downloads" to "The Long Wave"). It is likely that we will return to that 58- to 60-year cycle over this century.

Note here that as the world becomes more globalized, we are projecting this New Economy Cycle around global trends, with the next boom peaking around 2035–2036. For the United States, the cycle will be slightly different. The echo-boom birth cycle ended up in two distinct waves of birth booms: 1976–1990 and 1998–2008. The first wave of Echo Boomers will drive the Maturity Boom from the early 2020s into around 2035–2036, with that Spending Wave peaking around 2040–2042, just after the world peak. There will be a natural slowdown for about seven years into the mid- to late 2040s during the next Innovation/Inflation Stage. The United States will see a Growth Boom around the second wave of echo boomers into around 2057–2058.

By the late 2050s, the United States and North America are very likely to see long-term peaks in economic growth, much like Europe in 2008–2009 and Japan in 1990 (unless we see a major revolution in aging and life expectancy, which is likely between the 2010s and 2040s and could extend the U.S. boom into the 2060s). America's leading role is already plateauing at best and waning at worst. It certainly will wane by the 2060s, when India and much of today's emerging world will be at its height and China will be the plateauing or waning power in the East.

Spending Waves and Potential Growth in Different Regions of the World

In this section we are going to look around the world at the broad demographic trends in eight major regions: Europe, Eastern Europe/Russia, East Asia, Southeast Asia, South Asia, the Middle East/Northern Africa, sub-Saharan Africa, and Latin America/Caribbean. We will use the same Spending Wave projections we used for the U.S. in Chapter 2 and for the entire world earlier in this chapter, only in five-year age cohorts rather than the one-year cohorts used to describe patterns in the U.S., so the forecasts are a little less precise but still very clear and illuminating. We also highlight workforce growth past and present (for ages 15–64), which correlates closely in developed countries but is more appropriate for emerging countries, as we will explain later in this chapter.

On our website www.hsdent.com we offer a free global database where you can look up the Spending and Innovation Waves of any individual country as well as a summary of qualitative and quantitative indicators from public resources. We also offer new graphs tracking GDP per capita vs. urbanization and workforce growth trends that are more critical for emerging countries. Go to "Free Downloads" and then to "Global Demographic Trends Database." We simply could not fit all of these graphs and indicators into this book, so we offer this analysis for free online.

We will also show later in this chapter how urbanization is more critical to projecting growth in most emerging countries, which don't have the same leveraged earning and spending curves by age that developed countries like the U.S. do. So for emerging countries and regions, these Spending Waves represent more potential for growth if they develop more fully. Also, the workforce growth projections are better to focus on here because they tend to peak earlier, especially in Latin America. For more-developed regions like North America, Europe, East Asia, and Australia/New Zealand, the Spending Waves should work nearly as well as they have in the U.S. (and Canada's demographics are very similar to those in the U.S.). We'll start by looking at the other large affluent region in the developed world, Europe, which includes western, northern, and southern Europe.

Europe: The World's New Retirement Community

Europe is the most mature region with the most striking overall aging trends. Figure 6.7 shows how this major affluent region will peak by around 2010, after which the trends point down for decades and decades to come. The trends point down even more strongly after 2035. Europe will lag in growth in the next concerted global boom, from 2020/2023 onward, and play a major role in the likely temporary top in the world economy around 2035–2036, as will Eastern Europe/Russia and China due to steep drops in demographic and spending trends. Northern Europe/Scandinavia, France, and Great Britain hold up the best in Europe. The fastest spending declines and most rapidly aging populations will be Germany, Switzerland, Austria, Italy, Portugal, Greece, and Spain, roughly in that order. Spain peaks the latest, between 2020 and 2025, and then declines sharply. Germany's workforce growth already peaked, in 2000, and its decline steepens after 2015. Italy's workforce growth peaked in 2005 and its decline steepens after 2025. The northern and western regions have better government-sponsored health care, which keeps birthrates a bit higher, especially in Scandinavia. In Southern Europe, women get little or no help and hence have fewer kids. We cover this topic more in Chapter 9.

This spending peak between late 2007 and late 2009 marks a watershed for Europe. Most countries in Europe will see only slowing demographic spending trends from here out. Many will see actual declines in

Figure 6.7: Europe, Spending Wave Vs. Workforce Growth, 1950–2095

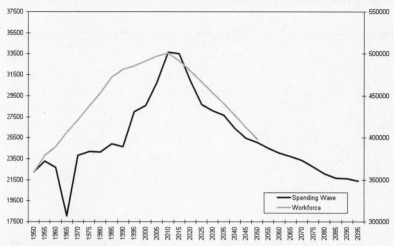

Source: United Nations.

population unless there are major changes in birth and/or immigration trends—and that does not appear likely, especially amid a deep downturn over the coming decade during which aging populations are less open to innovation and immigration and the capacity for higher birth rates declines. For the U.S., many forecasters believe this watershed will be the decline of Rome. That will be the case even more for Europe and Eastern Europe/Russia.

Eastern Europe/Russia: Cold and Cloudy Long-Term Outlook

Russia dominates this region in population and, consequently, the Spending Wave trends in Figure 6.8. Spending and workforce growth hit a plateau between 2000 and 2005 and should trend down into 2015, then bounce back a bit into 2030. But after 2035, Russia heads down sharply, following Europe. Russia is the only major country that has seen its life expectancy actually fall in recent decades, although that has improved as energy and commodity exports boosted its economy. This country is very dependent on energy and commodity exports and will struggle with a

Figure 6.8: Eastern Europe/Russia, Spending Wave vs. Workforce Growth, 1950–2095

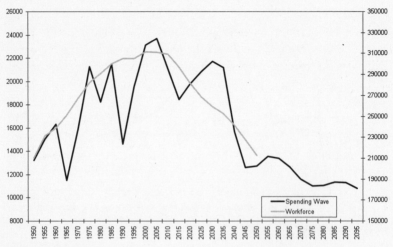

Source: United Nations.

commodity cycle likely to be weak off and on for at least the next decade, as we noted in Chapter 3. We project that Russia should see a last hurrah in the commodities boom from the early 2020s into the late 2030s. But outside of that, Russia should fade as a major world power somewhat in the coming decades and much more after 2035, just as India rises as a major new political and military power.

Leading countries in Eastern Europe like Poland, the Czech Republic, and Hungary have seen an entrepreneurial renaissance that has greatly improved their GDP per capita, but the demographic trends in these countries tend to point down into 2015, then back up again into 2030. Hence, Eastern Europe will likely fare better than Russia after a severe banking crisis between 2010 and 2012 or even into 2014. Eastern Europe is considered one of the "subprime" areas for loan defaults in European banks. We could see a more impressive rebound there, however, when most of the rest of the world likely rebounds, between 2013 and 2017.

East Asia: The Affluent but Aging and Slowing Leaders of Asia

East Asia includes Hong Kong, Japan, Taiwan, South Korea, and China, in order of descending affluence. These countries (and Singapore) have seen explosive development relative to the rest of Asia and now are the only truly wealthy countries outside of Europe and its offshoots in North America and Australia/New Zealand. But East Asia's population is aging almost as fast as that in Europe.

China will be the surprise of the century when it follows Japan and starts to lag in growth in the next boom, from 2020/2023 into 2035/2036, and it is already facing the greatest environmental challenges of any major nation.

China dominates the Spending Wave and workforce growth in this region due to its overwhelming demographics. China's Spending Wave (shown in Figure 6.20 ahead) shows a peak in 2015 and then a first significant fall in spending trends between 2020 and 2025. Then it has a minor echo boom until about 2035, after which spending will drop more markedly for decades to come, nearly as fast as Europe. Workforce

Figure 6.9: East Asia, Spending Wave vs. Workforce Growth, 1950–2095

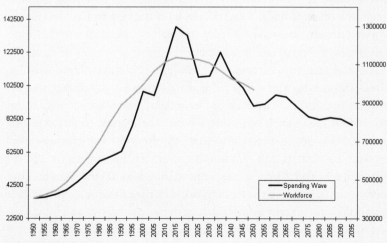

Source: **United Nations.**

growth plateaus between 2015 and 2025 and then starts to drop off substantially, but not as steeply as Europe. Recall our previous quote from Phillip Longman in this chapter: "China will grow old before it grows rich." China will have continued growth in urbanization trends as late as 2050, but its aging society would suggest that urbanization will not likely proceed as fast as it did in the past because, as we showed in Chapter 5, it is younger families that move and migrate. It is very possible that China will not reach the 80% urbanization levels, forecast by the UN, by 2050.

Japan is the wealthiest large country in Asia, but it is aging faster than any major country in the world—even Italy, Germany, Austria, Switzerland, and Russia. Japan's Spending Wave and workforce growth peaked between 1990 and 1995 and turned down from 2000 to 2005, as did its economy, stock markets, and real estate. It has a minor echo boom pointing up into 2020, then it ages rapidly for as far as the eye can see. But this global downturn will counter even that minor trend. The Japanese prefer not to have many children in its "most urban" society, which includes the largest city by far in the world, Tokyo. The Japanese also don't encourage immigration, as they love to preserve their very impressive and cohesive culture. But if its approach to those issues doesn't change—and it likely will not substantially—Japan will surprise the world with how its economy continues to slow, and will lead the world in population declines in the coming decades. Japan also will likely lead world demand for robots in the future to replace basic low-end labor that younger workers and immigrants often provide. South Korea fares the best in East Asia in the coming decade. Its Spending Wave will plateau into 2020 and then, on a lag, decline nearly as rapidly as Japan.

For convenience here we will include Australia and New Zealand in this section, as they represent affluent western countries though they reside farther south in East Asia and have their strongest trade with countries like China and Japan. Australia has the highest quality and best immigration policies of any western country. Its immigration is not slowing as much as immigration in the U.S. in this downturn, and the U.S. will see much bigger declines ahead. Australia has the most buoyant demographic trends in the western world during the coming slow decade and is the only western country that has a more persistent and mildly rising Spending Wave into 2040 or so. New Zealand has more of a demographic dip in the coming decade that resembles those in Canada and the

U.S., but then a gradual rise to new highs heading into 2035. Given their position close to Asia, these two countries should have the most potential going forward of any western affluent nations. Their Achilles heel is twofold:

1. Overall, Australia and New Zealand have the most overvalued real estate in the world because their populations are concentrated in urban, coastal areas where there is scarce land for development. Real estate has been late to peak and slow to drop thus far, but we see prices falling very significantly as the world downturn and depression takes hold between 2010 and 2012.

2. Like Canada, they both have strong commodity exports, which should be weak off and on for the next decade, and especially between 2010 and 2012–2014.

Southeast Asia: Continued Development and Steady Growth into 2040

Southeast Asia includes Indonesia, Singapore, Malaysia, the Philippines, Thailand, Vietnam, Cambodia, Laos, and Myanmar (Burma). This is another dynamic region for demographic growth and urbanization, and its Spending Wave in Figure 6.10 continues to point up strongly into around 2040, then tail off only slightly for decades to follow. Workforce growth plateaus between 2040 and 2045. This region already had a major currency and banking crisis between late 1997 and late 2002. And that crisis cleared the decks for steady growth, especially in Indonesia, the largest of these countries in population and a place where democracy and stability have resurged despite major natural disasters like the tsunami of 2004. Indonesia's Spending Wave and workforce growth point up later than those of its neighbors until around 2055.

Vietnam has seen the strongest growth and is often called "little China." It has seen strong education, urbanization, and export gains. Further infrastructure investments are needed to keep its boom going, but investors likely will continue to find the country attractive, given its track record and more open foreign investment policies. And Vietnam's Spending Wave points up the strongest into 2040. Thailand is more ur-

Figure 6.10: Southeast Asia, Spending Wave vs. Workforce Growth, 1950–2095

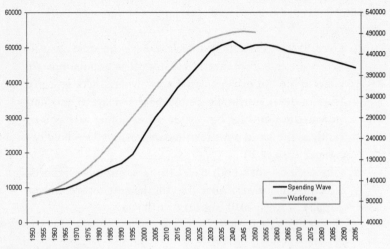

Source: United Nations.

banized and affluent due to strong tourism, but its Spending Wave peaks the earliest, around 2030. Its growth is likely the most limited in this region, and Thailand has had growing political instability in recent years.

The biggest opportunities in Southeast Asia should come from the successive development and urbanization of Cambodia first, then Laos—following Vietnam's growth model—and possibly Myanmar if its oppressive dictatorial regime is thrown out, which we think is likely over the coming decade in our adverse geopolitical cycle. Indonesia represents the largest country with steady growth likely into as late as 2055 or so.

At the extremes, Singapore is by far the richest country—an island city-state that is the trade and financial center for this region. But its demographics are more like those of the west and South Korea, with a spending peak by 2010, a decline into 2025, an echo boom rise into 2040, and then lower levels before a longer term slowdown. This area could continue to attract large numbers of immigrants during the tumultuous downturn ahead and in the boom to follow. Hence, its demographics could improve a bit. The Philippines, by contrast, has one of the lowest standards of living but the longest demographic rise into 2065–2070, much like India. This country has been a major source of migration to other countries as its workers have brought a strong work ethic to their quest for better wages in locations ranging from Hawaii to Dubai.

South Asia: The Greatest Growth Opportunity and the Next Major Demographic/Political/Military Power Center in the World

This region includes India, Pakistan, Bangladesh, Afghanistan, and by many definitions, Iran, which we include here. This region has more potential than any region in the world over the next 50 years.

Anyone who has followed our newsletter and our speeches in the last several years knows that we see India as the greatest single opportunity for growth, rise in urbanization, foreign direct investment, and real estate development. Between 2035 and 2050, India is likely to join the U.S. and China as one of the three "by far largest" economies and political/military powers in the world.

A simple visit to India would make clear to almost anyone that it holds the greatest potential for human development, and that the entire country is a massive "tear down" opportunity for real estate and infrastructure development. Except in the more modern areas of major cities, everything is worn and decaying, and this country suffers massively from lack of infrastructure that could help it leverage the largest population in the world. In rural areas people walk all day to get water and firewood and to graze their goats—because they don't have access to electricity, water, and wastewater treatment. And it takes forever to travel even 50 miles over its inadequate roads, which are shared by pedestrians, motorcycles, cars, buses, elephants, cows, and goats. But the people there are creative, find a way to recycle scarce resources, and make the best of a chaotic and low infrastructure environment. India has a higher standard of living than many other emerging countries at the same stage of development and urbanization, and it has more entrepreneurs per capita than China, which is at a higher stage of development. India also leads the emerging world in two complex industries that are otherwise the province of only major western countries like the U.S.: high technology software/services . . . and movies!

India's problem is the opposite of China's, where the government has strongly pushed government and foreign investment in infrastructure and business development. India's democracy makes it slower to act and achieve consensus and it has a history of bureaucracy and more socialistic ideals, from Gandhi forward, that have slowed the move of capitalism internally and for foreign business and investors. But in the end, India's democratic approach, along with more recent investments in roads and infrastructure, will likely give it an advantage over China, since India's organic growth may allow a more environmentally sustainable economy. But more important, India and the region it dominates have a very strong spending and workforce potential into 2065–2070, as Figure 6.11 shows. It also has the greatest concentration of present and future megacities, as we noted earlier in this chapter (we also show India's Spending Wave in Figure 6.22 ahead). Workforce growth is projected out only to 2050, but it is likely to plateau or edge up into 2065 or so. India also has the strongest potential urbanization trends of any major country in the world that is on a clear development path.

Pakistan has made more progress in growth and GDP per capita (as

Figure 6.11: South Asia, Spending Wave vs. Workforce Growth, 1950–2095

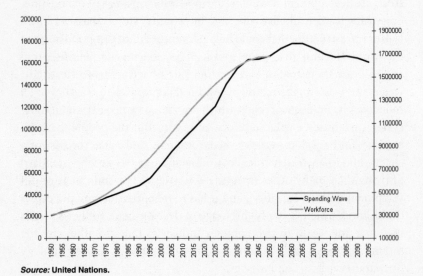

Source: United Nations.

we will explain further later in the book) than most would assume, given its recent political instability and its clashes with both India and Afghanistan. We think that Pakistan will tend to resolve its political instability over the coming difficult decade and emerge more as a follower of India's development path, though likely without as high a potential for affluence. Bangladesh, on the east side of the country, is impoverished and often encumbered by natural disasters, but it is also likely to follow India's development path on a lag. Iran's Spending Wave grows dramatically into 2035 before declining, and its younger, more educated population seems clearly on the verge of a revolution against its very conservative and cleric-run government. That is a very good sign. After it emerges from the tumultuous decade ahead, Iran could have very strong potential and perhaps even lead a democratic and free market revolution in both the Middle East and South Asia. Afghanistan is likely to be the slowest to come out of the dark ages and move onto a clearer development path. There is no question that instability will prevail there in the coming decade.

The Middle East and North Africa: Third World Countries with Strong High-End Oil Wealth—a Paradox That Requires a Revolution for Broader Advancement

This region includes Israel, Saudi Arabia, Turkey, Iraq, Egypt, and the North African countries along the Mediterranean coast and the very rich small gulf nations: the United Arab Emirates, Kuwait, Qatar, Bahrain, and Oman. This region's demographics are slightly stronger than those in South Asia, as Figure 6.12 shows. This region has become suddenly rich from massive oil reserves and revenues. But such growth has not generally extended very much into the broader population, which is still more backward in many respects than South Asia despite much higher urbanization (much of the extreme desert geography in the Middle East and North Africa doesn't accommodate a large rural population). And that is the biggest reason that terrorism has grown in this area and in the neighboring South Asian countries of Afghanistan, Pakistan, and Iran. Terrorist tactics have become popular weapons in fundamentalist religious cultures where living standards are low. Many people in these regions

Figure 6.12: Middle East/North Africa, Spending Wave vs. Workforce Growth: 1950–2095

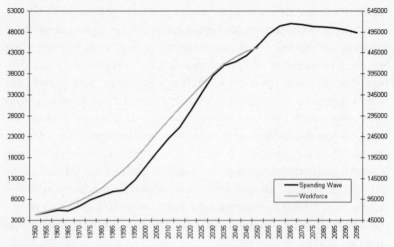

Source: United Nations.

want to lash out against progress that they both don't want and fear— and that also hasn't benefited their country, culture, or standard of living.

This region has always been a powder keg for ethnic/religious conflicts and warfare, and for good reason. Think about the movie *Lawrence of Arabia* for a minute. You have very tribal cultures that developed in a desert where water (and food from it) was the overwhelming scarcity. So what do you do? You fight fiercely over wells and every isolated oasis! And when you have to trade with feared rivals, you do so with the greatest possible mistrust and the most elaborate bargaining process!

In one early scene, Omar Sharif (as Sherif Ali) shoots someone who is poaching from his tribe's well, and then asks questions later! It's us vs. them, and the void of the desert keeps such tribes largely separate and less communicative. Scarcity breeds a "survival" mentality, and we all know how defensive and aggressive we can get when our survival is threatened! That is part of the long history of a region that actually was the cradle of the Agricultural Revolution 10,000 years ago, which was centered in Iraq, "The Fertile Crescent." After thousands of years of overcultivation and climate change, the Middle East and North Africa are now increasingly dry and desert. See our free special report "A Brief History of Human Evolution" at www.hsdent.com (go to "Free Downloads" and then to the report) for elaboration on such historical trends.

Israel is the richest broader-based country in this region, with a more westernized culture of education, technology, and work ethic. It is strongly allied with the U.S. but gravely threatened by the Muslim countries that surround it. Israel's Spending Wave points up into 2050–2055 due to birthrates that will be higher than those of any other westernized country, so it has considerable potential to improve an already high standard of living. Much will depend on how Israel weathers a difficult decade of turmoil, warfare, and revolution in this region. After 2019 we would be very bullish on Israel.

Turkey has the greatest potential in this region because it combines the best of the Muslim/Middle East and Southern European cultures. Istanbul has long served as a cultural and trading bridge between the two regions. Turkey's Spending Wave points up very strongly into 2040 and declines only slowly after that for decades. This country has been applying for European Union membership, which likely will be delayed in the downturn ahead as EU and neighboring countries increase trade and immigration restrictions. But Turkey may in the end be happy that it stayed out until the turmoil settles, since currency and trade disputes are likely before we enter the next, more concerted global boom, from 2020/2023 to 2035/2036, in which Europe and the EU will increasingly lag, not lead.

Egypt was one of the first countries to emerge and develop a higher standard of living due to its fertile Nile region and proximity to Southern Europe. It was also the second region to develop early-stage affluence, after Babylon and along with Greece and Rome, in the Agricultural Revolution in biblical times. Egypt's growth has been the least consistent, with urbanization trends that we will cover later in this chapter, and gyrations in its tourism industry and political landscape. Its Spending Wave points up very late into 2080. That is a good trend if this country can remain politically stable and continue to advance, urbanize, and expand its trade industry, particularly with South Asia.

Saudi Arabia is the geographically largest country and possesses the largest (at least at present) oil reserves and production capacity. Its potential Spending Wave and workforce growth ascend very dramatically into 2065 before declining. But this country's elite sector of western-like affluence and very backward cleric-educated populace—a young and highly impressionable one at that—diverge markedly. Iran is seeing the beginnings of a revolution from a more educated young population, but Saudi Arabia's young are not that educated or progressive—and somewhat terrorist oriented at worst. So the revolution here may take more time and involve more domestic turmoil over the coming decade. And as we know, Iraq is going through a similar revolution, between three very different ethnic/religious factions, precipitated by the U.S. invasion. The outcome of that revolution is uncertain and will likely take a decade or more to sort out as well. But then this region could follow South Asia in development from the 2020s or so forward, augmented greatly again by the next energy and commodities boom from the early 2020s into the late 2030s.

The big question in the Middle East is: Will alternative sources of energy be adopted widely enough in the next two to three decades to seriously cut into its high revenues and profits from energy exports? And the answer is likely: in developed countries, yes, but probably not enough in the emerging countries that will dominate growth until after the next commodity cycle peaks, near 2040.

The oil wealth in the Gulf, from Saudi Arabia to the smaller Gulf countries and cities such as Dubai, has created an enormous real estate boom and bubble, and there will be overcapacity and oversupply there for the next decade plus. But Dubai and other key cities in this region have established themselves with major infrastructure investments as the new trade, shipping, airport hubs and finance centers for transactions between Europe and Asia. And those investments should pay off long term after the real estate crash and oil implosion as Asia—especially India and South Asia—becomes the growth center of the next global boom.

Sub-Saharan Africa: Will It Join the Globalization Party or Wither into Further Poverty?

The one region that has the longest and strongest demographic potential for growth is obviously sub-Saharan Africa, as Figure 6.13 shows, with a Spending Wave that will grow until near 2100. Workforce growth correlates strongly into 2050 and would be due to accelerate after that. This region will not be as large as Asia in population, but it will be the second-largest and still has the highest birthrates, even as fertility trends decline worldwide. But high birthrates are a "Malthusian trap," or disadvantage (more people competing for limited land), unless you have rising technology for production and rising quality of life and life expectancies. High birthrates can result in a large young population that is more unproductive, expensive, and volatile. Lower standards of living, education, and health create fertile environments for violence, warfare, corruption, and disease.

Sub-Saharan Africa represents the birthplace of humanity, the evolutionary source of our most intelligent and innovative species. But it also has bred tribal warfare and corruption on a level with that in the Middle East, and this region of the world has been geographically isolated ever since the Agricultural Revolution. It was rediscovered in the late 1400s, when Europeans applied new technologies in sailing and weapons to colonize the region. But for the most part, this region was exploited for its commodity resources, not empowered by them, although it did gain

Figure 6.13: Sub-Saharan Africa, Spending Wave vs. Workforce Growth, 1950–2095

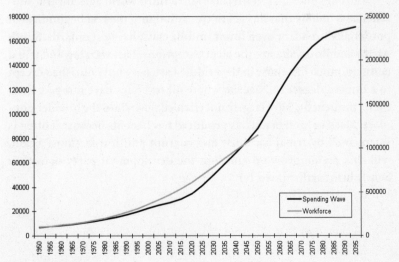

Source: United Nations.

somewhat from European investment in infrastructure and the application of new technologies.

South Africa has led a revolution in democracy and rising standards of living in this region. One of its key assets is Cape Town, a major European-dominated world trading port. This city rivals major coastal tourism magnets and is as attractive a place to live as San Francisco, Sydney, and Vancouver. South Africa is one of the few countries that has seen a major democratic revolution without a major war, thanks to leaders like Nelson Mandela. The "shantytowns" there often provide their residents free access to water and electricity but no major welfare after that, so immigrants are motivated to produce some income even though some of their basics are covered.

We think that this strategy, like "microfinance" (small loans to households that reliably pay them back after growing their local businesses), works better in emerging countries that naturally see high migration into their major cities. As it is, almost 50% of immigrants end up in slums that are often worse than the rural areas they migrated from. Botswana has followed South Africa's model to some degree and has benefited from rising eco-tourism. Nigeria has seen the greatest boom due to its oil exports, but like Saudi Arabia, it has passed few economic benefits along to its increasingly urbanized populace.

Most of sub-Saharan Africa is still a third world agricultural subsistence economy that has yet to transition into the real beginnings of potentially broad, or even lower middle class, living standards. South Africa and Botswana are the clear exceptions. Past warring and tribal cultures, much like those in the Middle East, have not flourished except to a limited degree in Nigeria, where oil revenues have jumped. Even there, the benefits have largely not trickled down into the broader populace. Massive foreign aid has produced few benefits because it often is intercepted by tribal warlords and corrupt political factions. Again, will this region grow up and join the development party or wither slowly into further poverty?

Latin America/Caribbean: Largely Urbanized and Lower Middle Class with Less Potential Outside of Continued Demographic Growth or Higher-Value-Added Industry

This region includes all of South America, Central America, Mexico, and the Caribbean. It is largely still emerging rather than developed and has, paradoxically, already high urbanization but lower than average GDP per capita and lower living standards than comparable areas in Asia. Like Africa, this area of the world was largely cut off from the Agricultural Revolution and the Industrial Revolution. Central America and northern South America (whose indigenous peoples include Mayans, Aztecs and Incas) saw an agricultural revolution of their own on a lag behind the one in the Middle East three thousand years ago. But in the 1500s, European invaders from Spain brought "guns, germs, and steel"—but mostly animal diseases—that wiped out their more modern and urban civilization.

But due to the growth of North America and trade with it, this region has largely urbanized since the 1950s and it has some of the largest megacities in the world, including Mexico City, São Paulo, Rio de Janeiro, and Buenos Aires. Bogotá and Lima will soon join them. This region has clearly prospered from earlier stage urbanization and from commodity booms like 1968–1980 and 1998–2008. But most of these countries have not transitioned more than nominally into higher-valued-added light and heavy industries and exports, and certainly not into information- or technology-based industries. This region has growing Spending Wave potential into around 2050–2055, but workforce growth here peaks a good bit earlier, by 2040, as Figure 6.14 shows. Here is where workforce growth forecasts reflecting higher urbanization and fewer young workers create the sharpest contrast with conditions in South Asia or Africa.

Brazil is clearly the largest country with the largest urban centers, and hence has the greatest opportunity for growth and foreign investment. Its Spending Wave peaks around 2055 but its workforce growth much earlier, by 2030. It is already over 80% urban, so there is little potential, beyond that in its moderately growing workforce and demographics, unless it enters into higher-value-added industries like manufactured wood products from sustainable and managed forest growth. Argentina and Chile have always been the richest countries outside of Puerto Rico,

Figure 6.14: Latin America/Caribbean, Spending Wave vs.
Workforce Growth, 1950–2095

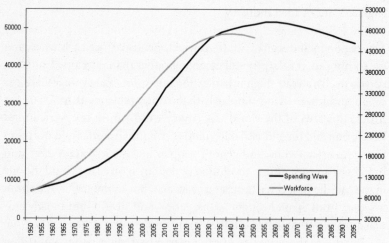

Source: **United Nations.**

which has close ties and trade with the U.S. and is more like a state. But
these countries are smaller in population and also already highly urbanized. Argentina's Spending Wave peaks later, around 2060, but its workforce growth plateaus around 2040. Chile peaks around 2040, with
workforce growth peaking a bit earlier. Chile, followed closely by Argentina, has the highest standard of living in Latin America outside of
Puerto Rico.

Mexico has the closest trade and immigration ties to the U.S. Its
Spending Wave peaks earlier, around 2040, but its workforce growth
peaks by 2030, likely due to high rates of emigration into the U.S. by
young cohorts. This situation is, paradoxically, an advantage for the U.S.,
as we have argued for a long time, even though many U.S. citizens constantly bitch about this trend, which makes the U.S. younger and Mexico
older! Colombia is the best up-and-coming country in Latin America,
after the drug wars and other sources of violence and crime subside. Rich
in resources, this country has close access to Miami's port and business
community, and high rates of immigration into the U.S. Peru could be
next along, followed by Uruguay and Paraguay.

A New Look at Emerging Markets That Will Dominate Future World Growth—How Rich Will They Become?

Thus far in this chapter we have looked at the potential periods for rising spending in different parts of the world, but emerging countries don't simply grow with demographics unless they begin the arduous process of developing the infrastructure and financial/legal/education systems that precipitate higher levels of urbanization and more specialized, value-added job opportunities. In fact, high birthrates and low levels of education and infrastructure only create the classic "Malthusian trap"—bigger populations with limited resources—which, as we mentioned previously, afflicted Europe for many centuries before the Industrial Revolution.

Urbanization and industrialization in the developed world ultimately created a "demographic dividend" with falling fertility rates (fewer expensive young people) and rising life expectancies (more productive people in the workforce and for longer). That is precisely why demographics became the key driver of economic growth and our Spending Wave indicators have been so accurate. But that demographic dividend is about to come to an end in most western and East Asian countries as their workers age past their most productive and biggest-spending years—past ages 46 to 50. This demographic dividend is just beginning in most emerging countries around the world, and it is where the opportunities will continue to emerge in the next 10 to 60 years.

We have clearly made the point for many years that the western and developed world is aging and will not see the growth that we have seen since the 1980s or the 1950s—or back all the way to our emergence out of the Dark Ages around 1000 AD, or even all the way back to the Agricultural Revolution over 10,000 years ago—the first "Big Bang" for urbanization and rising scale, specialization of labor, productivity, and wealth. But there is a modern "affluence and urbanization trap" of progress wherein more urban and affluent civilizations, despite their rising affluence, try to offset the cost of raising and educating their kids by having fewer of them. Hence, these populations ultimately age and slow down despite their high standards of living, and eventually lose that high standard of living, at least to some degree, because they have fewer young, innovative workers.

There are four stages of growth in the modern world since the Agricultural Revolution:

1. The early agricultural "subsistence" stage driven largely by commodity cycles and revolving around basic farming and herding;
2. Growing urbanization with more mechanized agriculture and, ultimately or at best, developing industrialization;
3. Middle class and affluent industrialized cultures that grow with high productivity and leveraged-earning cycles, which are pegged to more-leveraged, higher productivity demographic/generational cycles of aging. At best, these cultures develop their own information technologies;
4. The most urban and affluent civilizations age to the point where they begin to decline first in productivity and then in population—like Japan today, then Europe, Russia, East Europe, and China—and eventually North America—and so on around the world.

For the last two decades various authors and experts have been saying that the twenty-first century would be the Asian century, and yes, Asia, led by China, has been growing faster than the western world—and, more recently, so have many emerging countries in Latin America and the Middle East. But the growth rates in the western countries, from their leadership in the Information Revolution and massive baby boom generations, have allowed them to expand strongly as well. That trend is clearly peaking with the meltdown of the financial systems of North America and Europe, and more critically, the peaking of their massive baby boom Spending Waves. Growth outside of East Asia in the emerging world in the last decade has been due to the rising 29–30-year Commodity Cycle, which has peaked recently as well, and because of rising urbanization, which is now peaking in parts of East Asia, Latin America, and much of the Middle East—but not for many decades in most of Asia or Africa.

Urbanization represents the best single indicator of growing incomes in emerging countries that are dependent on commodity industries and exports to more developed countries. Urbanization is more powerful than demographic trends, which are more critical in devel-

Figure 6.15: Brazil, GDP per Capita vs. Urbanization

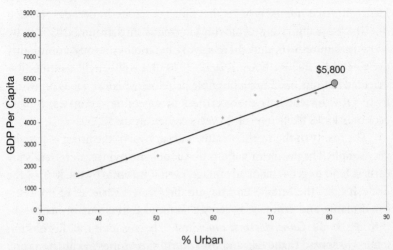

Source: United Nations. Maddison, Angus. *The World Economy: A Millennial Perspective.* Development Center Studies, OECD, 2001.

oped countries with growing middle class and professional workers, who drive those economies with sharply rising productivity and spending cycles as they age into their mid- to late 40s.

Our research into Brazil was the first "eye-opening" insight into the difference between more established, technology-rich developed countries and most emerging countries. Brazil is already more urbanized than the U.S. but with only about 20% of its income, or GDP, per capita! Figure 6.15 shows how Brazil's GDP per capita has grown largely in line with urbanization since the 1950s, when we could measure it, with some swings up and down, with the 29–30-Year Commodity Cycle that peaked in 1980 and again in 2008. Urbanization creates greater economies of scale in business and commerce, more access to infrastructure and education, greater sharing of ideas and learning, and most important, greater specialization of labor and access to higher-paying jobs, which is the key to economic progress over history. This is generally true all the way back to the Agricultural Revolution, which created towns and then cities and then nations and, finally, the global economy that is just now emerging more fully. Brazil's economy has seen some industrialization, but it is largely still in the commodity and resource sector of the world economy and has not made a clear breakthrough into the industrial and information sectors that offer substantially higher wages and value-added jobs. Hence, Brazil is not likely to get that much richer in the decades ahead. It does have strong rising demographic trends into around 2055, as we show in Figure 6.16, and there should be another strong commodity cycle between 2020–2023 and 2039–2040 that will benefit commodity-oriented nations like Brazil. But note here that when we focus on work-force growth, which is more critical in emerging countries, Brazil's economy looks likely to peak 25 years earlier, around 2030.

The reality of the world, wealth, and survival of the fittest is actually very simple. The people or nations that adopt and pioneer new trends the earliest tend to get a major advantage, even if it comes by the luck of the draw. It's like the Middle East having the greatest varieties of domesticated plants and animals, as Jared Diamond points out in his break-through book *Guns, Germs, and Steel*. The Agricultural Revolution tended to spread to the east and west due to similarities in climate as one traveled in those directions. Easier travel access throughout Europe and Eurasia also benefited those regions more than Africa. Then, farther down the road, Great Britain led the Industrial Revolution, as it already

Figure 6.16: Brazil, Spending Wave vs. Workforce Growth, 1950–2095

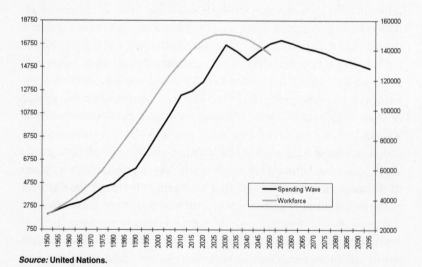

Source: United Nations.

had higher levels of urbanization and wage workers with a Protestant work ethic. What's more, as an island nation, Britain was forced to depend more on importing and exporting. This transition in Western Europe is best chronicled in the recent book *The 10,000 Year Explosion*, by Gregory Cochran and Henry Harpending.

The European and English-speaking nations today tend to have the highest per capita incomes—especially offshoot countries of the U.S., Canada, Australia, and New Zealand, which brought improved infrastructure, railroads, automobiles, and economic opportunities to new lands. These early moves into new technologies and economic structures gave them a technological edge, then a cultural edge, to support new business and social models, and over time, a genetic edge as well. (Unlike today, successful families didn't face enormous costs to raise children in an affluent society, and so had higher birthrates and survival rates, which favored the gene pool.) The Middle Eastern cultures that dominated in Persia from the Agricultural Revolution until the emergence of Greece and Rome, from 600 BC forward, had an advantage as well at first and then faded, although centuries later.

There is a simple logic that drives the "survival of the fittest" model in the modern world that has been especially pertinent since the Agricultural and Industrial Revolutions. Technologies change and accelerate faster than cultures, and cultures change faster than genes. It's kind of like comparing the mind (technologies), emotions (culture), and body (genes). That sequence of change gives a distinct advantage to the cultures and nations that adopt new technologies and business/societal models earlier. Their cultures change to support those new technologies and, eventually, so do their genes. These cultures also adapt more easily to new technology, business, and societal models, allowing them to achieve higher levels of value-added employment and productivity.

Agriculture is more sedentary than hunting and gathering, and forces you to settle down in one place and improve your land and assets. It also values a morning-to-evening work ethic. Hunting, meanwhile, favors careful plotting and quick, precise surges to make a kill, allowing longer periods of eating and relaxing and celebrating. I saw this clearly in South Africa by observing lions. They are the "kings of the jungle" (actually the plains or savannahs) because they have no predators other than man. They are strong, agile, and able to quickly calculate if potential prey is worth the massive short-term energy for a kill. And they know where to hang out for such opportunities. They exert enormous energy to make a kill—in a matter of minutes, at most—but are then set for days with food, and then they can largely sleep or lie around. They would appear to be lazy most of the time to us—but they are the most successful animal in their environment due to their unique "hunting and sprinting" skills. Hunter/gatherer societies that dominated for much of human history have been more that way and were highly successful in that environment, but didn't naturally have the more persistent work ethic required for farming, industry, and office work.

Even though the Agricultural Revolution started in the Middle East, where climate and other conditions for domesticating plants and animals were favorable, the harsher climates of Western and Northern Europe required a more persistent discipline, work ethic, and ability to innovate, and that eventually set the stage for the Industrial Revolution—the "Second Big Bang"—to emerge in Great Britain and then in Western and Northern Europe.

This is another important principle of human evolution: Stronger challenges to survival stimulate more highly evolved behavior.

Human evolution began in Africa, where our ability to walk on two legs, and our big brains and opposable thumbs for creating, emerged. A small group migrated out of Africa with unprecedented language and creative skills and populated the rest of the world. But they did that by settling over long periods of time in different areas with different challenges that forced new and specific changes in cultures and genes over time. The colder, harsher climates presented greater challenges and prompted innovations in everything from clothes making to cooperative strategies for hunting larger animals. In temperate climates and coastal areas, by contrast, the focus was on simpler beachcombing for shellfish or hunting for smaller animals. That is why cultures are so different around the world despite emerging from a common gene pool out of Africa. (See our free download *The History of Human Evolution and Economic Progress* at www.hsdent.com.)

Africa gave birth to human evolution, then the Middle East gave birth to the Agricultural Revolution. Western Europe then gave birth to the Industrial Revolution and the U.S. more to the Information Rev-

olution. The paradox is that now wealth in the world is distributed in reverse order: Africa is the poorest, then the broader Middle East (outside of oil revenues from the West), then Latin America (where agriculture emerged last, but also where much of the culture was wiped out by the Western invasion and diseases), then Asia (where agriculture spread the latest across Eurasia), then Europe, and finally the U.S., which is now the richest. The leader of each revolution tends to fall behind in the next, like General Motors going bankrupt today after leading the automobile and mass manufacturing revolution in the 1920s and beyond, while information industries like Microsoft and Google are rising to dominance.

This returns us to one of our most important fundamental principles of economic progress—the S-Curve from Chapter 2. The reason that 1% of the U.S. population controlled 47% of the wealth in 2007 (like 1929, this was a period of extreme innovation) is that we entered a new information age innovation cycle, and the most entrepreneurial and risk-taking 0.1% to 1% created the new companies that would dominate by adopting early and making major investments. (A lot of them, of course, failed, especially in 2000–2002, and there will be more of that to come until about 2013.) The same thing happened from the late 1800s to the Roaring 20s' bubble boom and then the Great Depression. From 1920 forward, after a massive innovation period and bubble boom, many innovative new companies failed in the survival-of-the-fittest challenge. Those failures peaked in 1933, at the worst of the Great Depression. General Motors became the leader in cars from the early 1930s forward despite Ford's dominance from 1907 (Model T) to the late 1920s (thanks to Ford's assembly line innovations in 1914). General Motors better understood the rising generation wave and income curve, and developed lines of vehicles, in different price ranges, that customers could grow into during the boom. But most important, Alfred Sloan, GM's president at the time, was perhaps most crucial to modern corporate innovation by decentralizing product divisions and financial controls, which gave GM a long-term edge and allowed it to best survive the 1930s shakeout.

So it is today, on a longer time scale, with the emerging world. These countries adopted agriculture first, and some, such as Japan, then South Korea, China, and India, adopted the Industrial Revolution later. Hence, they have less income and wealth because they were later adopters—just

Figure 6.17: The Wealth Curve
The S-Curve of Industrialization/Urbanization

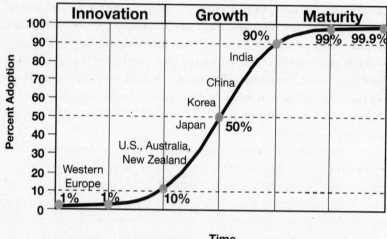

as everyday people in the U.S. do compared to the more innovative and higher-risk-taking entrepreneurs (the top .1% to 1% of earners) and the higher-educated professional sectors (10% plus) of the upper middle class in the U.S. and developed nations. Hence, the S-Curve also represents the Wealth Curve globally, as we show in Figure 6.17. Early Adopters take more risks and get the lion's share of the gains—and nature favors them for doing that in a survival-of-the-fittest challenge, but only if they survive the shakeout period that accompanies depressions, and many don't.

The emerging world is growing richer and will dominate growth in the decades ahead after this severe downturn and depression. But most are not likely to get anywhere near as rich as the leading developed countries have achieved in the last century!

China is leading the emerging world currently and will continue to urbanize, but its potential GDP per capita appears to be more like $8,000 to $10,000—not $30,000 plus. And its demographics turn against it from 2020 forward, and more dramatically after 2035. India is best positioned, with a minority British culture, to dominate growth and could rival the U.S. as an economy in the coming century. The same goes for China, although it will then fade sooner than expected. Even India would do well to eventually achieve today's level of $10,000 to $14,000 per capita GDP after decades of development. Europe, Eastern Europe, and Russia will clearly fade as major powers in the coming decades due to aging demographics and rising cultural complacency, although they will still have relatively high incomes, as Japan does today even after its peak in 1990.

Let's now look at the urbanization curve that came with the Industrial Revolution in the late 1770s, and at how the leading nations of today became rich initially. Figure 6.18 shows how Great Britain led that revolution and started to urbanize well before the steam engine, giving the country an edge. But Western European nations like France, Germany, Spain (and the Netherlands, followed by Belgium and others) followed suit on a lag. The Western European S-Curve of industrialization and urbanization hit the tipping point of 10% around 1850. Now most developed Western countries are at 80% to 90%, plus urbanization, and their incomes and wealth have grown dramatically. But such trends will clearly slow in the decades ahead due to aging populations and slowing Spending Waves.

Urbanized and with higher wages/skills and needs for import/export strategies, Japan was the first Asian nation to follow Great Britain. Japan

Figure 6.18: Urbanization Rates in Select Developed Countries

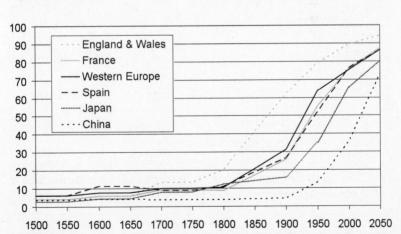

Source: Maddison, Angus. *The World Economy: A Millennial Perspective.* **Development Center Studies, OECD, 2001.**

accelerated from 1900 to the present and is still only at 70% urbanization, with levels of GDP per capita near those of the U.S. Japan's rapidly aging demographics will cause slower growth and urbanization in the decades ahead as younger people tend to migrate to cities and new areas of opportunity. China was next and accelerated in urbanization from 1950 onward—and, at 50% urbanization, still has a long way to go before it reaches 70% to 80%. But China's peaking demographics between 2015 and 2020 will slow both economic progress and urbanization far earlier than most economists would expect. But the point is, again, that urbanization, especially from industrialization, creates an S-curve of growth in income and wealth as measured by GDP per capita.

Urbanization is the key driver of GDP per capita growth after a country moves out of the rural, agrarian stage. But there is a big difference between urbanization that comes more from better mechanization and organization of agriculture and commodities than from higher-value-added industrial products and information services, as in Japan, Taiwan, South Korea, Singapore, and to a lesser degree, China.

Let's look first at the most successful large emerging country, China.

Figure 6.19: China, GDP per Capita vs. Urbanization

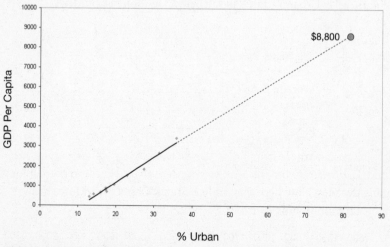

Source: United Nations. Maddison, Angus. *The World Economy: A Millennial Perspective.* Development Center Studies, OECD, 2001.

Figure 6.19 shows how GDP per capita in China was relatively flat until around 1950 and has since started to accelerate with growing urbanization, which was at 38% as of 2000 and likely closer to 50% today. GDP per capita today in China is still lower than in Brazil and most of Latin America, but it is accelerating faster due to the country's breakthrough into industrialization and very strong infrastructure development driven by a top-down government strategy. China's GDP per capita in U.S. dollars is only $3,400 as of 2000 and likely closer to $5,000 today. It's continued urbanization would suggest it could grow to only $8,800 by 2050. That is still nowhere near western standards of living. We tend to think that Chinese and Asians are smarter than us because they top the SAT scores and achievement levels in our country. But we are forgetting that we are seeing only the top .1% to 1% of their population who can afford to come over here to our best schools. We also forget that they are more highly motivated than we are to rise and succeed due to their past poverty. If you go to the rural and very poor areas of China, you will see the sources of that motivation!

A principle of growth in emerging countries is that they need more top-down planning and investment, typically around strong export industries, until incomes and education can grow to the point where the countries become more democratic and their economies are based on free-market principles. China has likely followed the top-down model for too long, at the expense of advances toward democracy and stewardship of its environment. India, by contrast, has not pushed hard enough from a "too bottoms-up and democratic" approach to business development.

But remember that China's Spending Wave peaks between 2015 and 2020, as shown in Figure 6.20, and then turns down faster than the U.S. and accelerates faster after 2035. That stems precisely from the "one child" policy China imposed in the early 1970s, in reaction to its fears of a "Malthusian trap." Shanghai is the first major city to encourage two children per family, but the positive impact of that policy won't be felt for many decades. Note here that, unlike Brazil, China's workforce growth trends are more in line with its Spending Wave projections. China will likely continue to grow into 2035, with the next concerted global boom beginning in the early 2020s, but its slowing demographics will counteract the effects of both its growth rates and continued urbanization, since

Figure 6.20: China, Spending Wave vs. Workforce Growth, 1950–2095

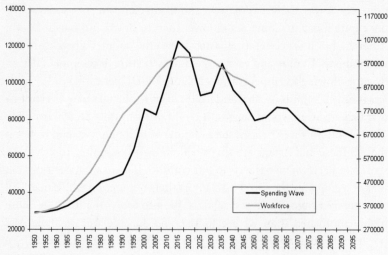

Source: United Nations.

fewer young people are available to migrate to urban areas. China's urbanization is likely to grow less than forecast by the UN and take a longer time to reach 80%. Its larger land area also would suggest lower urbanization than one would expect in island nations like Great Britain or Japan. And Japan's urbanization is still below that in most western countries, also likely due to an aging population that is less likely to migrate to urban areas or embrace political and societal changes needed to grow in the future.

Now let's look at India, our favored country for growth and international economic power over the coming five to six decades. Figure 6.21 shows how India started to accelerate into urbanization since 1980—30 years after China. And India's urbanization rates are only 28% in 2000 and likely just over 30% today, which means much more capacity to grow forward. Note that wireless phone penetration rates are very similar to urbanization rates, at 30% for India, 50% for China, and 80% for Brazil. India's GDP per capita is lower than China's, but it is possible that its acceleration could continue to be higher due to its lead in entrepreneurial companies (more entrepreneurs per capita than China despite its earlier stage of development) and its minor initial leap into high-tech industries

Figure 6.21: India, GDP per Capita vs. Urbanization—
High Growth Scenario

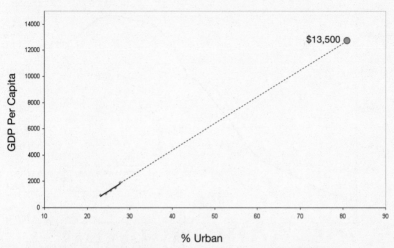

% Urban

Source: **United Nations. Maddison, Angus.** *The World Economy: A Millennial Perspective.*
Development Center Studies, OECD, 2001.

and movies. The truth is that India's emergence is still in an early enough stage that its recent economic acceleration could have been propelled by the emerging country bubble of the 2000s, with much of its growth coming from its minority of highly educated elite and British descendants. But India has one of the most compelling Spending Waves and workforce growth trajectories ahead: it accelerates dramatically and doesn't peak until around 2065 or so in Figure 6.22, and its culture is the closest in the emerging world to that of the U.S. in terms of middle-class lifestyles, aspirations, and pop culture entertainment (tacky commercials, soap operas, Bollywood and movie star fascination, synchronized line dancing, etc.).

According to demographic and urbanization projections, India continues to look like the growth story of the twenty-first century for businesses and investors, far more than China after 2020!

Sometime between 2065 and 2070, a decade after the U.S. echo boom matures and when the world's population is likely to peak, India is likely to rival or best the economic and/or military power of the U.S. China will still be very large but will likely begin to wane after 2035—following Eu-

Figure 6.22: India, Spending Wave vs. Workforce Growth, 1950–2095

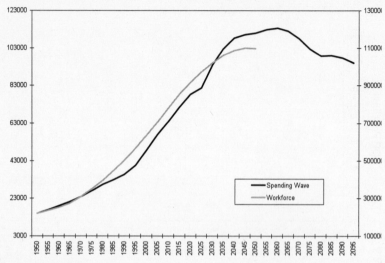

Source: United Nations.

rope, Eastern Europe, and Russia. The major economic powers in the world are likely to ultimately be India and the U.S., and then China. But it is possible that the U.S. will still dominate a bit if we can continue to innovate as we age, a strength due in part to massive immigration during the last few decades and high rates of entrepreneurial innovation. If India merely reaches 25% of our GDP per capita, which, with a population almost four times that of the U.S., is more than likely by 2065, its economy will be as large as ours or larger. The truth is India could achieve higher growth than that if it continues to rise in information-based technologies, cut its bureaucracy, and, like China, attract strong foreign investment. This seems to be the emerging trend there for now.

We will look at a few other emerging countries around the world to show the differences in development and GDP per capita rates with urbanization. Indonesia is another heavily populated country in Southeast Asia that is still more like Brazil and Latin America—a commodity-based country, but a less aggressive exporter. Its GDP per capita in Figure 6.23 was $3,200 as of 2000, at 42% urbanization; urbanization is now more like 50%. Indonesia's GDP per capita has risen with urbanization, which

Figure 6.23: Indonesia, GDP per Capita vs. Urbanization

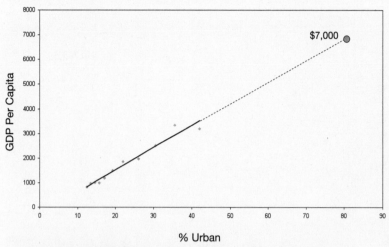

Source: **United Nations. Maddison, Angus.** *The World Economy: A Millennial Perspective.* **Development Center Studies, OECD, 2001.**

points to a GDP per capita decades ahead of $7,000. This country will also get only so rich unless it makes a leap into industrialization, which it hasn't thus far. Malaysia fares better. It has benefited from major urban cities like Kuala Lumpur and Singapore next door and has slightly higher rates of industrialization, but it is still largely a commodity-based economy. Malaysia's projected GDP per capita in Figure 6.24, at 80% urbanization, is $10,200—on the high end of the range for most emerging countries.

Next door to India is another large Muslim-based country that has higher birthrates and the potential to grow demographically even a bit beyond India. But Pakistan is a very troubled and unstable part of the world now and will likely be more so into our adverse 34–36-Year Geopolitical Cycle into 2019 or so. But instability is the inspiration for revolution. This country could be the next to follow Iran and set the stage for a more effective democracy and more infrastructure development. And it is hard to imagine that India's likely growth will not eventually spur a desire for growth and greater capitalism in Pakistan on a lag. Figure 6.25 shows potential for substantial growth for decades ahead: Pakistan's GDP per capita is only $2,200 with 34% urbanization as of 2000

Figure 6.24: Malaysia, GDP per Capita vs. Urbanization

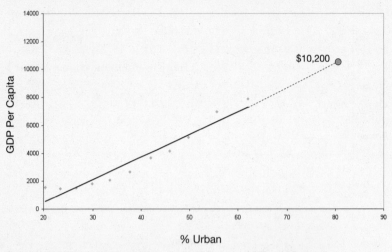

Source: United Nations. Maddison, Angus. *The World Economy: A Millennial Perspective.*
Development Center Studies, OECD, 2001.

Figure 6.25: Pakistan, GDP per Capita vs. Urbanization

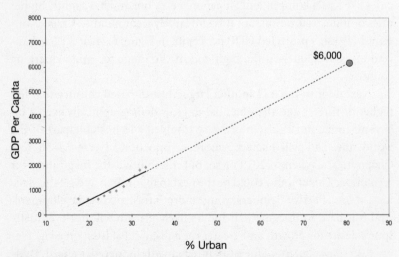

Source: United Nations. Maddison, Angus. *The World Economy: A Millennial Perspective.*
Development Center Studies, OECD, 2001.

but projected to grow toward $6,600 for many decades ahead. And this is a country that, because of its proximity to India, could accelerate that GDP per capita growth if it allies with India rather than elevating tensions with it. That is the sort of progress that tends to emerge in a more positive geopolitical cycle, which we project for 2019/2020–2035/2036.

If we look at the Middle East, it is more useful to measure a country, like Turkey, that is clearly emerging effectively and is not dependent on oil revenues. Figure 6.26 shows GDP per Capita of $7,000 at 66% urbanization as of 2000, and projections of $9,700 likely by 2040—higher than China and closer to Malaysia. If we go to Africa, the biggest success story there has been South Africa and Botswana, partially due to tourism and also to their mix of indigenous peoples and Europeans. South Africa's GDP per capita in Figure 6.27 is only $4,000 at 57% urbanization as of 2000, but projected to reach $6,400 by 2035 or so. That is higher than all other African nations, outside of Egypt, that are still mostly in the early agricultural subsistence stage—but still lower than most emerging countries' potential in Asia. But as in the Middle East, there is still a deep divide between rich and poor in South Africa. The poor are poorer than the average statistics would suggest, but still rising faster than their counter-

Figure 6.26: Turkey, GDP per Capita vs. Urbanization

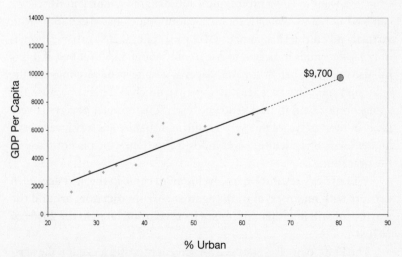

Source: United Nations. Maddison, Angus. *The World Economy: A Millennial Perspective.* Development Center Studies, OECD, 2001.

Figure 6.27: South Africa, GDP per Capita vs. Urbanization

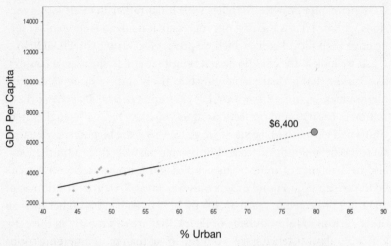

Source: United Nations. Maddison, Angus. *The World Economy: A Millennial Perspective.*
Development Center Studies, OECD, 2001.

parts in other areas of Africa. South Africa is the migration magnet for sub-Saharan Africa. That bodes well for future growth, but creates ongoing instability and potential class warfare.

If we want to cite a prototypical sub-Saharan country in Africa, we can look at Kenya, which is clearly a commodities-based economy with virtually no industrialization. Its GDP per capita, at 20% urbanization, is only $1,000 and is projected to rise to only about $3,000 at best if it hits full urbanization, like Brazil. And Nigeria, despite its oil revenues and the emerging megacity of Lagos, is not that much different, because the spoils do not tend to trickle down there. So continued poverty is very likely in most of Africa unless its countries urbanize and advance toward higher levels of agriculture and industrialization, which is not likely in the near future.

Will Africa's revolution in development come in the next decade in concert with major revolutions against corrupt dictators around the world—or will it wither and/or see its revolution later, in the 2040s or 2070s?

The Philippines is a Southeast Asian country still locked in the agricultural/commodity stage, despite rising urbanization, with little indus-

Figure 6.28: The Philippines, GDP per Capita vs. Urbanization

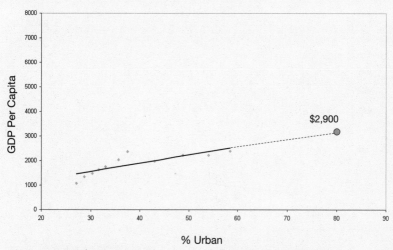

% Urban

Source: United Nations. Maddison, Angus. *The World Economy: A Millennial Perspective.* Development Center Studies, OECD, 2001.

trialization. Hence, it is one of the poorer urban countries in Southeast Asia, which has obviously been booming. Figure 6.28 shows a GDP per capita of only $2,200 with 59% urbanization, with projections of only $2,900 in the next few decades. This is why you see so many Philippine workers migrating around the world to better job and infrastructure opportunities. Blame for this lies not with their work ethic but with their country's corrupt and low-productivity economic system.

Most of Africa and parts of South America and Asia, like the Philippines, are still mired in low-paying manual-labor service jobs, despite gains in urbanization. This is a sign of strong corruption in government and business that keeps hard-working people from rising, but also from genetic traits that make them slow to adapt.

And finally, South Korea is the best example of an Asian country that has moved more fully into the industrialization stage, as Japan did before it. Island nations have little land for agriculture and have higher incentives to move into export/import enterprises and industrialization, as did Japan, and much earlier, Great Britain. South Korea has achieved more of an S-Curve pattern of growth in GDP per capita rather than showing a normal, straight-line trend. It has achieved $20,000 GDP per capita at

Figure 6.29: South Korea, GDP per Capita vs. Urbanization

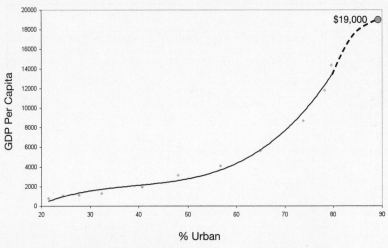

% Urban

Source: United Nations. Maddison, Angus. *The World Economy: A Millennial Perspective.*
Development Center Studies, OECD, 2001.

81% urbanization and could come close to catching up with Japan, as Figure 6.29 shows. Very few emerging countries make such achievements this late in the industrialization process. But Korea and Japan show how important and rare it is to move into industrialization and higher-value-added industries to achieve higher standards of living.

Accelerating GDP per capita, as has occurred in South Korea since 1980, is typically a sign of a potential breakout into higher value industries and jobs.

In the next two charts we look, based on just this first rough analysis of urbanization and GDP per capita relative to the U.S., at how large major emerging countries could grow relative to the U.S. in the decades ahead. These numbers will understate growth because they don't allow for inflation, and may understate growing productivity from technology growth. And the U.S. projections are a bit overstated, as immigration rates are now falling and not likely to live up to UN projections. We simply take the projected GDP per capita at rates of urbanization according to the UN and then adjust for population projections by the UN.

In Figure 6.30 we can see that by 2035, India gets close to the size of China. Also, China's growth rates are likely overstated a bit because its de-

Figure 6.30: Projected Real GDP—Select Emerging Countries

	2000	2020	2035	2050
USA	$ 8,096,707,618	$ 11,423,049,000	$ 14,059,963,000	$ 16,157,280,000
China	$ 4,339,317,450	$ 7,155,775,000	$ 9,066,576,200	$ 10,911,246,500
India	$ 1,991,346,900	$ 4,785,287,500	$ 8,403,334,500	$ 12,103,500,000
Indonesia	$ 657,511,840	$ 1,372,777,200	$ 1,725,968,400	$ 2,016,770,000
Brazil	$ 967,710,744	$ 1,275,211,100	$ 1,381,602,600	$ 1,442,179,200
Pakistan	$ 288,413,004	$ 633,323,600	$ 1,081,331,800	$ 1,541,897,000
Turkey	$ 497,187,260	$ 712,920,500	$ 901,294,900	$ 1,022,584,500
Malaysia	$ 183,212,928	$ 320,170,000	$ 388,320,400	$ 464,068,800
South Africa	$ 185,725,208	$ 289,690,500	$ 332,880,000	$ 363,532,800
Vietnam	$ 140,806,770	$ 225,425,300	$ 324,273,000	$ 446,664,000

Source: United Nations, HS Dent Foundation.

mographics are now slowing. The U.S. projections are also likely overstated, since they are based on UN assumptions of higher immigration, which we will have to adjust for in the future. But the bigger picture is that by 2050 India pulls well ahead of China and will likely be on par with the U.S. after immigration figures are adjusted lower. Indonesia, with the world's third-largest population, doesn't even come close, with one sixth of India's projected real GDP by 2050. Even Brazil projects to a mere 12% of India's economy by 2050, and countries like Malaysia, South Africa, and Vietnam will be much smaller despite strong growth rates, especially in Vietnam.

Figure 6.31 looks at growth rates in each major period, and they obviously decline over time as urbanization sees smaller relative gains. The highest growth rates in all periods are obviously in India again, then Pakistan (if it stabilizes), then in Vietnam (which is more likely to be stable). China's growth rates again are very likely to be a bit overstated after 2020 and more so after 2035, due to rapid aging and slowing demographic trends. U.S. growth rates are again a bit overstated as well due to lower immigration rates that likely lie ahead. Brazil and the rest of Latin America will likely see the slowest growth over time (outside of strong com-

Figure 6.31: Projected Real Growth Rates—Select Emerging Countries

	2020	2035	2050
India	4.48%	2.86%	1.84%
Pakistan	4.01%	2.71%	1.79%
Vietnam	2.38%	1.83%	1.61%
China	2.53%	1.59%	1.24%
Turkey	1.82%	1.18%	0.63%
Indonesia	3.75%	1.15%	0.78%
USA	1.74%	1.04%	0.70%
Malaysia	2.83%	0.97%	0.89%
South Africa	2.25%	0.70%	0.44%
Brazil	1.39%	0.40%	0.21%

Source: United Nations, HS Dent Foundation.

modity cycles from the early 2020s into the late 2030s) due to limits in urbanization rates—unless some countries industrialize at a much faster pace, although that is unlikely. If Africa grows in commodity and resource exports in the future, as it should, Latin America may be forced to industrialize or fall behind.

Another principle from history is that the countries near and south of the equator tend to focus more on lower-value-added commodity and resource industries, and those in the larger and broader lateral temperate zone north of the equator tend to lead in innovation and have higher standards of living.

Even the nations in the more temperate parts of the southern hemisphere, like Australia, New Zealand, Chile, Argentina, and South Africa, have led in standards of living beyond their ample resources. Cold, up to a point, is challenging and good for innovation and evolution, as we stressed earlier. That equation could change, however, with the wider use of air conditioning, as Singapore—right on the equator—has proved. Bogotá may follow suit.

Figure 6.32 summarizes the GDP per capita and urbanization statistics for many emerging countries—both in 2000 and when they are projected to peak at 80% urbanization. Again, since the UN doesn't project past 2050, we give the urbanization rates projected for countries that haven't hit 80% by then. But much of Asia, from China to Indonesia, and nearly all of Latin America and the Middle East will have reached 80% urbanization by 2050. When India's potential demographic trends and Spending Wave peak, at around 2065–2070, even India and other large Asian countries like Pakistan are likely to be 65% to 70% urbanized.

Peaking world population and slowing urbanization trends are likely to cause the next major global slowdown and depression between the late 2060s and the early 2080s, especially in the first half of the 2070s. A major commodity cycle is likely to be peaking by 2068– 2069 as well, and that will hurt still resource-oriented emerging countries, especially in Africa, the Middle East, and Latin America.

Figure 6.32: Summary of GDP per Capita and Urbanization with Projections, Select Emerging Countries

	Urbanization Rate in 2000	GDP per capita in 2000	Urbanization at 80%	Peak GDP per capita at 80%
Brazil	81.2%	$5,556	2000	$8,400*
South Korea	79.6%	$14,343	2000	$19,115*
U.S.	79.1%	$28,129	2005	$46,716*
Mexico	74.7%	$7,218	2020	$7,800
Czech Republic	74.0%	$8,630	2040	$9,700
Turkey	64.7%	$7,481	2035	$9,700
Iran	64.2%	$4,742	2035	$6,000
Malaysia	62.0%	$7,872	2025	$10,200
Philippines	58.5%	$2,385	2040	$2,900
South Africa	56.9%	$4,139	2050	$6,400
Indonesia	42.0%	$3,203	79.4% in 2050	$7,000
China	35.8%	$3,425	72.9% in 2050	$8,800
Pakistan	33.2%	$1,947	63.7% in 2050	$6,000
India	27.7%	$1,910	55.2% in 2050	$13,500
Vietnam	24.3%	$1,790	57.0% in 2050	$5,800
Kenya	19.7%	$1,020	48.1% in 2050	$2,800

*2008 GDP per capita from World Bank

Source: United Nations, World Bank, and Maddison, Angus. *The World Economy: A Millennial Perspective.* Development Center Studies, OECD, 2001.

The Truth Is, Income Gains by Age Are Very Limited in Most Emerging Countries

We have finally found standardized data on income by age in emerging countries, in the Euromonitor International report *World Income Distribution 2008/2009*. The only limitation is that the data is only in 10-year age cohorts rather than the 5-year and 1-year cohorts that we get for the U.S. Also, the data is pegged to income, not spending, although the two are very similar in trend and magnitude. Nonetheless, this data is much better than what we have found in the past.

Figure 6.33 shows most clearly why the Spending Wave is not the most critical indicator for most emerging countries. They simply don't have the leveraged earning and spending curves as they age that most developed countries do.

In the U.S., with 5-year cohorts, the rise is from near $10,000 to near $40,000, or an approximate increase of 400% from workforce entry into peak income and spending at around age 46. Out of four major emerging

Figure 6.33: Income by Age, 10-year Cohorts

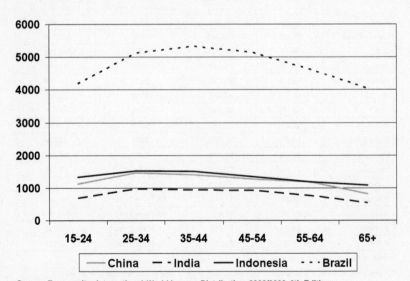

Source: Euromonitor International, World Income Distribution, 2008/2009, 6th Edition.

countries, Brazil's income is the highest on average due to much higher urbanization, but the rise is only minor and peaks in the age 35–44 cohort; in the U.S. the peak is in the age 45–54 cohort. The income rise in Brazil from the 15–24 level to the peak 35–44 cohort is only 27%. Crude data from an academic article on Brazil suggests that average income rises modestly from age 22 to age 29 and then plateaus to age 49 before declining. There is obviously only a short learning curve at first for what are, at best, largely manual or clerical jobs, and then a very flat curve indeed! The truth is income may rise 50% or a bit more from actual average workforce entry to the peak earning period, especially in more urban areas, but again that is nowhere near the rise in the U.S.

Indonesia, China, and India all have successively lower average incomes by age, in line with their lower urbanization. But again the rise in income is very minor with age. In China, India, and Indonesia, the actual peak is even earlier, at 25–34. That is typical today in most early stage emerging countries. But even in India and China, rougher surveys show that such income levels hold up until the late 40s before declining. Hence, the Spending Wave trends still suggest when an emerging country will see declining spending trends by age, and that is clearly after age 46–50, as in the U.S. and most developed countries! These emerging countries on average just don't accelerate that much higher after workforce entry. That also is true of most manual, agricultural or construction jobs in the U.S., a minority of which are taken by immigrants here. We also note in the final column the approximate rough peak income by age, based on an intuitive interpolation model we use.

Even though most emerging countries do not see nearly as high a peak in earnings and don't peak as late as countries like the U.S., their earnings still tend to drop off more sharply after workers reach their late 40s, so the lags we project in the Spending Waves for emerging countries still mark more where their countries will likely peak, while urbanization rates better forecast how much they will grow into those peaks. As Latin America demonstrates, most emerging countries do tend to peak later in income and spending, and at somewhat higher levels, as they urbanize.

Figure 6.34 shows the ratio of the peak income cohort to the entry level 15–24 cohort in select emerging countries, and for the most part we see the same story. We also include the U.S. as a benchmark, although

Figure 6.34: Ratio of Peak Income Cohort to Age 15–24 Cohort, 2007, Select Emerging Countries

	Ratio of Peak Income to 15-24	Peak Cohort	Estimated Actual Peak
South Africa	2.05	45-54	50
Saudi Arabia	1.93	45-54	46
U.S.	1.72	45-54	46-50
India	1.40	25-34	32
Colombia	1.37	45-54	50
China	1.30	25-34	32
Brazil	1.27	35-44	40
Chile	1.24	45-54	50
Mexico	1.17	35-44	37
Malaysia	1.15	25-34	32
Indonesia	1.14	25-34	32
Philippines	1.14	25-34	33

Source: Euromonitor International, World Income Distribution, 2008/2009, 6th Edition.

even it shows an increase multiple of only 1.72 (the real multiple is closer to 4) because of the very broad smoothing of the 1-year and 5-year cohort data in the U.S. Most emerging countries range from 1.14 to 1.30—very low and closer to Brazil at the higher end due to higher urbanization. India is higher, at 1.40, which is a very good sign given its early stage of development and urbanization. Hence, India is more likely to develop a steeper earning and spending curve by age and see a quicker rise in GDP per capita vs. urbanization in the future, as we forecasted in Figure 6.21. There are strong exceptions in countries like South Africa, where ratios are even higher than those for the U.S., at 2.05, and Saudi Arabia, at 1.93. But South Africa has a strong minority of wealthy Europeans and foreigners that skew income data, and oil revenues in Saudi Arabia flow mostly to the very top income earners and a lot of foreigner/immigrant professionals and investors.

What is clear here is that most emerging countries do not have the same leveraged income and spending cycles by age that drive most developed countries, which have much better and more established infrastructures, legal/financial systems, and consequently, higher-value-added professional, technical, financial, and managerial jobs. These emerging countries are bottom-feeders that tend to generate lower value-added profits and jobs still focused more on construction and resource industries despite rising urbanization. They are like our immigrants in the U.S., very hard-working but still well below middle class living standards, even adjusted for lower living costs in these countries.

We have already shown urbanization to be the key factor for most emerging countries, as opposed to Spending Wave projections alone. Figure 6.35 ranks emerging countries based on their highest real GDP per capita growth in the bubble boom, from 1995–2007, and looks at other factors we can measure that would contribute to such growth. Investment in infrastructure would be another factor we would like to measure, and we will continue to look for useful measures for our research.

Here we can see first that the greatest progress in real GDP per capita has been in China. No surprise here. But the next occurred in Vietnam—

Figure 6.35: Growth Factors in Emerging Countries, 1995–2007

	Real per Capita Income % Change 1995-2007	% Urbanization Change 1995-2007	% Secondary + Higher Education Change 1995-2007	% Change in Exports 1995-2007
China	167.17%	68.82%	39.64%	704.05%
Vietnam	119.89%	56.38%	50.70%	672.40%
Indonesia	72.99%	64.35%	31.20%	138.83%
Malaysia	61.89%	48.77%	30.50%	145.97%
Pakistan	60.38%	34.31%	22.91%	94.07%
Chile	47.03%	19.21%	31.00%	272.33%
India	45.34%	34.55%	16.84%	530.59%
Egypt	41.16%	25.63%	31.99%	182.89%
Mexico	39.98%	24.52%	35.33%	232.97%
South Africa	37.15%	31.10%	38.26%	160.57%
Philippines	34.64%	51.03%	35.82%	132.16%
Turkey	33.88%	32.16%	31.31%	320.77%
Nigeria	32.46%	73.47%	25.69%	435.16%
U.S.	21.43%	19.62%	5.02%	78.87%*
Brazil	19.96%	28.58%	34.96%	241.60%
Thailand	17.35%	22.64%	54.64%	153.99%
Argentina	16.89%	14.71%	22.54%	154.28%
Colombia	1.93%	30.26%	27.19%	154.58%
Saudi Arabia	-5.80%	51.29%	45.65%	358.30%

*1995-2006

Source: Euromonitor International, World Income Distribution, 2008/2009, 6th Edition.

"little China"—and then Malaysia and then Indonesia. All in Asia, despite the incredible commodities boom for Latin America, the Middle East, and Africa in this time period. Why? They have moved more into higher-value-added light-industrial and heavy industrial sectors. The second column measures the percentage increase in urbanization, and here is where we see a strong correlation with growth in real GDP per capita. The exceptions come more from the oil exporting nations like Saudi Arabia and Nigeria, where such commodity growth does not greatly trickle down to most households, even with high urbanization. These countries clearly don't tend to have the educational systems, infrastructure, or value-added jobs that take full advantage of rising urbanization.

The third column shows rises in education levels of high school and above, which is obviously important. But this category does not show as much variance among countries and does not correlate as clearly as does growth in urbanization. Demographic data from India shows that households with high school or secondary higher education make 37% higher salaries over those at elementary school levels, with graduate degrees making 89% more. In urban areas, 66.5% of residents have a high school or higher education whereas only 32.2% do in rural areas. So urbanization clearly drives higher levels of education as well. Surveys of incomes in urban vs. rural areas are also largely consistent with these findings in emerging countries like China, Brazil, and India, with 60% to 80% higher incomes in urban areas vs. rural.

Column four shows increases in exports. Export industries tend to support higher-paying jobs and encourage migration into urban areas—but more so when such jobs are more industrial than merely agricultural or commodity-based. This column shows very extreme changes, and a stronger correlation with urbanization. Since urbanization is something we can project more reliably into the future, and rising exports encourage rising urbanization, these two factors correlate to a significant degree. **Urbanization is still the best and most reliable overall predictor of GDP per capita.** India is an example of very high export growth, but not as rapid GDP per capita growth compared to China. China's exports are more industrial and a much larger percentage of GDP, hence they would have more impact. India is merely growing rapidly from a small base of exports that could grow to higher levels of GDP and higher value-added jobs in the future.

Given that there is relatively modest leverage in earning and spending curves in most emerging countries, workforce growth projections are, overall, a better measure of demographic growth potential than the Spending Wave—but both are still significant because many of these countries will reach both higher growth rates in income and spending by age as they become more middle class and offer more value-added jobs, and they will peak in incomes and spending later, more toward ages 46–50, as in the most urbanized areas in East Asia and, to a lesser degree, in Latin America.

Given the flatter earning and spending curves in most emerging countries, workforce growth (for ages 15–64) is really a better overall indicator than the Spending Wave. Figure 6.36 shows the projections for

Figure 6.36: Workforce Growth Projections, Emerging Countries, 2010–2035

	% Growth in 15-64, 2010-2035	Total 15-64 in 2035 (in 000s)
Nigeria	79.75%	155,049
Pakistan	71.68%	188,123
Saudi Arabia	55.42%	26,553
Philippines	49.07%	86,851
Egypt	46.97%	78,507
India	35.96%	1,061,287
Malaysia	34.57%	24,823
Colombia	27.80%	38,827
Turkey	24.13%	63,561
Argentina	21.57%	31,860
Indonesia	21.08%	189,308
Mexico	17.99%	85,515
Vietnam	17.37%	71,660
Brazil	13.33%	149,795
South Africa	12.30%	36,906
U.S.	10.78%	235,152
Chile	8.88%	12,780
Thailand	-0.85%	47,847
China	-2.33%	950,580

Source: United Nations.

the 15–64 population for select emerging countries from 2010 to 2035. The highest growth rates are similar to the Spending Wave projections, with countries in Africa (like Nigeria), then the Middle East (Saudi Arabia and Egypt), and the edge of South Asia (Pakistan). India still ranks on the higher end, with nearly 36% growth in the workforce in the next 25 years and the largest population projected in the future. But again note the total size of the workforce in 2035 by country, in the second column. India will by then have the largest workforce, at 1.06 billion, and China will come in a close second, with .96 billion. The U.S. is actually the third-largest workforce, at .235 billion (and again likely overstated a bit due to lower immigration than forecast), but with much higher GDP per capita. Then come Indonesia, Pakistan, and Brazil. After that only Nigeria rivals in workforce size, and most other countries are much smaller. Chile and Argentina are among the smallest.

Figure 6.20 showed the comparison of the Spending Wave in the past and future for China compared to workforce growth rates. In this country (as with Japan), the workforce and Spending Wave projections correlate very well, with the workforce projections actually holding up into 2020–2025, a bit later than the clearer Spending Wave peak around 2015–2020. Figure 6.16 showed the difference in a maturing urbanization country like Brazil, where growth would peak around 2030 instead of 2050–2055, a difference of 20 to 25 years. Argentina would similarly peak 20 years earlier, but Mexico would peak only 10 years earlier.

Latin America is more likely to peak around 2040, according to more-appropriate workforce projections, as opposed to 2050–2055 with the Spending Wave projections. This will also coincide with an approximate peak in the next commodity cycle around 2039–2040. So 2040 should represent a long-term peak for most of Latin America after a dynamic boom from 2020/2023 forward.

Many countries in South Asia, the Middle East, and Africa are likely to see workforce trends peak 10–20 years ahead of their potential Spending Waves, but that will be hard to determine for awhile because UN projections for workforce growth don't go past 2050. We have charts for Workforce Growth vs. Spending Wave projections for most countries in our Free Global Trends Database at www.hsdent.com. Go to "Free Downloads."

The most salient principles are:

1. Demographic factors and rising Spending Waves are the most critical factors for forecasting growth in the more affluent developed countries, with some differences attributable to political and cultural factors. Such demographic trends are highly projectable around the developed and already affluent world.
2. Urbanization is more critical for emerging countries, where earning and spending curves are much flatter and education, infrastructure investment, and export growth are more influential. But these factors are most driven by urbanization—and urbanization, like demographics, is much more reliable an indicator and easier to project into the future.
3. Workforce growth is generally a better indicator of demographic trends in emerging countries than The Spending Wave, which lags the birth index for the peak in spending and is variable and less leveraged in emerging countries anyway. Workforce growth also correlates well with developed countries, but the Spending Wave has greater definition of cycles.
4. There are generally four classes of countries emerging:
   - Still poor basic agricultural countries with less than $3,000 potential GDP per capita, like the Philippines, Afghanistan, and Kenya and most of the rest of Africa
   - Emerging lower-middle-class countries with $4,000–$8,000 GDP per capita like Pakistan, Indonesia, Brazil, and most of South America
   - Emerging upper-middle-class countries with $9,000–$14,000 GDP per capita like India, China, Vietnam, Argentina, Chile, Poland, and most of Eastern Europe
   - Upper-class countries like Israel, North America, Europe, Down Under, and East Asia with $15,000 plus GDP per capita.

Summary Conclusions and Opportunities from This Chapter

1. India has the most overall potential due to its size, long urbanization growth ahead, and strong, early stage progress and entrepreneurialism. India most needs strong government and foreign investment in infrastructure to better leverage its massive workforce and to improve its "ease of doing business" for foreign investors and domestic businesses. After 2020 India should lead the world in total growth and investment opportunities and should approach the U.S. in the size of its overall economy between 2035 and 2050. India could even exceed the U.S. in that category by 2065–2070, when the world peaks in population, demographic, and urbanization trends.

2. China will be the second largest economy after the U.S. for decades to come and may catch up to the U.S. in total GDP by 2035. But China's workforce and demographic spending trends slow after 2015–2020, and more so after 2035, and that will work against continued growing urbanization, which is driven largely by younger households. Those households will be diminishing in number, even faster. China's growth will clearly trail other strong countries like India after 2020 and China will face very strong environmental challenges. It will very likely lose its lead as the second-largest economy, ceding the spot to India, between 2035 and 2050, and almost surely by 2065–2070.

3. Pakistan is another large country that has already seen more progress than most would assume, and could accelerate if it moves beyond its present political instability (likely by 2020, at the end of our adverse geopolitical cycle) and gets the bug to be more like India, which we think is very likely.

4. Indonesia has made much progress politically and financially since the Southeast Asian crisis of 1998–2002. It is one of the few large emerging countries that looks set to continue to make steady progress for decades ahead. Much like India, this country needs to improve its "ease of doing business"

to attract foreign investors and to incentivize domestic businesses.

5. Turkey has the greatest growth prospects in the Middle East after the oil bubble burst. The Middle East has very strong demographics if it can modernize infrastructures and education for their broader workforce. This is still a big question mark at this point. It may take a decade of turmoil/revolution (as is beginning to occur in Iran) and low oil prices to force meaningful change.

6. Columbia and Brazil have the most potential for continued high growth rates in Latin America, but already high urbanization says that all Latin American countries will have to attempt to move into higher-valued-added industries and become less reliant on just commodity exports. Both the workforce and commodity trends should peak around 2039–2040 for Latin America, marking a major watershed for this region.

7. All of the commodity-oriented export countries in Latin America, the Middle East, and Africa are likely to do the best in the next commodity boom, from around 2020/2023 into 2039/2040. But Asian countries like India, China, Vietnam, and Malaysia that tend to move into higher-valued-added industries will still outperform the others, as they have in the past.

8. Southeast Asia includes the smaller giant Indonesia and has the potential to see Cambodia, Laos, and possibly Myanmar, follow Vietnam's growth example. These are countries to watch for signs they might be moving into a projectable development trend like India.

9. Sub-Saharan Africa has only seen major progress toward democracy and higher GDP per capita in South Africa and Botswana. Will the rest of that region join the development party—or continue to fall farther behind with corruption, warfare, and disease? Even Nigeria has benefited only from oil revenues, not from broader education and skills, despite rising urbanization, as is the case in most of the Middle East.

10. Emerging countries should target the largest high-growth

emerging economies, like India and China, rather than declining regions like Europe. North America and Australia/New Zealand are the more attractive export growth areas in the aging developed world.

11. The ultimate demographic message is that the developed world is slowing in GDP growth, but such aging societies have higher wealth to invest. The emerging countries have much higher urbanization and demographic/spending growth, but need to progress in a way that does not create the horrific pollution that marked China's growth miracle.

12. The ultimate "New Deal," as we describe in Chapter 9, is that the developed countries bring new green and high-technology investments in infrastructure to emerging countries in exchange for profits and trade agreements for commodities and lower-cost industrial goods, and for more-stringent pollution/carbon standards to combat global pollution and warming trends.

13. Major emerging countries like India, China, Brazil, and Indonesia should be outstanding proving grounds for new ecological win/win models, since these countries have large populations, substantial demographic growth, and abundant natural resources. For example, Brazil would not be depleting its greatest resource—its rainforests—if it were given the right incentives to replant trees and develop new, value-added industries around that.

Alternative Demographic Impacts and Scenarios

The spending projections in this report assume that birthrates continue to fall at rates similar to those in the past several decades. Once higher education, income, and urbanization trends set in, this tends to be the case. That is why demographic projection is such a reliable science. Our 500-year Mega Innovation Cycle suggests that world growth should continue to accelerate into around 2150 instead of 2065. There are three alternative scenarios that could occur and impact birthrates and mortality rates ahead and extend growth for decades or more ahead:

1. **Second Baby Boom in the Emerging World.** We could see a second baby boom, centering more on the emerging world. The massive baby boom in the West occurred after the Great Depression and World War II (a crisis that threw people back to the basics, like family) and an accelerated suburbanization shift. Currently, most of the migration in emerging countries is from rural areas into larger cities. It is possible that on an approximate 80- to 84-year Generation Wave lag on the first baby boom from 1934 to 1961, we could see a second baby boom from about 2016 into 2040 or so around suburbanization trends in emerging countries such as China and India (after migration to larger cities peaks). Such a baby boom would extend the spending trends into a later boom that peaks in more like 2090–2095 instead of around 2065—and extend the Innovation Wave into the early to mid-2060s, instead of around 2040. This obviously would create more bullish trends in the second half of this century. **But it is more likely that such a baby boom would come after the first serious depression in Asia, between the late 2060s and the 2070s.** A baby boom in the 2080s and 2090s would create a large new generation that would see revived innovation in the early 2100s and economic growth that could last into the 2160s or so. As in all demographic changes, the impacts mostly will be decades down the road, so that we can adjust our forecasts well in advance of the necessary investment and business strategy changes.

2. **Aging Revolution in the Developed World.** We could see a more accelerated aging trend as biotechnology innovations allow more people, first in the affluent countries, to live substantially longer—to age 100+ versus 80. The last leap in life expectancy occurred between the 1930s and 1960s, at four years of increase per decade. On our 80-year New Economy Cycle the next great leap should occur between the 2010s and the 2040s, especially while the global Innovation Wave is still rising and we see the full impacts of the biotech revolution and artificial intelligence, as Ray Kurzweil (*The Singu-*

larity Is Near) predicts will be the case into 2045. That would cause peaks in spending and productivity trends to come substantially later in life—in the 50s and 60s and beyond—and such trends would cause the projected population decline from slowing births to be less. Hence population could peak and begin to slow later than in the 2060s as is projected now—or population may not peak as expected if such trends spread fairly rapidly to emerging countries as well. **But it is very likely to take many decades for such progress in the most affluent countries to spread to the emerging countries.** As a result, the peak in spending overall for the world around 2065 should still stand with major developed countries like the United States, their Spending Waves extending into the 2060s instead of the 2050s. In this scenario, there also could be advances in fertility drugs that allow increasing numbers of people to have kids later in life, and that could further support the trends for a second baby boom in point 1 above. Then emerging countries that first have a second baby boom could follow on a lag with much longer life spans and extend long-term demographic growth trends into as late as 2150–2160 (in line with our 500-year Mega Innovation Cycle).

3. **Accelerating Adverse Environmental Trends.** We could see an array of negative trends that impact demographics, including rising war and terrorism, accelerating global warming and pollution affecting crops and flooding, and major pandemics. These trends likely would most adversely affect the emerging countries, would increase mortality rates, and could reduce the propensity to have kids as well. In this scenario, the peak in global spending and population could come earlier and the ensuing decline would be more dramatic.

Opportunities Given Likely Slowing Global Demographic Trends

As we mentioned earlier in this chapter, there are more countries that haven't effectively entered a successful development path than countries that have. The first opportunity for increasing global growth and regional opportunities is for more of the less developed countries to learn from the lessons of successful emerging countries from South Africa to United Arab Emirates to South Korea and to enter the rising productivity path to economic development. This requires the peaceful or not so peaceful overthrow of corrupt and dictatorial governments that often dominate these less developed countries and keep them in a poverty cycle. This also requires more stable, democratic, and accountable governments; enforceable laws and property rights systems; stable financial systems and markets; investments in basic infrastructures; and effective education systems. Free markets and truly democratic government can follow later, once the country is autonomous and capable of competing in world markets without government protection of industries, as protection typically is healthy in the earliest stages of development.

The most important revolution we will see in this extended global downturn will be that more and more constricting and corrupt dictatorships will fall, allowing more emerging countries to enter a sustainable development path—although many will try to strengthen their chokehold at first in the chaos of the downturn and commodities crash. The second will be the Second Industrial Revolution in the developed world, likely led by North America. The third will be greater cooperation between developed and emerging countries in solving major global issues like terrorism, global warming, and income inequality.

For the many large and more dominant developed countries from Europe to North America to East Asia and Down Under that are aging and slowing in demographics, the only path (other than the Aging Revolution in point 2 above) will be technological innovation and, to a greater degree, developing more effective organizations at all levels, from small businesses to large corporations to charitable organizations to governments. Since technological innovations are driven more by younger people between ages 20 and 24, the technological opportunities will be more challenging for aging Western nations, especially in Europe and Japan. But since older people from ages 45 to 64 have the power in management and organizational change, this is where the greatest opportunities will come from, as we discussed in Chapter 3.

One thing is sure: we have been increasingly moving into a global economy for the first time on a more pervasive level since the 1950s. Although there will at first be a greater backlash to globalization as countries grow more protectionist in trade policies at first and terrorism rises, increasing global challenges including pollution and global warming ultimately will force a broader and more effective level of global institutions to replace present ones, such as the UN, that have only limited effectiveness.

The paradox of this global crisis with its backlash against globalization is that the enormous challenges from terrorism to global warming to trade imbalances to currency and bank failures will force the leading countries to work together to create more effective global institutions and to foster the next, more global boom starting in the early 2020s. The best win-win way to do this is for the developed countries to make major infrastructure investments in the emerging nations in trade for cooperation on these issues.

We discuss these issues in Chapter 9. But first we will look in Chapter 7 at why the risks in investing cluster in time periods like this bubble bust ahead rather than being distributed normally or more at random—as a result, the portfolio diversification strategies you have been using will not protect you as you expect. Then in Chapter 8 we will look at the changes required in your portfolio, life, and business to survive and actually prosper in the Next Great Depression, which will bring the greatest bargains in investments since the early 1930s.

CHAPTER 7

The Clustering of Risks and Returns

Why Traditional Asset Allocation Strategies Will Fail Miserably in the Decade Ahead

TO ENJOY THE BENEFITS of an item, whether it is a meal, a home, or even an airline ticket, you or someone else must pay for it. The same is true for investment returns: the profits in your 401(k) or the capital gains on your home come at a price, whether you realize it or not.

The way that we pay for investment returns is by taking on risk. The risk is that you will not earn as much as you expected or, in some cases, that you will actually *lose* money. Some investments, such as stocks, can have dramatic swings in value. Bonds, on the other hand, tend to have less fluctuation than equities. There are also less obvious risks, such as opportunity cost: the return you could have gotten from investing either in something else or in nothing at all. The goal is to ensure that the price you pay for an investment—or the risk you take—is commensurate with the return that you expect to receive.

Most people intuitively understand risk, and we are always estimating the risks that we face. The last time that you jaywalked or ran a yellow light, you decided that it was "worth" taking the slight risk of getting hit by a car or being ticketed. In finance, we like more exact estimates. To quantify better the risk of stocks and other investments, the financial services industry has developed many tools. In addition to estimating the quality of the companies that stocks represent, investors look at charts and historical price moves, trying to determine the range of possible returns that an investment will earn. This involves estimating an average return that is expected and then how far from that average a return might deviate. After all this, we calculate whether an investment is "worth the risk" to us as individual investors. Unfortunately, it is the details of these calculations that are the problem. To estimate risk, we assume several things—and once we start making assumptions, the problems start to grow.

How to Be Smart and Still Lose $550 Million in One Day!

In the 1990s, a group of highly intelligent people came together and started a hedge fund with the rather dull and conservative name of Long-Term Capital Management (LTCM). The group included noted Nobel scholars and well-respected veteran Wall Street players. The objective of the hedge fund was to take advantage of discrepancies in relative pricing of different investments. For example, if two investments such as Treasury bonds and corporate bonds generally had a 1% difference, or spread, in their yield (one yielding 5% and the other yielding 6%) but currently there existed a 2% spread (one yielding 5% and the other yielding 7%), this group would put bets on transactions that made money when the spread fell back toward 1%, or what was considered normal. Another way of thinking about this is that the company looked for situations in which the prices of investments in relation to one another seemed irrational based on historical price trends and then made investments that would profit when the markets returned to a rational state of pricing. This type of investing is called *arbitrage.* Of course, the risk involved was that the irrational pricing—in this case the wider-than-average spread—could go the other way and widen even more, creating a loss.

To assess the risk of their investments and their overall portfolio, this experienced, intelligent, and successful group of people used some of the same basic principles that most individual investors are encouraged to use today. They used tools such as expected returns, standard deviations, and correlation coefficients. Based on these metrics, their portfolio was rock solid. According to their own marketing, the risk of a 10% annual loss in their portfolio was about 1 in 1,000 years. The risk of a 50% loss was approximately 1 in 10,000,000,000,000,000,000,000,000,000,000,000,000 years, or several billion times the age of our universe! Other, more conservative estimates put the risk of a 50% annual loss a little higher, at 1 in 1 billion or even 1 in 1 trillion years.

Much to the shock of LTCM and its investors, that "once in a billion years" event happened after just five years. The problem was that the risk models of LTCM were based on poor assumptions—as mentioned above, these are the same assumptions that are used today by many in the investment industry and by individual investors. First, they assumed that the distribution of returns for investments or portfolios was normal (we will get more into this later); second, they assumed that an event that had not happened before had a zero chance of happening in the future. Essentially, they expected investments to behave in the future in the same way that they had behaved in the past, with no allowance for shocks or unexpected future events. In this case, the seemingly impossible event was the default by Russia on its bond payments. This shows a fundamental disconnect between the models and reality—Russia, which was facing continual financial crises in the 1990s, was certainly capable of defaulting or doing something unexpected, yet the LTCM models had no way to assess that possibility. That kind of risk is simply incalculable, as was the risk of investor panic spreading across the globe.

As it turns out, the investment risks of LTCM were not normal, and its situation in mid-1998 looked a lot different from the recent past. LTCM had vastly underestimated the volatility of its portfolio and, therefore, had incorrectly assessed the chance of loss or even catastrophic loss. On August 21, 1998, LTCM lost $550 million. It incurred a loss of approximately 80% from January through August 1998, something that its models said was next to impossible. That should not have happened—but it did. The firm's looming insolvency threatened the stability of the international financial system. The best and brightest minds in finance needed a bailout by a consortium of Wall Street banks, negotiated by Alan Greenspan of the Federal Reserve.

All of this might give the impression that LTCM was run by a bunch of reckless "cowboys" with terribly misguided investing practices. Nothing could be further from the truth. Even after their incredible paper losses, when the owners of the company had to sell 90% of their shares and agree to oversight in order to receive the bailout, the investments eventually did what the managers had expected, returning to more rational relative pricing. The problem, as John Maynard Keynes is credited with saying, is that "the market can stay irrational longer than you can stay solvent."

It is also worth noting that these events took place in the mid-1990s, ending in late 1998. This is a period that in retrospect seems somewhat calm. This was before the technology bubble, before the dot-com bust, before September 11, before Enron, and before oil soared to almost $150 per barrel. We have obviously recently seen another example of how poor assumptions about risk led to the development of collateralized debt obligations or mortgage-backed securities. It was assumed that packaging a lot of bad loans together would reduce the risk, and the history of home prices would have suggested an extremely low chance of a substantial and extended decline. But we did see a major decline in home prices and that created the subprime crisis, which will impact our economy for years to come as home prices decline much more.

The Problem with LTCM Is a Problem That We All Face

LTCM suffered from problems associated with how we estimate risk in the financial world. First, it assumed that investment returns and correlations between investments would act as they have in the past. In essence, it assumed that nothing new would occur and that no relationships would change. Second, its approach assumed that the returns furthest from their expectations (large losses and large gains) were the least likely to happen or had the lowest chance of actually happening. Third, its approach assumed that investment returns are independent of one another, that each day's gain or loss happens in a vacuum, and that there could not be carryover, in which one day's results would affect the next day.

These assumptions, which led to the implosion of the great financial all-star team at LTCM, are the same basic assumptions that most investors rely on today, even if they don't know it. These assumptions are built into asset allocation models and portfolio optimizer programs. Just as these assumptions created a ticking time bomb in the investment portfolio of that hedge fund, they can be the death of the portfolios of individual investors as well. This chapter will identify how risk typically has been described in the investment world and will then show (1) how that measure of risk is little help for investors and (2) how the assumptions underlying many people's view of investment risk are just plain wrong.

The Black Swan

Swans are white—or at least every swan you've ever *seen* is white. But does that mean that, because you've never seen one, a black swan doesn't exist? This may seen like a silly question, but as Nassim Nicholas Taleb relates in his book *The Black Swan,* the problem is central to our understanding of risk.

To continue the analogy, consider this thought: You can spend your entire life observing millions of white swans, but these observations will never *prove* the theory that only white swans exist. Yet it would take the sighting of only one black swan to *disprove* the theory.

So what do bird feathers have to do with portfolio risk? The answer is . . . everything.

The stock market is often considered to be a form of casino gambling in which one side wins and one side loses. This is certainly a fair critique. The problem is that the stock market is actually *worse* than a casino. A casino is a closed system in which you can precalculate the odds and for which the rules do not change halfway through your hand of, say, blackjack. Your chances of drawing an ace will not be 4/52 on one hand and 10/51 on the next. Betting limits do not arbitrarily change at the poker table, and the number of red or black spaces on the roulette wheel does not change every time you spin the wheel. In the real world of finance, all of these things *do* happen. The stock market is not a roll of the dice, unless you can find a pair of dice with the ability to change shape as well as numbers in the air after it leaves your hand.

Taleb refers to this as the problem of induction. In finance, we base our view of what is possible on what has already happened. Our estimates of returns and volatility are based on the past and then presented as if these "odds" are truly predictable, like the rolls of the dice. We know that the odds of rolling any one number on a die are 1/6. We don't know what the odds of hitting a certain return in the stock market are. The problem is that the tools used in the industry assume that we do know the odds, and this assumption is dangerous. It lures investors into a false sense of security . . . until a "black swan" like the 1987 crash or the dot-com bust or the subprime crisis of 2008 comes along and reminds us that the future can be much, much different from the recent past.

The Basis of Traditional Investment Advice: Normal Distributions and Risk

Everyday life is full of risk, and yet we go about our daily lives as if we don't have a care in the world. Well, almost. What we really do is try to assess those dangers we face and then lower the possibility of a negative outcome. In short, we try to mitigate our risk. The chance of having an auto accident in any given year is 1/12.5, and the chance of being killed in some kind of motor vehicle accident is 1/5,800. Those chances increase with conditions such as nighttime, bad weather, or the driver's impairment (drunken driving, etc.). In order to mitigate this risk, many different groups—auto manufacturers, the U.S. government, advocacy organizations such as MADD, etc.—all try to help us be safer when we drive by equipping cars with safety devices, setting legal limits and regulations, and increasing awareness of dangers. On the other hand, the chance of being hit by a meteor while driving is infinitesimally small, so we don't often worry about whether our car will withstand the impact of an interplanetary object. It is a risk that we dismiss because it has such a slim chance, or low probability, of occurring. This is an extreme example of risk assessment—determining what is more likely and should be guarded against versus what is less likely and therefore can be safely ignored.

Everyone Expects to Make Money

When we invest, we expect to have a positive return on our investment. If we invest in a one-year CD from the bank that yields 3%, we know exactly what we will get back. However, many investments, especially equity investments, experience a wide variety of returns, including substantial losses or extraordinary gains. Our payback for putting our capital at risk in the stock market is the possibility of larger returns than would be earned on a CD from a bank. With equities we usually estimate our expected return by taking an average of past returns, and then we develop a range of possible outcomes around that expected return. For example, if we are investing in a large-company stock index, we are most likely estimating an annual return of approximately 9% after inflation, because that is about the historical average of large-company stocks over the last 80 years as measured by SBBI. However, we also know that it is uncommon for the large-company stock index ever *actually* to earn 9% (only twice in the last 80 years has the large-company index been within 1% of this number).

We Want Things to Be Normal

Knowing that the chance of the large-company index earning the average of 9% is small, we try to figure out the likelihood of the return's being within a certain range around our expected 9%. The expected return in a normal distribution is the historical average of the returns (also known as the mean). Once we know what to expect (the mean), we have to estimate the possible range of returns around that mean. Mainstream investment analysis assumes that returns are distributed in what is called a normal pattern or bell curve, which is also known as a Gaussian distribution, after the famous mathematician who described this pattern. In a normal distribution, most observations occur around the average or expected return. The farther away from the average, the less likely something is to occur; those points farther away from the expected return are said to have a lower probability of happening. This is very important: in a normal distribution with an expected annual return of 9%, earning 15% is more likely than earning 16% (because 16% is farther away from 9%, the expected number) and earning 20% is less likely than earning 16%. Figure 7.1 shows a normal distribution for annual stock market returns. Any chart that shows a normal distribution is also called a bell chart because of its bell-shaped curve.

This pattern is a mathematical wonder and describes the observa-

Figure 7.1: The Normal Distribution

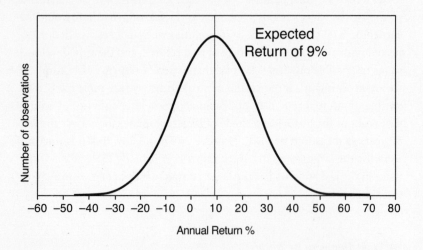

tions of many things in the world, such as the height of people in a country, the distribution of IQs among people, test scores earned by students in a class, or what happens in a game of dice. In fact, many of these risk tools originally were created to help gamblers determine the possibility of rolling certain numbers in dice games.

A normal distribution assumes that all of the data points are independent (like the idea that rolls of dice in a game are unrelated to one another) and that the observations are distributed identically. In other words, a bad year does not cause the next year to be good, and a good year does not cause the next year also to be good. Whatever happens in a given year (or day or month) is completely independent of what happened in the past or what will happen in the future.

Consider the examples of height and intelligence, or IQ. The fact that one person is tall does not cause another, unrelated person to be tall or short. The fact that a person is smart does not cause others to be smart or dumb. These attributes are independent.

In a normal distribution, you need only two pieces of information to determine the chance of any outcome. The two parameters are the mean, as described above, and the standard deviation. Without delving into mathematical minutiae, the standard deviation is a way to quantify how far a single observation is from the average or how far an observation de-

Figure 7.2a: The Normal Distribution, 68% of Occurrences

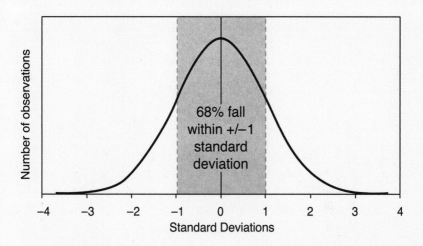

viates from the expectation. As you can see from the shape of the bell curve, most observations happen close to the mean, or within ±1 standard deviation (SD).

The numbers shake out like this:

- 68% of observations are within ±1 SD from the mean.
- 95% of observations are within ±2 SD from the mean.
- 99% of observations are within ±3 SD from the mean.

A bell curve with standard deviations is shown in Figures 7.2a through 7.2c.

Now apply this to the world of investing. For the large-cap index, using the period 1926 through 2004, the expected return is 9%, with a standard deviation of 19%.

Using this approach, we can give pretty good odds on what the market's return will be in any given year. Roughly 68% of the time, the market's return should fall in a range of –10% to 28% (the 9% average ±1 SD of 19%), and 95% of the time, the market's return in a year should fall within a range of –29% to 47% (±2 SD). Returns outside the range of –48% to 66% (±3 SD) are extreme and should happen less than 1% of the time—or less than once every hundred years!

A problem should immediately be apparent. If you want to be 99%

Figure 7.2b: The Normal Distribution, 95% of Occurrences

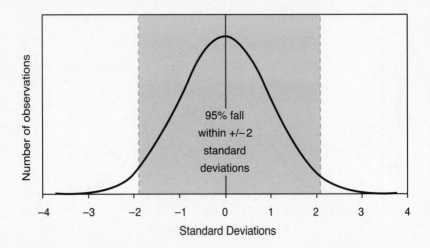

certain of what the return will be on your large-cap stock index in any given year, you have to be willing to accept a range that is more than 100 percentage points wide! Although this seems crazy, this is exactly the way that expected returns for stocks, bonds, and investment portfolios are developed. The reason the range is so wide is that the returns vary greatly from the expectation and the bell curve has to be drawn so that 68% of the returns are within ±1 SD. This leads to the data being almost useless; the expectation is 9%, but to be 99% sure of what you will get, you have to be willing to accept anywhere from –48% to 66%!

The problems don't end with an unacceptably wide range of possible annual returns; there is also the issue of "volatility clusters," which means that low-probability events seem to happen close to one another. Consider the string of positive returns during the tech boom of the late 1990s, followed by the grueling bear-market down years of 2000–2002. Were the positive years unrelated to one another? Is it just random luck that the market experienced several years in a row of high returns, or did the same underlying economic fundamentals of strong productivity, excitement over technology stocks, and the emergence of the Internet create a multiyear trend? Were the down years unrelated, or were they a string of months during which the markets had to wring out excess capacity and purge companies that had overstated their earnings as well as deal with

Figure 7.2c: The Normal Distribution, 99% of Occurrences

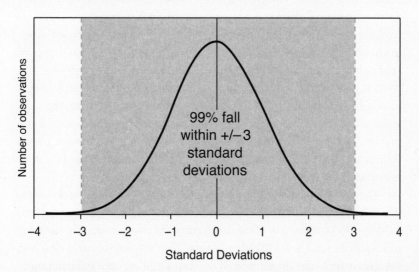

the new geopolitical realities that emerged? And what about market psychology? Did the strong boom years encourage investors to plow new money into the market, thus causing it to go even higher? And did investors' fear after the initial 2000 bust cause two more years of bear-market misery?

Feedback Loops—Both Positive and Negative

Normal distributions do occur and are valid when we are measuring such things as physical traits in gene pools or the sizes of stars in a galaxy. The distributions get less normal and more volatile when people or things interact in a network. Markets reflect the interactions of millions of people who imitate one another, learn from one another, and react to one another—as do the evolution of rumors, political elections and polls, the adoption of products and new technology, fashions and fads, and businesses competing in a marketplace. This brings us back to the five-curve principle in Chapter 2.

So, unlike height, IQ, and the rolling of dice, human interaction and market psychology clearly lead to a lack of independence when it comes to financial markets. At times it appears that the financial news is overwhelmingly positive and that securities seem to be moving up in price without stopping. During the late 1990s, although there were setbacks, it felt as if everyone was getting rich in technology stocks. The power of reinforcement to those who were making money, as well as the power of suggestion to those who were not invested in technology stocks, was tremendous. This dynamic created a positive feedback loop that strongly affected investors who otherwise would not have thought of buying such stocks. The more that stocks went up, the more investors entered the market, causing stocks to go up further—until that trend went to extremes and was simply unsustainable and there were no more investors available to buy.

The same is true on the negative side. The lower down stocks went, the more people panicked—until there was no one left to panic and sell. After the dot-com bust of 2000–2002, many investors stopped buying equities altogether. The financial press was full of stories of people who had lost everything. The negative feedback cast a pall over the financial markets in general and technology stocks in particular that has lasted for many years. This psychology arguably continued to influence investors as late as 2008, with stocks by many measures at that time undervalued versus bonds by 30% to 50%.

Why do market bubbles and crashes often go to such extremes? Because markets are made up of individual decision makers who are influenced by many different sources, reacting to events in their own lives as well as events in the world around them. These reactions can, from time to time, lead to irrational decisions, which are not accounted for in economic models or mathematical formulas. Economists assume that people are rational, and this is just not the case. Most people are rational at least some of the time, some more than others. Our irrational decisions occur when we make quick, intuitive decisions that are based on what other people like us are doing instead of on a deliberate, well-constructed plan that takes into account the likelihood of different events. We are the most social of any species and have a unique ability to perceive and imitate the actions of others. The more people see others like them buying or selling stocks (or buying an iPhone or wearing a new fashion), the more they feel that it must be the right thing to do, even if the cost of doing so is getting ridiculously low or high.

Figure 7.3: Consumer Adoption S-Curve

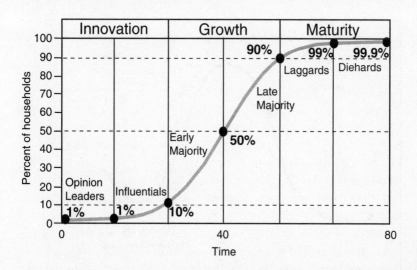

People imitate others in a progressive way—from opinion leaders to influentials to early adopters to early majority to late majority to laggards to diehards—until everyone has followed a trend, as we show in Figure 7.3. This is the principle of the S-curve, which is one of our most fundamental forecasting tools for the development of products, markets, and innovations. The trend of "following" appears to occur in financial markets as different levels of participants, from sophisticated traders to institutional managers to everyday investors, move progressively into a bull market, pushing prices ever higher, until there is no one left to enter. Investors tend to exit on the downside in the same progression, from more to less sophisticated. This is how positive and negative feedback cycles are created in financial markets. People join in when people just like them or just above them get in on the trend.

We Like Things to Be in Straight Lines

Another human bias that occurs in these feedback loops is the tendency of people to forecast in straight lines. If things have been going well for a while, people tend to forecast that things will continue to do well. If

Figure 7.4: The Human Forecasting Model

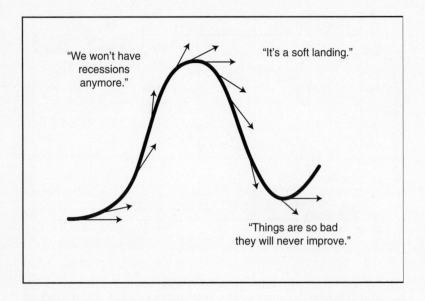

things have been difficult, then people tend to see difficult times ahead. This "Human Forecasting Model" (Figure 7.4) often can lead us to make poor decisions, because it ignores the natural ebb and flow of events. The markets move exponentially, not linearly, until they reach limits, and the markets move in cycles, up and down. There are few if any straight lines in the real world.

Notice that as a situation improves, people tend to infer that the situation will continue to get better, and vice versa. This linear thinking prevents people from seeing "around the corner." This leads them to see things as only getting better just as the situation is about to turn downward and also leads them to forecast difficult times just before things improve. In the investing world, this describes the misfortune of buying high and selling low. If a stock continues to move higher, the expectation is that it will only go up. The longer a stock goes up, the less risk people perceive. If a stock does nothing but sink lower, the expectation is that it will continue to fall, and the perception is that more risk is involved. This straight-line thinking creates a huge misperception of risk! As more people buy on the way up or sell on the way down, it reinforces the positive or negative sentiment, drawing even more investors into the fold and creating the herd mentality.

George Soros, the legendary speculator, takes the idea of dependence even further. Over his career as hedge fund manager, Soros observed what he called "reflexivity" in the markets. Changes in fundamentals, such as an unexpected boost in earnings, can drive stock prices higher. This is standard investment theory, but Soros has a new twist. Not only can fundamentals drive prices, but prices themselves can drive fundamentals. When a company's stock price rises, it finds itself with more investment capital that can be used for expansion or acquisitions. This, in turn, increases earnings and causes speculators to drive the stock price even higher. This virtuous cycle continues until it becomes unsustainable and collapses under its own weight, whereby a vicious cycle starts in the opposite direction: lower fundamentals beget a lower stock price, which further begets even lower fundamentals . . . We should reiterate that these are not the words of an idle academic. George Soros is one of the most successful speculators in the history of the financial markets, and he used this insight to make billions of dollars in profits.

This type of situation describes anything but "independent moves."

The Chaos of Change and Transitions: Where Did All the Pay Phones Go?

In addition to *dependent moves* in markets, strong volatility, both positive and negative, seems to come in waves or batches, which are diametrically opposed to what the normal distribution tells you *should* happen. However, normal distributions cannot take into account the changing environment of the business world and entire industries. As new technologies come to market, the financial system has to go through the process of evaluating what the new technologies mean in terms of opportunities as well as threats. Are there great productivity gains ahead? Are any businesses going to be marginalized? Who wins? Who loses? These are just some of the questions that are asked when something new is developed or introduced.

Just a decade ago, there seemed to be a pay phone on every corner. The spread of cell phones has decimated that business. Now, not only does Clark Kent not have a place to change into Superman, but if your cell phone dies, it is difficult to find a pay phone to use. The same is true of pagers—the cell phone phenomenon has all but killed the pager industry. How long did it take for the metamorphosis to occur? Did it happen neatly over a calendar year, or did it take several years? Which companies won? Which ones lost? When this sort of chaos surrounds an industry or market, the chance of increased volatility, both positive and negative, is much greater. We can see when such large changes are more likely by reviewing the S-curves of technological development and acceptance rates, which give us insight into when this type of volatility (positive and negative) might occur. Volatility increases during "phase transitions," when we are going from one technology to the next, one market to the next, one fashion to the next, one generation to the next, and so on.

The Record Is Worse on a Daily Basis

As if the problems with annual returns were not enough, the idea of normally distributed returns falls apart at shorter intervals. At the daily level, the approach fails completely, as we saw with the example of LTCM above.

Recall that for these statistical tools to work in the financial world, three things must be true:

1. Returns must be normally distributed (a smooth line can be drawn from the expected number to the farthest observation).
2. Returns must be independent of one another (one return does not influence another).
3. Volatility must be constant over time (the market doesn't go through periods that are more turbulent than others).

When it comes to investing in the short term, none of these necessary conditions is met! Not only are returns not normally distributed, but they are also absolutely dependent on prior returns, and anyone familiar with the markets knows that they can go through days, weeks, or even months of extreme turbulence followed by long stretches of relative calm.

What this means for investors is that (1) days with very high returns and very low returns happen more often than we are led to believe and (2) down and up days in the financial markets tend to be clustered together rather than occurring at random intervals. All of this adds up to a greater risk level than many investors are prepared for.

Figure 7.5 plots the daily returns of the Dow Jones Industrial Averages in 1998, the year of the LTCM implosion. The chart should quickly dispel any belief in the three criteria above. The volatility clearly is *not* constant, as it appears to explode in late August through November. Furthermore, extreme down days are followed relatively quickly by extreme up days, the former seeming to cause the latter. Clearly, they do not move independently. As noted mathematician Benoit Mandelbrot says, "markets have memories," and these memories create patterns that are far from random.

Figure 7.6 plots daily returns from October 1928 to the present. For most of the history of the U.S. stock market, daily volatility has been relatively small and uniform, less than ±2% per day, with a few larger-than-usual moves, as a normal distribution would predict. However, the late

Figure 7.5: Daily Price Changes—Dow, 1998

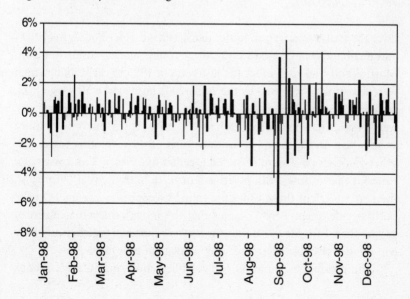

Figure 7.6: Daily Price Changes—Dow, 1928 to Present

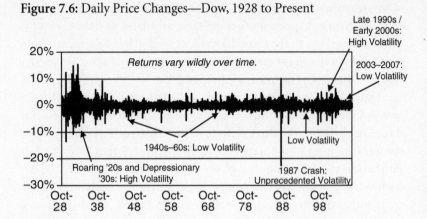

1920s and the 1930s tell a different story. Returns were all over the place in those years, routinely rising or falling more than 10% in a day several times. The late 1990s and early 2000s were more volatile as well, although they were less so than the 1920s and 1930s. One data point truly stands out: *October 19, 1987, the day the Dow fell 23%.*

Volatility Clustering

Over the past 80 years, our equity markets have experienced great runs and terrible crashes. Interestingly, these trends tend to occur in series. Most recently, we remember the fast years of 1995 to early 2000, which were disastrously followed by the 2000–2002 bear market. If we go back through the annual returns of the Ibbotson Large Company Index, there were 24 years in which the index had a negative return, but only 11 times was the year on either side of the down year positive. In other words, the other 13 down years were clustered together in series of 2 or 3 years at a time. Of the 11 times with positive returns in both the year before and the year after, 5 of those times the returns were below average. On the positive side, there were 17 times that the index achieved a return of greater than 20%. Eleven of these times were clustered together, and only 6 of these times were surrounded by smaller gains or losses.

One possible explanation for volatility clustering in investments, which is the same as saying that returns are dependent on one another, is the notion that there are underlying causes for investment returns that can take more than one period (in this case a year) to be fully realized. On inspection, this appears to be the case. In the early 1930s (negative effects), it was the full effects of the monetary policy, tariffs, and overbought equity markets. In the 1950s, it was the full effects of the GIs coming home and taking advantage of the GI Bill. In the 1970s, it was the full impact of the oil shocks and inflation. In the 1990s, it was the incredible productivity gains from the implementation of the Information Age, and then in the 2000s, it was the impact of the war on terrorism with the hangover effect of the excess capacity. In each of these instances, long-term economic drivers took time to be worked through and that affected the markets and returns.

For individual investors, the issue with volatility clustering is a double-edged sword. The investor could experience investment returns far in excess of expectations in back-to-back years or in a series of years or just as easily could have to deal with several years of losses in a row. Mostly, volatility clustering means periods of relative calm followed by market returns that are well away from any expectation in a financial plan. This is how many describe police work: hours of sheer boredom interrupted by moments of wild excitement! The good news is that by understanding cycles in our economy, such as generational spending, technology life cycles (S-curves), and repetitive cycles like the 4-year and decennial cycles, investors can anticipate when the periods of highest volatility might occur.

To illustrate how truly abnormal the stock market is, we plot the returns from Figure 7.6 on the normal distribution to see where they fall in Figure 7.7.

As you can see, Figure 7.7 is full of observations at the extremes of the bell curve, or the "tails." To fit them all on the graph, the bell curve has to be squeezed into a wedge! This type of chart is referred to as a "normal distribution with 'fat tails,'" and it means that the farthest reaches on both the positive and the negative sides are bigger than they should be. The model shows more returns than expected that are either very positive or very negative and that the model cannot explain. The curve is drawn differently, but there is no investment model that allows you to estimate your risk differently.

Figure 7.7: Stock Returns, Normal Distribution Assumed

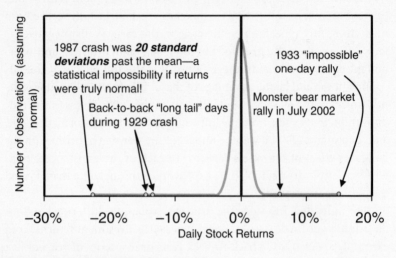

Fat Tails and Higher-Than-Expected Peaks

As we have established, stock returns are not normally distributed. The technical term for their distribution is *leptokurtic*. This means that the mean is more common than you would expect, but also that extreme events (fat tails) are far more common than you would expect. So the "true" distribution of stock returns has a much more sharply pointed peak and much wider tails as well as a skinnier middle than the normal bell curve.

Figure 7.8 illustrates the difference between a normal distribution (in black) and a leptokurtic distribution (in gray). Leptokurtic distributions can vary in terms of the fatness of the tails and the pointedness of the peak. For example, the actual distribution of historical stock returns is a little less exaggerated than Figure 7.8 would suggest. Our intent was to make it clear that the curves are not the same shape; therefore it is *not* sensible to assume that they are in calculating risk.

This is just the beginning, however. Not only is the variation around the mean much wider and wilder than current tools assume, but the mean also is shifting constantly! Depending on what time frame is used, the average return on the stock market will be vastly different. To give a case in point, imagine calculating returns for the period of, say, 1930 to

Figure 7.8: Reality Versus Normal

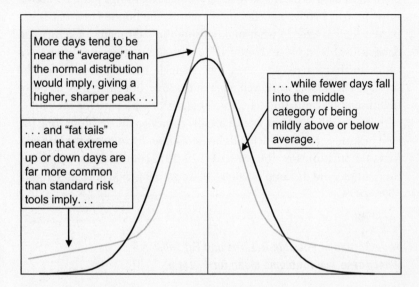

More days tend to be near the "average" than the normal distribution would imply, giving a higher, sharper peak . . .

. . . while fewer days fall into the middle category of being mildly above or below average.

. . . and "fat tails" mean that extreme up or down days are far more common than standard risk tools imply. . .

1999. Now imagine that you take the average for the 1930 to 2002 period, too. Which do you think will be higher? One period includes one of the worst bear markets in history—the Nasdaq bust—and the other does not! This is a problem known as "nonstationarity." In order for statistical tools based on the bell curve to make sense, the returns and standard deviations have to be stationary. In other words, they cannot vary over time. Of course, we know that these conditions do not hold! The mean and standard deviation are in a perpetual state of change. Bottom line: Take all estimates of financial returns and risks with a grain of salt.

If investment returns do follow a normal distribution pattern, then the 1987 crash never should have happened—literally not once in over 1 billion years. The problem is that the stock market is full of "once every billion years" days, even though we have only about 80 to 100 years' worth of reliable data. So what does that actually mean? Suffice it to say, the returns of the stock market are not normally distributed. This means that mainstream investment tools are flawed. What is the typical answer from CNBC commentators when a tremendous downdraft hits the market? "We didn't expect that" or "We never anticipated three down years in a row" or some other response that clearly shows an inability to quantify the risk of the markets ahead of time. The normal distribution does explain most days in the marketplace. As noted regarding Figure 7.7 above, most returns behave and fall nicely within the bounds of what is expected. This is exactly what makes using these estimates of returns so dangerous. Investors get comfortable with the markets until there is a shock to the system, and then they struggle to assign blame for the mishap. These tools work well most of the time, but when they fail, they fail miserably. Unfortunately, it is the investor who pays for the failure with lost wealth. This lost wealth usually comes on the heels of a long period of steady growth, which lulls investors into discounting the possibilities of dramatic losses: the crash of 1929–1932 coming after 1925–1929, for example, and the drop of 2000–2002 occurring right after the gains of 1996–1999.

Wide Spread of Possible Returns and Fat Tails: What These Two Problems Mean for Investors

Obviously, there is no value in purchasing an investment with an expectation of returns that ranges from –48% to 66%. This is gambling, not investing, and this is most likely not what people think they are buying when they turn over their life savings to a financial advisor. What they think they are buying is a relatively stable investment (after all, it *is* a U.S. large-company stock index, the "best of the best" blue chips) that will return them approximately 9% adjusted for inflation. Why? Because that is what the financial software tells them. If a financial planner said, "I am almost certain that your allocation to a large-company stock index could return anywhere from a loss of almost 50% to a gain of over 65%, but most likely it will be around 9%," most of us would think he was crazy. We would not base our financial future, our children's college funding, or any other major decision on such a wide spread. And yet this is exactly what we do.

Most financial plans have a constant rate of return that has to be agreed on by the financial planner and the client so that the software can develop how a portfolio might grow. What rate do you use? Whatever rate it turns out to be, it has a tremendous impact on the illustration in the financial plan. If you invest $100,000 and you assume that you will

Figure 7.9a: Stock Returns, 1966–1970

		$100,000
1966	−13.52%	86,485
1967	11.42%	96,365
1968	11.19%	107,152
1969	−12.93%	93,293
1970	6.89%	99,719

Figure 7.9b: Stock Returns, 1976–1980

		$100,000
1976	5.76%	105,760
1977	−8.07%	97,223
1978	4.49%	101,593
1979	1.19%	102,804
1980	12.63%	115,791

Figure 7.9c: Stock Returns, 1986–1990

		$100,000
1986	16.99%	116,990
1987	−10.61%	104,577
1988	7.56%	112,487
1989	17.76%	132,468
1990	−1.17%	130,914

Figure 7.9d: Stock Returns, 1996–2000

		$100,000
1996	15.83%	115,830
1997	23.85%	143,459
1998	25.39%	179,876
1999	13.42%	204,023
2000	6.89%	189,320

earn 9% per year, then at the end of one year you will have $109,000. At the end of five years you expect to have roughly $153,860. However, this is just theoretical. The reality could be vastly different. Consider the table of returns and growth of an investment of $100,000 in Figures 7.9a through 7.9d on page 265, based on inflation-adjusted total returns for the S&P 500.

Note that if you had invested $100,000 at the beginning of each five-year period, in only one of them would you have made $153,860 or more, and if you had chosen to start your investing in 1966, you would not even have retained the original $100,000! In short, the wide spread of possible returns renders most financial plans useless.

In addition to dealing with returns that are far from the average, investors have to deal with the fact that their returns are not just a simple calculation of average; instead, their returns are geometrically linked. This means that the return of one year has an impact on how the returns of future years affect wealth. As a simple example, think of starting with $100,000 and earning −30% in the first year and +40% in the second year. The average return is 5% per year (−30% + 40% = 10%, and 10% ÷ 2 = 5%), but the return earned on the investment is actually −1% per year ($100,000 − 30% = $70,000, then $70,000 + 40% = $98,000). So although academics discuss average returns as if these large losses and gains are nothing more than numbers on a page, investors have to live with the outcomes and how these returns can sometimes devastate a portfolio.

Fat Tails: The Returns Least Expected Happen
More Frequently than Anticipated

If you expect 9% from an investment and you receive 40%, then life is pretty good. You can think more seriously about buying that new car, retiring a bit early, or even slowing down your savings because you have the odd problem of having "saved too much." But what of the opposite: If you expect 9% and receive −30%, then what? Do you scale back your retirement plans? Sock away more money? Or just work longer? This is the problem with the fat tails in the distribution of investment returns. Because the expected return means so little and the occurrence of very high returns and substantial losses is so prevalent, the ability of individual investors to create an intelligent plan that extends five, ten, or twenty years into the future based on the vagaries of equity markets is almost nonexistent. Without some reasonable estimate of what an investment will mean to our portfolios, there is no way to create a reliable plan. The variables are too great, especially on the downside.

Not many people complain about making too much money. While saving too much can impact your current standard of living, it is not what we would think of as a problem. The other end of the spectrum, saving too little, is all too common. When it comes to retirement, most of us are trying to figure out how to plan for the unknowable, which is how long we will live and how much it will cost. Once we have rough estimates of these two things, which are hard enough to calculate, then comes the second daunting task: determining how much to save. Simply put, the amount we need to save is based on how much we think we will need, how many years we can invest, and how much we think we will earn on our investment. It takes a lot of homework to make several of these estimates, but the last one, how much we will earn, is anybody's guess. Not only do extreme returns occur more frequently than we think, but they have long-lasting implications.

The problem with suffering an unanticipated loss (who expects a loss when the average is a gain of 9%?) is that you then have to make up not only the loss, but also the profit that you expected to earn that year but didn't. You have to get back on track with your financial plan. In our example above, we showed how an investment of $100,000 would have fared in several periods. Look at 1966. In that year the expectation was to earn 9%, so $100,000 would have grown to $109,000. Instead, there was a loss of 13.5%, so the balance after one year was $86,484. Not only do we have to make up the loss of $13,500, but we also have to make up for the $9,000 we had anticipated earning that year. Our true loss is the combination of the two, or $22,500. Now we stand at $86,484, and to get to what should be our end of year 2 balance (the original $100,000 earning 9% in year 1 and then 9% again in year 2, for a total of $118,810), we would have to earn over 37%! This is another way of looking at the impact of geometrically linked returns. It is at this point that we as intelligent investors start recalculating our entire financial plans. Do we work two more years? Do we scale back our standard of living? Or do we rely on the market "averages" to pull us through, and just blindly go into the next investing year hoping that it all evens out at the end? Who would base his or her financial future on such an approach?

The Unknown Unknowns

There are known knowns. These are things we know that we know. There are known unknowns. That is to say, there are things that we know we don't know. But there are also unknown unknowns. There are things we don't know we don't know.

—Donald Rumsfeld, former U.S. secretary of defense

Rumsfeld's words are difficult to follow, to say the least, but his point is true. We plan for things that we know will occur, "known knowns," such as encountering a curve in the road while driving. Things that we know are possible but do not know when or if they will occur, such as having a traffic accident, are called "known unknowns." If you knew ahead of time that you would have a car wreck costing who knows how much money in repair bills, you would simply avoid driving that day. Naturally, we don't know, and this is why we buy insurance. The possibility of an accident can be prepared for, although the event might not occur.

It is the things in the final category, "unknown unknowns," that make life complicated. These are possibilities that we do not know about at all; we can't even imagine what they are, and therefore we cannot plan for them.

The September 11 attacks were an example of an unknown unknown, in that no one except fiction writers had ever thought that terrorists would be able to use a hijacked plane, much less more than one, as a missile to take down a building. Now that it has happened, it's a known unknown. This is probably the most famous unknown unknown in recent history, but the financial world is full of them. The markets are always finding new ways to take investors by surprise, on both the downside and the upside. This takes us all the way back to the story of LTCM at the beginning of this report, where a group of exceptionally smart, experienced investors ran straight into an unknown unknown— that a country of the economic size and power of Russia could default on its bonds—and this caused their portfolio to unravel.

What to Do Next

By now you should have a sense of the increased risk that is associated with investing in the capital markets, which is far greater than is typically discussed by the financial press and even by many financial professionals. From the higher frequency of large gains and large losses to the existence of unknown unknowns, investing can be treacherous business. So what can investors do to limit their exposure to such events? Stop investing? Stay in only those investments, such as CDs, that offer little volatility but also very small returns? If an investor can afford to take almost no risk and earn a correspondingly small return, then great. But many investors, in order to reach their financial goals, need to have the potential of higher returns that are associated with stocks. For these investors, the answer is to approach investing in the same way that you approach other areas of life.

First of all, it's important to focus on the known knowns. This is what HS Dent has attempted to do with our demographics-based models for understanding how our economy changes over time. Demographic trends affect inflation, earning and spending, saving and borrowing, productivity and innovation, home buying and real estate, and many other things. We also adopt new technologies in a predictable S-curve progression, and that makes technology bubbles more predictable.

We may not know with certainty what the exact growth rate of real GDP will be in any given quarter, but we can forecast the general direction and magnitude of major economic moves by tracking highly predictable demographic and consumer spending trends. Will we correctly call every bend and twist in the economy and markets? Of course not, but simply identifying the underlying long-term trends vastly improves our ability to assess the odds of achieving financial goals. Our approach does not eliminate risk, but it certainly allows for a better management of risk than naïve standard financial tools. It is what enables us to turn some of those unknown unknowns into known unknowns or better yet, known knowns in some cases.

There are also numerous ways to protect further against risks, both known and unknown. Most of us carry insurance on our car, on our house, and even on our lives and our health. Why? Beyond the fact that some of it is required by law, it also protects us in case we have a catastrophic loss. We carry insurance not because we expect large, expensive problems, but because we understand that they do happen and we want to avoid the risk of loss. Unfortunately, when it comes to our investment portfolios, most of us rely on the vague notion that "the market always goes up over time" as the only backstop against loss. However, there is a much better approach—it's called hedging.

Correctly hedging one's portfolio is a topic worthy of its own full-length report, since it can be very complicated. Many of the strategies that large institutions use to hedge their portfolios—such as futures strategies—are not efficient for individual investors. Some investors hedge by holding a position in a bear fund, which benefits when the market declines. Over the last ten years, many insurance companies have developed variable annuities that have available different types of guarantees to guard against the risk of huge losses or offer minimum increases in value no matter what happens in the marketplace. All of these approaches have a cost related to them, which must be weighed in light of the benefit being offered. The key insight is not to accept the proposition that investors cannot, or should not, take steps to guard against losses. As an investor, it is your money, your future, and your responsibility to protect yourself in the best way possible.

The most important issue is that we are now very likely to be entering the next strong and extreme period, in which risks cluster to the downside. That means that traditional asset allocation models are going to fail miserably. You need a different strategy for the most risky stage of the New Economy Cycle: the Next Great Depression!

In Chapter 8 we will look at how the four seasons of our 80-year New Economy Cycle affect risks and returns and the sectors of investment that do best. You don't just need a diversified portfolio, you need one for each season—and the season is about to change.

CHAPTER 8

Investment, Business, and Life Strategies for the Great Winter

How to Profit in a Deflationary Economy

Radically Different Strategies for the Most Difficult Season Ahead

FOUR IMPORTANT ISSUES are covered in this chapter, as we enter this once-in-a-lifetime era of deflation and the bursting of a major bubble boom:

1. During the winter or Shakeout Season from roughly 2008 to 2023, all traditional asset classes will deflate to larger or lesser degrees, causing most asset allocation models to fail miserably, as we started to address in Chapter 7. The clustering of risks to the downside hits more in this season than any other, as deflation of the various asset bubbles follows the bubble boom in the Growth Boom Season. Hence commodities, real estate, and stocks all will fall in the years ahead, with their worst declines in the first half of the coming decade. The only safe havens at first will be cash equivalents and high-quality bonds—even gold will deflate more than advance, likely after early 2010, despite its crisis hedge qualities in the past. The tops in these major investment areas and most businesses between late 2007 and mid- to late 2009 typically will not be exceeded again for two decades

or more. This is a long-term downturn, much like the past inflationary Innovation Season from 1969 to 1982 and 1930–1942, but with greater declines in more investment categories.

2. As we addressed in Chapter 4, these depression or winter seasons follow a three-stage progression, with the deepest deflation and bank and business failures occurring in the first deflation crisis stage, when the bubble boom finally busts, creating a shock wave that overwhelms the economic and financial system, especially given the extreme debt and leverage created in this bubble boom. This stage typically lasts 3 to 5 years (for example, 1930–1933, 1990–1992 in Japan, and 2008–2010 or 2008–2012 or 2010–2012 or 2010–2014 in this cycle). In the second stage, the economy and many investment sectors rebound, under strong government stimulus and with extreme oversold conditions, from the first major crash. The markets typically have a 3- to 5-year bear market rally in this second stage (for example, 1932–1937 in the United States, 1992–1996 in Japan, and likely mid-2012 to mid-2017 in the current U.S. cycle), and most economists and politicians will claim that the downturn is over. A final recession, which is often less extreme, sets in due to continued weak demographic and technology trends. This stage typically lasts 3 to 5 years (for example, 1937–1942 in the United States, 1997–2003 in Japan, and 2017–2020 or 2022 in the current U.S. cycle). Then the economy and stock market will be set for the next broad demographic boom—although most investment sectors tend to reach their ultimate bottoms in the first crash.

3. Just as we have seen, and will see, bubble after bubble in different stock, real estate, and commodity sectors until the broader bubble boom comes to an end between late 2009 and mid-2010, we will see a succession of spikes in bond yields as the crisis worsens in different areas, from T-bills to long-term Treasury bonds to corporate bonds and municipal bonds. We will also see buying opportunities at key cycle points such as late 2010 (minor or major), mid- to late 2012

(major), late 2014 (minor or major), late 2018 (minor), late 2019 to early 2020 (minor or major), and finally late 2022 (major) for reinvesting selectively in the best demographically favored stock and real estate sectors. The most powerful long-term buying opportunities for stocks are likely to come in mid- to late 2012 and mid- to late 2022. A broad-based commodity boom is not likely to reemerge until the early 2020s, although there will likely be a resurgence there as well in the second stage, between mid-2012 or late 2014 and mid-2017. Housing is more likely to bottom between late 2012 and early 2015 at the latest and then head back upward more steadily due to echo-boom generational buying patterns.

4. Your own life cycle will prompt you to make decisions in different areas of your investments and life as you age, as your business progresses, and as your children age. But the economy's present 80-year New Economy Cycle will tend to have a bigger impact on your risks and potential returns than your own life cycle will. The ultimate approach to financial planning requires combining your life cycle with the economy's broader life cycle. Given that this winter season has the greatest impact on investments, businesses, jobs, and major costs such as housing and health care, it is especially important to make changes ahead of and during key stages of this season. Coming after the expansive bubble boom, this season brings the reality of survival of the fittest: "What doesn't kill you makes you stronger." You must be prepared in advance to survive this most difficult season, like a squirrel storing nuts for winter—and there will be the greatest rewards for those who do prepare during this once-in-a-lifetime "great sale" in financial assets!

The Four Seasons of Our Economy: The 80-Year New Economy Cycle

In Figure 8.1 we repeat the New Economy Cycle from Figure 2.16 in Chapter 2. This represents the most important financial planning cycle

Figure 8.1: 80-Year New Economy Cycle

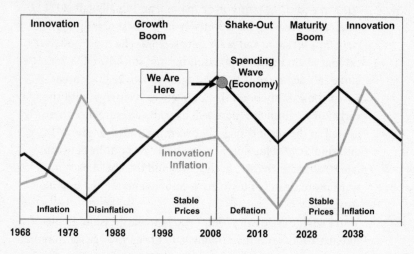

for your life, your investments, and your business. You don't have to catch all of the corrections and crises along the way in each major boom and bust to progress in your quality of life and your standard of living, but missing the changes in these seasons can be devastating. The entire gains of the Roaring Twenties boom and more were wiped out in just three years! One of the key points we make throughout this book and our research is that these seasons of the economy are largely predictable. Thousands of years ago, we learned how to chart and predict the annual weather seasons with great implications for agricultural planning and advances in our standard of living. Even before that we learned to track migration cycles for animals and to make clothes and store food in preparation for winter when we were in the hunting and gathering stage.

The most remarkable insight in modern times of unprecedented scientific advances and expanded predictability in most arenas is that economists, politicians, businesses, and investors still don't see clear seasons and cycles in our economy, stocks, bonds, real estate, and commodities— even though they follow similar longer-term seasons with regularity. The reason is that economists aren't scientists and haven't learned yet how to track what really matters long term in our economy. They focus on symptoms, not causes. They spend too much time analyzing government policies that end up being largely reactions to the very cycles that they fail to notice. The other reason is that such cycles are much longer term than our annual seasonal cycles in weather, and this makes them less obvious in most of our planning horizons. The most important economic cycles last 30 to 60 years or 40 to 80 years, and there are larger cycles that are just as predictable and that last much longer: 500 years (mega innovations); 5,000 years (cultural: towns to city-states to global); 100,000 years (climate swings and ice ages); and so on.

During the past century we saw major tops in our economy and stock markets about every 40 years: 1929, 1968, and recently in late 2007. Every 29 to 30 years, commodities have topped, as occurred in 1920, 1951, and 1980, and again in mid-2008. In our lifetime, the New Economy Cycle has developed over about 80 years in four distinct seasons, but before the early to mid-1900s it occurred about every 58 to 60 years. Rising middle-class populations from the Industrial Revolution stretched the old New Economy Cycle from the Kondratieff Wave (which simply comprised two 29- to 30-year Commodity Cycles) to the 80-year generation-based New Economy Cycle of today (with two 40-year generation boom and bust cycles) and we are likely to return to the 58- to 60-year cycle in the future as generational cycles recede in importance with falling birthrates around the world. For more on this topic go to www.hsdent.com to "Free Downloads" to "The Long Wave." However, we don't want to get too complicated here and confuse the key issues, which are more critical to your decisions now and over the next decade.

Different Strategies for Different Seasons

In our past books and especially in *The Next Great Bubble Boom* (Free Press, 2004), we discussed in greater detail how much risks and returns vary and whether different long-term asset classes and sectors, such as large-cap stocks, small-cap stocks, bonds, and international stocks, are favored during each season. We will not repeat that discussion here, as it is fully available in Chapter 7 of that book. If we simply go to Figure 8.1, we can understand the most important changes in trends that will impact our investment, business, and personal life/family strategies. We will start first with financial investment strategies.

The **Innovation Season** sees rising and ultimately peak inflation rates and radical new technologies and products, which first move into niche markets but ultimately will create prosperity and rising standards of living over the rest of the broader New Economy Cycle as these technologies and products move more mainstream. This season also sees rising inflation, because productivity trends are at their lowest point as a result of older long-term technologies and industries running out of steam and newer ones affecting only smaller niche markets. The old economy also is at its peak in demand for resources from the full mainstream saturation of the old-growth industries; hence commodities are inflated as well. Around 1980, we also saw the peak in the last 29- to 30-year Commodity Cycle. However, the largest inflationary trend in the 1970s was the peak entry of the largest generation in history into the workforce, which came at a great expense and with low productivity—and which just happened to coincide with the peak Commodity Cycle in 1980.

During the Innovation Season, large-cap stocks and long-term bonds are disfavored for thirteen to fourteen years, whereas small-cap stocks (innovations), commodities, and investments in third-world countries (due to the commodity boom) are favored. Real estate and short-term T-bills and bonds are favored by rising inflation as well (real estate correlates most closely with inflation and is in effect a leveraged hedge against inflation). Also, there are always some developed countries or regions of the world that are more favored by demographic cycles, as when Japan soared in the 1970s while North America and Europe slowed.

A diversified portfolio in small-cap stocks, real estate, commodities, Japan, emerging countries, and short-term fixed income would have given handsome returns in the otherwise low-return, high-risk Innovation Season from late 1968 to late 1982.

In the **Growth Boom Season** that follows the Innovation Season, the new, innovative generation grows up and earns and spends more money while adopting the new technologies into the mainstream. This creates the strongest boom in the economy with falling inflation rates—the best of all worlds. Ultimately, such trends create bubbles in stocks and other sectors of the economy due to high growth, high productivity and earnings, and low interest rates. During the Growth Boom Season that the United States has just been experiencing, starting in 1983 and continuing into 2009, large-cap stocks have been strongly favored, with small-cap stocks lagging but still doing well, due to the broad-based boom. Just ahead we will look at how small-cap stocks follow more of a 22- to 23-year lag on the Birth Index. Long-term bonds did great from 1980 to 1986, when inflation rates fell the most, and then continued to do well into mid-2003, with continued falling inflation and interest rates. During the final stage of this boom, long-term bonds have been up and down but have underperformed and should continue to underperform to an even greater degree from late 2008 into late 2009 as inflationary pressures return with the short-lived economic recovery and as commodities are likely to soar to their greatest heights for decades to come.

Real estate did well from 1983 to 1989, corrected a bit or flattened into the early to mid-1990s after the starter home boom cycle for the baby boomers, and then bubbled to extremes between 2000 and 2006 with the trade-up boom, extremely low interest rates, and the most liberal lending standards in history. Japan lagged horribly for most of the boom (until early 2005), and then the emerging markets, including China, India, Brazil, and Russia, experienced the greatest bubbles from 2001–2002 through late 2007. Commodities greatly underperformed until 1998 and have become the other great bubble since 2003. In our past books, we showed how focusing throughout this boom in large-cap stocks in the best demographic sectors—technology, Asia, financials, and health care—provided higher returns with S&P 500–like risks (Chapter 7, *The Next Great Bubble Boom*).

A diversified portfolio that included large-cap stocks, international and especially Asia (ex-Japan), real estate, and long-term bonds would have been a great strategy from 1983 to 2000, with a shift toward emerging markets, commodities, and short-term fixed income over the past decade to capture those changing cycles.

Now we move into the **Shakeout Season,** during which deflation and depression set in to puncture the enormous asset bubbles in the Growth Boom Season. The businesses in the new growth sectors that did not go under in the 2000–2002 crash will go under at this point, leaving only the fittest to survive long term and creating the next Fortune 500 leaders for decades to come. The asset sectors that did the best in the bubble boom generally crash and then underperform for most of this 13- to 14-year winter season. So changing long-term investment strategies is crucial at this transition. Long-term highs will be put in for most investment sectors between 2000 and 2009, as we described in Chapters 1 and 2: technology stocks during the bubble that peaked in early 2000, home prices between mid-2005 and late 2006, and financial stocks in mid-2007. Emerging markets peaked in late 2007; commodities peaked in mid-2008.

As we began to cover in Chapter 4, the Shakeout Season in the United States in the 1930s encompassed a three-stage progression, with the greatest crash from late 1929 to mid-1932. In Figures 4.22 and 4.23, we showed the progression of rising bond yields in different sectors as the devastating downturn unfolded. T-bills peaked in late 1929 as the boom peaked (Figure 4.22), followed by long-term Treasuries in late 1931 (Figure 4.23) as the downturn looked more ominous. Corporate bond yields peaked in mid-1932 at the worst of the crash, and, finally, municipals peaked in mid-1933 at the worst of unemployment and falling tax revenue (as we will show just ahead).

The bear market rally we forecast in the first edition of this book did occur and into our target range of 9,800 to 11,800. It has lasted a bit longer than expected, but is very likely to peak between October of 2009 and February of 2010. A less bearish and more likely scenario for stocks is shown in Figure 8.2. In this scenario the bear market rally in stocks is likely to peak near 10,000 on the Dow in late October or as high as 11,300 by late February 2010. Then we are likely to see a second crash to around 3,300–4,600 in late 2010, and then a retest of those lows around mid-2012. In the more bearish scenario in Figure 8.3, the market could crash as low as 2,300 by late 2010 and go even lower in mid-2012, as low as 800 to 2,300. This scenario is less likely.

The last **Maturity Boom Season** will come between early 2020 to 2023 and 2035 to 2036 and see a broad-based global boom that will favor Asian stocks the most (not including China, Japan, and South Korea), then U.S. stocks (especially small-cap in the earlier stages), emerging countries from Latin America to the Middle East to Africa, and com-

Figure 8.2: Dow Forecast: 2009–2023
Scenario 1

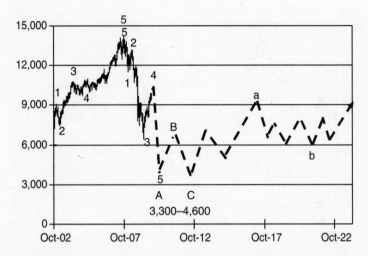

modities and broad-based real estate (especially commercial, apartments, and starter and trade-up homes). Long-term bonds generally will be in disfavor due to moderately rising inflation trends; short-term fixed incomes will be favored instead.

During the upcoming Maturity Boom Season from 2020–2023 to 2035–2036, a diversified portfolio in international and Asian stocks (not including China, Japan, South Korea, and Europe), U.S. small-cap and large-cap stocks, real estate, commodities, emerging countries, and short-term fixed incomes will perform the best. The areas to avoid will be East Asia; Europe, including Eastern Europe; and long-term bonds.

The Best Risk/Return Play Ahead Will Come in Long-Term Bonds . . . but Wait Until You See the Whites of Their Eyes!

When the battle comes, the best generals always have urged their soldiers to overcome their initial fears, which naturally impel them to fire too early, and instead wait until the opposing soldiers get close enough for a

Figure 8.3: Dow Forecast: 2009–2023
Scenario 2

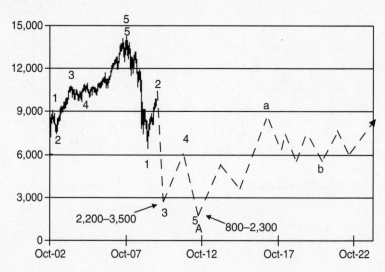

clear, high-impact shot. The truth is that when the next downturn begins to set in due to runaway commodity prices and a slowing in the United States followed by slowdowns in European and emerging economies, long-term bond yields from U.S. Treasury to corporate to international initially will decline slightly in anticipation of a slowdown and lower inflation rates. However, that situation will be a short-term trap at first!

In Chapter 4, we looked at how various bond yields spiked upward in succession as the fears of a worsening economy emerged. Even the highest-quality long-term U.S. Treasury bonds spiked upward between mid-1931 and late 1931 (peaking at 4.1%) as the downturn threatened the entire financial system—bonds that the U.S. government obviously would have to stand behind and provide greater guarantees upon (much as we saw on a minor basis again in 2008). But as things got worse, there was a "flight to quality" from corporate and municipal bonds back to Treasuries between late 1931 and mid-1932, just before the stock market bottomed and the worst was assumed for the economy. Yields on long-term Treasury bonds ultimately fell to 1.7% in late 1941. Corporate bond yields peaked in mid-1932, right at the bottom of the greatest stock crash in U.S. history, when there was the most fear about the impacts on U.S.

Figure 8.4: Corporate AAA to BAA Bond Yields, 1929–1932

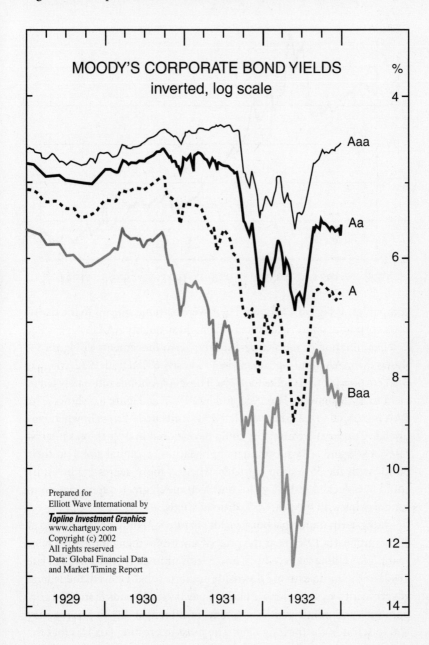

Figure 8.5: AAA Corporate Bond Yields, 1929–1942

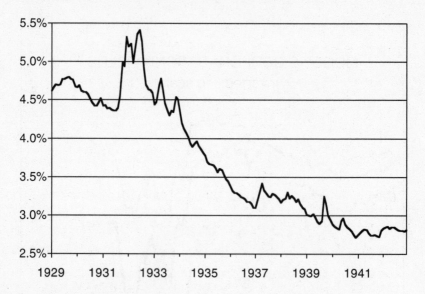

companies, as Figure 8.4 shows. There were extreme spreads in the rise of BAA corporate bond yields versus the highest-quality AAAs.

Examination of the sharpest shorter-term movements in Figure 8.4 shows that AAA bonds spiked in yield to nearly 6% in mid-1932, whereas BAA corporate bonds spiked to 13%. Those AAA bonds ultimately fell in yield to 2.7% between late 1941 and late 1942, as Figure 8.5 shows. The BAA bonds fell to 4.3% between late 1941 and late 1942, as shown in Figure 8.6. Conservative investors could have locked in twenty-year interest rates at 6% and seen substantial appreciation in capital gains on their bonds with the 55% drop in yields, whereas more aggressive investors could have locked in 13% yields and seen much greater appreciation in capital gains with the near-75% drop in yields.

Long-term municipal bond yields (Figure 8.7) didn't peak in yield at 5.3% until early 1933, near the peak of unemployment and with a one-year lag for falling tax receipts. Those yields ultimately fell to 1.9% in late 1942. In the more extreme downside scenarios that evolved, the federal government was seen as more likely to pay back its bonds than most corporations and municipalities due to its imminent ability to print money and to stand in for the long haul. The most interesting fact was that the

Figure 8.6: BAA Corporate Bond Yields, 1929–1942

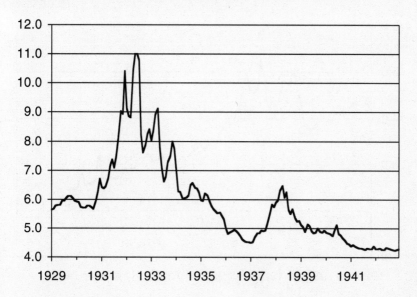

CPI bottomed in 1933 but long-term bond yields continued to fall into the early 1940s. This probably occurred because the Federal Reserve kept short-term rates near zero into the early 1940s. Once deflation set in, people's expectations moved in that direction for many years.

The key insight is that long-term bonds appreciate more like stocks in a deflationary downturn—but you first have to wait for bond yields to spike in reaction to the severity of the downturn in sector after sector. The best risk/return play in the Shakeout Season (or the first phase of a depression) is to hold cash and money market investments first, switch to longer-term bonds as yields spike, and then wait for everything else to fall in value. Your assets continue to be liquid and continue to appreciate until the greatest bargains in history unfold in sector after sector in stocks, real estate, and commodities! The greater truth is that as the best sectors, like corporate bond yields, spike the highest, you also start to see the first attractive investments in stocks. So you can decide to play it safe in bonds or be more aggressive in higher-yield bonds or select stock sectors again when the first major stock crash bottoms. In our scenario, the first such opportunity is likely to come in mid- to late 2010.

If we adjust this scenario for what occurred in the 1930s, highs in

Figure 8.7: Municipal Bond Yields, 1929–1942

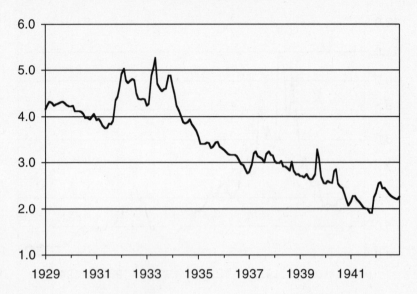

yields for various bonds and fixed-income sectors are likely to occur for long-term Treasuries (10-year to 30-year) between mid- to late 2010, in corporate bonds between late 2010 and mid-2011, and then in municipal bonds between mid-2011 and mid-2012. Again, the trickiest times will come between mid- to late 2009 and mid- to late 2012 in the first phase of the next crash and downturn, when even high-quality bonds will be in question as to their viability, given that the downturn is anticipated to be more extreme than anything we have seen since the early 1930s, mid-1970s, or early 1980s.

We looked at how large-cap stocks in the United States tend to correlate with the Spending Wave, a 46- to 48-year lag for peak spending, in Figure 2.3 of Chapter 2. Such a peak would come between late 2007 and late 2009 in the present baby-boom generational cycle. Small-cap stocks partly follow a different drummer. They benefit from the broad boom in generational spending, but they also follow innovation cycles from young, new generations entering the workforce—what we call the "yuppie impact." Figure 8.8 combines a 22- to 23-year lag on the Immigration-Adjusted Birth Index for peak innovation with the Spending Wave

Figure 8.8: Small-Cap Indicator, 1958–2030

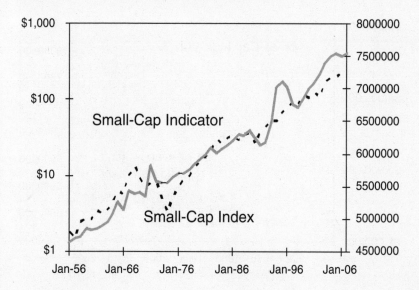

on a 46- to 48-year lag. Going forward, Figure 8.9 compares the fundamental trends that will favor large-cap or small-cap stocks over time.

Small-caps trounced large-caps from 1958 to 1983 during the baby-boom Innovation Cycle. Large-caps outperformed clearly from 1983 through 2000. Small-caps have had a slight edge from 2001 to 2006 and could fare somewhat better in the early stages of the downturn into 2013 or so. Both sectors should fare poorly overall into around 2020, when small-cap stocks may lead the next boom from 2020 into 2028 or so. Large-caps should be coming on strong as well after 2022 and will lead in the final boom from around 2030 to 2036.

Portfolio Allocations and Recommendations for 2009–2022

Since there is a wide range of risk and return profiles for different investors, we want to keep this simple here and focus on when to look for opportunities to reallocate to different parts of your portfolio. You need to sit down with a financial advisor or mentor and determine how much

Figure 8.9: Small-Cap versus Large-Cap, 1958–2058

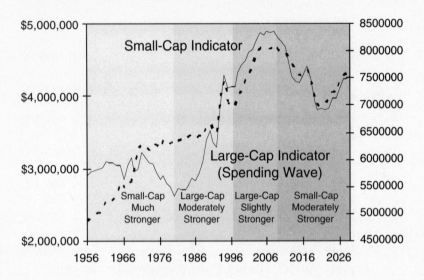

risk you should take and which sectors are appropriate for you and to what percentage. Conservative investors should focus more on T-bills and money markets; safe currencies such as the Swiss franc and Singapore dollar; high-quality Treasury, corporate, and municipal bonds; and the more conservative stock sectors, including large-cap multinationals, health care, and Japan. There can be substantial gains without the extreme volatility of stocks in this season simply through diversification within fixed income, including U.S. and international. Growth and aggressive investors can play a wider range of investments and have a well-diversified portfolio when desired in many sectors of stocks and bonds, both U.S. and international.

Simplest Overview of Areas on Which to Concentrate for Growth and Aggressive Investors

Late 2009/early 2010 to late 2010: Cash, money markets, or short the stock markets

Mid- to late 2010 to late 2022: Long-term bonds—Treasury, corporate, and international

Mid-2012 to mid-2017: Stocks: China, India, health care, technology, and multinational

Mid-2012 to early 2015 through 2020–2024: Real estate—starter
homes and vacation and retirement

Late 2022–2035: Stocks: India, emerging countries, and United
States; commodities; and real estate

Simplest Overview of Areas on Which to Concentrate
for Conservative Investors

Late 2009 to late 2010: Cash and T-bills, money market, and
funds

Mid- to late 2010 to late 2022: Long-term bonds: Treasury, corporate, and international

Mid-2012 to mid-2017: Stocks: Japan, multinational, and health
care

Late 2022–2035: U.S. large-cap multinational, health care, India,
and real estate

More Detailed Portfolio Allocation Strategies

Stage 1: The Great Crash and Bubble Burst

1. **Late 2009/early 2010:** Sell stocks and allocate to T-bills or
short the stock market without leverage. The dollar is likely to
rise and most foreign currencies such as the Swiss franc or
Euro should fall, so sell most foreign currency holdings.
Stocks are likely to peak between late October 2009 and late
February 2010.

2. **Early 2010:** Sell commodities, precious metals, and energy
stocks and allocate to T-bills or short the stock market. It is
harder to predict a top in commodities, as there could be
spikes from banking and geopolitical crisis between late 2009
and mid-2010.

3. **Mid- to late 2010:** Start to allocate to 30-year Treasury bonds
only after yields begin to spike.

4. **Late 2010 to mid-2011:** Allocate to 20-year corporate bonds when yields go to extremes; more conservative investors should focus on AAA corporate, more aggressive toward BAA.

5. **Mid-2011 to mid-2012:** Allocate to long-term municipal bonds when yields seem to be peaking, especially for high-tax-bracket investors.

6. **Late 2010 (optional):** Growth and aggressive investors allocate to Asian stocks (focused on China, India, South Korea, Japan, and Vietnam) and to multinational, technology, and health-care stocks in the United States. Conservative investors allocate more toward multinational and health care in the United States and Japan in Asia.

7. **Late 2011 (optional):** Sell stock allocations from late 2010 and reallocate toward T-bills or money markets and bonds.

Stage 2: First Recovery and Bear Market Rally

1. **Mid- to late 2012:** Make medium-term allocations into stocks and long-term bonds; growth and aggressive investors focus more on Asian stocks (China, India, Japan, South Korea, and Vietnam), multinational, and technology and health care in the United States, with minor allocation in long-term corporate, Treasury, or municipal bonds. Conservative investors focus largely on 10- to 30-year Treasuries and 20-year corporate AAA bonds, with minor allocations in multinational, health-care, and Japan stocks.

2. **Late 2011 to early 2015:** Look for selected investment opportunities in real estate, including apartments and starter homes for echo boomers on the early side and vacation/retirement homes for aging baby boomers on the later side. Trade-up homes may start to become attractive again by 2015.

3. **Mid- to late 2014:** Aggressive and growth investors can make greater allocations to leading stock sectors such as China, India, health care, multinational, technology, and financials on a likely short-term correction between late 2013 and late 2014 on the four-year cycle.

Stage 3: Final Recession and Slowdown

1. **Early to mid-2017:** All investors sell stocks in all sectors and convert largely back into long-term bonds and, to a lesser degree, into T-bills or money markets.
2. **Early 2020:** Aggressive and growth investors can selectively buy in leading sectors of stocks like health care, financials, and technology but not in East Asia (China, Japan, and South Korea), which is likely to correct into the early 2020s. This would be the best time to rebuy larger trade-up homes or Mc-Mansions.
3. **Mid- to late 2022:** Make long-term allocations back into stocks (U.S., international, and emerging markets), real estate, and commodities but again not into East Asia (China, Japan, and South Korea). Focus mostly on United States (large-cap and small-cap) and India; convert any desired fixed-income portion of your portfolio into T-bills or money market accounts due to long-term rising interest rates ahead.

Remember that in the back of this book we offer free periodic e-mail updates to our basic forecasts and investment strategies. We also have a monthly newsletter with more detailed strategies and updates.

From around mid- to late 2022 into 2035–2036, we should see a broad-based global boom again led more by India, Southeast Asia, and the United States, with East Asia (including China) and Europe lagging. This boom will not be of the magnitude of the great boom from 1983 to 2009, except possibly in India. Small-cap stocks in the United States also should do well into around 2028–2029. There is likely to be a substantial setback midway in this boom between 2028 and 2030, with the strongest bubble-like surge from 2030 into 2035. Commodity prices should enter a more concerted boom from around 2020–2023 into 2039–2040, benefiting emerging countries outside Asia, in South America, the Middle East, and Africa. Interest rates and inflation should rise generally from 2023 into 2040, favoring short-term fixed income over long-term bonds. Between 2035 and 2044, we are likely to see the next stagflation period and the next Innovation Season, which could extend into the early 2050s.

How Safe Are Your Bank and Investment Accounts?

A commonly neglected but very important question in addition to what assets should be held is where they should be held. Most of us use typical investment firms such as national or regional brokerage firms, the affiliates of banks, or do-it-yourself companies such as Scottrade and TD Ameritrade. But what happens if, during a severe economic crisis like the one we are forecasting, the company where you hold your investments and trade goes under? The Securities Insurance Protection Corporation (SIPC) is funded by brokerage firms and guards investors against loss due to fraud or misappropriation in the event that the investment company improperly takes your assets, but SIPC does not protect investors against market risk. The limitations on SIPC are currently $500,000 in assets, including a $100,000 limit on cash. Most investment firms carry additional coverage that increases these limits dramatically. Remember, SIPC is not the FDIC. The Federal Deposit Insurance Corporation guarantees the deposits at banks up to $100,000 and IRA accounts up to $250,000—beyond that you are at risk in accounts at a bank. The goal of the FDIC is to give depositors peace of mind so that there is no "run on the bank." The FDIC works to ensure the timely access to funds as well as the guarantee of deposits, so when a bank fails the FDIC works to make sure that depositors have uninterrupted access to their funds.

Even though SIPC guards against losses due to misappropriation and fraud, it does not guarantee a time frame in which an investor will regain control over his or her account and assets. When a brokerage firm goes under, the experience of the clients depends on the size of the brokerage firm, the state of the brokerage firm's record keeping, the types of securities the clients owned, and the speed at which the trustee overseeing the process works.

If a brokerage firm is small, the records of the firm are up to date and in good order, and there has been no fraud or misappropriation, then SIPC and the trustee will work to move the clients' accounts to a new brokerage firm intact. The clients will then have the choice of staying with the new firm or moving on to a different firm. This process can take as little as a week. If the failed brokerage firm is large or the records are in disarray, then it can take longer to determine what other firm or firms can take over the accounts as well as what each client owns, thereby extending the time between when the original firm fails and when clients can access their accounts. If there is fraud or misappropriation involved, clients must fill out claim forms, submit them to the trustee, and then wait through the process of the trustee appropriating the remaining assets of the firm and then supplementing those assets with funds from SIPC.

The real problem in all of this is time. In the midst of an economic crash, which would be a main reason for a brokerage firm to fail in the first place, it is imperative that clients have access to their accounts so that they can remain correctly allocated or on the sidelines as the situation warrants. If the process of regaining control over your investment account takes several months, as is entirely possible, you could see the market value of your investments drop dramatically. So even though SIPC coverage ensures that you get your securities back, it does not ensure the timing.

There are several caveats in the SIPC coverage that should be noted. If you own securities on margin, you have taken a loan from the brokerage firm. If the firm fails, it is possible that you will have an immediate, full margin call on your account. It is not guaranteed that this will happen, but it is possible. Also, SIPC does not cover items not listed with the SEC as securities, such as currency, investment contracts, limited partnerships, etc. Also, if a part of your holdings is proprietary products from that brokerage firm, it could complicate matters even further.

For more information on SIPC (Securities Insurance Protection Corporation), what it covers and what it doesn't, as well as the process, visit its website at www.sipc.org.

In your normal course of investing, there are two things you can do to protect your investment accounts. The first is to be vigilant in keeping copies of your records (statements, confirmations, etc.), since these will be necessary in the case of having to send a claim to a trustee. Because so many things are available electronically, this record should be much simpler to compile and keep updated than it was in the past. The second is to keep abreast of any research or reports on your brokerage firm itself. If a firm is having extreme difficulties due to CDO investments, capitalization rates, its own trading losses, or whatever else, then you should consider moving your account to a firm that you consider to be in a stronger financial position.

Business Strategies: The Ultimate Survival-of-the-Fittest Challenge

We have been warning business owners and managers for many years that this change of season ahead is the most important challenge and opportunity they are likely to face in their lifetimes. The shakeout, especially in technology and new growth industries that began in the early 2000s, will come to a final culmination, establishing a smaller number of leaders that will dominate for many decades to come. In Chapter 2 (Figure 2.12) we showed, using automobile companies as an example, how a similar shakeout cycle started in the early 1920s and peaked in the early 1930s. Many new car companies entered the market as the S-curve accelerated from 1% to 40% in 1919. With the first bubble crash from late 1919 into early 1922, about 20% of the companies went under or consolidated into other companies. Then the second crash narrowed the field by another 60%, leaving the leaders that dominated for many decades to follow.

It is important to reiterate here that there is a natural cycle after radical new technologies first begin to move mainstream. Bubbles develop in the stocks of these companies that allow great capital for expansion, acquisitions, and new initial public offerings (IPOs). This allows a maximum of experimentation in new products, applications, markets, and business models, given that no one really knows which applications are going to be the "killer" applications at first. The first crash shifts market share toward the best proven companies and models after the first bubble that gain greater scale, which allows them to lower costs and penetrate markets further until they become initially saturated near 90%. The second crash and depression narrow market share to the long-term leaders that have fully proved themselves. It is these larger companies that can lower costs further long term through massive scale and bring the new technologies and industries to much broader application and saturation in the Maturity Boom Season to follow.

This is the Darwinian process of free markets. These markets foster innovation and the expansion of many new companies through bubbles and then shake them down to the very fittest during the crashes and depressions that follow such bubbles. The Fortune 500 leaders of today emerged as leaders largely between the late 1920s and early 1930s. Hence, businesses have a few clear options for prospering during this exceptionally critical period:

1. Sell out by early to mid-2010, while your company can still fetch a strong valuation.
2. Get lean, mean, and liquid, using the shakeout to gain stronger market share at the expense of failing competitors, including acquiring them cheaply.
3. Sell the parts of your business that are least strategic long term and use the proceeds to acquire assets, market share, and companies in the areas best positioned for long-term trends during the downturn.

Option 1: Sell Your Business by Mid- to Late 2009

Option 1 is the most obvious. If you are looking at retiring anyway and you don't have family members who want to take over the business long term, sell by early to mid-2010. You may be considering retirement and selling down the road when it best fits your life cycle. However, you are likely to receive much less for your business if you try to sell in the years to come, so why not retire or start now and even consider starting a new business in the downturn, when new opportunities will open up at lower costs? Larger companies that are looking at selling to or merging with stronger companies as a long-term strategy should do so in 2009. Those who run new, emerging ventures may think that they will get a higher price if they prove their sales or profits for a few more years. But the truth is that the valuation you are likely to get for your company is likely to be cut in half or reduced by two-thirds or more between 2010 and 2012, so it is probably better to sell in 2009. Those in new ventures who are looking to partner with larger companies to expand their distribution should make such alliances before 2010 and should make sure to target the companies that are dominant and thus most likely to survive such a shakeout.

Option 2: Hunker Down and Use the Shakeout to Gain Share

In option 2 there is much to consider. First, cut costs to the bare minimum to be effective in all areas. Close down marginal operations that may be creating excess costs or have little potential ahead—or sell those operations if possible, as in option 3 below. Especially look at which operations are causing your overhead and fixed costs. That is where most businesses fail in their accounting and profitability assessments, as direct or variable costs are more obvious. They tend to allocate fixed costs and overheads somewhat equally across different products and market segments by sales, whereas some parts of your business tend to have much greater impacts than others. For example, allocate order processing and accounting costs by number of orders rather than by sales. Allocate building and office costs by actual square footage used rather than by sales.

Second, cancel plans for capital expenditures to expand nonessential operations. Preserve your capital and/or borrowing capacity first to survive the downturn in your sales, profits, and cash flow and, more important, to be able to acquire such assets more cheaply in the downturn by buying them from a bank or a struggling competitor. Also, to free up capital, sell off real estate assets that can be leased. Cancel plans to acquire office, warehouse, or industrial space; lease it instead. Structure your leases so that they don't go too far out. The ideal would be from mid-2011 to late 2012. You should be able to negotiate much more favorable long-term leases after the worst of the downturn hits, between late 2010 and late 2012. Store the new capital in liquid accounts for purchasing power during the downturn and/or to pay down high-interest debts to free up cash flow and borrowing capacity for the downturn. If you do this, you will be able to refinance at lower interest rates later.

Finally, in the late stages of this boom push to maximize your market

Figure 8.10: S-Curve, GPS Systems

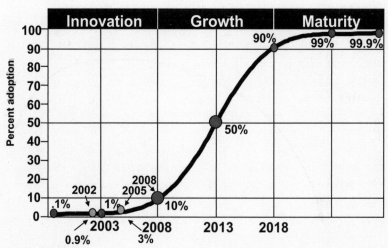

Source: Masterlink.

share in the most important segments of your business—in the places where you can dominate and lead in the future. Do this through short-term marketing expenditures rather than through long-term capital expenditures and commitments. Make alliances with the strongest partners (the ones who will survive) *before* the crash, because after the crash they will have more leverage over you.

As the crash and downturn set in, look for opportunities to acquire the customers of your competitors by cutting prices and showing the capacity to deliver uncompromised service in the downturn when your competitors are struggling to survive. Look to buy out your competitors and/or their key assets or customer lists when they are in trouble or failing. You may be able to do this directly from their bank at favorable terms if you can simply show that you have a much better chance of paying off a failing loan than they do. In other words, you may not even have to put any money down. Just having good cash flow and low debt service in a downturn may be sufficient to save a bank from having to write a loan further down than necessary. Many of your competitors may be happy to sell out to you at bargain prices or merge with you under favorable terms.

Figure 8.11: Beauty Salon Services, Spending by Age

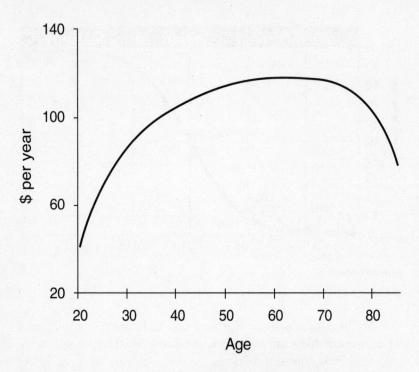

You will be able to acquire office, warehouse, or industrial capacity at low prices and much lower interest rates in the downturn.

Option 3: Sell Parts of Your Business and Hunker Down in the Best Segments

The smartest business leaders with whom we have consulted or who have attended our seminars have opted for a hybrid strategy, or the best of both worlds. They analyze their business for the segments where they do and can dominate, and the ones that are best positioned in demographic and technology/product life cycles. If your business is in the earlier stages of a new trend, between 1% and 10% on the S-curve, such as GPS systems for cars (Figure 8.10), you may decide that the growth potential outweighs the economic downside in the next few years. Even in this case, you might decide to sell to or partner with a company that can accelerate your growth rather than just going it alone in a difficult time. Or, let's say you have a beauty salon and your customers peak in their spending later than the economy does, as Figure 8.11 shows, and your experience tells you that women will continue to value your services and to spend even when they are cutting back in other areas. You may decide to hunker down and to continue to grow for the long term, despite a fall in valuation for your business ahead.

The point is to determine which parts of your business you want to keep and build up long term and which ones are questionable or unattractive. Focus on selling or closing down the least attractive segments to create capital, lower costs, and better cash flow for expanding market share and acquiring capacity from competitors at bargain prices in the downturn when competitors are struggling or failing and when the broader assets that you need go on sale, often from banks and foreclosures—especially real estate. Follow the strategies in option 2 above for gaining market share and assets in the best parts of your business during the downturn.

Summary Points for Businesses

1. Defer capital expenditures and loans until the worst of the downturn, when assets and real estate will be much cheaper and interest rates lower.
2. Identify the parts of your business that you want to keep and grow long term, and sell or close down everything else to create capital and cash flow to take advantage of the "great sale" in the downturn. Determine which parts of your business have the most favorable demographic or S-curve trends.
3. Cut all unnecessary costs now before the economy forces you to later.
4. Outsource nonstrategic functions for greater flexibility in the downturn.
5. Pay off high-interest loans now and refinance in the downturn at lower rates if you think that you will be creditworthy.
6. Where possible, choose fixed-rate loans into late 2010 or later

that switch to variable rates from there on (currently a 3/1 ARM, which gives you a fixed rate for three years and then converts to an adjustable short-term rate), saving refinancing costs.

7. Structure leases or loans to mature between mid-2011 and mid-2013 for the best leverage to renegotiate or to refinance.

8. Protect your personal assets from lawsuits through trusts and variable annuities where possible.

Personal and Family Life Planning and Strategies

It has become a standard part of financial planning to consider how your life and financial needs will change as you age and that your risk tolerance tends to decline as you get older and closer to retirement. Hence the standard approach is to diversify among higher-return and higher-risk asset classes when you are younger and toward lower-return and lower-risk assets as you get older. As a general rule, that makes sense. Also, people with higher incomes and assets often can afford to take greater risks, while those with lower incomes and assets should take less risk. But another important dimension of financial planning has largely been ignored.

The economy has its own cycle and its impact on your life and financial planning can be greater than your own life cycle. There are four different seasons that occur over a typical life span of 80 years in modern times. These seasons not only create different return and risk outcomes in your portfolio, but also affect your job and business opportunities and those of your kids and grandkids, including their education. The Shakeout Season ahead yields the lowest returns and the highest risks, but it also reduces the cost of living and the future costs of real estate and assets due to the unique deflationary trends in this cycle.

As we were considering for businesses above, you may have your own target for when you feel that you would like to retire and sell your business, but the economy's life cycle will determine the best time financially for you to sell your business. The late stages of the Growth Boom (late 1990s to late 2000s) were when you were likely to get the highest valuation for your business if you sold it. At this point in the economic sea-

sons, you are likely to get the most for your business if you sold it between late 2007 and mid-2009. If you wait just a few years into the Shakeout Season, the value of your business could plummet 50% to 80% and
not reach valuations, sales, or earnings at the top for a decade or two.

Your Retirement and Dream Home in the Exurbs, Downtown, or in the Boonies

Similarly, if you are looking at retiring and buying a house in South
Florida, the Caribbean, Arizona, Idaho, Vermont, or British Columbia,
why buy at or near the top of the greatest real estate bubble in your lifetime? As a general rule, the greatest bubble and speculation have come in
vacation/retirement areas. So, even though there is a second round of
baby-boom buying ahead from around late 2012/mid-2013 to 2024, the
greatest corrections will continue to come in these areas, especially from
2010 into mid-2013. First, remember that the strongest areas due to
migration trends in Chapter 5 are likely to be in the Southeast, the Southwest, the Rockies, and western Canada. If you are looking at the Caribbean, the best emerging new areas tend to be the Dominican Republic,
Costa Rica, Panama, and Vieques or Culebra in Puerto Rico.

The best strategy is to sell your present house by September 2009 and
either rent in the area where you presently live or, better, rent in the area
you desire to move to and make sure you love the area as much as you
think before you actually buy and settle down long term. You might end
up missing your kids and grandkids too much when you are out in Idaho
or Costa Rica. Maybe there isn't much to do and you get bored. Maybe
you get physical ailments you didn't expect and the great outdoors
doesn't look so alluring or you wish you were closer to better health care.
The vacation/retirement market is likely to make a strong comeback
from 2015 into 2024 on a 63-year lag as we showed in Figure 4.18 in
Chapter 4. So you shouldn't have to wait long to actually buy in most of
these areas, and low-maintenance condos typically will be selling at the
greatest discounts.

Even if you plan to stay in the area you are in to be near your kids,
grandkids, and friends, maybe you want to move a little farther out into
the exurbs (just outside the present suburban boundaries), where hous-

ing is a little more affordable or into an active retirement community that has access to medical services and assisted living if you need it down the road. Perhaps instead you want to move downtown, where you are closer to restaurants, theaters, and health care. Or maybe you are simply thinking of eventually downsizing to a smaller, more affordable, and lower-maintenance home. In this case sell your present home now and either buy the smaller one or, better, rent until it becomes more attractive to purchase. Even if you buy a smaller house now, you are reducing your exposure to downside risk. And a small percentage of our readers may simply be willing to sell their primary home now, rent, and wait to repurchase.

Whether you are thinking of moving locally or far away before or in your retirement, strongly consider selling your primary home now and renting until home prices crash further, especially until late 2012 to mid-2013. Then you can settle down there knowing you like the new area.

If you are financing a home between 2011 and 2015, it is likely that you will be able to lock in at a very low 30-year fixed rate; or, to be a bit more aggressive, look at a 5/1 ARM if you buy earlier or a 3/1 ARM if you buy later and look to benefit from falling short-term rates in the final slowdown from around mid-2017 into 2020–2023. Then convert back to a long-term fixed rate by 2023.

For automobile purchases, the same logic applies as with houses. If you are buying a car for use between 2009 and 2010, it is better to lease the car than purchase it, as the car is likely to be worth less when you sell it or turn it in. Let the bank take the risk of falling car prices! The best time to purchase a car will be between mid-2011 and mid-2013, when the economy is weakest; then you should be able to get a low interest rate and can feel good about owning the car, because the economy is likely to do better from 2013 into mid-2017 and because the car's value may be higher than the bank would assume on a lease. However, make sure your credit score is good, because lenders will continue to have higher standards for houses and autos.

Creating Retirement Income with Minimal Taxes and Passing Assets and Income to Your Kids and Grandkids

Now let's look at how you can maximize both your retirement income and the assets and income that you pass to your kids and grandkids. Maximizing your 401(k) and matching contributions is the first step, because this is about accumulation. Once you are through this stage, you move into distribution—where the greatest issues are making your cash flow match your needs and then ensuring that your assets pass along according to your wishes.

Variable annuities and variable universal life policies can be important tools for deferring taxes during your earning years, minimizing taxes during your retirement years, passing down assets to your kids and grandkids, and offering some protection against downside risk. These policies are often berated in the press for having excessive costs, but compared to the benefits for high marginal tax rate households and the potential downside risk protection through the use of living benefits, these policies can be more than worth their costs. Through living benefits, variable annuities are able to give investors the security of knowing that they will receive some sort of set benefit no matter what happens to the underlying investments. This type of protection will obviously be of tremendous importance to investors during the Shakeout Season we are about to enter!

As a professional or business owner, you also should investigate the ability to protect your assets against lawsuits through variable annuities and trusts. In a downturn like this, with so many businesses failing, creditors will end up suing anyone remotely connected to companies defaulting on debts. Just as with any other financial product, these types of products are not right for every person or every situation but are certainly worth considering when you are determining how to position yourself financially for the years to come.

One of the least appreciated advantages of variable annuities and variable universal life investment products is that you can make major changes to your long-term portfolio in an abrupt season change like the one just ahead without tax consequences. This could save you 15% to

40% of your portfolio value, which can then be reinvested and compounded tax free for years and decades to come.

A tremendous concern will be minimizing the amount you pay to the government both while you enjoy retirement and through your estate. This is an area that is very complex and is specific to your situation. For several years we have worked with Ed Slott, commonly referred to as "America's IRA Expert." Ed has published several books on the subject of how to position yourself appropriately for retirement and passing along your assets. Strongly consider reviewing his work; his website is www .irahelp.com, and he has been featured on the popular PBS program *Stay Rich Forever and Ever*.

One of the greatest trends you will face if you are a more affluent household is that marginal tax rates and business tax rates are almost certain to rise as this downturn creates enormous deficits for the federal government, not to mention state and local governments. In the last Shakeout Season, with the Great Depression of the 1930s and World War II, marginal tax rates accelerated dramatically from 25% at the lows in the 1920s boom to 94% in 1946, as Figure 8.12 shows.

As we move from the Growth Boom Season to the Shakeout Season, the political climate will shift much faster toward a "tax the rich and busi-

Figure 8.12: Marginal Tax Rates, 1913–2008

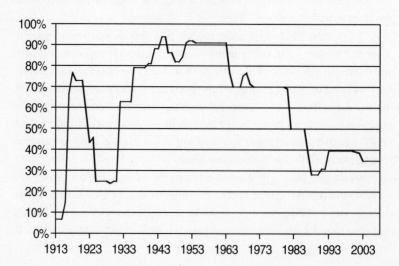

nesses" mandate, as we will cover more in Chapter 9. The entrepreneurs and professionals who gained the most by far in the Growth Boom Season will see taxes rising against them and will fall even more into disdain by the public in general. This is where tax planning becomes critical. Strategies for deferring income both earned and unearned, utilizing Roth IRAs where possible, skewing investments toward tax-free items such as municipal bonds, and minimizing your real estate footprint to avoid property tax all come into play. There is no substitute for strong financial planning in terms of taxes! Legislation to tax the rich is most likely to come very quickly, by 2011 to 2012, moving up not just ordinary income, but capital gains and dividend taxes and estate taxes, so this is a critical area to consider now!

Education and Career Planning for Kids and Grandkids

Now let's get even more practical when looking at how you can best help your kids and grandkids. Everyone wants their kids to get the best education. But are we that rational when it comes to this? Education costs are the only major sector of our economy that has gone up faster than health care costs, as we can see in Figure 8.13. However, there is a major difference between private and public schools and colleges, as we can see in Figure 8.14. There is a runaway bubble in private education costs, since we parents will pay almost anything to give our kids an edge and because these institutions can raise their prices with little decline in demand.

We will mortgage our house to get our kids in the best schools. However, the truth is that outside the very best and most elite schools, their higher costs don't tend to pay off. Education costs are getting so high that it is hard to justify them in long-term returns. It may be better to put the typical four-year private college costs of $150,000+ into a long-term investment fund for your kids. They could be millionaires by the peak of their careers just on the investment fund doubling every ten years or so!

The first insight is that more often than not, it is better to put your kids in a good public school or university, unless they are among the few potential stars whose Ivy League degree will get them into the very best jobs. With the Internet revolution today, young people tend to learn more

Figure 8.13: Growth in Education Versus Health-Care Costs

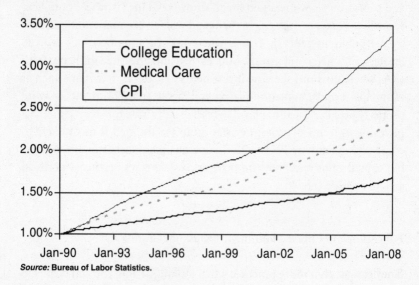

Source: **Bureau of Labor Statistics.**

from experts around the world and from their peers than they do in school anyway—and Internet college and education sites are booming! The second insight is that it is often better to have them go to a junior college, technical school, or public university for their basic education and then look at spending more on the best private schools for their advanced degrees if they have the necessary desire and capacity. If they attend local schools, you could save further by having them live with you. If your kid is very smart and hardworking, he or she can get into honors programs in these public universities and still get a leading-edge education. Their last degree will be more critical than the earlier ones if they are in an area of higher specialization of skills, as in the case of lawyers, doctors, and MBAs, so spend the money there.

Home-Buying Strategies for Your Kids and Grandkids

Kids and grandkids who are just getting married and looking to buy a home should wait for the worst of the housing downturn, which we pre-

Figure 8.14: Growth in Private Education Versus Public

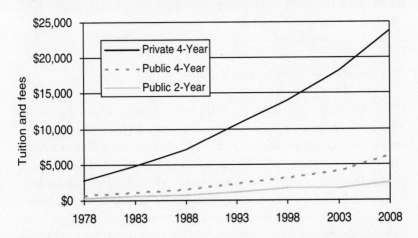

dict will occur between 2010 and 2013 or so, before investing in a house. They should continue to rent until they see home prices come back to the levels of 1996–2001 in their area, as we covered in Chapter 4. The starter home cycle should create appreciation again in that sector (albeit at lower rates than in the past decades) starting around mid-2011 to mid-2013, with continued growth for decades to come as the echo boom grows in such buying on a 31-year lag on immigration-adjusted births, as we showed in Figure 4.14 in Chapter 4.

Your kids or grandkids who are looking to buy a starter home should be able to do so at much lower prices between 2011 and 2013 and should be able to finance such homes at mortgage rates much lower than today—as low as 3% to 4% on a 30-year fixed mortgage between 2011 and 2020–2023.

Larger trade-up homes are likely either to continue to decline or to remain flat until 2015–2020 on a 37- to 42-year lag. Many younger, more affluent households may find that they can afford a larger home earlier in their life cycle as prices in this arena fall even more, but their appreciation potential may be less for some years to come versus that of more affordable starter homes. This sector is not likely to appreciate again until 2015 or so and is not likely to appreciate strongly until the early 2020s, as we showed in Figure 4.15 in Chapter 4.

The Deflation of the Education Bubble

There are likely to be some big changes in education ahead due to this Shakeout Season over the next decade. Just as with the housing or technology or emerging market or commodity bubble, there is an education bubble. Does it make sense that education costs should be rising so fast when education is an information-intensive industry during an unprecedented information revolution? Bureaucratic management structures, real estate intensity, and tenure-based systems have sustained high costs, while high demand from frantic parents has exacerbated the price spiral. Why can't greater parts of education be conveyed online with greater access to experts and peers around the world? Why do we need sprawling campuses with elaborate landscaping, buildings, libraries, etc., in an Internet world? Why should students be restricted to teachers and experts in a local area when they can have video and interactive feedback from around the world from the best experts, peers, and blogs?

Education can be delivered at radically lower costs through a combination of online programs, in-classroom programs, and internships with companies. However, it will take a shock to the system to force such changes in the most complacent, academic, and tenure-based system in our economy.

The real trigger for such changes will come from a combination of a decline in enrollments from 2009 to 2015 and a dramatic decline in our economy from 2010 to 2012 off and on into as late as 2020/2023. This is likely to create an actual fall in higher education costs, or at a minimum, a much slower rate of increase. Figure 8.15 shows the demographic trends in college enrollments by lagging immigration-adjusted births eighteen years for college entry. After 2008, the first wave of echo boomers will peak and there will be a seven-year decline into 2015. The

Figure 8.15: College Enrollments, 18-Year Lag on
Immigration-Adjusted Births

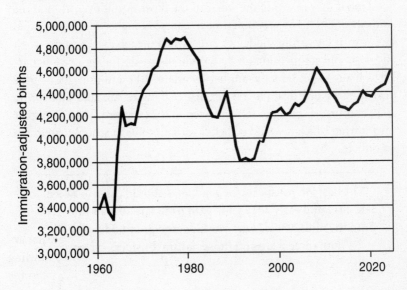

declining economy and lower portfolio returns for parents also will greatly increase price sensitivity for the first time. Finally, a dramatically declining economy will mean lower job prospects for future graduates and, hence, reduce the value of higher education for years to come.

We believe that the best time for your kids or grandkids to get advanced education will be between the fall of 2010 and the summer of 2012, when the economy is at its worst and enrollments are falling due to demographic trends. They will have better chances of getting into a good school and costs may fall somewhat, with scholarships more accessible. Conversely, it will be better for them to get into the workforce and get a good job with a growing company or institution by the summer of 2009, before the greater downturn sets in between late 2009 and late 2010, and to defer higher education for a year or more.

So, even if your kids or grandkids are already in junior college, technical school, or college, it may be better for them to take a break after the spring semester of 2009, get a job with a company that has good prospects, and wait until the downturn sets in to finish their education or get advanced degrees. They will be more likely to retain their jobs in the

layoffs that follow and you and they can wait until costs fall and it is easier to get into a better school. We would advise your kids staying with a
good job if they can until the worst of the downturn is over, around the
summer of 2012. The very best time to complete higher education would
be between the spring and fall of 2012, when the job market is the worst
and costs and competition for better schools are declining. The job market is likely to get better again between late 2012 and mid-2017 but is
likely to get worse again to a lesser degree between fall 2017 and spring
2020 and/or the spring or fall semester of 2022 onward. That is another
time during which it would be better for kids to be in school than in the
workforce.

**The best job prospects for graduates should come between
late 2012 and early 2017 and again from late 2020 or mid-2023
into the mid-2030s. Plan your kids' and grandkids' education
and careers around those natural business cycles.**

Long-Term Care Costs Likely Slowing or Declining:
Wait to Buy Your Policies

Health care is the other major cost bubble that is likely to burst or at least
slow down in this downturn, and for two reasons. First, this is another
area where we have low price sensitivity during this boom, as health is
such a high priority and more options become available over time that
we didn't have before, given advances in medical science and alternative
health care. Health care is becoming one of the largest sectors of our
economy and will continue to grow as baby boomers age into their peak
health-care spending years. Second, as with education, information technologies should be capable of cutting costs in this arena, given that this
sector involves information and is service intensive. Again, however, the
information technologies environment is one of very high levels of regulation, lawsuits, and bureaucracy that resist such changes. This is another
area that will see major reforms in government policies, as we will cover
in Chapter 9.

Strongly consider the new health savings accounts (HSAs) for health insurance, which allow you to buy the minimum insurance you need and pay for the rest out of your own tax-deductible investment account, which continues to grow if you do not use the funds. Look for options from companies like savedaily.com that allow full investment options. It is likely to be better for you to wait to buy or to upgrade long-term health insurance and long-term care policies until we see a major downturn in our economy and slowing or falling health-care costs. The cost assumptions assume strong rises for years and decades ahead. That probably will start to change by 2012 or 2013. Government policies also are likely to change more clearly after the 2012 election, and that will give you clarity as to what you will receive in the future from the government—and affluent households are likely to receive much less in benefits. So you can also better recalibrate your needs for health care from 2013 forward.

In Chapter 9, we will look further at how this downturn will affect government policies in the United States and globally. The next "New Deal" will come, especially from 2013 to 2014, as a massive mandate for change grows, much beyond Obama's appeal in the 2008 election. In fact, the next 250-year Revolution Cycle will begin to set in over the next two decades, very similar to the American Revolution and the Protestant Revolution before that, changing U.S. and global politics more than at any other time during most of our lifetimes and leading to a New Deal between developed and emerging nations into the early 2020s—and possibly something like World War III (likely in Asia) by the mid-2020s.

CHAPTER 9

The Political and Social Impacts of the Next Great Depression

The Coming Revolution and "New Deal" in the United States and Globally

DESPITE THE OBVIOUS broad benefits of this unprecedented U.S. and global boom, which began in 1983, great economic, social, and political issues have been building for decades:

1. Growing inequality in incomes and assets
2. Extreme debt levels for the government, businesses, and consumers
3. Extreme leverage and bubbles in financial markets and bank lending
4. Unsustainable benefit programs like Social Security and Medicare/Medicaid
5. Failing pension and benefit programs
6. Inadequate health-care insurance for a substantial portion of society
7. Pollution and global warming
8. Addiction to oil and coal
9. Rising terrorism and the backlash against globalization in many third-world countries
10. Resistance to rising immigration in the most successful countries, like the United States

11. Trade and currency imbalances
12. Corrupt dictatorships holding back the progress of many third-world countries
13. More recently: runaway oil, food, and commodity prices

Most politicians and citizens are well aware of these growing imbalances, but there are few feasible solutions to them, as the costs of dealing with them simply appear to be too prohibitive and against the grain of such progress in this boom. Hence we are collectively in denial on these issues and hoping that continued economic progress will eventually solve the problems. However, we will not see continued economic progress in the coming decade to bail us out!

That is the blessing of the difficult Shakeout Season we are about to enter. When the economy fails most dramatically and the deflation of the financial bubbles sets in, we are forced into a crisis mode, in which such economic, social, and political imbalances become even more extreme and the solutions become both much more urgent and more obvious. Real change always occurs in crisis or urgent times, and those times are when heroes emerge in politics, like FDR in the Great Depression and Winston Churchill in World War II! Of course, these changes will still be painful. As in the 1930s and 1940s, leading nations, such as the United States, and the new emerging nations will have to quickly develop sweeping changes to deal with these issues—hence a "New Deal" and a broader revolution in democracy and human rights and participation is coming over the next decade or two.

One of the more obvious symptoms of the success of the early stages of the information and globalization revolution of the past decades is that the rich have grown richer, as we can see in Figure 9.1, in the United States and in all developed countries to a large degree. As radical new technologies that change the very foundations of business, society, and politics arise, only the most astute or lucky take advantage at first on an early S-curve cycle. The enormous progress and growth of new industries and business models since the 1970s have accrued to the top 1% to 10% at the extreme (as wealth is more concentrated than income), and more broadly in incomes to the top 10% to 20%, the upper middle class, who are more educated and who have the skills to take advantage of these changes. This also occurred from the late 1800s into 1929, when the high-

Figure 9.1: Financial Assets Owned by the Top 1% of U.S. Households

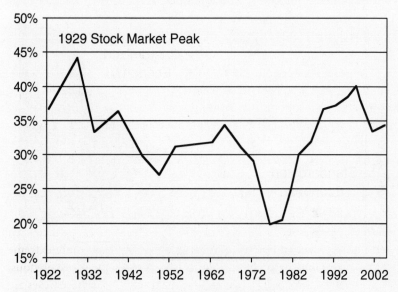

1929 Stock Market Peak

Source: Edward Wolff, as printed in Kevin Phillips, *Wealth and Democracy.*

est peak, 45% of wealth by the top 1%, was reached. But also note that between 1930 and 1976, the top 1% share dropped to 20%! On the 80-year New Economy Cycle, you can picture this as a longer S-curve cycle of adoption, as in Figure 9.2, showing the transition from the industrial-based standardized economy to the information-based customized economy over the last century.

In the Innovation and Growth Boom Seasons of the 80-year New Economy Cycle (from Figure 2.16 in Chapter 2), the rich get richer as new innovations first drive a new economy. About 80 years back, from the late 1800s into the Roaring Twenties, it was the robber barons, new industrialists like Carnegie, Ford, and Mellon, who became the new billionaires in today's terms by founding major new technologies, businesses, and industries. Today it is Bill Gates, Warren Buffett, Larry Ellison, Steve Jobs, and many more in the developed countries—including many new billionaires in the Middle East, China, and India. Into the Roaring Twenties, the new upper class was the first to move into the suburbs, which became the new lifestyle for decades to follow.

Figure 9.2: Standardized to Customized Economy

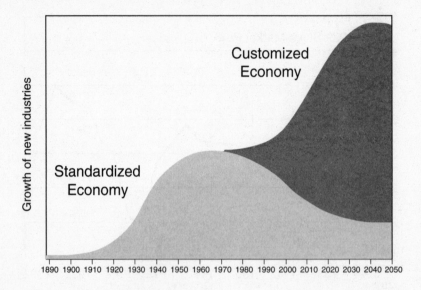

The point is that the new upper classes and innovators set the trends for the next New Economy Cycle, which unfolds over four seasons. In the first two seasons, income inequality grows, with the rich getting richer and the top income groups taking the lion's share of the gains. In the next two seasons, the gains pass through increasingly to broader income groups as the new technologies become more accessible and governments react in the Shakeout Season to favor the everyday worker and household, including trends like rising labor unions. From 1930 to 1976, the everyday household made greater gains than the upper class on average, and broad-based prosperity advanced more than at any other time in history in the developed countries! This will occur again from 2010 onward for many decades to come and spread to the emerging world to an even greater degree. Trickle-down economics does work. It just takes decades, not years!

So the first point is that it is natural for income inequality to grow and to reward the more entrepreneurial innovators and more highly skilled workers, who take more risks and who invest in the future, including their own education. But when the bubble boom finally bursts, these very people lose the most, as they own the most assets that deflate, then costs come down and make more things affordable to everyday people and the government naturally reacts with policies that tax the affluent more and favor the everyday worker and household. Unions also naturally grew to protect the average worker from excessive management power from the 1930s into the 1970s before they started to wane into this decade. Life expectancies also advanced more rapidly from the 1930s into the 1960s, creating more broad-based prosperity through longer work and productivity cycles for more people, because the rich have always tended to live longer.

Recall from Chapter 2 that the economy's natural mechanisms favor the extreme advancement of new technologies and business models through bubbles that raise sudden and extreme amounts of capital and leverage to support the maximum of new innovation into the Growth Boom Season, once such innovations first move to the mainstream. It is the Shakeout Season that pulls the rug out from under the economy and forces a survival-of-the-fittest test that narrows down companies in each sector to the few that can survive and create on an even greater scale to bring costs down to affordability for the masses. This creates a banking crisis and much consolidation in business, which creates high unemployment at first—but which then creates a more level playing field for broader progress for more people in the future. Hence, there is a method to the madness of bubble booms and busts!

Given that the economy already will evolve naturally to shift the advantages to more and more everyday people over the coming decades, we now come to the natural responses of government policies to the severe downturn ahead—the first depression since the 1930s. Remember that our theory is that governments don't primarily drive economic growth or change so much as they react to it—including short-term changes in fiscal and monetary policies and interest rates as the economy ebbs and flows. However, it is important that governments create the framework of laws, regulations, and financial institutions and also the basic infrastructures that allow such innovation and change in the first place. That is the biggest difference between most of the more advanced developed countries and the less developed emerging countries today, and this difference includes more democratic and transparent government and business practices in the advanced countries. That's why immigrants from

Mexico and Latin America—or from Africa or India—can move to countries like the United States and make major advances in their standard of living.

Rising Taxes and Growing Safety Nets for Everyday and Lower-Income Households

There have already been growing calls among the Democratic Congress and from Barack Obama to raise capital gains taxes and marginal rates on the top 1% to 2% of households (those making over $250,000 annually, who actually pay nearly 40% of federal taxes apart from Social Security at the present time). However, the extreme downturn we are forecasting between late 2009 and mid- to late 2012 will force this issue to the fore, and we will see major legislation emerge to raise taxes even higher on the more affluent between 2011 and 2014.

Ultimately, marginal tax rates are likely to rise on households making more than $100,000, which is the top 10%, not just the top 1%—and taxes eventually will rise for the top 20% to 40%, households making more than $60,000 to $70,000 annually.

The call for rising taxes and greater protection for everyday households will grow rapidly, given dramatically growing unemployment between 2010 and 2012 as the economy worsens, with an even more extreme mandate for change in the 2012 elections.

There also will be growing legislation for greater protection of households that are defaulting on mortgages and whose members are being laid off or losing health-care benefits. The federal government ultimately will have to take over a substantial share of mortgages, as the banking system will not be able to handle them. The government will have to support mortgage lending to everyday households as it did in the 1930s. It will have to become the "lender of last resort" to banks and consumers to an even greater degree than it did in the 1930s, as it has clearly started to in 2008.

Social Security and Medicare/Medicaid Finally Get a Reality Check

For decades, intelligent analysts and economists have warned about the obvious: that Social Security and, more so, Medicare/Medicaid benefits are not sustainable as our society ages and we approach a ratio of two workers for every retiree by around 2030. Of course, these ratios are even worse in Europe, Russia, and Japan. Politicians and most of society are simply in denial about this. There are always very rosy long-term projections regarding GDP growth and investment returns, which show that, after a difficult decade or so ahead as baby boomers retire en masse, the economy all works out by 2040 or 2050. Even the traditional 4% real GDP growth forecasts of the past are not realistic in an aging society with slowing growth. However, the real flaw is that they project such rosy rates of growth from the top of a long boom that is way overdue for a major correction in both growth and investment returns. These projections certainly don't take into account a "great depression" ahead, and that is what we will see.

By 2012 we could see GDP down 10% to 20% and unemployment as high as 14% to 16%. What will that do to payroll taxes for Social Security and Medicaid? What will that do to long-term projections for GDP and government tax revenues? It will quickly become obvious that Social Security and Medicare/Medicaid must be radically restructured for rationed benefits by need, with later retirement ages and higher payroll taxes or, more likely, with much higher payroll tax limits. The affluent will again pay most of the bill and get less of the benefits—but at least the next generation will not have to wait twenty years to address the sustainability of these programs, when it could be too late.

It is hard to predict the magnitude of the coming downturn on government revenues and social costs. However, real GDP declined nearly 30% from 1929 to 1933, as did consumer prices, whereas tax revenues in total declined 50%, with personal and corporate income and taxes down 69%. Our simple analysis assumes that this depression will be about half as bad as during the 1930s, since the unemployment and GDP downturns in recent recessions have been about half as bad as those preceding the Great Depression in the early 1900s. So 15% unemployment and a 20% plus drop in GDP are probably the best forecast, with government revenues down 40% plus—and it could be worse with all of the leverage and real estate overvaluation in this cycle. We will very likely see GDP no higher than 2009 in 2019, and possibly lower. Consumer prices probably will be lower in 2019 than in 2009, and government tax revenues are likely to be about the same in 2019 as in 2009—but with greater rises in expenses and benefits.

We predict that between 2013 and 2014, there will be a major overhaul of Social Security and Medicare/Medicaid—and that will be a good thing longer term. However, affluent households and taxpayers will be the big losers.

A Brief History of the New Deal in the 1930s

Franklin Delano Roosevelt (FDR) won the election in 1932 by a landslide, and the Democrats took control of both houses of Congress as the crash and record unemployment defeated Herbert Hoover and the Republican Party, which was the probusiness and lower-tax party during the Roaring Twenties. FDR had pledged a "New Deal" back at the Democratic convention in Chicago. Upon his inauguration on March 4, 1933, he gave his famous declaration, "The only thing we have to fear is fear itself," and then gave his first "fireside chat" on March 12. He immediately declared a four-day bank holiday on March 5. He summoned Congress to the "Hundred Days" session from March 19 to June 16 to generate many of the New Deal policies that would follow. On the first day of the session, Congress passed the Emergency Banking Act, which gave FDR broad powers over banks and foreign exchange. When a thousand banks reopened after the four-day holiday, national confidence rose, just as unemployment was rising toward 25%—an unimaginable level in today's economy. Remember that the Dow had fallen by 89.5% from September 1929 to July 1932, just before the election.

On March 31, 1933, Congress passed the Reforestation Relief Act, employing 250,000 men immediately and ultimately employing 2 million in total by 1941. On March 19, FDR took the United States off of the gold standard to allow the massive debt that would be required to stimulate and shore up the U.S. economy. On May 12, Congress passed the Federal Emergency Relief Act, which authorized major grants to states, and the Agricultural Adjustment Act for relief to farmers by use of subsidies for curtailing production. On May 18, the Tennessee Valley Authority (TVA) was established to construct dams and power plants there. Also enacted were, on May 27, the Federal Securities Act to regulate stocks and bonds; on June 6, the National Employment System Act; and on June 13, the Home Owners Refinancing Act, which was designed to provide mortgage funding and aid to home owners and which provided loans for around 1 million mortgages into mid-1936. On the final day of the "Hundred Days" session, Congress established the Public Works Administration (PWA) for the construction of roads and other public projects, as well as the National Recovery Administration (NRA) to promote fair trade (declared unconstitutional by the Supreme Court in May 1935), and passed both the Farm Credit Act and the Banking Act of 1933, which established the FDIC to guarantee banking accounts with deposit insurance, starting in 1934.

You can see how rapidly government will and must act in a crisis. The first round of the massive reforms of the New Deal was legislated in just over three months in early to mid-1933, right at the peak of unemployment at 25%! A similar response is likely to come by 2013, if not earlier.

Other notable reforms and legislation in 1934 included the Farm Mortgage Refinancing Act to assist farmers in refinancing their mortgages; the Import-Export Bank to encourage foreign commerce; the Securities Exchange Act to regulate securities transactions; the Corporate Bankruptcy Act to allow reorganization if two-thirds of creditors agreed; and the National Housing Act, which established the Federal Housing Administration (FHA) to insure loans for construction and renovation or repair of homes. Phase two of the New Deal began in 1935 and contained the longest-range reforms, including Social Security and the actual beginning of the Works Progress Administration (WPA) for further public works and infrastructure projects. The first major tax increase under FDR came on August 30, 1935, with rising inheritance, gift, and marginal tax rates that followed Hoover's broad tax increases in 1932.

In 1936, FDR won another landslide victory. In 1937, he was given the authority to add judges for those who refused to retire at age 70 and give "full pay" incentives for those who did retire. The purpose obviously was to create greater support for FDR's New Deal programs. However, there was a public backlash against this extreme assertion of power. The dramatic New Deal policies clearly had crested in momentum by then, and actually had crested during 1935.

The New Deal was largely in place by 1935; it focused on massive public works to stimulate employment, regulation of financial markets, expanded government support for mortgage lending, bankruptcy relief, unemployment benefits, and Social Security—with rising taxes on the affluent to finance these programs. It was about helping struggling households, workers, and farmers—and about raising taxes on the rich. This will occur again, especially in the presidential term between 2013 and 2016, if not starting in 2010–2012.

There was a strong boom and recovery between mid-1933 and late 1937, with the Dow almost quadrupling between mid-1932 and early 1937, largely as a result of such extreme stimuli to fiscal and monetary policies. This is similar to what occurs to a more minor degree when the government and Federal Reserve stimulate the economy after a more normal or moderate recession, as in 1990–1991 or 2001 or mid-2008 into mid-2009. The Federal Reserve lowered short-term interest rates from 6% in late 1929 to 2% in 1931 and ultimately lowered them to 1% between 1938 and 1946, but only after raising them abruptly in late 1930— which was later seen as a major error in monetary policy. The Fed lowered rates to 1% in the very minor downturn between 2001 and 2003 and to near zero in 2008. It is very likely to keep rates low between 2010 and 2012—and into at least 2019, after perhaps some substantial rate hikes between 2015 and 2017.

The Parallels and Differences Between the 1930s and the 2010s

You can see the obvious parallels between the 1920s–1930s and today. We have been in a bubble, wherein most have benefited but the greatest gains have gone to the top 1% to 20%, the new upper class and the superrich. The difference this time is that the economy started to slow a bit earlier in the cycle from the subprime mortgage crisis and rising oil and commodity prices. In the 1920s, we did not have a commodity bubble, as it had already peaked on its 29- to 30-year cycle back in 1920. The decline in commodity prices (a much larger percentage of the economy back then) and the strong productivity from the technology revolution caused interest rates to decline in the 1920s, much as they did in the 1990s bubble. Falling interest rates only increase speculation and bubble trends.

Although housing was slowing between 1925 and 1929, it didn't experience a bubble like today's; it didn't slow as quickly and the banks did not extend credit nearly as liberally as they did in the 2000s. And we didn't see such a banking crisis this early as in 2008. We will see three bubbles deflating—stocks, real estate, and commodities—and an extremely leveraged financial system that has to unwind and deleverage. This will add to the downside pressures in this Shakeout Season, especially in the first few years from 2010 to 2012.

The last time we saw these three bubbles peak in similar time frames was around 1835. We saw the greatest extended stock crash before the 1930s and early 1940s between 1835 and 1857, with a "great depression" bottoming around 1843.

That depression and the on-and-off depressions between the 1870s, the 1880s, the 1890s, and the 1930s fell into the long bottom of our 500-year Mega Innovation Cycle. The 29- to 30-year Commodity Cycle peaked around then, as did a technology cycle in canals and steamships and a dramatic real estate boom, as the U.S. government encouraged expansion from the East Coast into the Midwest through inexpensive land grants that fostered real estate speculation. As in the 1930s, the government responded to such speculation by raising interest rates and tightening lending policies, which made the crisis worse—a mistake that is not likely to be repeated fully again.

The fact that our economy and financial systems are more mature and sophisticated, and the continued strong long-term growth in emerging countries, will likely make this depression less severe. That is where the 500-year Mega Innovation Cycle, upward since the late 1890s, becomes important, despite its impacts long beyond our lifetimes and planning horizons. The greatest burden will still fall on the U.S. government (and on other governments), as it did in the 1930s, but even more so this time. The downturn for banks, businesses, and unemployment is not likely to be quite as bad as in the 1930s. Some major policy mistakes were made out of inexperience and a lack of simple economic wisdom, which caused the Great Depression of the 1930s to be worse than it needed to be—simply because the government did not know how to manage such a shakeout from the bubble excesses and mainstream technology explosion of the 1920s. Federal Reserve policy is kind of like a teenager learning how to drive—he or she overcompensates and overreacts at first. The biggest policy error came with the infamous Smoot-Hawley Tariff Act in 1930. The United States raised import tariffs by as much as 50% on a wide range of goods, and that invited trade retaliation around the world. Total world trade dropped 67% from 1929 to 1933! That is astounding, and it compounded an already weakening economy in the United States and worldwide. The Fed, after initially easing interest rates, raised them in late 1930, considering such austerity to be "bitter and necessary medicine." Bank failures accelerated after that ill-advised move. Taxes were raised on individuals, on corporations, and on luxuries such as alcohol out of necessity due to the growing federal deficit, and that certainly did not help the economy near term.

Although taxes will certainly rise, especially on the affluent and on businesses, the Federal Reserve should be much more supportive of the banking system this time around. It will likely become the "lender of last resort," as it did with Bear Stearns in 2008, unlike in the 1930s. However, even that move may be considered a mistake by the new president and Congress in 2009, as citizens and taxpayers guaranteed the debt of major banks and investors rather than merely protecting home owners. That may cause Ben Bernanke some trouble and may even cost him his job. This time, in contrast to the Bear Stearns deal, our government will be less likely to bail out investors and bondholders at taxpayers' expense. Instead the "bailouts" will be more to the benefit of the home owners through guarantees and subsidies.

The U.S. government did not enter the 1930s with commitments to cradle-to-grave benefit programs, and it was not facing an aging population with a falling ratio of workers to retirees. There was no major housing bubble in the 1920s to deflate, nor was there a falling dollar or a large level of debt in the hands of foreign governments, as the United States was a net creditor in 1929.

This shakeout or depression largely will revolve around restructuring the debt of the banking system, companies, and the U.S. government. It will require major increases in taxes on the affluent and on businesses and major subsidies and support to everyday households and workers. We will see major bank failures and mergers in distress, but not likely near the extremes of the 1930s. The government will be limited in its ability to inflate its way out of the downturn—not only because of failing bank loans that actually contract the money supply, but also because of the threat of the destruction of the U.S. dollar if foreign governments and investors who hold dollars lose faith in our policies and fail to continue to buy U.S. Treasury bonds—or worse, start to sell them.

It is in the interest of major governments around the world not to let the United States, the leading economy, fall into a greater depression than necessary and not to let the U.S. dollar totally collapse—those governments hold a lot of U.S. dollars. Hence they will tend to continue to hold and to buy U.S. Treasury bonds. However, the U.S. will leave them no choice if it becomes totally irresponsible and raises expenditures to stimulate the economy without raising taxes and bringing its long-term budgets back in line. Our government will be between a rock and a hard place—and that is a good thing ultimately. It will have to restructure its tax and entitlement programs in a manner that is sound long term to keep other governments from making a run on the U.S. dollar! That will mean that the U.S. government will have to restructure those massive debts such that they can profit long term to repay them.

Tax Policies in the Great Depression

In Figure 8.12 in Chapter 8 we showed how marginal tax rates fell dramatically in the 1920s after World War I and then increased the most dramatically in history from 1932 into 1944–1946—from 25% to 94%! However, our tax systems were much different back then. Very few people paid income taxes until World War II. The income tax was started only in 1913 to finance World War I. Due to high exemptions, only 2% of households paid income tax in 1913, with marginal rates ranging from 1% to 7%. As World War I progressed, the top rate was raised to 73% and capital gains went to 77%, yet still only 5% of households paid income taxes in 1917. In 1921, top rates fell to 56%; they then fell to 46% in 1924, and finally, to 25% in 1926—helping to stimulate the Roaring Twenties boom, as did the low inflation, interest rates, advancing technologies, and high productivity all occurring at that same time. Taxes were cut on the first $4,000 (above exemptions) from 2.0% to 1.5%, and estate taxes were cut from 40% to 20%. So, as in the 1980s, 1990s, and 2000s, taxes fell in an increasingly booming and low-inflation economy in the 1920s.

Supply-side economists argue that cutting tax rates is a key to stimulating the economy. What is most true is that a strong economy allows the government to cut tax rates as revenues rise and social costs fall. In turn, this means that a bad economy requires raising taxes, because government revenues fall and social costs rise, creating mushrooming budget deficits. Governments can keep taxes low and stimulate the economy in minor recessions such as those of 1990–1991 and 2001 but not in major ones like the 1970s or the Great Depression. Taxes rose across the board in the 1930s, and a major hike in Social Security payroll taxes came in the 1970s, although income tax rates did not rise, since they already were high.

Herbert Hoover was still in office through early 1933 and of course lost by a landslide, as we remarked earlier. But even this probusiness president raised taxes in 1932 due to rising deficits. The top marginal rate soared from 25% to 63%; on the low end, the rate went from 1.5% to 4.0%. However, the low-end taxes still were applied only to affluent people at that time, not the everyday person. FDR continued to raise top income tax rates to 79% in 1936 and ultimately to 94% in 1944 to finance World War II.

In 1937, a 2% payroll tax was first instituted for Social Security, and that hurt businesses. The top corporate income tax rate rose from 11% in 1929, to 12% in 1930, to 13.75% in 1932, to 15% in 1936, to 19% in 1938, to 38.3% in 1940, to 44% in 1941, to 53% in 1942. The biggest tax rates for business and the broadest for individuals came during World War II. In fact, it was not until 1942 that the majority of households paid income tax. Marginal rates went up to 13% on the first $2,000 (for the first time hitting more of the middle class) and to 82% on those earning $200,000 or more. The number of taxpayers went up from 3.9 million in 1939 to 42.6 million, or 60%, in 1945.

The Great Depression and World War II created a major advance in the role and size of the federal government. Public debt rose by $23.8 billion, whereas private debt fell by $8.5 billion from 1932 to 1940. Federal versus state and local taxes rose from 16% of the total in 1940 to 51% in 1950. Government employment was larger in 1940 than 1929, whereas private employment was still lower.

Figure 9.3 shows how much the federal government's income tax revenues fell: 69%, from $2.4 billion in 1930 to $750 million in 1933 due to the severity of the downturn—despite sharply rising tax rates. Corporate and individual taxes were nearly equal back then and they dropped similarly. Total government revenues, including excise and customs taxes, fell from $4 billion to $2 billion, or 50%. Excise taxes on things like liquor rose the most in the 1930s. Never before had the U.S. government seen such a shock to tax revenues. There was no way not to raise taxes, even though raising them obviously would hinder the recovery! State and local governments began to institute income taxes and raised taxes as well in the 1930s.

Figure 9.3: U.S. Revenues from Corporate and Individual Income Taxes, 1925–1940

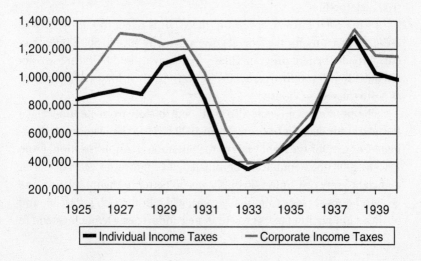

Rising Taxes from 2010–2011 into 2016

Obama is claiming to target only the top 1% to 3% (incomes over $250,000), but that will not last. The top 20% to 40% will see tax rate increases by 2014 on incomes as low as $60,000 to $75,000. Exemptions will continue to be eliminated for affluent households. Capital gains taxes first are likely to return to 25% to 30% and ultimately to rise to 50% to 70%. The Social Security limit on payroll and earned income will rise from the present $102,000, and ultimately that limit is likely to be lifted altogether. That could represent one of the greatest broad taxes on the affluent (a rise of 12.4% on all earned income).

We have been warning affluent people and business owners that there will naturally be a backlash in public and government sentiment against them when the bubble boom finally busts. Entrepreneurs are worshiped in a bubble boom for advancing technologies, innovation, and jobs—even though the rich are getting richer much faster than the everyday household. However, when the tide turns and unemployment, health-care, pension, and investment plans fail, those in everyday households get angry and blame the very entrepreneurs, financial wizards, and businesspeople who created the bubble. In the 1930s, FDR increasingly demonized business leaders and investors as "economic royalists" and "privileged princes" seeking a "new despotism" and "industrial dictatorship."

In the Next Great Depression, the GDP is likely to fall by 15% to 20%; tax revenues for the federal government, by 40% to 50%. If that occurs, broader benefit programs like Social Security and Medicare/Medicaid quickly will put forth crisis projections for their long-term viability, as we discussed previously.

The political landscape also will tend to shift from Republican to Democrat for decades to come. From 1932 to 1968 the Democrats dominated, except for the eight years of the Eisenhower administration. From 1969 to 2008, the Republicans dominated, except for four years of Carter and eight years of Clinton. Republicans do better in the innovation and growth boom seasons (about 40 years), wherein the rich get richer and business innovation favors growth in new industries. Democrats tend to control when the economy is in the Shakeout and Maturity Boom Seasons, wherein benefits pass more to the everyday worker.

In this coming depression the United States (and many developed nations) will have to fight rising terrorism and deal with greater global tensions and rising trade protectionism, while global warming is likely to accelerate its impacts on weather. Those things we will have to deal with as they arise. But the one predictable thing our government can do in this period of very high unemployment and business/debt restructuring is to make major investments in long-term infrastructures. In the 1930s unemployment stayed above 14% for ten years. This time it may be more like above 9% for ten years. But that creates a lot of idle capacity, which can be used for local and national projects to benefit the future, as occurred in the broad public works projects in the Great Depression. This time infrastructure investments are even more critical, as infrastructure has deteriorated in many areas and we need new infrastructure for a world that faces grave threats from pollution and congestion.

The clearest and best policy for dealing with this necessary and protracted period of high unemployment and business/debt restructuring is for governments at the national, state, and local levels to make the most critical infrastructure investments required for the future while labor is freed up. The benefits will be much greater than mere unemployment benefits, which only stimulate spending and allow households to cope near term.

This will also likely be seen in retrospect as a blessing in disguise, as we have not kept up with our infrastructure needs in the boom. The federal government should spearhead this effort and make major grants down to the state and local levels. But in keeping with sound policies and the huge deficits they will generate, the U.S. government should also participate in the benefits and revenues that accrue long term. With the already large deficits and huge foreign debts we have, we cannot just run massive deficits without both raising taxes and creating long-term revenues to pay off those debts—otherwise we will kill the U.S. dollar (which many valued trading partners are holding) and mortgage our kids' futures.

Our government spends only 2.4% of its GDP on infrastructure compared to 5.0% in Europe and 9.0% in China, as Fareed Zakaria showed in his CNN *GPS* show in July 2008. Not only are we not keeping up with our infrastructure, from water to wastewater to roads to bridges and levees, we need new technologies in all these areas and new infrastructure for alternative energy that can deal both with the energy crisis and with the pollution crisis. Global warming is only a symptom of a much bigger environmental crisis that has been emerging especially since World War II, as we will discuss just ahead. Worldwide growth has accelerated and encompassed emerging countries with much larger populations. We cannot grow as we did in the past, when resources and energy were abundant. It's not just resource scarcity; the carbon and pollution impacts are even more threatening to our quality of life and standard of living—as China is fast becoming aware. Developed nations will have to invest in emerging countries to deal with pollution and trade issues, as we will discuss ahead as well.

Investing in new technologies that revitalize and expand long-term infrastructure, including alternative energies, is perhaps the greatest way that government can help spur private investment and innovation, which in turn helps to counter the inevitable slowing demographic trends and the aging of our society.

Growing Trade and Economic Protectionism

We are not coming into this downturn with the sharply rising tariffs that we had in the 1930s, but there is rising public sentiment for curbing the outsourcing of jobs and goods overseas and curbing immigration. Both of these are natural reactions that will occur but are not the best intermediate- or long-term policies. Immigration naturally will decline, with fewer opportunities and jobs in a declining economy. On top of that, the public, led by Lou Dobbs, of course, will start demanding stricter immigration laws and enforcement. Immigration dropped to nearly zero in the early 1930s after reaching its highest relative rates in U.S. history between 1907 and 1914. This will happen again—it's just that we may not drop quite so far.

Calls for greater trade protectionism and the combating of unfair competition from countries like China are already growing in the latter stages of the boom. Imagine how strong those demands will be from voters in the downturn. Emerging countries like China will feel their vulnerability in trade with North America and Europe and thus will become more protectionist regarding the West, while at the same time strengthening their trade alliances with neighboring countries. We are likely to see growing trade blocs in emerging countries that still have stronger demographic trends: in East Asia and Southeast Asia, the Middle East and North Africa, Latin America, and sub-Saharan Africa.

We certainly won't see world trade collapse by 67%, as we did in the early 1930s, and we should hope that we and most other countries do not adopt such strong trade protectionist policies. However, world trade could drop by 25% to 40%. It is inevitable that a drop will occur at first. Only down the road will the smartest countries realize that freer trade and greater specialization are the way out of this downturn. By the early to mid-2020s, meaningful steps will be taken back toward an even more global economy, with stronger global institutions to enforce such policies.

The 250-Year Revolutionary Cycle

The information revolution and especially the Internet dictate that the world must and will become more intertwined and connected. Yes, this downturn will increase trade protectionism and barriers to immigration, as well as a backlash against globalization (including terrorism) in third-world countries that are not benefiting from world growth. But we think that these regressive trends, including terrorism, are likely to peak by 2015, or by 2020 at the latest. There will be an increasing revolution within developed and emerging countries between 2012 and 2015, and between more emerging countries between 2015 and 2023, toward greater freedom rather than less. The downturn, with growing terrorism and unrest, like 9/11, may be seen as an excuse to tighten surveillance and further limit individual rights at first and to increase our military strength and presence around the world. However, the great majority of voters in the United States increasingly will favor less U.S. intervention overseas and freer trade between 2013 and 2020 and onward.

The apparent errors and unpopularity of the Iraq War, as costly as it has been financially and to our reputation in the world, may in the long term be seen as a blessing in disguise, not because we brought democracy and peace to the Middle East but because U.S. citizens decided to stop being global policemen.

However, there will be a battle back and forth on this issue for several years, first around individual privacy versus national intelligence and around national security versus intervention in overseas affairs. The more progressive policies are very likely to win, especially from around 2015 onward as we likely increasingly win the war on terrorism and lean toward greater privacy and freedom and less world intervention, except when we or our close allies are threatened directly.

The American and French revolutions represented the political side of the last 250-year Revolutionary Cycle. Americans overthrew what they deemed to be unfair control over their destiny and "taxation without representation." They overthrew the British monarchy in America. Then the French overthrew their monarchy, and monarchies have been declining in power ever since. Meanwhile, the Industrial Revolution was just beginning in Great Britain to create a small but rapidly growing middle-class workforce that would change the dynamics of our economy (to generation-based innovation and growth cycles) and to spread democracy and capitalism increasingly across the more developed world. Now this revolution is spreading to the emerging world, which has five times the population of the developed world and is still growing.

Similarly, the Protestant Revolution began 250 years earlier, in the early 1500s, starting with Martin Luther and extended by John Calvin. This movement questioned and increasingly countered the all-powerful Catholic Church while creating a new grassroots ethic of hard work, saving, and conservative morals. This movement and the work ethic blossomed most in the new American colonies, to which many Puritan believers fled to start a new world. They were the ones who most led the next 250-year Revolutionary Cycle in the mid- to late 1700s (after 90% died in the earlier colonies—the typical price of radical innovation).

The coming revolution will look to create an even greater level of democracy and participation around the power of the Internet. Politicians will get faster feedback from blogs and Internet polls. Local institutions and governments will gain more power at the local level while power paradoxically grows at the global level. More people and groups will become activists on the Web and take control over more projects and issues at the local and national levels. More campaign contributions and hence more power will come through the Web.

Green Networked Companies and Institutions

We have been arguing for over a decade that the reengineering trend in corporations was missing the greater principle of organizational change. Networks are driven by the users or customers. They operate from the bottom up, not the top down. They innovate more horizontally than vertically. Information technologies are now powerful, wireless, and affordable—so that information for making decisions can be put right in the hands of frontline workers or even the customers themselves, who, like "browsers," can access and customize products and services from the organization's broad resources of products and services (and strategic alliance partners), or "servers." Such an organization can produce more directly to demand (as Dell has done for decades) and operate more in real-time response (like our stock exchanges). Accountability—including profitability and specifically the profitability of every customer—can be pinpointed to individuals or to small frontline teams. The biggest reason that this has not occurred so far is that most managers like to control and to dominate people. (What's the use of being rich or powerful if you can't be a jerk?) This Shakeout Season will bring greater stresses to business and government institutions and force these changes to occur more radically and more quickly.

Management is the problem, not the solution. Our brightest people should be designing and mediating networks of information and relations that allow companies and institutions to run in "real time" with no bureaucracy and from the bottom up or customer back, like the New York Stock Exchange. The same principle comes environmentally. Companies should be able to profit by eliminating huge waste streams in their antiquated business designs dating back to the 1800s and early 1900s, when resources were abundant and cheap. That will eliminate much of the pollution we create and will best counter the potential global warming threat.

As we mentioned in Chapter 2, there is also a "green" movement that now has the attention of venture capitalists and Thomas Friedman. There are huge opportunities in technologies and designs that conserve energy and natural resources and greatly lower pollution. The commodity bubble and the growing threats of global warming are making this level of innovation essential. It is very likely that sooner or later there will be greater taxes on pollutants and carbon emissions, much like those which Europe has already implemented for decades and which have led to much lower environmental impacts there than in the United States and China.

It is important to see global warming as a huge symptom, not the root problem. The problem is simple. Developed countries have grown to astounding levels of wealth since the Industrial Revolution, when resources were plentiful and population levels much lower. However, we are largely using the same technologies, production organizations, and energy resources as were used back then. If the rest of the world continues to develop as fast as China is developing, we will destroy life as we know it!

Now, these resources are not abundant and the pollution impacts are becoming overwhelming. Emerging countries are growing much faster and literally will threaten existence as we know it. The pollution levels in China would horrify us in the United States, although the Chinese have achieved only a $5,000 per capita income (a sixth of ours) and are still at only 41% urbanization versus a potential for 80%—and they have more than four times our population! And consider India, Indonesia, Pakistan, and Africa, with billions more people and low per capita incomes and minimal energy use thus far. Thus, business as usual is no longer an option, and the huge "symptom" of global warming may finally be the event that forces the world, not just Western Europe and California, to respond. It is our opinion that global warming is more likely to be an exponential trend, as greenhouse gases stay in the atmosphere for something like 100 years—creating a cumulative effect that is hard to slow down, with only minor reductions in gases in the coming decades. More radical changes are needed, and we will still tend to see substantially rising pollution impacts and perhaps temperatures for decades to come anyway.

The next decade could continue to see growing hurricanes, flooding, and tsunamis from weather changes and earthquakes, as well as corresponding droughts elsewhere. It's not that there aren't some benefits to global warming, with longer agricultural seasons in many areas. It's that most of our present infrastructures and real estate are in areas that may be more disadvantaged, especially along coastlines in more developed and emerging countries. And there may even be a short-term cycle toward cooling that alleviates warming to some extent. And very long term, the cycles point toward cooling rather than warming. But massive pollution is still the major issue!

The real solution is twofold: (1) a radical redesign of our production and organization systems, and (2) a "new deal" between the developed and emerging countries.

Paul Hawken, Amory Lovins, and L. Hunter Lovins first presented a comprehensive view of the new business model for how we produce goods in their book *Natural Capitalism* (1999)—they called it "The Next Industrial Revolution." Actually, the first to introduce this approach clearly were James Womack and Daniel Jones in *Lean Thinking* (1996). They were studying the leading-edge industrial designs of Taiichi Ohno, the father of Toyota's production system. Ohno's overriding principle was eliminating waste, which he defined as "any human activity that absorbs resources but creates no value." Now Peter Senge, the organizational expert who wrote *The Fifth Discipline* (1993), has a new book out on this subject, *The Necessary Revolution* (2008). And Thomas Friedman has a new book, *Hot, Flat, and Crowded* (2008).

We have become proficient at creating waste and at wasting natural resources, especially energy. That made sense when such resources were cheap and plentiful and we were small in number. Now information is cheap and plentiful. We need to use information and real-time network-based production and organizational designs to eliminate systematically all waste in our systems, and that means (1) producing in real time to meet customer demand, (2) establishing continuous-flow systems, (3) eliminating inventories, (4) sourcing locally, (5) making decisions on the front lines, (6) cutting bureaucracy and unnecessary steps in production and processing, (7) simplifying and right-sizing tasks, and (8) selling long-term services rather than onetime products.

Obviously, some industries are easier to do this in than others. The reason that the New York Stock Exchange is a real-time network organization today is that it is almost totally information based. It prices every stock, bond, and commodity every second of the day with almost no bureaucracy. Somebody rings the bell at 9:30 A.M, runs, and gets the hell out of the way! Where is the management? You almost never see the managers unless they are standing with their best clients at the opening or closing bell. The users drive the system and get real-time quotes, confirmation of trades, and updates of accounts. All concerned know how much profit or loss they make every minute and every day at all levels.

The real revolution in business and organization is yet to come. The 250-year Revolutionary Cycle predicts an industrial/business/service/government revolution in the coming decades much like the Industrial Revolution of the late 1700s and the American and French revolutions. But in an increasing service economy, the revolution in our government and service institutions will be even greater and more radical, at both the global and the local levels. New network organizational structures will attack most of our major issues, from inequality of incomes to global warming. This will create the single most profitable trend for decades to come.

We will not regurgitate our whole argument here, as we cover "The New Network Corporation" in four chapters, 5 through 8, of *The Roaring 2000s*. We strongly encourage businesspeople to read the three books mentioned above as well. There is already a clear road map to this revolution in production and business organizations that is succeeding today. History has shown that it is the coming stages of the 80-year New Economy Cycle—like Sloan's new corporate model at GM in the 1920s, which spread to the mainstream into the 1950s and 1960s—that will make the greatest difference in long-term productivity and in bringing greater rewards to everyday workers by raising their productivity and lowering the costs of the products and services they buy. Most people are not aware that new technologies such as automobiles, oil, and electricity actually reduced pollution in major cities from the late 1800s forward. Now they are the major polluters.

By having more frontline and everyday workers make decisions and operate like small businesses within corporations and companies, their value added will accelerate and be more measurable—in turn leading to higher incomes and reducing the income gap between the rich and middle class or poor today.

The New Deal Between Developed and Emerging Nations

There is also a great gap in incomes between emerging and developed countries, despite major leaps in progress in countries such as China and India. Of course, these gaps are much greater in many largely undeveloped countries in the still struggling and increasingly unstable third world. The challenge to help the poorest countries is great, as massive aid programs have seemed to do little to help—largely because most of the money just ends up back in the hands of corrupt governments or warlords. The problem in most of these countries is that dictators and corruption block access to technology and learning, so the people cannot advance as do those in China, India, Vietnam, or South Africa. However, there is the potential for the major developed countries and the successfully emerging countries to cooperate to deal with world issues like pollution and global warming, terrorism, unfair trade practices, and corrupt governments.

The most obvious potential comes in areas like carbon emissions. The paradox here is that the emerging countries are growing the fastest and have the least efficient technologies, which are increasingly contributing the most to pollution and global warming—they cannot afford the cleanest technologies and the environment is not a national priority compared with raising the basic standard of living. These countries obviously will contribute much more toward environmental problems as they grow at exponential rates for decades to come.

The obvious "new deal" here would be for developed countries to make major investments in emerging countries' infrastructures for energy, electricity, and water/wastewater. This approach would have a much greater impact on reducing global pollution than having the emerging countries try to make their own technologies more clean and efficient. Such infrastructures would also help to accelerate development in the emerging countries and help to close the income gap to some degree as well—with greater global GDP and trade as a result.

This is an example of a clear win-win solution. In exchange for major investments such as these and others, the developed countries also could get agreements for fairer trade or to help police the terrorism in the less developed countries that may be affecting the rest of the world, and so on. They may also get a share in the returns of these projects. Recall that much of the focus for economic stimulation and job creation came from government-backed infrastructure programs in the 1930s. In 2008, despite campaigning for "not negotiating or talking with terrorist nations," the Bush administration actually got North Korea visibly to abandon its nuclear capacities in (at first) trade for economic aid and lifting trade sanctions.

The governments of the more affluent developed countries will fund major infrastructure projects at home and in emerging countries to accelerate progress on pollution and global warming and stimulate employment in depressed times. This also will represent a means for the developed countries to get emerging countries to cooperate on issues like terrorism, fair trade, and pollution.

Emerging countries such as China are making alliances with resource-rich countries in Southeast Asia, Latin America, the Middle East, Russia, Canada, Australia, and Africa, as their high-growth and commodity-intensive economies require such resources for growth. However, the developed countries naturally will try to increase their alliances with emerging countries for trade and military cooperation, as China and India are building up their armed forces, especially their navies. The truth is that China will be the dominant military power in Asia in the coming decades. Ultimately, however, India will have the largest population and economy, and likely the most military power by the time we move into the 2040s–2060s. China's growth rate will slow down temporarily after 2009, again to a greater degree after 2020, and dramatically after 2035. Hence the smartest developed countries, especially the United States and the United Kingdom, ultimately are likely to ally more with India over time—if it ever comes to a choice, and it likely will.

The most probable major wars in trade or military affairs are likely to come from among China, India, Russia, and the Middle East. China and India increasingly will be the rising major powers in the world, along to some degree with Russia; Russia is a declining country that still has vast natural resources, which makes it a potential acquisition target first for China and later for India. The Middle East is a rising area with energy resources at least for some decades into the future, and is likely to follow the lead of Dubai as a growing trade hub between Europe, Asia, and Africa. The United States and Europe may get dragged into some of these wars, and the next major war cycle is due around the early to mid-2020s on the 80-year New Economy Cycle. Similar broad generational cycles from William Strauss and Neil Howe show a very broad global challenge from the early 1990s (9/11) into the early to mid-2020s, as the millennial generation comes of age in growing numbers—much as the Bob Hope generation saw from the 1920s through World War II.

The echo-boom or millennial generation is due to face a world crisis much as the Bob Hope generation did in the Great Depression and World War II. There are two major birth surges for this generation: 1976–1990 and 1998–2007/2008. The first group is coming of age during the rising threat of terrorism from 2001 to likely around 2012 to 2014. The second group could see something like World War III, which is more likely to focus on rising Asian nations. The big question is how involved countries like the United States will be in international military affairs by the 2020s, or even whether the United States will become a target. We are likely to be less interventionist by then but could still be forced into a war, much as we were in World War II.

The Greatest Challenge: Aging Societies

Many of the financial issues discussed above arise from a slowing in long-term growth (and even outright decline in many countries) and falling entitlements as the ratio of workers to retirees falls. Phillip Longman was the first to address this issue broadly in *The Empty Cradle* (2004). Most people simply can't grasp that affluent countries like Japan, Germany, Italy, Spain, and Greece could lose up to half of their population in fifty years. It's worse for Russia, because the Russians aren't just failing to have enough kids but are also drinking themselves to death, with declining life expectancy (one way to control the excessive retiree population). However, that is approximately what the clear trends in births and deaths suggest! As we showed in Chapter 6, even South Korea, Hong Kong, Singapore, and China face this crisis much sooner than most would assume. Ultimately this will occur in North America and eventually in the emerging countries as they become more affluent and urban and have fewer kids as well.

There are a number of potential and likely solutions to the aging crisis in the developed world:

1. Higher immigration from cultures with higher birthrates, as has occurred in the United States and parts of Europe and Australia/New Zealand.
2. More births through subsidized child care (as in Scandinavia and northern Europe) or through cultural and corporate support for women who work and have kids (ample corporate-subsidized and private child care and support from husbands in sharing the tasks), as in the United States.
3. An aging revolution, wherein people in developed countries not only live much longer, but are productive and work until they are much older. If life expectancy advances as much in the next four decades as it did between the 1930s and 1960s, it could extend toward 100 or higher; peak spending and productivity could come well into the early 60s, with retirement in the mid-80s. Life expectancy could advance more than that, given the potential of biotechnology, nanotechnology, and robotics.
4. Advances in fertility that allow people who live longer to have babies later, and, hence, to have more children over their lifetimes on average.

In Chapter 6, we also addressed the potential for a second baby boom, likely in emerging countries after a world crisis, just as the 1930s and World War II spawned the last great baby boom worldwide. Crises like these seem to cause people to stop taking the value of family for granted and to have more kids. This could occur to some degree in the 2020s and 2030s. However, it would seem to us more likely to occur after the next greater depression and crisis likely in the 2070s—and that would lead to a more dynamic economy in the first half of the next century. That would also put us more in line with an expected continued growth and inflation cycle into around 2150 on our 500-year Mega Innovation Cycle. However, the potential baby boom and demographic revolution are too far away for present concerns.

The real question is: What is likely to occur in reaction to slowing births and declining/aging populations in the next few decades? First, let's examine the problem a little more closely. In Figure 6.1 in Chapter 6 we showed how birthrates in general are falling almost everywhere around the world and predictably, making future trends largely predictable. Figure 9.4 shows the very clear trend between rising standards of living (and urbanization) and birthrates. The decline comes

Figure 9.4: Fertility Rates Versus GDP per Capita

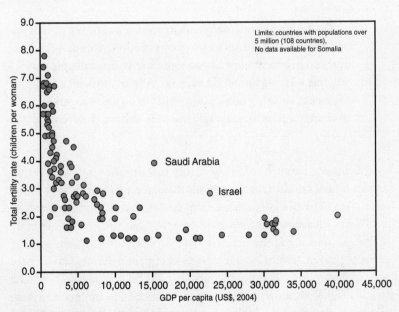

Source: CIA World Fact Book (www.cia.gov).

quickly as you move to $5,000 in per capita GDP and to a lesser degree to $10,000.

An affluent society like ours needs about 2.1 births per household just to replace itself over time (replacement level is slightly higher in emerging countries with higher mortality rates). The lowest birthrates today are in places like Hong Kong at 1.00, Singapore at 1.08, and Taiwan at 1.13. Japan is at 1.25, Germany 1.41, and Russia 1.40. Italy, Greece, and Spain are around 1.3. In Scandinavia, where there is strong state support for paid maternity leave and child care, birthrates are 1.70 to 1.85 per household. England is also stronger at 1.70. France and Australia are at 1.75, and New Zealand is at 2.01. Canada is much weaker than the United States and Northern Europe at 1.55, but western Canada is much stronger. The United States is the strongest at 2.10, due to a culture (rather than a government) that supports working women and high immigration from Mexico and South America, countries with higher birthrates on average. That's why population growth for the U.S. and Australia/New Zealand is still strong for decades ahead, whereas most of Europe, Russia, and East Asia decline significantly by 2050.

Declining population is disastrous for a country, as innovation declines well before economic trends— and you just can't have an economy where most people are in a nursing home! Yet aging trends are difficult to reverse, as an aging population tends to be more adverse to change and is increasingly less able to have children.

We already see such countries as Russia, Australia, and Norway giving substantial bonuses for households that have a second child or more, but it takes more than that. (See a great article, "No Babies?," in *The New York Times Magazine,* June 29, 2008). Norway has the highest birthrate in Europe, and it has the greatest state support for mothers, with 54 weeks of paid maternity leave and 6 weeks of paid paternity leave. There is a 4,000-euro bonus, and state-subsidized child care is common. The paradox is that although 75% to 80% of women in Scandinavian countries work, they have the highest birthrates in Europe. It is the state and cultural support for working women that makes the difference. A 2006 Eurobarometer survey by the European Commission showed that the average woman desires to have 2.36 kids. That is perfect, since it allows for replacement and mild growth over time. However, urban society makes it difficult for women to do so, with rising burdens of work and child care.

Contrast Norway with Italy, in which only 50% of the women work, but the birthrate is 1.30. The tradition there is for women to stay home when they have kids, but they get little or no state support and little support from their husbands, who work full-time. Young people also stay with their parents longer, due to low pay in entry-stage jobs. Hence they tend to have fewer kids later. A much greater proportion of births in Italy is to parents in their late 30s and 40s than in most countries. Surveys also have shown that women who have to do more than 75% of the housework are not likely to want to have another child. In more progressive countries, such as the United States and those in Scandinavia and Northern Europe, men share more in the household tasks when both spouses work; that makes it feasible to have an extra kid.

There are two models that work for supporting more children in affluent urban societies: the Northern European model, with strong state and husband support for the wife, and the laissez-faire U.S. system, wherein private companies and the husband provide more support. The truth is that countries with a higher percentage of women working have higher birthrates than those with a lower percentage. However, the women need help and support to achieve that, and it is a worthwhile investment.

The more traditional, old-fashioned countries in Southern Europe, Russia, and Eastern Europe are less likely to see innovative reforms that support both higher birthrates and working rates for women. You need to become modern all the way, not just urban with outmoded traditional gender and family values. East Asia also is not likely to reverse its very low birthrates, as traditional gender values tend to rule there as well. More countries should study and adopt the successful models of Northern Europe, the United States, and New Zealand.

The Immigration Solution Will Not Be Popular in a Strong Downturn

The immigration solution is less likely to be embraced, with perhaps some exceptions such as Australia. The reason is simply that affluent countries, especially the United States, have already seen strong immigration trends for decades in this unprecedented boom, which is causing a backlash from lower-level workers who fear competition over jobs and also a broader cultural backlash. It's hard to take in a sizable minority that has different values and language so rapidly. In Europe, many of the immigrants are from Muslim countries and don't assimilate easily—and European culture is harder to assimilate into compared with the American "melting pot" of long-standing immigration from all parts of the world.

We have been forecasting that the slowdown in the U.S. and world economies would lead to major falls in immigration rates, as occurred in the 1930s, when immigration dropped to nearly zero after the highest rates in history just two decades before. The incentive to immigrate into a declining economy will drop, and the backlash in a rising unemployment environment will grow exponentially. Ultimately, immigration will look more attractive to affluent nations after they suffer economic and demographic slowing in the next decade. We expect immigration rates to pick up again in the 2020s and 2030s but probably not to the rates we saw in the 1980s to 2000s.

The best models for immigration come from such countries as Australia and Canada, which encourage selective immigration for the skills that are needed. However, given the projected population declines of 35% to 50% in many European and East Asian countries, immigration rates would have to be too high to work long term anyway.

The Aging Revolution: More Substantial Increases in Longevity in the Next Four Decades Are Actually Likely

Again, we can get unique insights from looking back over our 80-year New Economy Cycle. Increasing life spans come both from medical advances and from higher standards of living. Medical advances counter premature deaths for children and for adults from lower cancer and heart disease rates, as do safer cars, airplanes, and work machinery. Higher standards of living are equally if not more important. It's pretty hard to get seriously injured working in an air-conditioned office doing paperwork with health-care benefits (although paper cuts can be a bit nasty), whereas working on farms, in mines, or on fishing vessels is another story. Obviously, we also have much better health-care benefits and more potential solutions—and that is the biggest reason health-care costs (including unnecessary bureaucracy and litigation) are rising so much: there are simply more solutions and results versus 20 or 50 years ago.

In the last 80-year New Economy Cycle, advances in our longevity accelerated to 4 years per decade between the 1930s and 1960s, as new technologies and middle-class, suburban lifestyles finally moved fully into the mainstream. In the last four decades, that rate slowed down to 1.5 years per decade. That means we are due for the next aging revolution from around the 2010s to the 2040s or so. This time we could see advances of 4 years or more per decade. Again, we would not be surprised to see an average life span closer to 100 and retirement closer to 85 by 2050, in the more developed countries at first. That sounds bad, since it would mean more old people. However, the truth is that it would advance the peak spending and productivity ages likely into the late 50s or early 60s. That would mean that the peak in the echo-boom Spending Wave in the United States would be more like the mid- to late 2060s instead of the mid- to late 2050s, more in line with India's likely peak.

It wasn't an accident that the greatest advance in our standard of living in history accompanied the greatest advance in our life spans in the last century. An aging revolution would raise our standard of living and allow more people to work more productively and longer, to earn more, and to accumulate more wealth. Longer life spans also would increase the odds of having more children per household, especially with advances in fertility enhancements.

If you really want to get excited about the potential aging revolution, just read Ray Kurzweil's book *The Singularity Is Near* (2005). He sees a combination of biotechnology, robotics, and nanotechnologies that will greatly change human life and artificial intelligence by the 2040s. It is hard to grasp how truly exponential technological progress is until you look back at long-term history, as we and Kurzweil have done. More progress was made in the last century than in the 1,000 years before, and more progress was made in the last 200 years than in the 10,000 years before. It is better to overestimate technology than underestimate it. How many people born in the early 1900s would have anticipated even remotely what would happen in their lifetimes?

The only limitation we see to exponential technology progress ahead is demographics. Although technology clearly grows exponentially over time, it still grows in leaps and then slows (much as the ancient Greek and Roman civilizations were followed by the Dark Ages). Young people, especially those ages 20 to 24, are the key drivers of radical innovations. Global innovation should continue to have strong tailwinds into around 2040, due to growth in areas such as India and the Middle East. However, after that, slowing young populations and aging societies are likely in turn to slow innovation and technological progress for decades, until there is a potential second major baby boom in the emerging world, which is most likely to occur between the late 2070s and late 2090s—too far out for our time horizons.

Human population has grown exponentially for at least 50,000 years. Figure 9.5 shows the growing human population bubble over the last 3,000 years, wherein it is more measurable. When population exploded

Figure 9.5: The History of World Population Growth

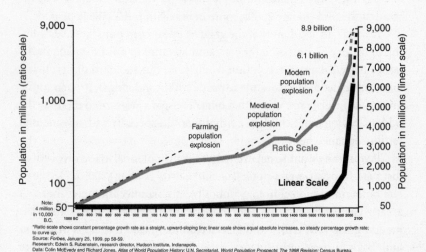

*Ratio scale shows constant percentage growth rate as a straight, upward-sloping line; linear scale shows equal absolute increases, so steady percentage growth rate; to curve up.
Source: Forbes, January 25, 1999, pp 58-59.
Research: Edwin S. Rubenstein, research director, Hudson Institute, Indianapolis.
Data: Colin McEvedy and Richard Jones, Atlas of World Population History; U.N. Secretariat, World Population Prospects: The 1998 Revision; Census Bureau.

from 1,000 BC into AD 200, the Greek and Roman empires blossomed, as did innovations in technologies. Population accelerated to a lesser degree again between AD 800 and 1200, with strong growth and expansion out of the Dark Ages, when population slowed to nearly zero for many centuries. The last surge in population began in the 1700s, and that saw the Industrial and American revolutions and nonstop technological innovation ever since. If human population peaks around 2065, as the best forecasts of present trends in births and longevity strongly suggest (see Figure 6.2 in Chapter 6), then innovation and economic growth will slow and ultimately even decline. For more information go to www.hsdent.com to "Free Downloads" to "The Long View."

That is why it is important that the more affluent countries—and down the road, the emerging countries—take seriously this challenge of aging societies and utilize new technologies to offset the demographic decline both by encouraging higher birthrates and longer work spans and by continuing to advance the standard of living through infrastructure investment and technological innovation to create more sustainable growth and offset the slowing in population.

Terrorism Should Peak by 2014, and World War III Could Come in the 2020s

We have noticed that terrorism cycles have seen escalating major attacks about every eight to nine years: 1993, 2001, and now likely 2009–2010. Hence we think it is likely that there will be a larger event somewhere between November 2009 and May 2010, when we expect the next crash most likely to accelerate. Such geopolitical events could cause term spikes in gold and oil prices between late 2009 and early to mid-2010. However, we also think that terrorism is a trend that will die of its own success, just as bubbles do. The more the terrorists succeed, the more we and the world will tend to unite to fight them—and they are on the wrong side of the growth and progress equation.

Unfortunately, U.S. foreign policy has ignored the same principle the other way. The more we interfere in Arab and Islamic countries' affairs, the more they can enlist terrorists to attack us, since we have failed to understand how they see globalization and Western values as a threat to their long-standing cultures—even though they would do better to change and modernize than fight such trends. This is no different from the South fighting the North in the Civil War. The North was the rising industrial power and the South was the waning agricultural power—and the new technologies and lifestyles were certain to win in the long term due to their rising demographics and technological productivity. However, the North underestimated the resolve and resistance of the South, and it was a difficult war and transition. The terrorists and more backward cultures will not win this war against globalization and more modern/progressive values in the end—but they will put up a strong fight first!

Information technologies will increase public reaction against more backward, dictatorial, and oppressive regimes from parts of Asia to the Middle East, Latin America, and Africa. Cell phones and the Internet are the greatest enemies of these regimes, since those leaders will no longer be able to fool most of the people most of the time, just as television and greater economic and military power in the United States and Europe eventually brought down the Soviet Union. However, the makers of U.S. foreign policy need to "better understand our terrorist enemies" and the countries that we try to help to achieve democracy and higher standards of living. They are not like us!

It was one thing to discipline a rogue dictator like Saddam Hussein, who attacked an ally and a strong oil resource. We attacked decisively, expelled him from Kuwait, and then left. The only criticism of that war campaign was that we could have done more damage to Saddam's forces on their retreat. However, to invade and interfere in an Arab and Muslim country with its different religion and values was suicidal from the beginning, especially given the very different factions in Iraq, which would be hard to unite. A responsible and phased exit from that war seems to be the best course—but sooner rather than later. If the United States does that, and if we or a major ally is attacked in a substantial way, we expect the world to unite further against the terrorists. In the end, the terrorists don't have the resources or technology to win, and again, they are on the wrong side of global evolution and progress.

The failure of the Iraq War was not solely due to the U.S. attacking Iraq without stronger international backing and better intelligence (or ignoring the latter). Saddam Hussein, like Mahmoud Ahmadinejad of

Iran more recently, was violating clear codes of international conduct—and many European nations were reluctant to confront and to discipline those actions, partly out of a "wimpy" aversion to conflict and war and partly due to defense contracts with Iraq and similar rogue nations. If there had been stronger unilateral actions by the UN, the United States would not have been as compelled to act or as justified in attacking Iraq. However, there is a bigger problem in global politics and the UN. China and Russia are part of the "Big Seven" nations that control the UN, and they tend to decide with the rogue dictators, since they are more that way themselves and don't want to be disciplined and controlled, either. Also, China relies on many of these rogue dictatorships for natural resources.

The leading developed countries of the past and the leading emerging countries of the future need to realize that they have greater common interests than conflicts, in areas from terrorism and rogue dictators to pollution and global warming. We need global institutions with more legitimate power and authority than the UN—which is largely a joke, to be frank. The coming depression will increase trade protectionism, terrorism, pollution violations, and conflict until the leading nations—including China, India, and Russia—decide that it is better to cooperate than to compete and that globalization and freer markets are the solution, not the problem.

We do expect terrorism to rise in a world in economic decline, with greater unemployment as well as trade protectionism, and in retreat on environmental issues. It was no accident that World War II grew out of the Great Depression. Hitler never could have persuaded a largely civilized people to do what he did in the booming 1920s or 1950s. Hard times and unemployment create dissatisfaction and unrest, and that leads to rising crime (as we showed in Chapter 4), warfare, nationalism, and conflict—and in this case, terrorism. We really aren't ready for World War III yet, as major new countries have not emerged to the point that they have the military capacity to challenge the United States or to fight such a war. That would be due more on an 80- to 84-year cycle, much as occurred for the American Revolution, the Civil War, and World War II—and now, around the early to mid-2020s. By the 2020s and 2030s, we are likely to see a greater buildup in the armies and navies of China and India, as is already occurring. They could end up fighting over resources in Russia, the Middle East, or even North America.

Our best forecasts from our cycles are that we are likely to see a major terrorist event or a series of geopolitical tensions between late 2009 and mid-2010 and that terrorism in general is likely to continue to grow into 2014 to 2015 due to rising unemployment and unrest in the world, including falling oil and commodity prices between 2010 and 2012–2015, which could further destabilize the Middle East. However, we also expect the developed countries to unite further in this cause, to begin to turn back the tide, and to start winning that war by 2014 or 2015 onward. We expect that threat to be largely over by 2020. We also expect developed countries to cooperate more with emerging countries and make larger investments in them to improve infrastructures in exchange for greater cooperation regarding terrorists, fair trade, and pollution and global warming issues between 2014 and 2024.

One of the best ways to protect your family from the floods, tsunamis, and hurricanes that may be likely from continued climate change, and to protect yourself from rising terrorism and global conflict, is simply to choose not to live in cities that are high targets for terrorism or in coastal areas. Inland, medium-sized cities and regions will be the safest—places like Austin, Texas; Tucson, Arizona; Birmingham, Alabama; Salt Lake City, Utah; Albuquerque, New Mexico; or Raleigh-Durham, North Carolina. These are also among the cities in the "sweet spot of growth" and the areas of greatest domestic migration, as we covered in Chapter 5, for more buoyant growth, lower crime, and less real estate devaluation—as well as fewer failures of banks and municipalities.

Let's sum up the political, social, and organizational changes in the coming winter and Shakeout Season, and the longer-term trends from our "Grand Hierarchy of Cycles":

1. We need a revolution in business and political organization that will meet the crisis in oil and commodity prices, pollution and global warming, trade protectionism, inequality in incomes, lagging infrastructure investments, and terrorism.
2. This will require new and more legitimate, powerful, and broadly supported global institutions than ones such as the UN today at the macro level.

3. This also will require a revolution more at the micro level in network and real-time, bottom-up, zero-waste organizations at all levels to meet the greatest crisis and systems failures since the 1930s.

4. We have seen radical innovations in technologies and new industries in the innovation and growth boom seasons, as expected in the 80-year New Economy Cycle.

5. Radical political, social, and organizational changes will now occur in the Shakeout and Maturity Boom Seasons from 2008 to around 2036, which will create broader-based progress than has occurred thus far into 2009, both within developed countries and, to a greater extent, within emerging countries.

6. These radical organizational changes, along with major investments in infrastructures, will best address the key issues and imbalances facing the world today, more than will superficial political reactions to and short-term social benefits of the crisis ahead. For now this revolution will continue to be led by the United States, with increasing leadership from China and ultimately from India; Europe is contributing much to the "green" revolution.

7. India will be the largest country and will very likely rival or exceed the United States in economic and military power by the 2060s, surpassing China after the 2030s.

8. Affluent nations, followed by emerging nations, will have to address more seriously the grave challenges of aging societies by utilizing new technologies, political incentives, and organizational models, some of which are already succeeding in a small minority of countries.

9. In the end, globalization, free trade, migration, and greater cooperation among leading developed and emerging countries will be the answer, but greater conflict, trade protectionism, anti-immigration policies, and terrorism will accelerate first between 2010 and 2015, and perhaps as late as 2020.

10. The next "new deal" within developed and emerging coun-

tries will begin to emerge between 2012 and 2015, as will a "new deal" between developed and emerging countries increasingly between 2014 and 2023.

11. The next era will see great progress in technologies and organizational efficiencies but will not see the same concerted global progress that we saw from the 1950s into 2007–2009 and especially from 1983 to 2000, wherein developed countries advanced and emerging countries such as China and many others advanced even faster.

12. The next boom, from 2020–2023 into 2035–2036 and again from around 2052 into 2065–2069, will be more mixed, with many affluent nations slowing and more emerging nations advancing; the affluent nations will have more weight in overall GDP and the emerging countries more weight in growth rates and potential.

13. The next great depression after this one is very likely to occur from the late 2060s into the 2070s and will be more dramatic and centered in South Asia, the Middle East, and Africa.

14. We have just witnessed the greatest boom in history, especially from 1983 to 2007–2009. We will not likely see the same again from 2010 into the rest of this century. We will have to be smarter to grow and to advance in the coming decades, especially in the most affluent nations.

15. Although there will undoubtedly be great booms ahead in many emerging countries between now and at least the 2060s, many such countries have long-standing cultural limitations that may limit their ability to achieve standards of living as high as those in the most developed countries, including environmental challenges from rapid growth in countries with much larger populations than those of the West.

16. It may take a great revolution in cultures and a second great baby boom in the emerging world to create the next great boom or "golden era" between 2100 and 2160, which would lead to a more dynamic world economy that could rival the unprecedented world boom from the 1950s into 2007/2009.

17. The Middle East and Africa could end up being the leading

areas of the world, completing a cycle of growth and progress that initially began for human evolution and progress in these areas and that initially could peak around 2150–2160 on the 500-Year Mega Innovation Cycle.

18. A broader global boom from the 5,000-Year Civilization Cycle is likely to continue in untold ways long past the peak of the 500-year cycle as technologies and human progress continue exponentially long term—especially beginning in the 2400s onward.

We don't wish to overwhelm you with very-long-term predictions that will get less clear and definable going into the future. However, we do want to impress on you the powerful impacts of recurring short-term, intermediate, and long-term cycles, which do predictably impact the future and your life—even in a more complex and faster-changing world. New information and innovations have only increased the predictability of natural cycles and our standard of living, including our ability to harness such cycles for rising human progress—as we covered in the Prologue. Ray Kurzweil is another author who has successfully predicted long-term technology trends accurately in the past. In this book, we have focused on the next several years and decades, which will impact your life, business, and investments and those of your children.

Best of success to you! And please keep in touch with us through our free periodic updates and services on our website at www.hsdent.com, and through our newsletter and publications that are listed at the end of this book.

Index

affluence: and aging, 350, 351; and
   comparison of New Deal (1930s)
   and Next New Deal, 330, 333;
   and financial assets owned by
   top 1% of U.S. households, 323;
   and fundamental trends that drive
   the economy, 68; and global
   demographic trends, 178, 201–3,
   205, 207, 209, 210, 215, 216, 219,
   221–24; and immigration, 352; and
   impacts of Next Great Depression,
   322–27, 328, 336, 341, 350, 351,
   352, 359, 360; and New Deal
   (1930s), 330, 334; and Shakeout
   Season, 68; and stages of growth,
   216; and technology cycle, 59
Afghanistan, 36, 205, 207, 245
Africa: commodities from, 78;
   and fundamental trends that
   drive the economy, 49; and global
   demographic trends, 180, 181,
   183, 193, 194, 197, 220, 221, 231–32,
   233, 236, 237, 242, 244, 245, 247;
   immigration from, 326; and
   impacts of Next Great Depression,
   342, 346, 347, 356, 360–61; Next
   Great Depression in, 288, 299,
   360; and Next New Deal between
   developed and emerging countries,
   346, 347; terrorism in, 356. *See
   also* sub-Saharan Africa; *specific
   nation*

age/aging: and birthrates, 350–51; as
   critical to growth, 44; and
   fundamental trends that drive the
   economy, 63–64, 139, 181; and
   global demographic trends, 177, 181,
   183–85, 190–94, 197, 198, 199,
   201–3, 215, 217, 223, 224, 226, 228,
   235, 238–44, 248, 249–50, 251; and
   housing, 118; and impacts of Next
   Great Depression, 347–51, 352–55,
   359; and inflation, 44; and
   migration/immigration, 139,
   140–42, 144, 145, 146; and New
   Economy Cycle, 352, 353; and
   productivity, 44; and spending, 13,
   44, 49–53, 238–44; and stages of
   growth, 216; and strategies for Next
   Great Depression, 306
aggressive investments, 296–97, 298, 299
Agricultural Revolution, 208–9, 211, 212,
   213, 215, 216, 217, 218, 219, 220
agriculture: and Civilization Cycle, 81–82;
   as driver of economy, 20; and
   environment, 343; and fundamental
   trends that drive the economy, 44;
   and global demographic trends, 219,
   221–22, 224, 231, 232–33, 245; and
   New Deal (1930s), 329, 330; and
   New Economy Cycle, 284; and Next
   Great Depression, 284, 343; and
   Revolutionary Cycle, 91; and U.S.
   Civil War, 356

Alabama, 143, 149, 151, 154, 160, 166, 167, 169, 358

American Revolution, 46, 87, 89, 175, 319, 340, 344, 355, 357

Annual Cycle, 98–99, 100

annuities, variable, 280, 308, 311–12

apartment housing, 115, 116, 117, 126, 136, 142, 173, 298

Argentina, 193, 213–14, 236, 241, 243, 244, 245

Arizona: housing in, 114; and impacts of Next Great Depression, 358; migration/immigration in, 142, 143, 149, 151, 155, 156, 160, 163, 170, 171, 173

Arkansas, 166

Armstrong Cycle (8.6 year), 97–98

Asia: bubbles in, 21; and commodities, 78; and comparison of Next Great Depression and Great Depression (1930s), 128; and Empire Cycles, 84; and fundamental trends that drive the economy, 49; and global demographic trends, 14, 179, 180, 181, 183, 189, 216, 221, 233, 237, 242, 247, 249; and hierarchy of cycles, 93; immigration from, 164, 171; and Next Great Depression, 128, 287, 288, 289, 298, 356; and Revolutionary Cycle, 89; terrorism in, 356. *See also* East Asia; South Asia; Southeast Asia; *specific nation*

asset allocation: assumptions about, 256–57; and fundamental trends that drive the economy, 72; for New Economy Cycle, 14, 280, 281–319; for Next Great Depression, 14, 280, 281–319; traditional, 253–57, 280. *See also* return; risks

assets, passing of, 311–13

Australia: aging in, 348, 350; and global demographic trends, 175, 180, 194, 198, 202–3, 236, 245, 248; and impacts of Next Great Depression, 346, 348, 350, 352; and Next New Deal between developed and emerging countries, 346

Austria, 198, 202

automobiles, 11, 54, 55, 57–58, 59, 219, 221, 302, 310

baby-boomers: and commercial real estate, 125, 126; and crash of 2008, 17; and cycles, 18–19, 40; and debt crisis (2010–2012), 18; debt of, 22; and fundamental trends that drive the economy, 46, 48, 63–64, 68; and global demographic trends, 196, 216; and Great Depression (1930s), 126, 127, 128; and housing, 13, 108, 120, 121, 122, 124, 126, 136, 173; and Innovation Stage, 65; and migration/immigration, 146, 171–72; and New Economy, 65; and Next Great Depression, 126, 127, 128, 298, 327; retirement of, 18, 22, 128; savings of, 18, 22, 23; and Shakeout Season, 68; spending by, 13, 18–19, 21–24, 40, 47, 73, 121, 125, 127, 216; in workforce, 63–64

baby booms, 249, 250, 348–49, 354, 360. *See also* baby-boomers

Bahrain, 188, 207

bailouts, 17, 29, 255–56, 332. *See also* rescue plans; stimulus, economic

Bain & Company, 7–8, 9

Bangladesh, 189–90, 205, 207

bankruptcy, 27

banks/banking: bailout of, 58; and Commodity Cycle, 34–35; and comparison of Great Depression (1930s) and Next Great Depression, 128, 132, 133, 134; and comparison of New Deal (1930s) and Next New Deal, 331, 332; and crash of 2008, 17, 24; crisis/meltdown in, 17, 18, 24, 26, 27, 29, 30–35, 37; and debt crisis (2010–2012), 18, 19, 26, 27, 29, 30–35; failures of, 17, 18, 19, 31, 58, 68, 69, 72, 102, 108, 121, 133, 252, 282, 332, 333, 358; and fundamental trends that drive the economy, 68, 69, 72; and future scenarios for stocks and economy, 102; and geopolitics, 36, 37; and global demographic trends, 200, 203, 252; and Great Depression, 31, 128, 132, 133, 134; and impacts of Next Great Depression, 321, 325, 326, 358; and Innovation Cycle, 86; and New Deal (1930s), 328, 331, 332; number of, 134; and real estate, 30–34, 107–8, 110, 114, 119, 121, 132, 136; safety of accounts in, 300–302; and Shakeout Season, 68, 69; stabilization in, 17; stages in cycle of, 137; and stock crashes, 31; and strategies for Next Great Depression, 282; and "survival of the fittest" battle, 58; and technology cycle, 58

bear markets: and Decennial Cycle, 95; and fundamental trends that drive the economy, 68; and future scenarios for stocks and economy, 101, 102; and Great Depression (1930s), 128; and Next Great Depression, 128, 282, 298; and phases of depressions, 68; and Seasonal Cycle, 100; and Shakeout Season, 68; of 2000–2002, 262–63, 264

Bear Stearns, 332

beauty salon services, 306, 307

Belgium, 223

benefit programs, 333, 336. See also specific program

Bernanke, Ben, 332

biotechnology, 182, 191, 348, 353. See also technology

Birth Index, 21, 22, 65, 116, 118, 119, 142, 194, 245, 287, 294. See also births/birthrate

births/birthrate: and aging, 348–51, 355; and debt crisis (2010–2012), 22; and fundamental trends that drive the economy, 44; and global demographic trends, 177, 178, 182, 183, 184, 186, 191–92, 196, 198, 199, 209, 211, 215, 219, 229, 248, 250; and impacts of Next Great Depression, 347, 348–51, 355; and Next New

Deal between developed and emerging countries, 347; and strategies for Next Great Depression, 285, 315, 317. See also Birth Index

black swans, 257–58

Bob Hope generation, 9, 18, 39, 40, 44, 45–46, 65, 68, 347

bonds: and comparison of Next Great Depression and Great Depression (1930s), 129; and cycles, 40; and debt crisis (2010–2012), 19, 35; and fundamental trends that drive the economy, 72; high-quality, 72, 129, 130, 281; high-yield, 293–94; long-term, 129, 130, 286, 287, 289, 292–93, 297, 298, 299; and recommendations for Next Great Depression, 296, 297, 298, 299; and risk and return, 253; short-term, 286; and strategies for Next Great Depression, 281, 282, 286, 287, 288–95, 298. See also type of bonds

booms: predictions about, 35–36. See also specific boom

Botswana, 186, 212, 231, 247

Brazil: bubbles in, 287; and fundamental trends that drive the economy, 48, 53; and geopolitics, 80; and global demographic trends, 48, 181, 186, 193, 213, 217–18, 225, 228, 232, 235–37, 238–44, 245, 247, 248; and strategies for Next Great Depression, 287

brokerage firms, safety of accounts with, 300–301

bubbles: and baby-boomer generation, 18–19; and comparison of New Deal (1930s) and Next New Deal, 330, 331; and cycles, 20, 38, 40; and debt crisis (2010–2012), 26; and Decennial Cycle, 94–95; and depression, 57; and determining risk and return, 264; and forecasting methods, 5, 73; and fundamental trends that drive the economy, 46, 48, 66–67; and Geopolitical Cycle, 81; and global demographic trends,

bubbles (*cont.*)
221, 241; and impacts of Next Great
Depression, 321, 324–25, 336; rules
of, 33; and Shakeout Season, 66–67;
and strategies for Next Great
Depression, 282, 287, 288, 302, 303;
and technology, 54, 57
Buffett, Warren, 323
bull market, 81, 93, 102, 128
Burma. *See* Myanmar
Bush, George W., 28, 346
business: and comparison of Great
Depression (1930s) and Next Great
Depression, 132, 133; and
comparison of New Deal (1930s)
and Next New Deal, 332; and cycles,
40–41; and debt crisis (2010–2012),
19, 29, 30, 33, 41; and Decennial
Cycle, 94; demonization of leaders
of, 336; failures of, 19, 30, 33, 125,
132, 133, 136, 282, 311; and
fundamental trends that drive the
economy, 67, 70; and global
demographic trends, 182–83, 196;
green networked, 341–45; and
impacts of Next Great Depression,
322, 325, 341–45, 358, 336–37; and
Maturity Boom Season, 70; and
migration/immigration, 140, 150,
172–73; new models for, 70, 89–90;
and recommendations for Next
Great Depression, 302–8; revolution
in, 343–45; and Revolutionary Cycle,
89–90; and science of forecasting,
8–9; selling of, 303–4, 306–7, 308–9;
and Shakeout Season, 67; and
strategies for Next Great Depression,
282, 302–8; summary points about,
307–8; taxes on, 334, 336. *See also*
real estate: commercial

California: housing in, 114;
migration/immigration in, 149–61,
164, 165, 169–70, 171, 173
Cambodia, 203, 204, 247
Canada, 144, 171, 173, 198, 202, 203, 219,
309, 346, 350, 352

capitalism, 19, 20, 84–85, 87, 90–92, 206,
340
Caribbean, 197, 213–14. *See also specific
nation*
cash, 72, 99, 129, 281, 293, 296, 297, 307
cell phones, 59, 60, 267–68, 356
Central America, 189, 213, 309. *See also
specific nation*
Champy, James, 89
children, 177, 202, 215, 219, 225, 250,
348–49, 350–51, 353. *See also*
births/birthrate
Chile, 193, 213–14, 236, 240, 241, 243,
244, 245
China: aging in, 14, 179, 185, 202, 216,
235, 239, 246, 348; bubbles in, 21;
cities in, 186; commodities in, 36, 80;
and debt crisis (2010–2012), 29;
democracy in, 185; echo-boomers in,
185, 193; environment in, 201, 206,
246, 248, 338, 342; foreign
investment in, 228; and fundamental
trends that drive the economy, 48,
53, 71; GDP in, 179, 186, 187, 222,
224, 225, 231, 235, 237, 241, 242, 245,
246; and geopolitics, 36, 79, 80; and
global demographic trends, 14, 176,
177, 179–81, 184–86, 189, 190, 193,
195, 197, 198, 201–2, 205, 206, 216,
221–28, 231, 234–37, 238–44,
245–49; government in, 206, 225;
growth in, 34, 36, 201, 205, 225, 227,
234–36, 241, 243, 244, 246, 248; and
history of long-term cycles, 82; and
impacts of Next Great Depression,
337, 338, 339, 342, 345, 346, 347, 348,
357, 359, 360; income/affluence in,
205, 221–22, 224, 238, 239, 240, 241,
242, 323; industrialization in,
221–22, 224, 225, 242, 247;
infrastructure in, 206, 225, 337;
innovation in, 185; as major political
and military force, 205, 228, 346,
347, 357; migration in, 185, 186; and
Next New Deal between developed
and emerging countries, 345, 346,
347; productivity in, 185; and

recommendations for Next Great Depression, 297, 298, 299; rural areas of, 225, 242; and Shakeout Season, 69; slowing in, 14, 48, 69, 180, 190, 197, 201, 222–23, 224, 225, 227–28, 246, 346, 347; spending in, 179, 184–85, 201–2, 225, 226, 244, 246; and stages of growth, 216; standard of living in, 185, 186, 225; and strategies for Next Great Depression, 287, 288, 289; technology in, 185, 360; and terrorism, 357; trade with, 36, 202, 241, 242, 339; urbanization in, 185, 202, 222–27, 237, 239, 241, 246; workforce in, 201–2, 225, 226, 244, 246

cities: and global demographic trends, 186, 188–90; growth rates of, 167; with highest population growth, 166; and impacts of Next Great Depression, 358; "in the middle," 161–62, 165; mega, 161–66, 188–90; and migration/immigration, 140, 143, 148, 149, 155, 159, 161–66, 167, 173; as most attractive for migrants, 153, 154; and real estate, 135; size of, 161–66; smaller, 155, 162–63; "sweet-spot," 162, 164, 358; and terrorism, 358; traffic congestion in, 168

Civil War, U.S., 89, 356, 357
Civilization Cycle (5000-year), 12, 81–83, 285, 361
climate, 43–44, 218, 220, 236, 285, 342–43. See also environment; global warming
Clinton, Bill, 336
Cochran, Gregory, 219
Cold War, 79
collateralized debt obligations, 256
Colombia, 214, 240, 241, 243, 247
Colorado, 143, 149, 157, 160, 170, 171, 172
commodities: booms in, 35–36, 78; bottom in, 108; bubbles in, 21, 34, 78, 104; and comparison of New Deal (1930s) and Next New Deal, 330–31; and crash of 2008, 17; and debt crisis (2010–2012), 19; and Decennial Cycle, 95; and deflation, 108; and fundamental trends that drive the economy, 49, 72; and Geopolitics, 37, 80; and global demographic trends, 180, 192, 193, 195, 199–200, 203, 210, 211, 213, 216, 217–18, 224, 228, 229, 232–33, 236, 242, 247, 248, 251; and Great Depression (1930s) compared with Next Great Depression, 128; and impacts of Next Great Depression, 322, 342, 358; and migration/immigration, 171; and new and recurring cycles for forecasting, 73; peaks in, 4; price of, 104, 192, 193, 299, 322, 330–31, 348, 358; and recommendations for Next Great Depression, 296, 297, 299; and science of forecasting, 4, 6, 7; speculation in, 35; and strategies for Next Great Depression, 281, 282, 283, 286, 287, 288, 289; and terrorism, 358. See also Commodity Cycle (29–30 year)

Commodity Cycle (29–30 year): and comparison of New Deal (1930s) and Next New Deal, 330–31; and debt crisis (2010–2012), 34–36; as driver of economy, 20; and evolution of forecasting methods, 7, 12, 43; and fundamental trends that drive the economy, 62, 70; and Generation Cycle, 81; and Geopolitical Cycle, 81; and global demographic trends, 180, 193, 194–95, 216, 217, 218, 237, 244; and hierarchy of cycles, 92; and Maturity Boom Season, 70; as new cycle, 7, 103; and Next Great Depression, 104, 285, 286, 355; overview of, 75–78; and Spending Wave, 81, 104; and stages of growth, 216; and terrorism, 355
complexity, dealing with, 1–2, 3–4, 9
Congress, U.S., 147–48, 326, 328–29, 332

Consumer Expenditure Surveys, 49, 116, 119, 123, 126
Consumer Price Index, 130, 131
contrarians, 5
cooperation, global, 181, 251, 252, 345, 346, 357, 358, 359
Corporate Bankruptcy Act (1934), 329
corporate bonds, 282, 288, 290–92, 293, 294, 296, 297–98
corporations. *See* business; corporate bonds
corruption. *See* crime/corruption
Costa Rica, 309
crashes: and comparison of Great Depression (1930s) and Next Great Depression, 128; and comparison of New Deal (1930s) and Next New Deal, 331; and Decennial Cycle, 94; and determining risk and return, 264; forecasting recovery from, 73; and future scenarios for stocks and economy, 102; and Geopolitical Cycle, 104; and global demographic trends, 180; next biggest, 102; and phases of depressions, 68; and Presidential Cycle, 97; and recessions, 31; and Shakeout Season, 68; and strategies for Next Great Depression, 288, 290, 302–3, 305. *See also* Great Crash (2008–10)
credit: bubbles in, 21, 24, 26–30, 31, 38, 40–41, 121; and cycles, 21, 38, 40–41; and debt crisis (2010–2012), 18, 24, 26–30, 41, 121, 129; and fundamental trends that drive the economy, 48, 58; and Innovation Cycle, 86. *See also* mortgages
crime/corruption: and global demographic trends, 211, 212, 214, 232, 233, 247, 251; and Great Depression (1930s), 133, 135; and Next Great Depression, 133, 135, 322, 345, 357, 358; and terrorism, 357, 358
culture; and global demographic trends, 219, 220, 223, 227, 245
currency, 30, 36, 203, 252, 281, 296, 297, 301, 322. *See also* dollar, U.S.

cycles: alternating stages in, 92; basic, 43–44; as basis for forecasting, 4–5; and bubbles, 20; and determining risk and return, 271; and evolution of forecasting methods, 12; and government, 20; hierarchy of, 6, 12, 13, 15, 92–93, 358–61; as immutable, 20; and impacts of Next Great Depression, 361; intermediate-term, 6, 7; key points about, 103–5; new and recurring, 14, 73–105; new research about longer-term, 178–82; Newton's theory of, 3; predictions about, 19–20, 21; prevalence of, 19; and science of forecasting, 6; seasonal, 18–19, 21, 37–41, 61; short-term recurring, 93–101; and strategies for Next Great Depression, 285. *See also specific cycle or type of cycles*
Czech Republic, 186, 200, 237

Davis, Ned, 11, 93, 96, 99
debt: of baby boomers, 22; and GDP, 24; private versus public, 24, 26–30; restructuring of, 18, 20, 27–28; total U.S., 28
debt crisis (2010–2012): and cycles, 18–19, 21, 37–41; as global turndown, 23; principles about, 24–41; and role of government, 17–18
debt/deficits, 58, 321, 328–29, 333, 335, 337
Decennial Cycle, 11, 93–95, 97, 99, 100, 104, 107
deficits; and debt crisis (2010–2012), 18, 29–30
deflation: and banking crisis, 137; and commodities, 35, 108; and cycles, 21, 39, 40–41; and debt crisis (2010–2012), 19, 23, 24, 26–30, 33, 35, 37; and depression cycle, 137; and fundamental trends that drive the economy, 48, 66–69, 71, 72; and geopolitics, 37; and Great Depression (1930s), 127–36; and

hierarchy of cycles, 93; and Innovation Cycle, 86; and Next Great Depression, 127–36, 282, 293, 308, 322; and real estate, 107, 109, 110–11, 113, 121, 136; and Shakeout Season, 66–69

Delaware, 151, 160

Dell, 64, 89, 341

democracy: and capitalism, 90–92; and global demographic trends, 185, 203, 206, 207, 212, 225, 229, 247, 251; and impacts of Next Great Depression, 322, 325, 340, 356; and Revolutionary Cycle, 89, 90–92; and terrorism, 356

demographics: and aging, 44, 349, 354, 355; alternative scenarios concerning, 248–50; and cycles, 38; and Decennial Cycle, 93; and determining risk and return, 279; as driver of economy, 9; and Empire Cycles, 84; as forecasting tool, 7–10, 11, 74, 178–82, 245, 279; and fundamental trends that drive the economy, 44, 49, 70, 71; and Geopolitical Cycle, 79, 81; global, 53, 70; global trends in, 13–14; and immigration, 352; and impacts of Next Great Depression, 338, 349, 352, 354, 355, 356; and inflation, 9; and Innovation Cycle, 86–87; and Maturity Boom Season, 70; new research about, 178–82; and opportunities in slowing demographic trends, 250–52; and real estate, 107, 109, 111, 115–24, 136; and Revolutionary Cycle, 92; and strategies for Next Great Depression, 282, 286, 307, 317; and terrorism, 356; trends in global, 175–252. *See also* births/birthrate; immigration; migration; population; *specific nation*

depression: and bubbles, 57; and comparison of New Deal (1930s) and Next New Deal, 331, 333; and cycles, 19, 38, 40–41; and debt crisis (2010–2012), 26, 29; and fundamental trends that drive the economy, 66–69, 71; and future scenarios for stocks and economy, 102; and Geopolitical Cycle, 79; and global demographic trends, 195, 196, 222, 237, 249; and impacts of Next Great Depression, 325; and Innovation Cycle, 86; predictions of, 19–20; and Revolutionary Cycle, 89; and Shakeout Season, 66–69; and stages of technology, 57; stages/phases in cycle of, 57, 68, 137; and strategies for Next Great Depression, 303. *See also* Next Great Depression; *specific depression or nation*

Diamond, Jared, 218

Dobbs, Lou, 338

dollar, U.S., 19, 30, 31, 35, 102, 332, 333, 337

Dominican Republic, 309

Dow Jones Industrial Average "Dow": between 1928–1942, 102; bottom in, 15, 288; and crash of 2008, 17; and Decennial Cycle, 93; and determining risk and return, 269, 270; and forecasting methods, 9, 10, 11, 12, 73; and fundamental trends that drive the economy, 47; and future scenarios for stocks and economy, 101–2; and New Deal (1930s), 328, 330; and Next Great Depression, 288, 289, 290, 297; predictions about, 20–21; S&P 500 correlation with, 9

Dubai, 48, 121, 188, 189, 210, 347

earnings. *See* income/earnings

East Asia: aging in, 350, 351; and fundamental trends that drive the economy, 46, 71; and global demographic trends, 179, 180, 181, 189, 193, 197, 198, 201–3, 215, 216, 243, 245; and immigration, 352; and Next Great Depression, 289, 299, 339, 350, 351, 352; population in,

East Asia (*cont.*)
350; and Shakeout Season, 69; slow down in, 48, 69; and trade, 339. *See also specific nation*

Eastern Europe: aging in, 216, 223, 351; and fundamental trends that drive the economy, 48; and Geopolitical Cycle, 79; and global demographic trends, 180, 189, 192, 197, 198, 199–200, 216, 223, 228, 245; and Next Great Depression, 289, 351; and stages of growth, 216. *See also specific nation*

echo-boomers: and aging, 353; and cycles, 41; and debt crisis (2010–2012), 41; and fundamental trends that drive the economy, 46, 49, 68, 70; and global demographic trends, 180, 181, 185, 193, 196, 197, 201, 202, 204, 227; and Maturity Boom Season, 70; migration of, 139–74; and Next Great Depression, 283, 298, 315, 316, 347, 353; and Next New Deal between developed and emerging countries, 347; and real estate, 118, 120, 126; and Shakeout Season, 68

economics: paradoxes in, 14; and science of forecasting, 2–7, 8–9; trickle-down, 324

economists, 284–85

economy: drivers of, 9, 20, 139; future scenarios for, 101–3; peaks in, 4; and science of forecasting, 4; seasonal cycles of, 18–19, 21, 37–41; standardized to customized, 324. *See also* New Economy Cycle; *specific nation or topic*

education: and college enrollments, 317; costs of, 313, 316, 317, 318; deflation of bubble in, 316–18; and employment, 317–18; and global demographic trends, 176, 177, 241, 242; growth in, 314, 315; for kids and grandkids, 313–14; and Next Great Depression, 313–14, 316–18, 324

Egypt, 194, 207, 209, 231, 241, 243, 244

80-year cycle. *See* Generation Cycle; New Economy Cycle

elections: of 1932, 328, 334; of 1936, 329; of 2012, 68–69, 319, 326, 327; and fundamental trends that drive the economy, 68–69; and health care, 319; midterm, 95–96; and Presidential Cycle, 95–97; and science of forecasting, 6; and Shakeout Season, 68–69; and strategies for Next Great Depression, 319

Elliott Wave patterns, 75, 100–101

The Elliott Wave Theorist, 97

emerging countries: aging in, 238–44, 359; bubbles in, 21; bull market in, 81; classes of, 245; commodities in, 34–36, 78, 104; and cycles, 38; and debt crisis (2010–2012), 34–36; and Decennial Cycle, 95; demographics in, 38; and fundamental trends that drive the economy, 53, 71; GDP in, 245, 359; and Geopolitical Cycle, 81; and global demographic trends, 14, 179–81, 184, 186, 190–93, 195–98, 210, 212, 215–37, 238–44, 245, 247–48, 249, 250; and impacts of Next Great Depression, 322, 324, 325, 339, 340, 342, 345–47, 348, 350, 354, 355, 357–58; income in, 238–44, 245; Maturity Boom Seasons in, 359; and New Deal (1930s), 331; Next New Deal in, 14, 331, 342, 345–47, 359–60; and recommendations for Next Great Depression, 287, 288, 289, 290, 297, 299, 338; and Revolutionary Cycle, 87; and Shakeout Season, 359; slowing in, 290; spending in, 215–37, 238, 245; stocks in, 35; technologies in, 360; and terrorism, 357–58; urbanization in, 215–37, 245; workforce in, 215–37, 245. *See also* third world countries; *specific nation*

Empire Cycles (2500-year), 83–84

employment/unemployment: and aging, 350–51, 355; bottom in, 15; and

comparison of Great Depression (1930s) and Next Great Depression, 127, 128, 129, 130, 132, 133, 135; and comparison of New Deal (1930s) and Next New Deal, 332; and debt crisis (2010–2012), 30, 33; and education, 317–18; and fundamental trends that drive the economy, 63, 68; and future scenarios for stocks and economy, 102; and Geopolitical Cycle, 79; and global demographic trends, 181, 215, 217, 218, 219, 233, 234, 239, 241, 242, 243; in government, 335; and impacts of Next Great Depression, 325, 326, 327, 336–38, 346, 350–51, 352, 355, 357, 358; and migration/immigration, 140, 145, 146, 150, 158, 168, 352; and New Deal (1930s), 328, 329, 330, 332; and Next New Deal between developed and emerging countries, 346; between 1923–1943, 132; and real estate, 111, 116, 124–25, 136; and Shakeout Season, 68; and stages of technology cycle, 58; and strategies for Next Great Depression, 288, 292, 317–18; and terrorism, 357
energy: alternative, 76, 127, 338; and bubbles, 78; and global demographic trends, 180, 199, 210; and Next Great Depression, 296, 297, 338, 342, 343, 345; and Next New Deal between developed and emerging countries, 345. *See also* oil
England, 82, 85, 350. *See also* Great Britain
entrepreneurs, 40, 200, 221, 222, 228, 246
environment: and Civilization Cycle, 83; and Geopolitical Cycle, 80; and global demographic trends, 181, 201, 206, 246, 248, 250; and Next Great Depression, 321, 338, 341–42, 344, 345, 357, 358, 360; and Next New Deal, 14, 344, 345; and terrorism, 357. *See also* global warming
Euromonitor International, 238

Europe: aging in, 198, 199, 216, 223, 251, 348, 350, 351; banking in, 200; and fundamental trends that drive the economy, 48, 71; GDP in, 186, 187, 245; and Geopolitical Cycle, 79; and global demographic trends, 175, 179, 180, 183, 186, 189, 192–93, 197, 198–99, 216, 219, 220, 221, 223, 227–28, 245, 248, 251; and immigration/migration, 143–44, 148, 352; infrastructure in, 337; and Next Great Depression, 286, 289, 290, 299, 342, 348, 350, 351, 352, 360; population in, 350; service workers in, 145; slowing in, 23, 180, 192, 198–99, 227–28, 248, 286, 290; spending in, 23, 198–99; and stages of growth, 216; and trade, 339; urbanization in, 223; worker-retiree ratio in, 327; workforce in, 198–99. *See also* Eastern Europe; *specific nation*
European Commission, 351
European Union, 209

families: formation of, 116–18; life cycle of, 21, 23; and strategies for Next Great Depression, 308–19
family values, 351
Federal Deposit Insurance Corporation (FDIC), 300, 329
Federal Housing Administration (FHA), 329
Federal Reserve Board/System: and fundamental trends that drive the economy, 68; and Great Depression (1930s), 129; and interest rates, 32, 58, 68, 108, 293, 330, 332; and LTCM bailout, 255; and New Deal (1930s), 330, 332; and Next Great Depression, 129, 293; and Next New Deal, 332; and Presidential Cycle, 96; and real estate, 108; and Shakeout Season, 68; stimulation of economy by, 129, 330
feedback loops, 263–65
financial sector; investment in, 12, 287, 288, 298, 299

financial system. *See* banks/banking

5000-Year Cycle. *See* Civilization Cycle

fixed income, 286, 287, 289, 294, 296, 299, 300

Florida: migration/immigration in, 142, 143, 149, 151, 152–53, 155, 163, 166, 167, 168, 169, 171, 173; real estate/housing in, 114, 152, 153

"following" trend, 264–65

Ford, Henry, 88, 323

Ford Motor, 221

forecasting: assumptions in, 254–57; and bubbles, 5; challenges concerning, 15, 104; and change and transitions, 267–78; and complexity, 1–2, 3–4; contrarian, 5; cycles as basis of, 2, 4–5, 6, 19–20, 43–44; and demographics, 7–10; errors in, 4–5; evolution of, 10–13, 43, 361; fundamental indicators of, 6, 11, 12; of global demographic spending trends, 190–97; and hierarchy of cycles, 92–93; and Human Forecasting Model, 265–67; and information revolution, 43; of key trends, 53; lessons learned from, 15; and life cycles, 2, 3–4, 6–7; new and recurring cycles for, 73–105; and new research about longer-term trends, 178–82; refinement of, 6; science of, 2–10, 284–85; straight-line, 4–5, 265–67, 268; and tools for determining risk and return, 254–67; typical, 268. *See also specific tool*

foreign investment, 205, 206, 213, 228, 246, 247, 252

Fortune 500, 288, 303

40-year cycles, 7, 93, 94, 196, 285

4-year cycle. *See* Presidential Cycle

France, 82, 198, 223, 350

French Revolution, 46, 340, 344

Friedman, Thomas, 342, 343

Gaussian distribution. *See* normal distributions

gender values, 350–51

General Electric, 70, 89

General Motors Corporation, 57, 58, 70, 88–89, 221, 344

Generation Cycle (80–84 year): and Commodities Cycle, 81; and debt crisis (2010–2012), 21–24; as driver of economy, 20; and fundamental trends that drive the economy, 44–53, 62; and Geopolitical Cycle, 81; and global demographic trends, 176, 216, 221, 249; and hierarchy of cycles, 92, 93; as new cycle, 14, 18, 20; and Next Great Depression, 93, 285, 294–95, 340, 347; and Next New Deal between developed and emerging countries, 347; predictions about, 20–21; and Revolutionary Cycle, 89; and science of forecasting, 7; and short-term recurring cycles, 93; and spending, 45–53; and stages of growth, 216

genetics, 219, 233

Geopolitical Cycle (32–36 year): and Armstrong Cycle, 98; and changes in forecasting, 11, 12, 43; and Commodity Cycle, 81; and crashes, 104; and debt crisis (2010–2012), 27, 35, 36–37; and fundamental trends that drive the economy, 69, 70; and Generation Cycle, 81; and global demographic trends, 180–81, 193–94, 204, 229, 231, 246; and Great Depression (1930s), 133, 135; and Maturity Boom Season, 70; as new cycle, 73, 103; and New Economy Cycle, 81; and Next Great Depression, 103, 104, 133, 135, 358; overview of, 78–81; and Shakeout Season, 69; and social unrest, 133, 135; and Spending Wave, 81. *See also* terrorism; *specific nation*

Georgia, 143, 149, 151, 154, 163, 166, 168

Germany, 82, 143–44, 198, 202, 223, 347, 350

GI Bill, 271

global warming: and Civilization Cycle, 83; and fundamental trends that drive the economy, 44, 71; and

Geopolitical Cycle, 80; and global demographic trends, 181, 248, 250, 251, 252; and impacts of Next Great Depression, 321, 341, 342, 343, 345, 358; and Maturity Boom Season, 71; and Next Great Depression, 337, 338; and Next New Deal, 14, 345, 346; and terrorism, 358

globalization: backlash against, 181, 252, 321, 339; and Civilization Cycle, 83; and cooperation, 181, 345, 346, 357, 359; and demographics, 70; and evolution of forecasting methods, 12; and fundamental trends that drive the economy, 70–71; and global demographic trends, 180, 181, 188–89, 210–12, 251–52; of govermental systems, 83; and government structures, 71; and impacts of Next Great Depression, 321, 322, 339, 340, 355–56, 357, 358, 359; and Maturity Boom Season, 70–71; and Next New Deal, 14; of real estate, 121; and terrorism, 355–56, 357

Globalization Cycle (5000-year), 84, 86, 87

gold, 35, 37, 76, 104, 281, 328

Google, 221

government/political system: and Civilization Cycle, 83; and crash of 2008, 17; and cycles, 19, 20, 41; and debt crisis (2010–2012), 17–18, 20, 22–23, 27, 29–30, 41; employment in, 335; and fundamental trends that drive the economy, 71; and global demographic trends, 177, 225, 232, 233, 245, 246, 251; globalization of, 71, 83; and health care, 318, 319; and impacts of Next Great Depression, 324, 325–26, 327, 340–41, 345, 346; and Maturity Boom Season, 71; and New Deal (1930s), 328–30, 331–32, 334, 335; and Next Great Depression, 337–38; and Next New Deal, 331–32, 346; and predictions, 20; and real estate, 127; and Revolutionary Cycle,

89; role of, 17–18, 325, 335; size of, 335; and strategies for Next Great Depression, 282, 318, 319

Great Britain, 198, 218–19, 220, 223, 226, 233, 340

Great Crash (2008–10), 17, 19, 24, 40–41, 94, 101, 297–98

Great Depression (1930s): and baby booms, 348; brief history of, 328–30; cause of, 31; comparison of 2010 and, 330–33; and cycles, 19, 38; financing of programs during, 59; as following bubble boom, 57; and fundamental trends that drive the economy, 68; and global demographic trends, 221, 249; housing during, 32, 128, 132; immigration during, 145, 329, 352; Next Great Depression compared with, 127–36; public works programs during, 337, 346; role and size of government during, 335; Roosevelt as hero of, 322; and science of forecasting, 7; and Shakeout Season, 66, 68; and strategies for Next Great Depression, 290, 292, 294; taxes in, 312; and terrorism, 357; trade during, 338

Greece, 82, 198, 347, 350

"green" movement, 341–45

Greenspan, Alan, 255

Gross Domestic Product (GDP): and aging, 350; and debt, 24; and debt crisis (2010–2012), 27, 29; in emerging countries, 245; and global demographic trends, 183, 197, 200, 206–7, 213, 217, 222–25, 227–37, 240, 241, 242, 244, 245–48; in Great Depression (1930s), 131–32, 327–28; and Next Great Depression, 131–32, 327–28, 336, 345, 349, 350, 360; and Next New Deal between developed and emerging countries, 345; urbanization as key factor in, 224, 242

Gross National Product (GNP), from 1921–1946, 131–32

growth: and aggressive investments, 296–97, 298, 299; and cycles, 38, 61; forecasting of, 245; and fundamental trends that drive the economy, 44, 55; and global demographic trends, 195–96, 197–252; and immigration/migration, 148; and Revolutionary Cycle, 340; simple trends as drivers of, 8–9; stages of, 216. *See also* Gross Domestic Product; Growth Boom Season/Stage; immigration; migration

Growth Boom Season/Stage: and Empire Cycles, 83; and fundamental trends that drive the economy, 65–66, 70; and global demographic trends, 197; and impacts of Next Great Depression, 323, 325, 359; and politics, 336; and Shakeout Season, 66; as stage in New Economy Cycle, 64; as stage of technology cycle, 56, 57; and strategies for Next Great Depression, 281, 286–87, 308–9, 312, 313

Hammer, Michael, 89
Harpending, Henry, 219
Hawken, Paul, 88, 343
health care: costs of, 318–19, 353; and global demographic trends, 198; growth in, 127, 314; and Next Great Depression, 287, 296, 297, 298, 299, 318–19, 326, 336, 353
health insurance, 321
health savings accounts (HSAs), 318–19
hedge funds. *See* Long-Term Capital Management
hedging, 280
Henry Ford generation, 7, 65
Hong Kong, 175, 176, 186, 201, 348, 350
Hoover, Herbert, 328, 334
housing: and age, 118; and baby-boomers, 13, 173; bubbles in, 20, 21, 107–14; and cycles, 41; and debt crisis

(2010–2012), 19, 22, 31–32, 33–34, 41; decline in, 13; and determining risk and return, 256, 279; foreclosures on, 128, 133, 134; and fundamental trends that drive the economy, 48, 50–51, 53, 70; in Great Depression (1930s), 32, 128, 132; and inflation, 110; key points about, 136–37; for kids and grandkids, 314–16; and Maturity Boom Season, 70; and migration/immigration, 142, 152, 155, 156, 158, 160, 161, 163, 173; and New Deal (1930s), 331, 332; and Next Great Depression compared to Great Depression, 128, 132; and Next New Deal, 331, 332; overvaluation in, 109, 111, 132; predictions about, 20; price of, 31–33, 108–12, 113, 114–16, 122, 123, 132, 156, 158, 256, 288, 314, 315; and recommendations for Next Great Depression, 297, 298, 299; replacement costs for, 110; and safest cities from terrorist attack, 358; speculation in, 120, 122, 136; starts in, 110–11; and strategies for Next Great Depression, 283, 287, 288, 309–10, 314–16; trade-up, 22; and where to live in Next Great Depression, 135; during World War II, 32. *See also* real estate; *type of housing*

Howe, Neil, 65, 347
Human Forecasting Model, 265–67
Hungary, 200
hunter/gatherer societies, 219–20

Ibbotson Large Company Index, 270
Idaho, 143, 149, 151, 156–57, 160, 172, 173
Illinois, 151, 158, 159, 161, 173
immigration: and aging, 348, 350; and assimilation of immigrants, 148, 352; backlash against, 321, 352; barriers to, 339; and cities, 163; and Civilization Cycle, 83; and cycles, 21; and debt crisis (2010–2012), 22; as driver of economy, 139; from

1820–2006, 147; and family life cycle, 21; and fundamental trends that drive the economy, 45, 46; and geopolitics, 36; and global demographic trends, 192, 199, 202, 204, 209, 212, 214, 228, 234, 235, 239, 240, 241, 244; during Great Depression (1930s), 338, 352; and housing, 111; illegal, 36, 145, 146, 148; and impacts of Next Great Depression, 321, 325–26, 338, 339, 348, 350, 352, 359; peaks in, 145, 146; reasons for, 145, 150; restrictions on, 140, 146, 147–48; slowing of, 140, 144–48, 164, 165, 173; social costs of, 144; states/cities attractive for, 153, 155, 168–69, 170; and taxes, 144; volume of, 166–71. *See also* migration; *specific nation or state/geographical sector of United States*

income/earnings: and comparison of New Deal (1930s) and Next New Deal, 330; and debt crisis (2010–2012), 21; and determining risk and return, 279; in emerging countries, 245; and financial assets owned by top 1of U.S. households, 323; fixed, 286, 287, 289, 294, 296, 299, 300; and fundamental trends that drive the economy, 49, 50, 51, 53; and Geopolitical Cycle, 80; and global demographic trends, 216, 217, 219, 221–22, 223, 224, 225, 238–44, 245, 248, 251; and housing, 116; and Innovation Cycle, 86; and lower-income households, 326; and new and recurring cycles for forecasting, 74; and Next Great Depression, 287, 321, 322–25, 326, 336, 345, 358; and Next New Deal between developed and emerging countries, 345; and S&P 500, 74, 75

India: aging in, 239, 354; bubbles in, 21; bull market in, 81; commodities in, 36, 80; culture of, 227; democracy in, 206, 225; foreign investment in, 228,

246; and fundamental trends that drive the economy, 48, 53; GDP in, 223, 227, 228, 235, 237, 242, 245; and geopolitics, 36, 80, 81; and global demographic trends, 14, 180, 181, 186, 189–90, 192–95, 197, 200, 205–6, 207, 210, 221–22, 225, 227, 231, 234–37, 238–43, 244, 245, 246, 247, 248, 249; government in, 246; growth in, 14, 34, 36, 205, 210, 222, 227, 228, 229, 234, 235–36, 241, 242, 243, 244, 246, 248; immigration from, 326; income/affluence in, 205, 221–23, 238, 239, 240, 241, 242; industrialization in, 221–22, 247; information technology in, 228; infrastructure in, 205, 246; as major political force, 200, 205, 227, 228, 231; and Next Great Depression, 287, 297, 298, 299, 342, 345, 346, 347, 354, 357, 360; and Next New Deal between developed and emerging countries, 345, 346, 347; population in, 228, 244; rural areas of, 205, 242; spending in, 205–6, 227, 237, 240; standard of living in, 205; technology in, 227, 228; and terrorism, 357; trade with, 36, 241, 242; urbanization in, 205, 206, 227, 237, 239, 240, 241, 246; workforce in, 205–6, 227, 242, 243, 244, 246

Indiana, 151, 159, 161

Indonesia: commodities in, 78, 80; and environment, 342; and global demographic trends, 181, 186, 203, 204, 228–29, 235–37, 238–44, 245, 246–47, 248; and impact of Next Great Depression, 342

Industrial Revolution: and fundamental trends that drive the economy, 46; and global demographic trends, 175, 213, 216, 218–19, 220, 221–22, 223, 251; impact of, 342, 355; Next, 343, 344; and Revolutionary Cycle, 87, 88, 340, 344; Second, 251; and stages of growth, 216; and strategies for Next Great Depression, 285 industrialization: and global demographic trends, 175–77, 215–18, 222–25, 229, 232–33, 234, 236, 241, 242, 247, 248. *See also* Industrial Revolution

inflation: and age, 44; and Commodity Cycle, 77; and comparison of New Deal (1930s) and Next New Deal, 333; and cycles, 18, 39–40; and debt crisis (2010–2012), 19, 23, 24, 26–30, 36; and demographics, 9; and determining risk and return, 279; and fundamental trends that drive the economy, 62–65, 67–68, 71; and future scenarios for stocks and economy, 102; and geopolitics, 36, 79, 80, 81; and global demographic trends, 194–97, 234; and Great Depression (1930s), 128, 133; and Growth Boom Season/Stage, 66; and housing, 110; and Innovation Cycle, 85, 86; and migration/immigration, 145; and New Deal (1930s), 334; and New Economy Cycle, 62–65; and Next Great Depression, 128, 133, 286, 287, 289, 290, 299–300; and science of forecasting, 9; and Shakeout Season, 67–68. *See also specific nation*

information: and cycles, 38, 361; and determining risk and return, 271; and global demographic trends, 196, 213, 216, 218, 220–21, 224, 228; and health care, 318; and Innovation Cycle, 86; and making predictions, 43; and Next Great Depression, 322, 339, 341, 344, 356, 361; revolution in, 216; and Revolutionary Cycle, 84, 86, 90, 316; and stages of growth, 216; and stages of technology cycle, 60; and terrorism, 356

infrastructure: and aging, 355; and cycles, 20; and fundamental trends that drive the economy, 68; and global demographic trends, 176, 181, 186, 203, 205, 206, 210, 212, 215, 217, 219, 225, 229, 233, 240, 241, 242, 245, 246, 247, 248, 251, 252; during Great Depression, 345, 346; and New Deal (1930s), 329; and Next Great Depression, 325, 337–38, 343, 345, 346, 355, 358, 359; and Next New Deal between developed and emerging countries, 345, 346; and real estate, 127; and Shakeout Season, 68; and terrorism, 358

innovation: and aging, 181, 350, 351, 354, 355; and climatic cycles, 44; and cycles, 20, 38, 41, 61, 92, 361; and debt crisis (2010–2012), 27, 28, 41; and determining risk and return, 279; and Empire Cycles, 84; and fundamental trends that drive the economy, 44, 46, 62–66, 70, 71; and global demographic trends, 177, 178, 181–82, 184, 185, 194–200, 221, 222, 228, 236, 249, 251; and Growth Boom Season/Stage, 65–66; and impacts of Next Great Depression, 323, 324, 325, 336, 338, 340, 341, 350, 351, 354, 355, 359, 361; and Maturity Boom Season, 70; and New Economy Cycle, 60–65, 359; and politics, 336; and recommendations for Next Great Depression, 300; and Revolutionary Cycle, 88, 89, 91–92; slowing of, 181; as stage of technology cycle, 56; and strategies for Next Great Depression, 282, 286, 294, 295, 303. *See also* Innovation Cycle (500-year Mega); technology

Innovation Cycle (500-year Mega): and aging, 349; and Capitalist Revolution, 84–85; and comparison of New Deal (1930s) and Next New Deal, 331; and forecasting methods, 6, 7, 12; and fundamental trends that drive the economy, 62; and global demographic trends, 196, 197, 248, 249, 250; and history of long-term cycles, 84–87; and Next Great Depression, 285, 294, 295, 349, 361; and seasonal cycles, 38; and Shakeout, 86

Intel Corporation, 57, 58, 64

interest rates: and cycles, 18, 40; and debt crisis (2010–2012), 18, 28, 29; and Federal Reserve Board, 58, 68, 108, 293, 330, 331; and fundamental trends that drive the economy, 68; and Geopolitical Cycle, 80, 81; and Great Depression (1930s), 127, 128–30, 133; and New Deal (1930s), 330, 334; and Next Great Depression, 127, 128–30, 133, 287, 292, 293, 299–300, 307, 310, 325; and Next New Deal, 330, 331; and real estate, 108; and Shakeout Season, 68; and stimulation of economy, 32. *See also* specific nation

international bonds, 290, 297
international stocks, 297, 298, 299
Internet, 5, 10–11, 59, 62, 82–83, 339, 340, 356
investments: conservative, 297, 298; and debt crisis (2010–2012), 19; fixed, 131; and fundamental trends that drive the economy, 72; growth and aggressive, 296–97, 298, 299; for Next Great Depression, 72; recommendations for 2009–2022, 295–300; safety of, 300–302; strategies for, 19, 35. *See also* returns; risks; type of investment
Iran, 37, 186, 205, 207, 210, 229, 237, 247, 356–57
Iraq, 36, 80, 207, 208, 210, 340, 356, 357
irrationality, 256, 264–65
Israel, 37, 176, 186, 207, 209, 245
Italy, 198, 202, 347, 350, 351

Japan: aging in, 20, 28, 33, 202, 216, 224, 226, 251, 347, 350; birthrates in, 183, 350; and bubbles, 114; children in, 202; and debt crisis (2010–2012), 29; debt in, 20, 23, 28; and Decennial Cycle, 95; deflation in, 114; downturn in, 47; and evolution of forecasting methods, 10; and fundamental trends that drive the economy, 47–48, 53; GDP in, 224; and global demographic trends, 175,

177–80, 183, 189, 192, 193, 197, 201, 202, 216, 221–24, 226, 233, 234, 244, 251; government in, 20, 28; growth in, 224; housing in, 33; and impacts of Next Great Depression, 347, 350; income and wealth in, 221–22, 223; industrialization in, 221–22, 233; inflation in, 112; interest rates in, 112; migration in, 224, 226; in 1990s, 197; population in, 202; real estate in, 20, 23, 28, 48, 111, 112–13, 202; and recommendations for Next Great Depression, 296, 297, 298, 299; retirement in, 33; and Shakeout Season, 69; slowing in, 14, 20, 23, 28, 69, 178, 192, 202; spending in, 48, 49, 202; and stages of growth, 216; stock market in, 20, 23, 28, 47–48, 49; and strategies for Next Great Depression, 282, 286, 287, 288, 289; trade with, 202; urbanization in, 223–24, 226; U.S. compared with, 114; worker-retiree ratio in, 327; workforce in, 202, 244

jobs. *See* employment/unemployment
Jones, Daniel, 343

Kentucky, 166
Kenya, 232, 237, 245
Keynes, John Maynard, 256
known knowns, 279, 280
Kondratieff Wave, 14, 62, 77, 92, 196, 285
Kuala Lumpur, 229
Kurzweil, Ray, 249–50, 353, 361
Kuwait, 188, 207, 356

labor unions, 324, 325
Laffer, Arthur, 74
Laos, 203, 204, 247
Latin America: commodities from, 78; and fundamental trends that drive the economy, 49; and global demographic trends, 180, 193, 197, 198, 213–14, 216, 221, 225, 228, 235–36, 237, 239, 242, 243, 244, 247; immigration from, 326; and Next Great Depression, 288, 339, 346, 356;

Latin America (*cont.*)
and Next New Deal between developed and emerging countries, 346; terrorism in, 356; and trade, 339. *See also specific nation*

LDCs (less developed countries), 178, 179, 325. *See also specific nation*

leadership, 66–69, 71–72, 359

Lehman Brothers, 17

leisure travel, 126

leptokurtic distribution, 272–74

life cycles, 2, 3–4, 6–7, 71, 283, 308

life expectancy, 45, 178, 182, 183, 191, 197, 199, 211, 215, 249, 250, 325, 348, 352–55

lifestyle, 194, 323, 353

Long-Term Capital Management (LTCM), 254–57, 268, 269, 278

long-term care costs, 318–19

long-term cycles/trends, 4, 6, 8, 12, 81–93

longevity. *See* life expectancy

Longman, Phillip, 186, 202, 347

Louisiana, 154–55, 167, 168, 169

Lovins, Amory, 88, 343

Lovins, L. Hunter, 88, 343

macro cycles/trends, 3, 4, 6

Malaysia, 193, 203, 229, 230, 231, 235, 236, 237, 240, 241, 242, 243, 247

"Malthusian trap," 215, 225

Mandelbrot, Benoit, 269

margin calls, 301

marriage, 50, 53, 116–18, 142

Massachusetts, migration/immigration in, 151, 160, 161, 173

Maturity Boom Season/Stage: and Empire Cycles, 83, 84; and four-season cycles, 38, 61; and fundamental trends that drive the economy, 69–71; and geopolitics, 81; and global demographic trends, 196; and New Economy Cycle, 64, 69, 70; and Next Great Depression, 288–89, 303, 337, 359; and Spending Wave, 69–71; and technology, 56, 57, 69–71; from 2023–2036, 70

Medicare/Medicaid, 29, 321, 327–28, 336

Merchant Revolution, 87

Mexico: and global demographic trends, 186, 189, 193, 213, 214, 237, 240, 241, 243, 244; immigration from, 36, 147, 164, 168, 171, 326, 350

Michigan, 151, 158, 159, 161

micro cycles/trends, 3, 4, 49–50

"microfinance," 212

Microsoft, 221

Middle East: aging in, 354; commodities from, 78, 80; and fundamental trends that drive the economy, 49; and Geopolitical Cycle, 80; and global demographic trends, 180, 181, 183, 189, 193, 194, 197, 207–10, 212, 216, 218, 219, 220, 221, 231, 237, 242, 244, 247; Next Great Depression in, 288, 299, 339, 346, 347, 354, 356, 357, 358, 360–61; and Next New Deal between developed and emerging countries, 346, 347; terrorism in, 356, 357, 358; and trade, 339; wealth in, 323. *See also specific nation*

Midwest, U.S., 149–51, 332

migration: and baby-boomers, 171–72; benefits of, 13–14; and cities, 140, 143, 149, 155, 159, 161–66, 167, 173; and convection current, 149–61; as driver of economy, 139; of echo-boomers, 139–74; in Europe, 143–44; and global demographic trends, 176, 185, 186, 192, 205, 212, 224, 226, 232, 233, 242, 249; growth of, 140–44; in-, 151, 152–55, 156–57, 160, 162, 166–71; key points about, 139–40; motivation for, 149–50; and Next Great Depression, 135, 309, 358, 359; out-, 151, 157–61, 165, 170; patterns of, 149–61; and real estate, 111, 127, 135; reasons for, 141; summary about, 172–74; and terrorism, 358; volume of, 166–71; waves of, 143. *See also* immigration; *specific state or section of United States*

Mississippi, 167, 169

modernization, 176, 177, 178, 180, 181, 186, 247, 356
money market investments, 293, 294, 296, 297, 298, 299
money supply, 26, 133, 333
Money Velocity, 27
Moore, Stephen, 74
mortgage-backed securities, 256
mortgages: and debt crisis (2010–2012), 22, 29, 33–34; defaults/foreclosures on, 33–34; and demographics of real estate, 118, 119, 121, 133, 134, 136; and housing bubble, 108, 110, 113–14; and New Deal (1930s), 329, 330; and Next Great Depression, 310, 313, 315, 326; subprime, 12, 13, 256, 321, 326, 330; write-off of, 29
motorcycles, spending for, 51
municipal bonds, 282, 288, 292, 294, 296, 298, 313
Muslims, 209, 352, 356
Myanmar (Burma), 186, 203, 204, 247

Nasdaq, 10, 11, 60, 102
National Association of Realtors, 119
national security, 147, 340
Netherlands, 82, 183, 223
Nevada: housing in, 114; migration/immigration in, 142, 143, 149, 151, 155, 156, 160, 163, 170, 171, 173
New Deal (1930s), 14, 319, 328–35
New Economy Cycle (80-year): and aging, 352, 353; asset allocation models for, 280, 281–319; components of, 60–61; and evolution of forecasting methods, 10, 11; and fundamental trends that drive the economy, 60–65, 69, 70, 71; and Geopolitical Cycle, 81; and global demographic trends, 196, 249; and hierarchy of cycles, 92; and impact of Next Great Depression, 323, 324, 344, 347, 352, 353, 359; importance of, 283–84; and inflation, 62–65; and innovation, 62–65, 86, 359; and Maturity Boom Season, 69, 70; as new cycle, 14, 38;

and Next New Deal between developed and emerging countries, 347; and Revolutionary Cycle, 88, 89, 344; and science of forecasting, 5, 6, 7; seasons/stages of, 7, 64, 71, 283–89; and Shakeout Season, 89; and strategies for Next Great Depression, 283–89; and technology, 359
New Jersey, 149, 151, 160, 161
New Mexico, 143, 151, 155, 160, 170, 358
New York City, housing in, 114
New York State, 149, 150, 151, 160, 161, 173
New York Stock Exchange (NYSE), 341, 344
New Zealand, 175, 180, 198, 202–3, 219, 236, 245, 248, 348, 350, 351
Newton, Isaac, 2–3
Next Great Depression: asset allocation strategies for, 72, 280, 285–302; business strategies for, 302–8; and commercial real estate, 126; creation of, 93; and debt crisis (2010–2012), 34; and fundamental trends that drive the economy, 53, 68–69, 71; and future scenarios for stocks and economy, 101–3; and Generation Cycle, 93; Great Depression (1930s) compared with, 127–36; and hierarchy of cycles, 93; and housing, 108, 113, 119, 121, 135; and investment recommendations for 2009–22, 295–300; and Next New Deal, 330–33; personal/family life strategies for, 308–19; political and social impacts of, 321–61; and Shakeout Season, 68–69; stages in, 282; strategies for, 281–319; and taxes, 336–38; and terrorism, 357. *See also specific cycle*
Next Industrial Revolution, 343
Next New Deal: between developed and emerging countries, 14, 345–47, 359–60; emergence of, 14; and global demographic trends, 248; and impacts of Next Great Depression,

Next New Deal (*cont.*)
      345–47, 359–60; New Deal (1930s)
      compared with, 330–33; overview of,
      319
Nigeria, 186, 212, 232, 241, 242, 243, 244,
      247
Nikkei Index, 47–48, 49
nonstationarity, 273
normal distribution, 14, 255, 258, 259–63,
      267, 268, 271, 272–74
North Africa, 180, 189, 207–10, 339. *See
      also specific nation*
North America: aging in, 216; and global
      demographic trends, 175, 179, 180,
      189, 192, 197, 198, 216, 245, 248, 251;
      and Next Great Depression, 286, 357;
      slowing in, 192, 248, 286; and stages
      of growth, 216; and terrorism, 357.
      See also specific nation
North Carolina: cities in, 358; and
      impacts of Next Great Depression,
      358; migration/immigration in, 143,
      149, 151, 153, 155, 160, 163, 166, 167,
      173; and terrorism, 358
North Dakota, 151, 157–58
North Korea, 36, 186, 346
Northeast, U.S., 149–61, 173. *See also
      specific state*
Northwest, U.S., 156–57, 170, 171, 172.
      See also specific state
Norway, 350
nuclear weapons, 36, 346

Obama, Barack, 68–69, 313, 319, 326, 330,
      332, 336
Ohio, 151, 159, 161
Ohno, Taiichi, 343
oil: bubbles in, 21; and Commodity Cycle,
      75–77, 104; and comparison of New
      Deal (1930s) and Next New Deal,
      330–31; and debt crisis (2010–2012),
      34, 35, 37; decline in, 35; and
      determining risk and return, 271;
      and forecasting methods, 11, 73; and
      fundamental trends that drive the
      economy, 48; and geopolitics, 37, 80;
      and global demographic trends, 186,

192, 193, 207–10, 212, 221, 232, 240,
      242, 247; and Next Great Depression,
      104, 321, 322, 348, 358; price of, 13,
      34, 73, 76–77, 104, 186, 192, 193,
      322, 330–31, 358; and spending, 13;
      and terrorism, 348. *See also* energy
Oman, 188, 207
opportunity costs, 253
Oregon, 143, 149, 151, 156, 160, 170–71,
      172, 173
organizations: green networked, 341–45;
      impacts of Next Great Depression
      on, 341–45, 359, 360; new models
      for, 89–90; and Revolutionary Cycle,
      88–90
outsourcing, 83, 90, 158, 307, 338

Pakistan: and Civilization Cycle, 82; and
      environment, 342; and geopolitics,
      36; and global demographic trends,
      186, 189–90, 193, 194, 205, 206–7,
      229–30, 235, 236, 237, 241, 243, 244,
      245, 246; and impact of Next Great
      Depression, 342
Panama, 309
Paraguay, 214
pay phones example, 267–68
Pennsylvania, 151, 159–60, 161
pensions/benefit programs, 321, 336. *See
      also specific program*
personal/family life; and strategies for
      Next Great Depression, 308–19
Peru, 214
Pete Peterson Foundation, 29
phase transitions, 267–68
Philippines, 203, 204–5, 232–33, 237, 240,
      241, 243, 245
Poland, 186, 200, 245
political system. *See* government/political
      system
politics, 14, 200, 207, 209, 246, 336–37,
      356, 359. *See also*
      government/political system
population: and aging, 349, 350, 354–55;
      bubble in, 53, 354–55; decline in
      world, 183; as driver of economy,
      139; and global demographic trends,

202, 203, 228, 234, 237, 246, 248, 250; history of world growth in, 354, 355; and impacts of Next Great Depression, 349, 350, 354–55, 360; projections of world, 185. *See also* demographics; *specific state or nation*

portfolio optimizer programs, 256–57

Portugal, 198

potato chip spending, 49, 50, 51

Prechter, Robert, 97, 100

predictions. *See* forecasting

Presidential Cycle (4-year), 6, 95–97, 99, 100, 104–5, 107

prices: of commodities, 104, 299, 322, 330–31, 348, 358; and cycles, 18; and debt crisis (2010–2012), 19; and determing risk and return, 267; and Empire Cycles, 83; and global demographic trends, 186, 192, 193; and impacts of Next Great Depression, 327, 328; and Innovation Cycle, 85; irrational, 254; and migration/immigration, 152. *See also* housing: price of; oil: price of

production system; revolution in, 88–89, 343–45

productivity: and age, 44, 348, 353; and cycles, 40; and debt crisis (2010–2012), 21; and determining risk and return, 271, 279; and forecasting methods, 73; and fundamental trends that drive the economy, 44, 53–54, 63, 64, 65, 66, 70, 71; and Geopolitical Cycle, 80; and global demographic trends, 176, 178, 185, 194, 215, 216, 217, 219, 233, 234, 250, 251; and Growth Boom Season/Stage, 65, 66; and Maturity Boom Season, 70; and migration/immigration, 173; and New Deal (1930s), 331, 334; and Next Great Depression, 286, 287, 325, 344, 348, 353, 356; and Next New Deal, 331; and stages of growth, 216; technology as source of, 53–54; and terrorism, 356

protectionism: and debt crisis (2010–2012), 36; and fundamental trends that drive the economy, 70, 71; and Geopolitical Cycle, 80; and global demographic trends, 181, 252; and Maturity Boom Season, 70, 71; and Next Great Depression, 337, 338–39, 357, 358, 359; and terrorism, 357

Protestant Revolution, 85, 87, 319, 340

Public Works Administration (PWA), 329

public works programs, 329, 330, 337, 346

Puerto Rico, 213, 214, 309

Qatar, 188, 207

real estate: bubbles in, 18, 21, 30–34; collapse of, 23, 78; commercial, 33, 124–27, 136; and comparison of Great Depression (1930s) and Next Great Depression, 128, 132–33; and crash of 2008, 17; and debt crisis (2010–2012), 18, 19, 23, 30–34, 35; and Decennial Cycle, 94; and demographics, 107, 109, 111, 115–24, 136; and determining risk and return, 279; and environment, 343; and fundamental trends that drive the economy, 67, 68, 72; and global demographic trends, 202, 203, 205, 210; globalization of, 121; and Great Depression (1930s), 128, 132–33, 135; and impact of Next Great Depression, 343, 358; key points/summary about, 126–27, 136–37; life cycle of, 115–16; and migration/immigration, 140, 148, 150, 152, 153, 155, 159, 160, 161, 164, 165, 169, 171, 172–73; and New Deal (1930s), 331; and Next New Deal, 331;overvaluation of, 165; and Shakeout Season, 67, 68; speculation in, 32, 108, 120, 122, 136, 331; and strategies for Next Great Depression, 281, 282, 283, 286, 287, 289, 297, 298, 299, 307, 308, 309–10, 313; and terrorism, 358; and where to live in real estate (*cont.*)

  Next Great Depression, 135. *See also* housing

recession, 21–24, 31, 32, 40, 63, 79, 102, 282, 299, 330, 334

"reflexivity" in markets, 267

regulation, 19, 29

rental housing, 115, 116, 117, 118, 119, 126, 136, 142, 173, 310, 315

replacement costs, 110

rescue plans, 102. *See also* bail-outs; stimulus, economic

resort hotels, 126

retirement: and aging, 348; of baby-boomers, 18, 22, 128; and commercial real estate, 125; and crash of 2008, 17; and debt crisis (2010–2012), 18, 19, 22; and determining risk and return, 277; and fundamental trends that drive the economy, 65, 68, 71; and Great Depression (1930s), 128, 129; housing, 122–24, 126, 136, 173, 297, 298, 309, 310; and migration/immigration, 139, 140, 141–42, 152, 153, 167, 171–72, 173; and Next Great Depression, 128, 129, 297, 298, 308, 309–10, 311–13, 348; and Shakeout Season, 67–68; and spending, 44. *See also* Social Security

return: assumptions about, 254–57; and change and transitions, 267–78; constant rate of, 274, 276; determination of, 257–58, 279–80; expected, 254, 258–59, 260, 261–62, 274, 276–78; least expected, 276–78; and Next Great Depression, 283, 286, 293, 308, 327; typical views of, 258–67, 268; understanding of, 14; wide spread in possible, 274, 275, 276

Revolutionary Cycle (250-year): and forecasting methods, 12; and global demographic trends, 196; and history of long-term cycles, 86, 87–93; as new cycle, 14; and New

Economy Cycle, 344; and Next Great Depression, 339–45; and Next New Deal, 319; overview of, 339–41

revolutions; and global demographic trends, 232, 247, 251

Rhode Island, 160

risk: assumptions about, 254–57; and change and transitions, 267–78; and impacts of Next Great Depression, 324; protecting against, 279–80; quantification of, 253–67; and strategies for Next Great Depression, 281, 283, 286, 293, 308, 311; typical determination of, 253–67, 268; understanding of, 14, 253–54

Roaring 20s, 24, 34

Roaring 2000s, 21

Roaring Twenties, 7, 57, 221, 284, 323, 328, 334

Rocky Mountain states: migration/immigration in, 139, 143, 149–61, 166, 170, 172, 309; and real estate, 135. *See also specific state*

Romney, Mitt, 7

Roosevelt, Franklin D., 69, 322, 328–30, 334, 336

rural areas; and global demographic trends, 205, 225, 242

Russia: aging in, 202, 216, 223, 347–48, 350, 351; birthrates in, 350; and commodities, 78; and fundamental trends that drive the economy, 48, 71; and Geopolitical Cycle, 79; and geopolitics, 36; and global demographic trends, 180, 183, 189, 192, 193, 197, 198, 199–200, 202, 216, 223, 228; and LTCM model, 255, 278; and Next Great Depression, 287, 346, 347–48, 350, 351, 357; and Next New Deal between developed and emerging countries, 346, 347; population in, 350; slowing in, 180, 228; and stages of growth, 216; and terrorism, 357; worker-retiree ratio in, 327. *See also* Soviet Union

S-curve cycles/trends: and change and transitions, 268; and Commodities Cycle, 81; and determining risk and return, 263, 265, 279; and forecasting methods, 8, 9, 10, 11; and fundamental trends that drive the economy, 65; and Geopolitical Cycle, 81; and global demographic trends, 194, 221, 222, 223, 224, 233; and Growth Boom Season/Stage, 65; and new and recurring cycles for forecasting, 73; and Next Great Depression, 305, 306, 307, 322, 323; present-day, 59–60; and Revolutionary Cycle, 92; of technology, 54–60, 92

S&L crisis, 119

S&P 500, 9, 22, 23, 74, 75, 276, 287; and dollar, 31

Saudi Arabia, 186, 194, 207, 209–10, 212, 240, 241, 242, 243, 244; and debt crisis (2010–2012), 29

savings, 17, 18, 22, 23, 26, 40, 41, 52–53, 279

Scandinavia, 198, 350–51. See also specific nation

Scottrade, 300

seasons, 61, 62, 100, 308. See also specific season

SEC. See Securities and Exchange Commission

second homes, 114, 120. See also vacation homes

Securities and Exchange Commission (SEC), 301

Securities Exchange Act (1934), 329

Securities Insurance Protection Corporation (SIPC), 300–301

Senge, Peter, 343

September 11, 2001, 36, 37, 73, 80, 97, 278

service industry, 145, 147, 159

Shakeout Season/Stage: and comparison of New Deal (1930s) and Next New Deal, 323, 331, 332; and cycles, 38, 40–41, 61; Empire Cycles, 83; and fundamental trends that drive the economy, 66–69, 70, 71; and global

demographic trends, 222; impacts of Next Great Depression, 322, 324, 325, 337, 341, 358–61; and Innovation Cycle, 86; and New Economy Cycle, 64, 89; and Revolutionary Cycle, 88–89; and strategies for Next Great Depression, 79–80, 281, 293, 302, 303, 304–6, 308–9, 311, 312–13, 316; and technology cycle, 56, 57, 58

Shiller, Robert J., 13, 31, 109

shopping centers, 116–18

short-term cycles/trends, 4–5, 6, 8

simple trends, 8–9

Singapore: aging in, 348, 350; birthrates in, 350; and global demographic trends, 175, 176, 183, 186, 201, 203, 204, 224, 229, 236; and impacts of Next Great Depression, 348, 350; urbanization in, 224

SIPC. See Securities Insurance Protection Corporation

60-year cycles, 6

Sloan, Alfred; 70, 88, 89, 221, 344

Slott, Ed, 312

Slovakia, 186

Smoot-Hawley Tarrif Act, 332

Social Security, 29, 321, 326, 327–28, 329, 330, 334, 336

social unrest, 133, 135, 181, 358

Soros, George, 267

South Africa, 48, 345; and global demographic trends, 186, 194, 212, 219–20, 231–32, 235, 236, 237, 240, 241, 243, 247

South America, 189, 213, 233, 245, 299, 350. See also specific nation

South Asia, 360; and global demographic trends, 179, 180, 181, 183, 189, 197, 205–7, 209, 210, 244. See also specific nation

South Carolina, 142, 143, 149, 151, 153, 160, 167, 173

South Dakota, 158

South Korea: aging in, 348; and fundamental trends that drive the economy, 53; and global demographic

South Korea (cont.)
trends, 175, 176, 186, 189, 193, 201, 202, 204, 221–22, 224, 233–34, 237; and Next Great Depression, 288, 289, 298, 299, 348; and Shakeout Season, 69; slowing in, 69

Southeast Asia, 299, 339, 346; and global demographic trends, 179, 180, 181, 189, 197, 203–5, 233, 247. See also specific nation

Southeast, U.S.: cities in, 162–63, 165–66, 173; migration/immigration in, 13, 139, 143, 149–61, 162–63, 165–66, 169, 170, 173, 309; and real estate, 135. See also specific state

Southwest, U.S.: cities in, 162–63, 165–66, 173; and determing risk and return, 267; and Geopolitical Cycle, 81; migration/immigration in, 13, 139, 143, 149–61, 162–63, 165–66, 169–70, 173, 309; real estate, 108, 120, 122, 136; and real estate, 135. See also specific state

Soviet Union, 177, 356. See also Russia

space/satellites, 83

Spain, 198, 223, 347, 350

speculation: in commodities, 35; and comparison of New Deal (1930s) and Next New Deal, 331; and cycles, 40; and debt crisis (2010–2012), 35; real estate, 32

spending: and age, 13, 44, 45–53, 238–44, 348, 353; by baby boomers, 13, 18–19, 21–24, 40, 47, 73, 121, 125, 127, 216; and Commodity Cycle, 81, 104; and crash of 2008, 17; and cycles, 18–19, 21, 38, 39, 40, 41; and debt crisis (2010–2012), 18, 21–24, 27, 41; and Decennial Cycle, 94; and determining risk and return, 279; as driver of economy, 139; and family life cycle, 21; and forecasting methods, 10, 12, 73, 182; forecasting of global demographic, 190–97; and forecasting of global demographic trends, 245; and fundamental trends that drive the economy, 45–53,
62–64, 68, 69–71, 279; and generational cycles, 45–53; and Geopolitical Cycle, 81; and global demographic trends, 176, 178, 181–252; and Great Depression (1930s), 127–28; and Growth Boom Season/Stage, 63–64; household, 47; and housing, 116, 117, 118, 121; insight about, 21–24; on leisure travel, 126; and Maturity Boom Season, 69–71; and migration/immigration, 142, 150, 173; for motorcycles, 51; and Next Great Depression, 104, 127–28, 294–95, 296, 306, 337, 348, 353; and oil, 13; peak in, 51–52; projection of global, 191; and real estate, 125; and Shakeout Season, 68, 69; and short-term recurring cycles, 93; and stocks, 183; and workforce, 245

Spending Wave. See spending

stagflation, 67–68, 300; and cycles, 39–40

standard deviations, 260–61, 262, 263, 273

standard of living: and aging, 349, 352–53, 355; and cycles, 360; and drivers of economy, 20; and Empire Cycles, 83; and fundamental trends that drive the economy, 55, 71; and global demographic trends, 176, 177, 181, 182, 185, 186, 190–91, 194, 196, 205, 208, 209, 211, 212, 214, 215, 225, 234, 236, 241; and Innovation Cycle, 85, 86; and Next Great Depression, 284, 286, 338, 345, 349, 352–53, 355, 356, 360; and Next New Deal between developed and emerging countries, 345; and Revolutionary Cycle, 87; and terrorism, 356

starter homes, 22, 114, 116, 118–21, 126, 132, 142, 173, 287, 289, 297, 298, 315, 316

stimulus, economic: and crash of 2008, 17; and cycles, 41; and debt crisis (2010–2012), 18, 19, 20, 22–23, 26, 27, 29, 30; failure of, 69; and forecasting, 20; and fundamental trends that drive the economy, 68,

69; and interest rate, 32; in New Deal
(1930s), 346; and Next Great
Depression, 282, 324, 346; and Next
New Deal between developed and
emerging countries, 346; in 1920s,
334; and role of government, 17; and
Shakeout Season, 68, 69
stocks: and Annual Cycle, 98–99; and
Armstrong Cycle, 98; bubbles in, 21,
34, 36, 77–78; buying opportunities
for, 104, 105; and Commodity Cycle,
77; crash of 2001 in, 32; crash of
2008 in, 17, 30; and cycles, 40,
100, 104, 128; and debt crisis
(2010–2012), 19, 23, 26, 30, 35,
37; and Decennial Cycle, 93–94, 95,
104; in emerging countries, 35;
forecasting about, 20, 182, 183; and
forecasting methods, 6, 9, 11, 15, 73,
74; and fundamental trends that
drive the economy, 46–47, 49, 64,
65, 66, 67, 68, 69, 71, 72; future
scenarios for, 101–3, 104, 105; as
gambling, 257–58, 274; and
geopolitics, 37, 78–80, 81, 104; and
global demographic trends, 180, 183,
193, 194, 202; and Great Depression
(1930s), 128; and Innovation Season,
64, 65, 66; key points about, 104;
large-cap, 286, 287, 289, 294–95,
296, 299; lows for, 15, 102, 105;
and New Deal (1930s), 331; and
New Economy, 64, 65; and Next
New Deal, 331; peak in, 26; and
Presidential Cycle, 95–96, 97; rally
in, 17, 34; and recommendations for
Next Great Depression, 296, 297,
299; and risk and return, 253; and
Shakeout Season, 68, 69; small-cap,
286, 287, 289, 295, 296, 299; and
Spending Wave, 183; and strategies
for Next Great Depression, 104, 281,
282, 283, 286, 287, 289, 294–95, 296;
and 3.3 Year Cycle, 97. *See also* bear
markets; bull markets; crashes; Dow
Jones Industrial Average; Great
Crash; S&P 500; *specific sector*

straight lines, forecasting in, 265–67, 268
Strauss, William, 65, 347
sub-Saharan Africa, 180, 189, 194, 197,
210–12, 232, 247, 339. *See also
specific nation*
suburbanization, 249
Sudan, 186
"survival of the fittest," 41, 58, 72, 90–92,
218, 219, 221, 222, 283, 302–8, 325
Switzerland, 198, 202

"tails," 271, 272–74, 275, 276–78
Taiwan, 175, 176, 186, 201, 224, 350
Taleb, Nassim Nicholas, 257
Tapscott, Don, 89, 90
taxes: and Annual Cycle, 99; and
fundamental trends that drive
the economy, 68, 69; and
migration/immigration, 142, 144,
148, 167, 171–72; and New Deal
(1930s), 327–28, 329, 332, 333–35;
and Next Great Depression, 288, 292,
311–13, 325, 326–28, 336–38, 342;
and Next New Deal, 332, 333; and
Shakeout Season, 68, 69; and
technology cycle, 58–59. *See also
type of tax*
Taylor, Frederick, 88
TD Ameritrade, 300
technology: and aging, 353, 354, 355;
bubbles in, 21, 54, 55; and change
and transitions, 268; and
Commodity Cycle, 77, 81; and cycles,
18, 38, 39–40, 54, 61; and debt crisis
(2010–2012), 19, 34, 41; and
Decennial Cycle, 93; and
determining risk and return, 262–63,
264, 279; as driver of economy, 9, 20;
in emerging nations, 359, 360; and
Empire Cycles, 83, 84; forecasting
about, 20–21; and forecasting
methods, 8–9, 10–11, 12, 73, 74; and
fundamental trends that drive the
economy, 44, 53–60, 65–66, 69–71;
and Geopolitical Cycle, 79, 80, 81;
and global demographic trends, 177,
178, 181–82, 185, 194, 195, 196, 205,

technology (*cont.*)
209, 211, 212, 213, 216, 219, 227,
228, 234, 248, 249, 251; and Growth
Boom Season/Stage, 65–66; and
health care, 318; housing bubble
compared with, 107–14; and impacts
of Next Great Depression, 322–26,
336, 338, 341, 342, 344, 345, 352–55,
358–61; and Innovation Cycle,
84–85, 86–87; and Maturity Boom
Season, 69–71; and migration/
immigration, 157, 173; and New
Deal (1930s), 331, 332, 334; and
New Economy Cycle, 359; and Next
New Deal, 331, 332, 345; and
recommendations for Next Great
Depression, 297, 298, 299; and
Revolutionary Cycle, 87, 92;
revolutions in, 54; and S-curves,
54–60, 92; and Shakeout Season, 69;
as source of productivity, 53–54;
stages of, 9, 56, 57, 71; and stages of
growth, 216; and strategies for Next
Great Depression, 282, 286, 287, 288,
302, 303, 318; and terrorism, 356.
See also innovation; Internet
Tennessee, 151, 154
Tennessee Valley Authority (TVA), 329
terrorism: and Civilization Cycle, 82, 83;
and debt crisis (2010–2012), 37; and
determining risk and return, 271;
and fundamental trends that drive
the economy, 70, 71; and geopolitics,
37, 80; and global demographic
trends, 181, 207–8, 210, 250, 251,
252; and Great Depression (1930s),
133, 135; and Maturity Boom
Season, 70, 71; and migration/
immigration, 147; and new and
recurring cycles for forecasting, 73;
and Next Great Depression, 133, 135,
321, 337, 339, 345, 346, 347, 355–58,
359; and Next New Deal, 14, 345,
346, 347; peak in, 339, 340
Texas: and impacts of Next Great
Depression, 358; migration/
immigration in, 143, 148, 149,

151, 155, 156, 163, 166, 167–68, 171,
173
Thailand, 186, 203–4, 241, 243
third world countries, 45, 78, 286, 321,
322, 339, 345. *See also* emerging
countries
30-year cycles. *See* Commodity Cycle
3.3 Year Cycle, 97, 105
trade: and Civilization Cycle, 83; and
commodities, 36; and debt crisis
(2010–2012), 30, 36; and global
demographic trends, 181, 183, 189,
192, 199, 202, 209, 210, 213, 214, 216,
219, 225, 233, 242, 245, 248, 252,
22371; during Great Depression,
339; and New Deal (1930s), 332; and
Next Great Depression, 322, 337,
338–39, 345, 346, 347, 357, 358, 359;
and Next New Deal, 14, 332, 345,
346, 347; and terrorism, 357, 358
trade-up housing, 22, 118–21, 122, 136,
287, 289, 298, 299, 315–16
transportation, 127
Treasury bills, 128–29, 282, 286, 288, 294,
296, 297, 298, 299
Treasury bonds: bubble in, 104; and
comparison of New Deal (1930s)
and Next New Deal, 333; and
recommendations for Next Great
Depression, 296, 297, 298; and
strategies for Next Great Depression,
282, 290, 294; and technology cycle,
58; yields on, 128–30
Treasury Department, U.S., 29, 102, 290
Turkey, 186, 189, 207, 209, 231, 235, 236,
237, 241, 243, 247
20-year cycles, 93, 94, 97

United Arab Emirates, 48, 186, 188, 207
United Kingdom, 346
United Nations (UN), 183, 184, 185,
191–92, 202, 226, 234, 235, 237, 244,
252, 357, 358
United States: age in, 239–40; birthrate in,
350; debt of, 28; and fundamental
trends that drive the economy,
48–49; GDP in, 235, 237, 244; and

global demographic trends, 180,
183, 192–93, 194, 196–97, 198,
220–21, 234–37, 238–41, 243, 244,
246; growth in, 236, 241, 243;
immigration in, 36, 202, 228, 234,
235, 239, 241, 244; and impacts of
Next Great Depression, 359;
income/affluence in, 221, 238,
239–40, 241; innovation in, 20, 194;
as major political force, 228; next
boom in, 48–49; population in, 350;
reemergence of, 69; slowing in, 290,
351, 359; spending in, 238; standard
of living in, 20; and trade, 241;
urbanization in, 237, 241; workforce
in, 238, 239, 243, 244. *See also specific
state or topic*
United Van Lines, 150–51
unknown unknowns, 278, 279
urbanization: in emerging countries,
215–37, 245; as forecasting tool, 245;
and global demographic trends, 176,
177, 178, 185, 186, 197–98, 202–6,
209, 213–17, 219, 222, 223–24,
226–37, 239, 240, 241, 242, 243, 244,
245, 246, 247, 248; importance of,
241, 245; as key factor in GDP, 224,
242; and stages of growth, 216
Uruguay, 214
Utah, 143, 155, 160, 170, 358

vacation housing, 120, 121, 122–24, 126,
136, 173, 297, 298, 309
Vermont, 160
Vietnam: and fundamental trends that
drive the economy, 48; and
geopolitics, 36, 79, 80; and global
demographic trends, 186, 193, 203,
235, 236, 237, 241, 243, 245, 247; and
Next Great Depression, 298, 345; and
Next New Deal between developed
and emerging countries, 345
Virginia, 168–69, 173
volatility, 255, 257, 262, 263, 267–78, 296

war, 70, 89, 181, 211, 247, 250, 347
Washington State, 156, 170, 172, 173
wealth. *See* affluence
Wisconsin, 151, 158, 161
Wolff, Edward, 323
Womack, James, 343
women, 198, 348, 350–51
workforce: and debt crisis (2010–2012),
21–22; and fundamental trends
that drive the economy, 63–65,
68; and global demographic
trends, 194, 197–252; and green
networked companies, 341;
and immigration/migration,
147; and innovation, 63–65; and
New Economy Cycle, 63–65; and
Next Great Depression, 286,
317–18, 341; and real estate
bubble, 125, 127. *See also*
employment/unemployment
Works Progress Administration (WPA),
329
World War I, 77, 333–34
World War II: baby boom following, 348;
Churchill as hero of, 322; and
comparison of Great Depression
(1930s) and Next Great Depression,
132; and cycles, 39; financing of
programs during, 59; and
fundamental trends that drive the
economy, 45, 70; and global
demographic trends, 249; housing
during, 32; and Maturity Boom
Season, 70; and Revolutionary Cycle,
89; and Shakeout Season, 68; stock
market during, 101; and taxes, 312,
333, 334, 335; and terrorism, 357;
U.S. involvement in, 347
World War II generation. *See* Bob Hope
generation
World War III, 319, 347, 355–58
Wyoming, 172

Zakaria, Fareed, 337–38

Get the Most Accurate Predictions from the World's Smartest Economist in the HS Dent Forecast Newsletter.

If you trust Harry Dent's enormous capacity to see, understand, interpret and advise on our global economic future, then you won't want to be without his newsletter!

If what you read in this book got your attention, and you want to avoid your own financial meltdown in the coming years and make a *fortune* despite these troubled times, then you need to stay informed through Harry Dent's monthly newsletter.

This will allow you to continually and accurately react to market conditions, such as the direction of mortgage rates, real estate prices, the prices of oil/gold/commodities, trends in the stock market, inflation, the federal budget, currency, unemployment and much more. Imagine having vital information to assist you in making the right choices, at the right time, throughout these dangerous economic times! Such a newsletter is not just valuable; it is invaluable!

"Your April 2007 newsletter was . . . simply put . . . terrific! Keep up the good work . . . you and your organization are making a difference in my family's life. We better understand the financial context within which we make investment decisions and plan for our future. Thank you." —Steven Miller, Wilmington, NC

"As an entrepreneur, I find the knowledge in HS Dent's Monthly Economic Forecast extremely helpful in targeting new business ventures. From upcoming technologies to understanding the right demographic for our targeted marketing or whether or not I should expand my business or take a step back, Dent's economic forecast has provided me with an excellent benchmark for making critical strategic decisions." —Steve H., Sequoia Unlimited, LLC

For only $349 per year (only $30 more for the Audio/MP3 version), you'll have ongoing access to Harry Dent's decades of experience and research. Few others possess his understanding of how the economy works, as well as the tools needed to accurately forecast what lies ahead. It is this body of knowledge and these forecasting tools that are shared with you each month in his newsletter. You can in turn use this information to make more informed life decisions regarding your finances, real estate, employment or your business, and even family affairs. In effect, Harry Dent becomes your own economic research team, your own economic think tank, from which you can gain insight.

Plus, You'll Get Free Updates, As Needed, Between Issues . . .

To thrive in this hostile environment, you'll need to know what important, even critical economic events are happening every day, and how Harry Dent suggests you react to these events on a moment's notice. Your newsletter subscription includes FREE e-mail updates. These updates will come as needed between newsletter issues. So as a newsletter subscriber, you'll miss nothing important. If something critical happens, and in the months and years ahead, this could be often, you'll know about it and what to do about it <u>instantly</u>!

If you want this kind of high-level assistance, call now. You can choose a very affordable one- or two-year subscription. Plus, you can also get an audio version of the newsletter, so you can listen to it anywhere.

See What People Are Saying . . .

"Harry's latest November update is excellent. Very well presented, with just the right balance of detail and overall concepts. It makes me feel confident in the depth of your team's analysis, and I appreciate the work that goes into that. Keep on doing great updates as we move into the coming economic transitions." —L.W. Bardell

"I have found Harry Dent's newsletter absolutely invaluable. It helped me not only make a great deal of money, but to avert a financial disaster. I first became a subscriber around 2001, and through his newsletter I was not only able to make a great deal of money buying beachfront real estate as investments before the real estate boom really got started. Then, thanks to his newsletter, I sold all my investment properties two months before the peak, and then put the profits into real estate in India, where I'm already up 150% to 200%." —A.J., Fort Lauderdale, FL

90-Day Risk Free Trial
Call Now to Subscribe: 1-888-307-3368
Or email to hsdentforecast@hsdent.com

Call Now to Get FREE Periodic Book Updates Directly from the Author, Harry Dent!

By e-mail, Harry Dent will periodically keep you abreast of what's happening in our economy, so you'll be able to counterbalance the views and news of the often misinformed major news sources.

As follow-ups, with news, information and advice, Harry Dent will continue to bring you a timely sense of what's truly happening in the economy and in the market.

To get these very important FREE updates, you need to call the number below and get on the list now! This way you'll be updated on what's happening with the economy so that you can take advantage of the many opportunities available and survive the possible problems that these turbulent times can throw at you.

As you've seen, entire countries, blue chip companies and large global banks can falter and fall without warning.

This is a VERY volatile environment! Having Harry Dent, one of the best economists in the world, with uncanny accuracy, by your side, and at important junctures, will bring you incredible piece of mind. It will also give you the ability to wade through the toughest times we've seen in decades . . . and even help you profit from it.

Call Now to Sign Up . . . It's Free! 1-888-716-1115
Visit www.hsdent.com/freeupdates and
fill out the form provided to receive free book updates.

Or mail your name, e-mail address (required, as updates are distributed via e-mail), address, and phone number now to:

HS Dent Book Updates
15310 Amberly Drive, Suite 390
Tampa, Florida 33647